THE OSWALD AFFAIR

THE
OSWALD
AFFAIR

AN EXAMINATION OF THE
CONTRADICTIONS AND OMISSIONS
OF THE WARREN REPORT

LÉO SAUVAGE

TRANSLATED FROM THE FRENCH
BY CHARLES GAULKIN

THE WORLD PUBLISHING COMPANY
CLEVELAND AND NEW YORK

Published by The World Publishing Company
2231 West 110th Street, Cleveland, Ohio 44102

Published simultaneously in Canada by
Nelson, Foster & Scott Ltd.

Published in France, March 1965
by Les Editions de Minuit, Paris

FIRST PRINTING 1966
Copyright © 1966 by Léo Sauvage

Library of Congress Catalog Card Number: 66–25889

Printed in the United States of America

In the photo insert, plates 2, 4, 8, 9 were furnished by Associated Press. Plate 15 was furnished
by Wide World Photos, Inc.

CONTENTS

INTRODUCTION 1

Chapter 1   Did Oswald Have an Alibi?   19
Chapter 2   The Chicken Bones Mystery   35
Chapter 3   The Italian Rifle Mystery   49
Chapter 4   Bullets, Experts, and the Mystery of the Irving Gunsmith   61
Chapter 5   Fingerprints, Witnesses, and the Mystery of the Oak Cliff Policeman   73
Chapter 6   The Mystery of the Texas Theater   95
Chapter 7   The Mystery of the Useless Crosses   118
Chapter 8   The Problem of the Brown Paper Bag   126
Chapter 9   Marina Oswald Identifies a Rifle   140
Chapter 10   Marina Oswald Identifies a General   148
Chapter 11   Marina Oswald Accuses Her Husband   169
Chapter 12   The Mystery of the Russian Widow   181
Chapter 13   The Assassination of Lee Oswald   190
Chapter 14   The Trial of Jack Ruby   197
Chapter 15   Oswald and the Law   204
Chapter 16   Oswald and the Truth   219
Chapter 17   Oswald and the Press   229
Chapter 18   Oswald and the Mathematician   243
Chapter 19   Lee Harvey Oswald   258
Chapter 20   Three Theories   273
Chapter 21   Some Questions of Evidence   285
Chapter 22   Four Ideas   303
Chapter 23   The Clipboard Mystery   332
Chapter 24   The Eight Proofs of the Warren Report   353

AMERICAN POSTSCRIPT   399

THE OSWALD AFFAIR

Let General de Pellieux allow me respectfully to point out that a piece of evidence, whatever it may be, cannot have any value and cannot constitute scientific proof before it has been subjected to cross-examination. . . .

FERNAND LABORI, defense attorney
at the trial of Émile Zola.
Paris, February 17, 1898

INTRODUCTION

JOHN F. KENNEDY, the 35th President of the United States, was assassinated on Friday, November 22, 1963, in Dallas. This, alas, we know for sure; and we can also say with certainty that it happened at about 12:30 P.M., Texas time.

But everything else—all that was said after 12:30 P.M., Friday, November 22, 1963, in Dallas—soon appeared subject to doubt. By the end of the next week, indeed, the investigators had presented us with so many errors, contradictions, and obvious improbabilities that on November 29 I cabled my newspaper in Paris: "If I were asked today to compile a list of the established facts in this case, I would reply that the only one we are absolutely certain of is the fact that President Kennedy was assassinated on November 22 in Dallas."

The President had attached great importance to his journey to Texas. In the 1960 elections he had defeated Richard Nixon there by only 46,233 votes out of 2,311,845, and there was a possibility that the Republican candidate might even carry the state in 1964. Increasingly violent attacks were directed against him from the militant right, including a faction of his own party; yet he was at the point—with Lyndon Johnson at his side—of neutralizing certain influential groups that had supported his opponent in 1960.

This was because the President of the United States has some powerful trump cards; he is the man, for instance, who decides which states to favor with federal funds. Texas had little to

1

complain about. Houston, for example, had become the astro-
nauts' headquarters, and now the official reason for the President's
trip was the inauguration of a space medicine center in San An-
tonio. The three other Texas cities on his itinerary in those two
days (Fort Worth, Dallas, and Austin) had likewise tasted the
federal manna in various ways, and the President hoped to find
in Texas something besides the venom of hostile Birchers, authori-
tarian old ladies, reactionary doctors, crusading millionaire oil-
men, and assorted maniacs of the extreme right.

The situation appeared to be especially favorable in Dallas,
where the business world was starting to react against the excesses
of the fanatics. Many Republicans were among the 2,500 guests
invited to the banquet that was to have honored the President and
Mrs. Kennedy at the Trade Mart on Stemmons Freeway. It was a
Republican, moreover, who was to have presided over the affair:
Erik Jonsson, leader of the powerful Dallas Citizens' Council.

Coming from Fort Worth (where they had spent the night and
then had breakfast with 2,000 guests of the Chamber of Commerce), the Kennedys arrived at the Dallas Airport that Friday
morning at 11:40 A.M. It was a sunny day and a large crowd was
out to greet them. The President and his wife took their seats in
the back of the Presidential Continental, its top removed, and
Governor Connally sat with his wife on the folding seats in front
of them. The President's limousine was followed by a car full of
Secret Service agents, then by the open Lincoln carrying Vice
President and Mrs. Johnson and Senator Ralph Yarborough. All
were smiling and happy, anticipating a successful visit.

The motorcade left the airport at 11:50 and slowly advanced
through the friendly crowds, without a discordant note. It arrived
at 12:28 at the intersection of Main and Houston streets, where it
turned right, and at 12:29 at the intersection of Houston and
Elm streets, where it turned left. And then it was 12:30, shots
rang out in the streets, and John F. Kennedy collapsed on the seat
of the car, mortally wounded.

The Houston-Elm corner is dominated by a seven-story building, massive and ugly, topped by a billboard advertising an auto-
rental firm. This is the Texas School Book Depository, which

stocks and distributes books in cooperation with a number of publishing firms. At the moment of the shots many spectators looked up at the building, and several saw a rifle pulled in from a window on the fifth or sixth floor. But from this point on, we enter the domain of the Dallas "facts": a shifting, slippery, uncertain world where everything, or nearly everything, must be questioned. That is the object of this book.

At first, the investigation must have appeared extraordinarily efficient to most Americans as they watched on 60 million television screens.

An hour and a half after the shooting, the police announced that they already had a suspect: an employee of the Texas School Book Depository, Lee Harvey Oswald, 24 years old, "admitted Marxist," and president of the local chapter of the Fair Play for Cuba Committee. This pro-Castro organization, with headquarters in New York, quickly stated that it had no local chapter in Dallas, but nobody paid attention to that since the police were by then releasing details on the arrest of Oswald. His arrest, said Captain Will Fritz, chief of the Dallas police homicide bureau, had taken place in a theater as a film was being shown; having just learned that a policeman had been slain in the same neighborhood, Fritz added that the suspect before being subdued had defended himself by firing his revolver and had killed a police officer.

These "facts" appeared the following day in the early editions of many newspapers around the world. In France, for instance, an American wire service—whose managing editor later claimed the agency had "resisted a spurious barrage" of false reports and "circulated nothing erroneous"—distributed the following story:

> The police arrested Lee H. Oswald, strongly suspected of being the assassin of President Kennedy. Officers Tippit and McDonald learned from an employee of the Texas Theater that a suspicious individual wearing a brown shirt had entered the dark theater, and they rushed inside. Tippit ordered him to surrender and fired a warning shot. The suspect replied with revolver shots and killed Tippit. McDonald threw himself on the murderer and the two men

toppled on a seat. McDonald received a knife wound in the
face, but the suspect was subdued and arrested. Oswald was
led away by the police, weeping and shouting. . . .

Thus our wire service had even furnished Oswald with a knife,
which was not listed in Captain Fritz's catalog. Soon afterward, in
any case, the police were obliged to admit that Tippit had been
killed in a different place. But since they appeared as positive
about the identity of Tippit's killer as if the officer had been shot
down in front of his colleagues in the theater, the image of Oswald
killing a policeman to escape arrest remained in the public mind
as the reflection of an established fact.

This was only one of the countless distortions that characterized
the Dallas investigation. The fact that some of them were almost
immediately recognized as such did not prevent the local authorities from declaring the following day that Oswald was not only a
suspect but was indeed the assassin. "It's in the bag," Fritz declared. "It's a cinch." And Henry Wade, the District Attorney:
"I have sent men to the electric chair with less evidence."

Lee Harvey Oswald, however, was not sent to the electric chair.
He was killed by a bullet in the stomach, fired at point-blank
range as he walked handcuffed between two detectives through the
basement of Dallas police headquarters on Sunday, November 24,
1963, at 11:21 A.M. This, indeed, is one other fact that cannot be
disputed; the murder of Lee Harvey Oswald, the first man in
history to be killed live on television, was witnessed by millions.

That Sunday night, at the end of a press conference that will
remain a perfect example of contempt for law and truth and fairness, District Attorney Wade—appointing himself judge and jury
—pronounced the posthumous condemnation of the man executed in the morning. "Without any doubt he is the killer," he
said. Then, remembering that it would be more suitable to speak
of Oswald in the past tense: "There is no question that he was the
killer of President Kennedy." A few hours earlier, Police Chief
Jesse Curry had declared the case "closed": For him, the death of
the accused evidently had canceled any further requirements of
justice.

What do we know about this man whom Dallas proclaimed the assassin of the President while Jack Ruby's revolver dispensed with the need to prove it in court? Keeping to the elements more or less supported by documents, we can retrace the main episodes of Lee Harvey Oswald's brief and unstable existence as follows.

Born in New Orleans on October 18, 1939, two months after his father had died, Lee was placed in an orphanage at the age of three. His older brother and a half brother born of Marguerite Claverie's first marriage had been sent there previously. When the mother remarried in 1945, she took Lee to Dallas, then to Fort Worth. In 1948 her third husband divorced her. The child was often left to himself while Marguerite Oswald (she had taken back the name of Lee's father) tried feebly to earn a living as a saleswoman or office worker. In 1952 she went to New York to look for a job. Lee, then 13, soon got into trouble with the authorities, since he preferred to watch television rather than go to school. A psychiatrist recommended treatment, even confinement in a special institution, but Mrs. Oswald refused. In 1954 mother and son returned to New Orleans, and in July 1956 they moved to Fort Worth again. On October 24, 1956, six days after his 17th birthday, Lee went to Dallas with his mother's approval to enlist for three years in the Marines.

The young serviceman, whose schooling had been erratic, became interested in electronics and in June 1957 received the rating of radar operator. He also decided to learn Russian, but failed the language course admission test; from then on he studied alone during his leisure time. He served in Japan, then in California. He would have been promoted if not for two brushes with military justice, one of them for "possession of an unregistered personal weapon" (a pistol).

In the summer of 1959 Oswald obtained an early release from the service for family reasons: His mother, who had been working in a Fort Worth store, was injured in an accident and had to remain in bed for six months. But Lee stayed with her only three days. He told her he wanted to travel and work on a ship. On October 16, 1959, two days before his 20th birthday, he made his appearance in Moscow as a tourist. On the 31st of the same month he showed up at the United States Embassy, announced that he had decided to become a Soviet citizen, and said he wanted to "dissolve" (the expression used in the diary he kept at the time) his American citizenship. The Russians, according to Oswald's diary, refused to naturalize him but did give him a job. He arrived in Minsk on January 7, 1960, to work in a radio factory. In his diary he described himself as a "metal worker" and "checker."

The Embassy heard from Oswald again in February 1961. In a letter he said he wanted his passport back in order to return to the United States. In July 1961 he visited the Embassy and received the passport—valid only for his return to the United States.

Meanwhile, on April 30 in Minsk, Oswald had married Marina Nikolaevna Pruskova, a 19-year-old pharmacist's assistant. In August the couple started proceedings to get a visa to leave the Soviet Union, and Lee bombarded the Embassy with letters, this time to obtain an immigration visa for his wife. In January 1962 he even wrote to Senator John G. Tower, Republican, of Texas: "I bessech you, Senator Tower, to rise the question of holding by the Soviet Union of a citizen of the U.S., against his will and expressed desires." Things were further complicated by the birth of June Lee Oswald, on February 15, 1962, in Minsk. But by May 1 all problems had been solved; the ex-turncoat had even obtained a loan of $435.71 from the Embassy to help him return to the U.S. The Oswald family arrived in New York by boat, from Rotterdam, on June 13, 1962.

With the assistance of a representative of the Traveler's Aid Society, Lee flew the following day with his wife and baby daughter to Fort Worth and the home of his brother, Robert. He had trouble finding a job, since people in town knew of his Soviet adventure. A metalworking factory eventually hired him. The following October he quit and found another job in Dallas as an apprentice photo printer. He rented a small furnished apartment in the Oak Cliff section of town, and Marina joined him there with the child. But this lasted only until April, when he was fired for incompetence.

Again hunting a job, Oswald went to New Orleans on April 24,

1963, leaving his wife and daughter with Ruth Paine. Mrs. Paine, separated from her husband, lived with her two small children in a four-room house in Irving, not far from Dallas. A Quaker, she had met the Oswalds through friends and had taken a liking to Marina. Besides, having learned Russian in college, she was glad to have a chance to practice the language.

In New Orleans, meanwhile, Lee had been hired as a machine oiler at a coffee-roasting plant and had rented an apartment. He telephoned his wife on May 9 and told her to come. The next day Mrs. Paine packed everybody in her station wagon and drove to New Orleans. But on July 19 Lee lost the job—once again, it seems, for incompetence. When Mrs. Paine visited them on September 20, the three Oswalds were living on his unemployment payment of $33 a week, and Marina was expecting another child in a month.

Ruth Paine wasted no time. She loaded Marina, June Lee, and the family belongings into her car and took them back to Irving. Lee said he was leaving to look for work in Houston. The women heard nothing from him until October 4, when he telephoned to say he had been unable to find anything in Houston and was back in Dallas.

In fact, he had not been in Houston but in Mexico, where he had gone to the Cuban and Soviet consulates to ask for visas—for himself with no mention of his wife and child. The two embassies later said they had told him it would take time, and Oswald had departed angrily.

He returned to Dallas on October 3 and took a room at the Y.M.C.A. At Mrs. Paine's invitation, he spent the weekend in Irving, then went back to Dallas to resume his job hunt. After a week in another inexpensive rooming house, he moved on October 14 into an $8-a-week room at 1026 North Beckley Avenue, where he gave his name as O. H. Lee. The next day, thanks to a tip given to Mrs. Paine by a neighbor, Oswald was hired for $50 a week (under his real name) as a stock clerk, filling book orders at the Texas School Book Depository. It was a temporary job, and he knew it would last only until Christmas, but Mrs. Paine told me he seemed happy. When Oswald called to tell her about the job, he even said—for the first time—"Thank you."

Of Oswald's political activities we do not know much. But the Fair Play for Cuba Committee—while maintaining that it had no Dallas chapter and that Oswald was not authorized to speak in its name—confirmed that its New York office had received a request for leaflets from Oswald in April 1963 and that the material had been sent on April 19 to a Dallas post-office box.

A month earlier, on March 20, Klein's Sporting Goods of Chicago had mailed to the same post-office box an Italian Mann-licher-Carcano carbine, ordered by a certain A. Hidell. The police later said that Oswald carried false papers with the name Hidell; facsimiles were given to the press. The false credentials of Alek James Hidell bore Oswald's photo. The signature of Hidell was obviously (the "H" especially was characteristic) in Oswald's hand.

Oswald also received literature from the Fair Play for Cuba Committee at a New Orleans post-office box. A membership card, issued in his own name, was mailed by the organization to the same post-office box on May 28, 1963. Carlos Bringuier, a representative of a group of anti-Castro Cubans in New Orleans, said that at the beginning of August Oswald had gone to him to offer his services as an ex-Marine. But on August 9 Bringuier found him distributing pro-Castro leaflets in the street. New Orleans police records show that on that day there was a fight between pro- and anti-Castro groups and that Oswald was fined for disturbing the peace. Interviewed on August 21 on a local radio station, as a result of the incident, Oswald declared that he was "Marxist but not Communist."

In Dallas, on November 26, Assistant District Attorney William Alexander announced that the police had discovered among Oswald's belongings a box containing letters from Communist Party headquarters in New York. One of these, written on the letterhead of the Communist Party of America, thanked Oswald "for past services." On November 29, after President Johnson had signed the executive order appointing "a commission to report upon the assassination of President John F. Kennedy," both the Communist Party and the Fair Play for Cuba Committee turned over to the commission their correspondence with Oswald. Finally, the Trotskyite weekly, *The Militant,* disclosed that a certain Lee H. Oswald of Dallas had paid a dollar for an "introductory subscription." The subscription had been renewed in May 1963 from New Orleans.

According to the police, Lee Oswald arrived at the Depository Building on the morning of the assassination with a package containing the rifle received on March 20. He had been hiding the rifle in a blanket among his belongings stored in Mrs. Paine's garage in Irving. When his fellow workers went out to the street to watch the motorcade pass, Oswald declined to join them. Once he was alone, he set himself up in a corner by a sixth-floor window facing Elm Street, piling boxes around him and against a window facing Houston Street (to keep out of sight of the building across the street). Then he arranged some boxes in front of him as a gun rest and used another to sit on as he waited, with rifle aimed. When the President's car was in range, he fired three times, killing Kennedy and wounding Connally. He then hid the rifle, went to the second-floor lunchroom, drank a bottle of Coca-Cola, and left the building. Arriving at his room on North Beckley Avenue, he picked up a jacket and a revolver and departed quickly. On Tenth Street he spoke with a policeman seated at the wheel of a patrol car pulled up to the curb. When the officer got out of the car, Oswald shot and killed him. He was arrested shortly after in a theater where two war films, *War Is Hell* and *Cry of Battle,* were playing, after the cashier had notified police that a customer was acting in a suspicious manner.

How do we know all this is true? We do not. For a long time we had only the word of the Dallas police for it, together with the incoherent, uncorroborated, or self-contradictory affirmations of District Attorney Wade in his press conference of November 24, 1963. Now, since September 27, 1964, we also have the Warren Report, whose conclusions were supposed to have been the result of a painstaking *new* investigation, but were made known in advance through managed leaks and official indiscretions.

Some Americans were shocked by Wade, or at least uneasy at the District Attorney's scorn for the rights of the accused, but

more were indignant about the doubts and criticism raised in
other countries by the investigation. Even when they admitted
that Oswald had been prematurely convicted in Dallas they considered it premature to defend him against Washington. Wasn't
it right to await the results of the FBI probe? Wasn't it proper
to trust in the special commission headed by Chief Justice Earl
Warren, ordered by President Johnson "to satisfy itself that the
truth is known as far as it can be discovered"?

   In the December 3, 1963, *New York Post,* liberal columnist Max
Lerner began a dispatch from Paris: "With the FBI inquiry and
with the wise choice of a Presidential commission of inquiry
headed by Chief Justice Warren, perhaps the amateur investigators
into the Kennedy assassination will now take a much needed rest."
Lerner did not ignore the realities of Dallas. He admitted that in
the beginning there was a "tissue of guesswork, ignorance and
contradictions in which the law enforcement officials were caught
by the reporters." But instead of praising the reporters for having
exposed the "tissue," he preferred to deliver a sermon criticizing
correspondents for having concocted "an elaborate plot by hypothesis, at best conjectural, often the sheerest fantasy, which has
been fed not only to audiences in Russia and Eastern Europe, but
in France and Italy and even as far as India."

   Lerner's advice that the "amateur investigators" take a vacation
would have been justified, no doubt, by the FBI's entry into the
case and the creation of the Warren Commission if the transfer
to Washington had put an end to the methods of Dallas. But it
immediately touched off an intense propaganda campaign, a true
brainwashing drive designed to convince the public that there
was no need to await the results of these new investigations in
order to be sure of Oswald's guilt.

   On the day Lerner's sermon appeared, the *Post* and the other
afternoon papers in New York were running huge headlines about
the "probable conclusions" of the "secret" FBI report: Oswald
was indeed the assassin and had acted alone. While noting the
Justice Department's statement that the FBI report would not be
submitted to President Johnson and the Warren Commission for
several days, the newspapers nevertheless quoted "government

sources." As anyone in a city room knew, the leak had come directly from the FBI, which was not even polite enough to wait until its report was in the hands of Chief Justice Warren.

On December 9 the Justice Department finally announced that, on instructions from the White House, the FBI report had that day been submitted direct to the Warren Commission. The Department spokesman added that the Commission had insisted that nothing be made public until it had "reviewed the document and taken whatever action it may feel appropriate." This was duly reported in the *New York Times* of December 10; the Washington story telling about the Commission's wishes, however, was headed: "OSWALD ASSASSIN BEYOND A DOUBT, FBI CONCLUDES." The subhead: "HE ACTED ALONE AND DID NOT KNOW RUBY, SAYS REPORT TO WARREN INQUIRY PANEL." And the television news program took up the same theme: The FBI report confirmed that Oswald was the assassin.

This was clearly a poor beginning. Despite all that had been said and written—and even preached from the pulpit—against the denial of justice in the Dallas "trial by television," now the same kind of denial was under way in Washington. And this time under the auspices of the Justice Department, with no "Texas cowboys" to blame and with the aggravating circumstance that in Washington, having had the opportunity to ponder the precedent, the Department certainly knew what it was doing. Wasn't the FBI consciously forcing the hand of the Warren Commission, just as the Dallas authorities had been in fact forcing the hand of a future jury if there had been a jury for Lee Oswald?

Nothing happened, though; the few papers that had protested the public statements from Dallas did not protest those from Washington, which were infinitely more cynical.

At most there was a timid remark in the *New York Post* editorial panegyric of December 11, titled "The Warren Commission Goes to Work." The remark, lost in the hosannas of tribute, was that "it would seem appropriate to urge that all government agencies —whether the FBI, the Secret Service or any others connected with the case—cease 'leaking' self-serving stories and let the

Warren Commission proceed without pressures of any form." A December 12 Washington dispatch in the *New York Herald Tribune,* giving new details about the "secret" FBI report again attributed to "government sources," contained the following: "It was further learned that Chief Justice Warren has strongly advised officials of investigation agencies against leaking items of information to the press. He was reported disturbed at piecemeal revelations and speculation surrounding the assassination."

But the matter went no further, and at no time was there any question of taking administrative measures against those responsible for the official "indiscretions," nor was there any threat of resignation on the part of the Chief Justice in order to impose such measures.

Chief Justice Warren became upset only later on, in July 1964, when the *Dallas Morning News* published long extracts from Oswald's diary (he called it his "historical diary"), written while he was in the Soviet Union. This time Marina Oswald protested; having already banked $80,000 since her husband's death and willing to obtain more, she found herself suddenly cut off from a source of revenue. Mrs. Marguerite Oswald, for her part, had managed to sell letters from her son to *Esquire,* which attached enough importance (and price) to them to hide a good portion of Yvette Mimieux's bare breasts on the cover of the May 1964 issue with a pasted-on promotional notice: "Exclusive! Lee Oswald's Letters from Russia. 8 Pages with Footnotes By His Mother."

Oswald's "historical diary," whose last page was written in March 1962, obviously tells us nothing about the assassination of President Kennedy; it only confirms the mental instability of its author and is most remarkable for its incredible spelling errors. But it was nevertheless a secret document, and the FBI, which had never been asked to explain the leaks about its own report, was officially ordered to find out where the photocopies of Oswald's journal had come from. The *Dallas Morning News,* however, refused to divulge the source, and the matter rested there.

Marina Oswald, incidentally, must have obtained some compensation in the meantime, since the "historical diary" appeared in full, with facsimiles on the cover, in the July 10 issue of *Life*. The magazine introduced it as "one of the most important pieces of evidence studied by the Warren Commission in its effort to unravel the character and motives of President Kennedy's assassin," and added: "Though Oswald's widow did not provide *Life* with the diary, it is printed here in full with her permission." True enough, *Newsweek* stated on July 13 that the Oswald diary had been offered to it indirectly, as to other publications, for a price of about $1,000. Considering the current rates, it was not a very high figure.

In any case, long before the Report was published, the secrets of the Warren Commission had become no more confidential than the stock market reports.

In the same month, July 1964, the *New York Journal-American* published the stenographic transcript of the statements made to Chief Justice Warren by Jack Ruby in his Dallas jail cell, and two other dailies printed an account of his statements made to the FBI while he was submitting to a lie-detector test. Half a dozen newspapers and magazines already had disclosed (quoting "reliable sources") that the conclusions of the Warren Report would confirm those of the FBI. Though the *New York Times* complained in an editorial that the "spate of advance disclosures" would tend to weaken confidence in the Commission, it had itself published, on June 1, a Washington story headlined: "Panel to Reject Theories of Plot in Kennedy Death." The author of that story, Anthony Lewis, knew by this time that the Report was going to say "the President was killed by one man acting alone, Lee H. Oswald."

This publicity show, which included several acts contributed by Warren himself, also presented the then Attorney General, Robert F. Kennedy, in two remarkable appearances. The first of these raised hopes, the second destroyed them.

On March 26, 1964, the Justice Department invited correspondents to Kennedy's office for an important announcement. The newsmen found there a former colleague who had been with the *Baltimore Sun*, a young writer named William Manchester. The author of four novels and three biographies—one of them,

Portrait of a President (published in 1962), about John F. Kennedy—Manchester ·had been commissioned by the Kennedy family to prepare "an extensive account describing the events of and surrounding the death of President Kennedy on November 22, 1963." He explained that Pierre Salinger, then White House Press Secretary, had first contacted him about the project on February 5 and that he had later gone to Washington to confer with Robert Kennedy. Both Salinger and Kennedy had told him that the initiative had come from the President's widow. Manchester said he expected to devote three to five years to researching and writing the book.

Before leaving the Justice Department, the reporters received copies of a statement signed by Mrs. Kennedy. In it, the mission of William Manchester was summed up in these terms: "Because versions of what occurred Nov. 20–25 already have appeared and because it is understood other articles and books are in the course of being prepared for later publication, these arrangements were made with Mr. Manchester in the interest of historical accuracy and to prevent distortion and sensationalism."

Much as one would like to avoid any such sensationalism, it was impossible to disregard one plainly sensational fact: Both the agreement between Manchester and the Kennedy family, and the statement describing the purpose of that agreement, completely —even ostentatiously—ignored the existence of a Presidential Commission already charged with the responsibility of determining "historical accuracy." Salinger had telephoned Manchester on February 5; the Warren Commission had begun its sessions on February 3 and was questioning the first witness, Marina Oswald. But on February 4 Warren had told some journalists that certain elements of the inquiry might never be made public "in your lifetime." The Manchester arrangement, in these circumstances, suggested a challenge to the Warren Commission—a challenge all the more impressive in that the operation was being carried out under the direct auspices of Attorney General Robert Kennedy.

And then, on June 29, 1964, while visiting Poland, Kennedy suddenly proclaimed in Krakow that "there is no doubt" about the Dallas crime, that his brother had been slain by "a misfit named Oswald," and that the assassination was "the single act of one person protesting against society."

After this, it was difficult to understand why Manchester should go on searching until 1967 or 1969 for the "historical accuracy" known already to Robert Kennedy by June 29, 1964. It was even harder to understand why the Attorney General had given him the assignment in the first place if he did not intend to wait for his findings before drawing conclusions. Where, by the way, did Kennedy obtain his conclusions? At the end of his *New York Times* story on Kennedy's astonishing remarks in Poland, Arthur J. Olsen noted: "The Attorney General is known to be fully acquainted with the findings of the Warren Commission. It is presumed by persons close to him that the commission's report will reflect the views expressed by Mr. Kennedy today." But not to mention the breach of confidence, if the Warren Commission was indeed the source, the Commission's investigation was far from completed in June 1964. The Krakow declaration thus put the finishing touch on the edifice of unsubstantiated assertions that turned the crime of Dallas into the scandal of Washington.

Publication of the Warren Report did not bring that scandal to an end. On the contrary, the Report made it permanent, for it proved that the Commission, on the pretext that it was a board of inquiry and not a court, had ignored not only the rules of procedure but also the principles of justice suited to a court. The Commission states that Lee Harvey Oswald killed President Kennedy. What difference is there, *morally,* between stating that someone committed a murder and pronouncing him guilty? The Commission answers that *legally* there is a difference:

> The procedures followed by the Commission in develop-
> ing and assessing evidence necessarily differed from those
> of a court conducting a criminal trial of a defendant present
> before it, since under our system there is no provision for
> a posthumous trial. If Oswald had lived he could have
> had a trial by American standards of justice where he would
> have been able to exercise his full rights under the law.

A judge and a jury would have presumed him innocent until proven guilty beyond a reasonable doubt. He might have furnished information which could have affected the course of his trial. He could have participated in and guided his defense. There could have been an examination to determine whether he was sane under prevailing legal standards. All witnesses, including possibly the defendant, could have been subjected to searching examination under the adversary system of American trials.

Reading this reminder of what a genuine trial of Lee Oswald might have been, one could believe that the Commission regretted that such a trial was no longer possible. But why then did the Commission fail to uphold at least those safeguards provided for in a trial that could still be applied even in the absence of the accused?

The Foreword of the Report defines the Commission's role as follows: "The Commission has functioned neither as a court presiding over an adversary proceeding nor as a prosecutor determined to prove a case, but as a factfinding agency committed to the ascertainment of the truth." Thus, the Report explains, the Commission listened to hearsay evidence that would not have been admitted by a court, but which could help to "uncover all the facts." The Report, however, does not explain why the Commission chose to reject time-tested methods clearly designed not only to protect the accused but also to help in "developing and assessing evidence." The Commission, for instance, not being a court, had a perfect right to hear the wife of the accused. I cannot conceive of any valid or honest reason why the Commission—freely prescribing its own rules of procedure—should have excluded the possibility of subjecting such a "witness" to cross-examination.

"The evidence reviewed above identifies Lee Harvey Oswald as the assassin of President Kennedy," we read on page 375 of the Report.

Throughout this book the reader will find a review of that review. Because of the necessity of taking into account both the

main lines of the inquiry and its successive stages, I fear the order
may often seem less logical than chronological. This is because
what is pejoratively known as "the Dallas investigation" cannot
be erased and, in fact, has not been erased. The Report retains
the essentials of that investigation yet refuses to admit there were
points it did not retain. It was therefore necessary to expose, subject by subject and step by step, the foundations upon which the
local investigators constructed the case against Oswald, and upon
which the Warren Commission continued to pile variations,
contradictions, and impossibilities. But it was also important to
retrieve, identify, and confront the various speculations that
more than once constitute the Commission's only "facts" and
remain the main counts of its indictment and conviction of
Oswald.

Publication of the full transcript of the Commission hearings
on November 23, 1964, contributed more complications: It
brought revelations that, ignored or suppressed in the Report,
contradicted it in the most unexpected places, often destroying
one affirmation in the course of testimony that dealt with other
matters.

The panegyrists of the Warren Report will not reproach me,
however, for my literary imperfections—repetition, going backward, leaping ahead. They will say that I am wrong in speaking
of indictment and conviction, when the Commission only intended
to uncover the truth. But what is the difference as long as the
Commission, on such a basis, claims the right to call someone
an assassin? The Report, to be sure, tells us that because it is
no longer possible to establish Oswald's mental state at the time
of the assassination, the Commission "did not draw conclusions
concerning Oswald's legal guilt." The Commission does not
reach a verdict; it merely states a fact. The distinction is very
subtle; while refraining from any verdict of my own, I shall
merely state that it is also very hypocritical.

I will add just two more sentences by way of personal introduction, to indicate why I neglected many other things to concentrate on the Oswald affair.

Before publication of the Warren Report, there was the irresistible reaction against the audacity of those who loudly proclaimed the dead man's guilt but asked those who had doubts to keep silent. After the Report, there was something even more irresistible: the feeling that, in this case, silence would give consent to injustice.

1

DID OSWALD HAVE AN ALIBI?

THE OSWALD AFFAIR started with an incredible, monstrous failure to carry out the most elementary police routine. "Nobody moves!" is the automatic command of any policeman arriving at the scene of a crime. If this had been heard and heeded at the Texas School Book Depository, a number of questions would not have arisen or would have been easier to solve.

The police, in this case, did not even have to arrive: They were already there. Dallas Police Chief Jesse E. Curry, who had been riding in the motorcade, said on television that he had had no trouble locating the source of the shots and that from his car ahead of the President's he had "immediately" radioed orders to have the Depository Building "surrounded and searched." This statement was later shown to be untrue by a check of the police radio log; Curry himself, when he appeared before the Warren Commission, said that someone else gave the order. In any case, the place was swarming with police, and still Oswald got out.

Boasting of the efficiency of his department in arresting Oswald less than two hours after the crime, and several miles from the scene, Curry found it perfectly normal that Oswald had not been arrested by such efficient police the moment he walked out of the building. Hadn't Captain Will Fritz given the necessary explanation? They let Oswald leave, Fritz said, because the Depository manager had identified him as an employee.

Even if it really happened in that manner, this would seem a strange way to seal off a building in which the assassin of the President of the United States was believed to be hiding. In addition, the explanation given by Fritz was totally false.

19

Oswald, in fact, was "discovered" by the police not at the moment he walked out the front door but while he was in the second-floor lunchroom. Motorcycle Officer Marrion L. Baker was the first policeman inside the building. He ran upstairs, revolver in hand, with Depository Manager Roy S. Truly. Stopping at the door to the lunchroom, Baker saw a man standing near a vending machine with a Coca-Cola bottle in his hand. Truly came up and recognized Oswald. He told the officer that Oswald was an employee and the two men continued running up to the floors above.

When Oswald left the building later, nobody took notice of him, nobody stopped him, nobody even bothered to ask his name.

Where were the police? Many foreign reporters asked that question the next day, and the fact that the Soviet news agency Tass also brought it up on November 26 does not affect its validity. At any rate, if Oswald was able to get out so easily, anybody could have done so.

The fact is that the Texas School Book Depository, after the murder of the President, remained as open as a railroad station.

Truly told me that when he came back down with the motorcycle officer he found "a real crowd" on the ground floor, "maybe 15 or 20 people or more." Some, he said, were "reporters, photographers, employees who worked on other floors." Others were "just people from the street, I suppose."

We know today that many persons entered the building after the assassination, saying they were employees returning from lunch or from watching the motorcade. Others left, saying they were reporters—or without saying anything at all, simply because they carried professional-looking cameras that had given them entry. If the assassin was not Oswald, and if for some reason he had not left in the first few minutes, as had Oswald, he still could have made use of the coming and going to slip outside. Soon enough, anyway, the police would no longer be bothering with anything not related to Oswald.

Indeed, this is perhaps the most suggestive aspect of the mystery of the open doors on Elm Street, more intriguing than all the "locked rooms" of detective novels.

Normally, the man who fired at Kennedy from the sixth floor of the Depository would have had little chance of escaping. The shots could not have failed to attract attention to the building where they had come from. With so many police in the motorcade and on the sidewalks, there would not have been enough time to get down from the sixth floor and out any of the doors before they would be under guard. There would be no hope of getting away over the roof, either, since the building is in the open, with no adjoining structures.

But the situation would be different if the assassin had reason to believe that soon after the murder the police would have someone else under arrest or would be chasing someone else around the city; that is, if he knew that everything had been arranged in advance to lead quickly to Lee Harvey Oswald.

The police did not even seek to establish who was in the building at the time of the shooting. It has since been determined that several employees had remained inside, but when Captain Fritz issued his famous "It's in the bag" Saturday night, he cited as one of the reasons the simple fact the Oswald *was* in the building. The importance he seemed to attach to this gave the impression that Oswald was there *alone*. Wade did the same the following day.

The notion of an Oswald alone in the building led to some curious conclusions. The French weekly *Le Nouveau Candide,* for example, asked American author Chester Himes, who lives in Paris, to comment on the events in Dallas: Himes delivered the opinion that the complicity of the police was proved by Oswald's presence in a building that had been "officially evacuated" (the term appears four times in the article). True, our novelist did not seem much concerned with accuracy; he cut the interval between shots to "a tenth of a second" and said the shooting took place as the motorcade was "leaving the tunnel" and not, as the rest of the world had it, when it was about to enter. But even if he did confuse the Dallas police with the FBI and mistake an insinuation for a communiqué, Chester Himes had some excuse for stating that "if one believes the FBI, the building had been evacuated a few hours earlier."

Two witnesses, as I said, testified to the presence of Oswald in the second-floor lunchroom: Depository Manager Truly and Motorcycle Officer Baker. In summing up their statements for press and television Saturday afternoon, Chief Curry added on his own an unexpected bit of news. He said there had been "other people" in the cafeteria at the time.

It is worth repeating, because it gives all the more weight, that the entire lunchroom episode was presented by the authorities as evidence *against* Oswald.

In his memorable press conference on Sunday, November 24, District Attorney Wade related it in the following way: "A police officer, immediately after the assassination, ran in the building and saw this man in a corner and tried to arrest him; but the manager of the building said he was an employee and it was all right. . . ."

By stressing that Oswald barely escaped arrest "immediately after the assassination," the District Attorney evidently wished to give the impression that the suspect had virtually been caught in the act.

He reinforced this impression by leaving out the fact that the place where Oswald had been "cornered" was by the vending machine in the lunchroom, not near the sixth-floor window. Whatever Wade's intention may have been, it was now official that Oswald's encounter with Baker and Truly had taken place "immediately after the assassination."

I believe I know why the Dallas police as well as Wade emphasized this point, leading Bob Considine, for instance, to write that Oswald had been questioned inside the building "almost before the smoke from the assassin's gun had disappeared."

Captain Fritz said on Friday afternoon that Oswald had been stopped when he tried to leave the Depository, but had been allowed to go after Truly identified him as an employee. Newsmen learned from Truly that this was untrue; the identification had taken place in the lunchroom and Oswald then had left the building without being seen. This would have permitted Oswald to claim that he had left the building *before* the shooting and had re-entered *after* it had happened. There was reason for concern, because the authorities learned Friday night about a photo taken by J. W. Altgens of the Associated Press at the moment the shots were fired. It showed a man curiously resembling Oswald standing on the steps in front of the Depository. Apparently this man was another employee, named Billy Lovelady; but until that was established the accusers must have been holding their breath.

Nothing developed to support the singular statement by Chief Curry that Oswald was not alone in the lunchroom. This was neither repeated nor ever retracted, at least not by Curry. The Warren Report dismisses it as an anonymous "speculation," without mentioning that its author was the Dallas police chief.

Despite my efforts, I was never able to meet Officer Baker, but I did have several talks with Roy Truly. When I asked him about the time it took for Baker and him to reach the lunchroom, he replied:

> I saw the officer running up just as the last shot was fired. It was so quick that I think he wasn't riding in the motorcade. He must have been on foot, near the building. In any case, it was immediately after the shots. I thought, I don't know why, that he wanted to check the roof. The front elevator only goes up to the fourth floor, so I led him right back to the rear of the building where the service elevators go up to the top. But both of them were stopped on the upper floors, so we took the stairway next to them.

When I talked with him later to verify some other points, Truly abruptly told me that the report about the Coke bottle had not come from him. "I arrived behind the policeman, who blocked the doorway to the lunchroom," he said, "and from where I stood I couldn't see if Oswald held something in his hand." Nevertheless, the story given out by the local authorities was that when Oswald was "caught" in the lunchroom he was standing near the machine holding a Coke bottle.

Let us retrace what Oswald must have done if he was the assassin who had just shot Kennedy from a sixth-floor window:

First he had to cross the entire width of the floor from the window to the stairway in the back, skirting the piles of boxes that blocked a direct path. Next, after hiding the rifle, he had to go down four flights of stairs, cross a landing and pass through a vestibule into the lunchroom, go to the machine, take a coin from his pocket, operate the machine, remove the bottle, and open it. He also must have regained his breath, since Truly and Baker did not say he was panting or gave any sign of having been running. Truly, on the contrary, was struck by Oswald's calmness.

In a reconstruction of the events in *Time* we find a passage describing Oswald's actions after the lunchroom episode, in the imaginative style characteristic of that magazine:

"Carrying his Coke, Oswald ambled into a nearby office. A switchboard operator said, 'Wasn't that terrible—the President being shot?' Oswald mumbled something unintelligible, went out of the office, walked down the steps and slipped through the crowd outside."

This is not the moment to reflect on the psychological deductions one might draw from Oswald's ambling into a nearby office instead of making a fast getaway. But Truly verified the details of this account. FBI agents, he told me, had received the information during the week after the assassination, when they questioned all Depository employees in Truly's presence. It was not a switchboard operator, however, who had spoken to Oswald, but another woman working in that office next to the lunchroom.

Now, before ambling in with his Coke, Oswald must have come down from the sixth floor to get it. Like that of the lunchroom, the door of the adjacent office was always left open, as I later learned. Wouldn't the woman who heard Oswald mutter something incomprehensible have heard him go into the lunchroom and operate the machine? Truly did not know, nor did he remember whether the question had been asked.

If Oswald had fired the three shots from the sixth floor, did he have enough time to reach the lunchroom before Truly and Baker arrived on the second floor?

From Roy Truly's original account I had gathered that the officer led the way up the stairs and that Baker was already at the door of the lunchroom with his revolver in hand when Truly caught up with him. But in February 1964, when I took advantage of the Ruby trial to see Truly again at his office, he gave me the following version:

> I was running ahead of the policeman, showing him the way. I had already passed the landing and was starting toward the third floor, holding open the door to the stair-well, when I noticed that Baker wasn't behind me. I went back down to the landing and it was then that I saw him from behind, looking into the lunchroom. I ran toward him. He pointed to Oswald, who seemed calm but a little dazed. ᵃ⁻ ' he asked me without turning around if I knew the man. I told him who it was, and then we left Oswald in the lunchroom and went back to the stairway.

It would have been interesting to know why Baker went off to the right when he arrived at the second-floor landing instead of following Truly up the stairway to the left.

Since I was unable to meet Baker, I asked Truly about this. He believed the officer was attracted by a noise in the lunchroom: "Maybe Oswald had just slipped in there when he heard us coming." But in that case Oswald could have continued down the hall past the lunchroom, around a corner where he would not be seen, and down the front stairway to the main entrance. When I suggested this to Truly, he shrugged his shoulders: "He probably didn't think about it, that's all."

The Warren Report's explanation does not solve the mystery, and the transcript of Baker's testimony before the Commission rather complicates it.

There is, for instance, the diagram of the second floor, provided by the Commission (see Illustrations section of this book). One of the indications given in it is not correct. Baker is placed close to the door between the landing and the vestibule that serves as the entrance not only to the lunchroom but also to a large business office and to the long corridor leading to the front stairway and elevator. But Officer Baker had no reason to be at the place marked by a cross in the diagram, and in fact he was not there: He was following Truly from one stairway to the next, which put him in the northwest corner of the landing, a good

distance from the door. The diagram's error is confirmed by the
account given on the opposite page in the Report:

> As Baker reached the second floor, he was about 20 feet
> from the vestibule door. He intended to continue around
> to his left toward the stairway going up but through the
> window in the door he caught a fleeting glimpse of a man
> walking in the vestibule toward the lunchroom.

I retraced Baker's route, and it seemed to me that taking the
quickest way from one stairway to the next (Baker's idea at this
time was to get to the roof as quickly as possible) it would require
a rare combination of circumstances to see anyone go from the
vestibule into the lunchroom. As Truly stated in an affidavit for
the Commission, the door from the landing to the vestibule is
kept closed by a special mechanism. There is a small window at
the top, but the always open door of the lunchroom is not opposite
the vestibule door and the distance between them is only about
2 feet. Anyone running up the stairway would have to be in a
precise spot on the landing to see a man in the vestibule, and
would have to be there at the exact second the man inside was
taking his first step away from the window.

I do not wish to exclude the possibility of such a coincidence,
and I realize that reflections or shadows could have appeared at
the window. But there is more. Baker was behind Truly, who saw
nothing himself. It follows that if Oswald had just come down
from the sixth floor, he had already entered the vestibule before
Truly arrived at the landing. But since a mere step toward the
lunchroom would have sufficed to put Oswald beyond the limited
field of vision offered by the window, Baker could have seen him
only if Oswald had stopped and waited behind the vestibule door.
This does not seem plausible.

The difficulty is so obvious that the Report is unable to ignore
it: "Since the vestibule door is only a few feet from the lunchroom
door, the man must have entered the vestibule only a second or
two before Baker arrived at the top of the stairwell. Yet he must
have entered the vestibule door before Truly reached the top of
the stairwell, since Truly did not see him. If the man had passed

from the vestibule into the lunchroom, Baker could not have seen him." Quite so, but the Report goes no further—as if a statement of the problem amounted to an answer, so that there could be no reason to continue the discussion.

For once, nevertheless, the Commission tried to find out by asking the proper questions, but to no avail. The questioning was conducted by David W. Belin, assistant counsel of the Commission, with the active participation of one of the best-known members of the panel, former CIA Director Allen W. Dulles.

> *Mr. Belin.* When you started up the stairs what was your intention at that time?
> *Mr. Baker.* My intention was to go all the way to the top where I thought the shots had come from, to see if I could find something there, you know, to indicate that.
> *Mr. Belin.* And did you go all the way up to the top of the stairs right away?
> *Mr. Baker.* No, sir; we didn't.
> *Mr. Belin.* What happened?
> *Mr. Baker.* As I came out to the second floor there, Mr. Truly was ahead of me, and as I came out I was kind of scanning, you know, the rooms, and I caught a glimpse of this man walking away from this—I happened to see him through this window in this door. I don't know how come I saw him, but I had a glimpse of him coming down there.
> *Mr. Dulles.* Where was he coming from, do you know?
> *Mr. Baker.* No, sir. All I seen of him was a glimpse of him go away from me.

The Commission was to obtain nothing more on this point from Marrion L. Baker, who admitted that "from this window, you know, you can't see too well," and faithfully repeated the same story under further examination:

> *Mr. Belin.* What did you see that caused you to turn away from going up to the third floor?
> *Mr. Baker.* As I came out of that stairway running [*note*

that Baker says "running" and not "walking"—L.S.], Mr. Truly had already gone on around, see, and I don't know, as I come around——

Mr. Dulles.   Gone on around and up?

Mr. Baker.   He had already started around the bend to come to the next elevation going up, I was coming out this one on the second floor, and I don't know, I was kind of sweeping this area as I come up, I was looking from right to left and as I got to this door here [*meaning when his eyes reached the door, since he soon confirmed that he had not actually gone near it*—L.S.] I caught a glimpse of this man, just, you know, a sudden glimpse, that is all it was now, and it looked to me like he was going away from me.

Although Officer Baker was unable to specify what had led him to the lunchroom, he at least provided some useful information about the Commission's approach toward the question formulated in the title of this chapter. Comparing Oswald's minimum elapsed time with the maximum time of Truly and Baker, is there a chance that Truly and Baker have furnished Oswald with an alibi? That is, if Oswald had to come down from the sixth floor, would Truly and Baker have reached the lunchroom *before* Oswald?

To sum up the main points to consider: While the piles of boxes on the sixth floor would have made Oswald take a zigzag course from the window to the stairs, Truly and Baker were able to run the distance in a straight line, from the entrance to the same stairway. Next, the two went up one flight, while Oswald had to descend four, *then* cross the landing into the lunchroom, *then* work the Coke machine, *then* catch his breath. (Truly and Baker could go on panting.) Who took longer?

I asked this question in *The Reporter* of January 2, 1964, and repeated it in the March 1964 issue of *Commentary*. At that time nobody had asked Truly to run up the stairs to see how fast he did it. And among the many newsmen camped outside the Depository during the investigation none of them ever saw a motorcycle officer rush in under the eyes of inspectors with stopwatches.

The Report confirms, implicity but plainly, that this indispensable verification, neglected by the Dallas police, was likewise not carried out by the FBI, which had been ordered by President Johnson to conduct an "independent" inquiry.

We are told, in fact, that the re-enactment of the movements of Truly, Baker, and Oswald took place under the supervision of one of the Commission's attorneys. The Report itself does not say when it took place, but we know that the Commission, created on November 29, 1963, did not begin recruiting a staff until after December 16. Devoting the month of January to the study of documents, the Commission began its investigation and hearings only at the start of February. The accusations of the Dallas police had been made public on November 22. The no less accusing conclusions of the FBI were spread around on December 3 and definitively leaked out on December 9, when the five-volume record of its probe went to Chief Justice Warren.

Thus it is established beyond a doubt, through the efforts of the Commission (which, however, criticizes no one and does not even appear to recognize the anomaly of it), that, like the "cowboys" of Dallas, the investigatory arm of the Justice Department did not bother to determine whether the man accused of killing the President of the United States might have had an alibi.

Did the tests later undertaken by the Commission (on March 20, 1964, as we learn indirectly from the complete record published November 23, 1964) remove all doubts on this subject?

Before giving the stopwatch results, the Report makes some adjustments aimed at reducing the time Oswald would have needed to reach the lunchroom and increasing the time required by Baker and Truly. The Report thus denies that Oswald had a bottle of Coke in his hand when Baker saw him. I didn't invent the Coke story, nor did any of my colleagues. It was given out by the Dallas police, and there was even a variation that had Oswald drinking from the bottle rather than holding it. According to the written statements of Captain Fritz and FBI Agent James W. Bookhout, both reproduced in the Report, Oswald mentioned the bottle of Coke during his questioning on Friday. Supposedly this was checked out with Baker. If Baker ever challenged Oswald's statement, Fritz, Curry, Wade, and the rest have kept a strange silence about it. As I said, I was never able to contact Baker and I don't believe my colleagues were any luckier. Thus it was necessary to await the Report, and the last line on page 151, to learn that according to Baker "the man had nothing in his hands."

We have to accept the Commission's word; but to those who might be shocked by my skepticism, I recommend a look at page 679 of Volume XXVI of the Commission's Hearings and Exhibits. There they will find Exhibit No. 3076, the photocopy of a handwritten deposition made by Marrion L. Baker on September 23, 1964, to the FBI. The text, in his initial version: "On the second floor where the lunchroom is located, I saw a man standing in the lunchroom, drinking a Coke." Though still clearly legible, the words "drinking a Coke" have been crossed out. Sure enough, Baker put his initials above the words crossed out; this means he deleted them himself. It also means that, in his spontaneous recollection, Officer Baker remembered Oswald holding a Coke and that FBI Special Agent Richard J. Burnett (to whom Baker's "voluntary signed statement" was made) had to remind the witness that his memory did not conform with what the Warren Report was going to state four days later.

I must add one further remark. "Truly also noted at this time that Oswald's hands were empty," we read on page 152 of the Report. In January 1964, when Truly talked to me over the phone, his story was quite different. "From where I stood," he said, "I couldn't see if Oswald held something in his hand."

Concerning the time it took for Baker to reach Truly at the entrance of the building, the Report comments that the actual time probably was longer than the 15 seconds clocked in the reenactment. Yet Truly told me that the officer rushed up so quickly that he must have been "on foot, near the building." Baker himself told the Commission that when the shots were fired, he was about "180 to 200 feet" away and immediately "revved that motorcycle up." He added that when he got off his motorcycle a few yards from the entrance, people were "falling and rolling around down there," which suggests that very few seconds had elapsed since the last shot. He "ran straight to the entrance," and the speed at which Truly and Baker raced inside is indicated by the fact that Baker "bumped into Truly's back" when Truly stopped at the swinging door leading to the main room on the ground floor.

There were two tests. In the first, the Report says, Baker reached the second-floor landing in 1 minute, 30 seconds. In the second test he ran the course in 1 minute, 15 seconds. As for Oswald's time:

> Special Agent John Howlett of the Secret Service carried a rifle from the southeast corner of the sixth floor along the east aisle to the northeast corner. He placed the rifle on the floor near the site where Oswald's rifle was actually found after the shooting. Then Howlett walked down the stairway to the second-floor landing and entered the lunchroom. The first test, run at normal walking pace, required 1 minute, 18 seconds; the second test, at a "fast walk" took 1 minute, 14 seconds. . . . Howlett was not short winded at the end of either test run.

Thus, taking the longest time of Howlett-Oswald (1 minute, 18 seconds) and the shortest time of Baker (1 minute, 15 seconds), Oswald would have arrived *three seconds after Baker*. In other words, *Oswald would have had an alibi:* The testimony of Motorcycle Officer Marrion L. Baker of the Dallas Police Department would establish that he could not have been at the sixth-floor window when the shots were fired.

Even if we take the shortest time of Howlett-Oswald (1 minute, 14 seconds) and the longest time of Baker (1 minute, 30 seconds), Oswald would be only 16 seconds away from his alibi, according to the Commission's statement—and forgetting about the Coke, as the Commission wants us to do.

The stairway, incidentally, is located in the *northwest* corner and to get there Howlett must have continued along the north wall; there is obviously (and regrettably) an error in the text quoted above. Without going into this, the fact remains that the assassin had to detour around his own barricade of boxes and that, in addition, it takes a little longer to hide a rifle than to "place it on the floor." There is also the fact that, according to one of the Commission's star witnesses, the assassin did not immediately withdraw his rifle after firing, but "maybe paused for another second as though to assure hisself that he hit his mark." In short, further reductions can be made in that maximum interval of 16 seconds separating Oswald, in the hypothesis most unfavorable to him, from an alibi.

When we examine certain aspects of the exchange between Baker and Assistant Counsel Belin, it even becomes apparent that the interval could easily be reduced to zero.

Belin was the man who had supervised the re-enactment of the movements of Baker and Oswald on March 20, 1964. The questioning of Baker took place five days later. This interrogation brought out some suggestive data that are missing, misstated, or confused in the account prepared for the public, known as the Warren Report.

Describing the Commission's efforts to check on a possible alibi for Oswald, the Report begins by stating that Baker and Truly were asked to repeat their movements from the time the shots were fired "until Baker came upon Oswald in the lunch-room."

A glance at the diagram is enough to confirm that Oswald could not have entered the lunchroom without passing the land-ing where Truly was to arrive with Baker. Baker's time, therefore, should not have been clocked to the moment when he reached the lunchroom but to the time when Truly emerged on the landing, since Oswald by then must have been on the other side of the vestibule door. In the same paragraph, however, the Report says the watch was stopped at "Baker's arrival on the second-floor landing." This would not be accurate either, because the time should have been clocked up to the arrival of Truly, not Baker; but since the two men were close together, one might ignore the difference. In any case, there is a regrettable contradiction be-tween the beginning and the end of the paragraph, concerning a question of alibi in which every second counts. It is a shocking surprise to discover, futhermore, that the second and only acceptable version of the re-enactment is contradicted by the Commission's own records.

Here are the Report's words: "On the first test, the elapsed time between the simulated first shot and Baker's arrival on the second-floor stair landing was 1 minute and 30 seconds. The second test run required 1 minute and 15 seconds.[359]"

The number indicates one of the many notes at the end of the Report: It refers us to page 252 of Volume III of the Hearings. Not a single word on that page permits the conclusion that Baker's time was clocked until his arrival on the landing. On the contrary, we have this:

> *Mr. Dulles.* I want to get clear in my mind and for the record, it [*the re-enactment*—L.S.] started at the first shot and when did it terminate, when you saw Oswald?
>
> *Mr. Baker.* When we saw Oswald.
>
> *Mr. Dulles.* When you saw Oswald?
>
> *Mr. Baker.* Yes, sir.

In short, if we are to believe Baker's direct testimony, rather than the Report's deceptive use of it, the Commission surreptitiously let the stopwatch run until Baker reached the entrance of the lunchroom, and indeed—since Baker speaks of "we" without provoking questions—until Truly, several seconds later, joined him there.

As for Belin, his questioning of Baker following the exchange with Dulles shows that he is after something else. The Commission already has shortened Oswald's time by suppressing the Coke bottle. It now remains to delay the arrival of the two witnesses who, unwittingly, might have provided the accused with an alibi and destroyed the whole case from the start.

> *Mr. Belin.* Were we walking or running when we did this?
>
> *Mr. Baker.* The first time we did it a little bit slower, and the second time we hurried it up a little bit.
>
> *Mr. Belin.* Were we running or walking, when we moved, did we run or walk?
>
> *Mr. Baker.* From the time I got off the motorcycle we

walked the first time and then we kind of run the
second time from the motorcycle on into the building.

Mr. Belin.   All right. When we got inside the building
did we run or trot or walk?

Mr. Baker.   Well, we did it at a kind of trot, I would say,
it wasn't a real fast run, an open run. It was more of a
trot, kind of.

Mr. Belin.   You mentioned the relationship between
what we did on March 20 and what actually occurred on
November 22. Would you estimate that what we did on
March 20 was the maximum or the minimum as for the
time you took?

Mr. Baker.   I would say it would be the minimum.

The Report, as I said, mentioned the "good trot" of Baker and
Truly on November 22, and even the fact that Baker bumped
into Truly in his haste. But in dealing with the re-enactment the
Report gives only the subjective interpretation drawn from
Baker by Belin, that is, the conclusion that the time clocked on
March 20 was the minimum time required. The Report does not
mention what the transcript shows—that Baker said "we walked"
in the first test, the one invoked to prove there was no alibi. It is
psychologically unlikely that on November 22 Baker was excited
enough to draw his revolver, yet content to *walk* up the stairs
without hurrying. Baker himself had told Belin that he "came out
of that stairway running," and Truly had told me that he was
"running" too.

It is a fundamental principle of American law, as of modern
law in general, that any uncertainty, any ambiguity, should be
interpreted to the advantage of the accused. Rectifying the negligence of the FBI, the Commission headed by the Chief Justice
of the United States conducted tests that—distorted as they were
—left at most a margin of a very few seconds in one case, and in
the other resulted in an incontestable alibi for Oswald. The only
conclusion of the Commission is that "Oswald could have fired
the shots and still have been present in the second-floor lunchroom when seen by Baker and Truly."

2

THE CHICKEN BONES MYSTERY

THE WRITER OF DETECTIVE STORIES who wants to keep his readers never lets question marks and unexplained clues linger after the words "The End." One would think the public would be no less demanding when confronted not by fiction but by a real-life investigation, and above all when the victim is the President of the United States. But the Dallas investigators did not grant world opinion the same consideration shown by any good novelist for his readers. Hence the mystery of the chicken bones.

When they entered the sixth-floor storage room, the police found leftovers of a meal near the window from which the shots apparently had been fired: a partly eaten piece of fried chicken, an empty soda bottle, some chicken bones in a paper bag, and an empty cigarette package.

This discovery, announced by Captain Fritz on Friday afternoon, not only demonstrated the cold-blooded premeditation of the assassin but signified also that he had set himself up for a prolonged wait well before the arrival of the motorcade. Nobody doubted that the one who ate the chicken was the assassin, and some even wondered whether the police would pump Oswald's stomach to prove he was the culprit. Chief Curry nobly declared the next day that such methods would not have been "constitutional," and added that there was already enough proof of Oswald's guilt without pumping his stomach. But like his associate Will Fritz, he appeared absolutely convinced that the chicken meal was Oswald's.

35

That same Friday afternoon, however, Captain Fritz disclosed triumphantly that no less than six witnesses had seen Oswald in the building shortly before they went out to watch the Kennedys go by. One of these witnesses, he stressed, had invited Oswald to join them, but the suspect had refused; Fritz seemed to attach great significance to the fact that Oswald asked the witness to send the elevator back up.

Some wondered later how a manually operated elevator could be sent up with nobody inside. In the meantime most American newspapers published side by side—without seeing anything strange about it—both the story of Oswald's chicken and the report that he had been with six witnesses until shortly before the assassination.

While Oswald could have grabbed his rifle quickly and placed himself in firing position after the others had left, he hardly had time for a picnic, even assuming he had the appetite. Thus the chicken bones, added to the empty cigarette pack (Oswald did not smoke), took on capital importance. Since they could not be related to the suspect, they indicated the presence of another man near the window.

Was this other man an accomplice? Was he the real assassin whose place Lee Harvey Oswald was to have taken in the electric chair?

I don't know whether the Dallas police ever asked themselves these questions. But we know now that Fritz and his homicide bureau did not conduct any laboratory tests on the chicken remain and did not look for tooth marks (Fritz could have borrowed this idea from the manual of Söderman and O'Connell used in American police academies, without waiting for the Soviet criminologist I. Karpets to suggest it in *Izvestia*). Neither did any of the captain's men think of making plaster casts of the chicken pieces before throwing them in the garbage.

By Monday, November 25, the chicken bones had been dropped from the investigation. When I asked Jim Bowie, Wade's first assistant, about this, he brushed the question aside with a wave of his hand:

"Oh, that chicken," he said, plainly surprised at my interest.

"It was old. It wasn't Oswald who ate that. It was somebody else, the day before. The bones weren't fresh."

"Did they find the one who ate the chicken the day before, near the sixth-floor window?"

"I don't know. I don't think so."

"Did they look for him?"

"I think so. . . ."

My conversation with Bowie took place on November 27. On December 8, a number of American papers published a story by Gene Roberts, originally written for the *Detroit Free Press*. In the middle of it was the following paragraph:

> The storage room seemed made to order for an assassin. It was cluttered with rows of book cartons, some of them in stacks six feet high. Five Depository employees had worked in the storage room until noon, covering its floor with plywood. One of them, Bonnie Ray Williams, walked near the window at the 10 o'clock smoking break, downed a bottle of pop, chewed on a piece of chicken. This killed the theory that the assassin had eaten while waiting in ambush. . . .

This information, mentioned in passing as if it had been common knowledge for some time, was in fact a "scoop," the kind of sensational and exclusive bit of news that American reporters usually don't play down.

I had never heard until then of Bonnie Ray Williams or of the five men who had worked until noon that morning on the sixth floor, and when I checked with other reporters they said it was news to them, too. Gene Roberts was certainly not the only one to have noticed that the storage room was "made to order for an assassin," but he was the first to discover that no place could have been less suited to the assassination *that morning*, because half an hour before the first shot was fired five men were still moving things around to repair the floor. How could such a major piece of information have been ignored or forgotten for two weeks?

It was ignored, in any case, by the president of the Depository, Jack C. Cason. Explaining to the *Dallas Morning News* on the day of the assassination that the sixth-floor room was a little-used storage area, he concluded, said the *News:* "President Kennedy's killer could have been holed up in that sixth story hideaway for as long as four days without anyone bothering him. . . ."

It was forgotten, as well, by the manager of the Depository, Roy Truly, when a few days later he discussed the advantages of the sixth floor as an assassin's lair without mentioning the existence of Bonnie Ray Williams and his companions. That did not keep him from confirming Roberts' story when I spoke to him in January. "Maybe I left some things out when I talked to you reporters," he added, to explain why he had not alluded to it in his own statements. "Yes, it's possible that I forgot that, there were so many things to remember and we were all so upset."

Well, let us assume that Bonnie Ray Williams had his lunch at 10 o'clock in the morning and that this humble worker did not think about the six hours' work still ahead, which might have led him to save the rest of the chicken for later. But his unexpected appearance at the scene of the crime along with his companions suggests new questions. Since it now appeared that Oswald could not have used the "facilities" of the storage room when there was such unusual activity on the floor, where did he hide his rifle between 8 A.M. and noon? At what time, by what route, did he retrieve the weapon and bring it to his position by the window?

It was not, I hasten to add, the belated disclosure of Bonnie Ray Williams' mid-morning appetite that "killed the theory that the assassin had eaten while waiting in ambush."

Gene Roberts, who obviously received the cooperation of the Dallas authorities in preparing his story, meant Oswald when he wrote "assassin"; but the theory that "the assassin had eaten while waiting in ambush" had lost all probability two weeks earlier when Fritz announced that witnesses had been with the suspect shortly before the motorcade arrived. I had cabled this to my newspaper on November 23.

In Appendix XII of the Report, titled "Speculations and Rumors," which claims to contrast "the most widespread factual misunderstandings" with "what the Commission has found to be the true facts," the Commission cites two of these "speculations" relating to the chicken bones mystery. According to one, "It is probable that the chicken lunch, remains of which were found on the sixth floor, was eaten by an accomplice of Oswald who had hidden on the sixth floor overnight." The other "speculation": "Laboratory tests showed remains of the chicken lunch found on the sixth floor were 2 days old." It is regrettable that the Commission did not take up the "factual misunderstanding" committed by Jim Bowie, the assistant D.A. of Dallas, who had told me, though without any reference to laboratory tests, that the chicken had been eaten "the day before."

The Warren Commission definitively sets aside the initial statements of Captain Fritz, even lists them among the "incorrect or inaccurate" hearsay items and unverified leads mentioned in the eight pages (out of 888) devoted by the Commission to criticism of the Dallas procedures. "Police sources," the Report declares, "were also responsible for the mistaken notion that the chicken bones found on the sixth floor were the remains of Oswald's lunch." But while the Report confirms Gene Roberts' exclusive story and explains away the chicken bones mystery with the same *deus ex machina* named Bonnie Ray Williams, it introduces variations that raise two new problems for every problem it claims to solve, as did the investigation criticized by the Commission.

The chicken, says the Report in opposing its "true facts" to the speculations quoted above, was eaten by Bonnie Ray Williams. But Bonnie Ray Williams, it goes on, left the bones on the sixth floor "shortly after noon on November 22" and not during the smoking break referred to in the amended story of the Dallas authorities, made public by Roberts.

The Dallas detectives had Bonnie Ray Williams eating at 10 o'clock in the morning because they had to fit the bones into the pattern imposed by Captain Fritz, who had said that Oswald was with other employees on the sixth floor shortly before the motorcade passed; none could have eaten lunch there at that time. The story of the 10 o'clock break apparently had not been ready when I talked to Bowie on November 27, so he tried to get rid of the bones by aging them a day. The Commission prefers to dispose of the timetable imposed by Fritz, and does so by simply sweeping his statements, and the affidavits of witnesses that led to those statements, into the Report's basket of anonymous "speculations and rumors." As to the "true fact," here it is: It was "about 11:55 a.m." when Oswald was seen for the last time on the sixth floor, by an employee named Charles Givens.

Thus it became possible that Bonnie Ray Williams, whose meal threatens to weigh for some time to come on the stomachs of the official investigators, could have eaten the chicken "shortly after noon on November 22." The Commission does not bother with Williams' colleagues on the sixth floor that morning, who had helped maintain the fiction of Williams' 10 o'clock meal up to the time the Report was published. The Commission does not pause, either, to consider the fact that Bonnie Ray Williams himself had said nothing at all about any meal at first, when the chicken bones mystery was widely discussed in newspapers and on television; he then went along with the 10 o'clock version, only to end by agreeing with the "shortly after noon" account. The Report, finally, retains Williams' statement that it took him "5, 10, maybe 12 minutes" to eat, and that the meal took place on the sixth floor "at least 15 minutes before the assassination."

But where exactly on the sixth floor? The question had never arisen before September 27, 1964. It popped up abruptly with the publication of the Report, because the Report—without saying so—upsets a part of the record that had seemed established once and for all.

The discovery of the leftovers near the assassin's window was one of the first bits of news made public by the Dallas police. It was confirmed by the federal agents who went to the sixth floor. Later, while there were several accounts of the origin and significance of the chicken bones, the place where they had been found was never disputed. Now, 10 months later, the Report was out, telling us in Chapter VI ("Investigation of Possible Conspiracy") that Williams had dined "in the area of the third or fourth set of windows from the east wall," and even specifying that "at this point he was approximately 20–30 feet away from the southeast corner window."

Did Williams, for some reason of his own, take the leftovers to the corner window before rejoining some of his colleagues on the floor below? No: "Williams," the Report continues, "left the remains of his lunch, including chicken bones and a bottle of soda, near the window where he was eating."

All this becomes completely incomprehensible when one notices how vague the Report manages to be while pretending to be precise. If Williams left the remains near the window where he had eaten, why doesn't the Report tell us exactly which window it was? Why does it waver between "the area of the third or fourth set of windows" and limit itself to stating the "approximate" distance to the southeast window, give or take 10 feet? We have no hesitation in believing (as we learn from Volume VII of the 26-volume record) that the Dallas detectives removed the leftovers without first marking their location on the floor. But the Report says nothing about it, nor does it explain how the Commission arrived at its estimates in the absence of such information.

What the Hearings reveal on this point is not likely to improve our opinion of the Commission, its methods, and its "facts."

True enough, Volume III gives us the testimony of Bonnie Ray Williams. Assistant Counsel Joseph A. Ball asked him, "Where did you eat your lunch?" And Williams replied: "I ate my lunch —I am not sure about this, but the third or the fourth set of windows, I believe." Along with Helen Louise Markham and Howard Leslie Brennan, whom we will soon meet, Williams— a young Texas Negro, unsure of himself, plainly anxious not to displease his white interrogators—belongs to the unlikely crew of Commission witnesses whose testimony would be reduced to shreds in five minutes of cross-examination. But we know this was a risk not taken by the Commission, which took care to prevent any such cross-examination.

For purposes of reference and for another reason, I will quote a brief passage from Williams' testimony. He had just stated that after finishing his meal on the sixth floor, he descended to the fifth floor by the east elevator. Ball reminded him that, according to the FBI, he had declared on November 23 that he had used the

stairs, not the elevator, and then on January 14 had said he had
gone down in the west elevator. The exchange went on:

> *Mr. Ball.*   The other day, when I talked to you in Dallas,
> on Friday 20 March——
>
> *Mr. Williams.*   Yes, sir.
>
> *Mr. Ball.*   And at that time were you able—did you re-
> member which elevator it was?
>
> *Mr. Williams.*   Which elevator I had?
>
> *Mr. Ball.*   What you had come down from six to five on.
>
> *Mr. Williams.*   As I remember, I first said I wasn't sure.
> After the fellows said they brought the west elevator up,
> I said I must have the east elevator.
>
> *Mr. Ball.*   Is it fair to say now that you don't have any
> definite memory of whether it was the east or west
> elevator?
>
> *Mr. Williams.*   Yes, sir. I believe that would be true.

My special reason for choosing this passage was Ball's disclosure
that he had conversed privately with the witness four days before
his appearance at the Commission hearing. Appendix VI of the
Report contains the Commission's rules concerning the questioning of witnesses. They deal in part with the authority given to
staff members to question witnesses on their own, but always in
behalf of the Commission and at its direction, under set rules of
procedure, including the stenographic transcription of all that is
said. There is nothing in Appendix VI to suggest that staff members were allowed to confer with witnesses scheduled to appear at
a hearing in order to assist in preparing their testimony.

Returning to our chicken, we have been told that Williams left
the remains of his meal near the place where he had eaten. The
Commission questioned the policemen who had searched the sixth
floor and had found or seen these remains. When the Report states
as an established fact that Williams ate "in the area of the third or
fourth set of windows from the east wall," is this because the
police changed their original story and were led to confirm that
it was indeed there, and not near the corner window, that the
chicken bones were found?

Let us begin with Captain Fritz, author of the theory that Oswald was savoring a piece of fried chicken while waiting for the President to appear on the telescopic sight of his Mannlicher-Carcano. When Fritz was questioned by the same Joseph A. Ball (apparently without a preparatory visit to Dallas), Commission member John J. McCloy interrupted:

> *Mr. McCloy.* When you went in, Captain Fritz, and you saw the site which Oswald is alleged to have fired the shot from——
>
> *Mr. Fritz.* Yes, sir.
>
> *Mr. McCloy.* Did you see any signs of a lunch there, a chicken there?
>
> *Mr. Fritz.* No, sir; I will tell you where that story about the chicken comes from. At the other window above there, where people in days past, you know had eaten their lunches, they left chicken bones and pieces of bread, all kinds of things up and down there. That isn't where he was at all. He was in a different window, so I don't think those things have anything to do with it. Someone wrote a story about it in the papers, and we have got all kinds of bad publicity from it and they wrote in telling us how to check those chicken bones and how to get them from the stomach and everything.

Captain Fritz thus denies having anything to do with a story dozens of reporters and millions of TV listeners had heard him tell. But there is something more amazing: On April 22, 1964, the date of the above testimony, the head of the Dallas homicide bureau, responsible for the investigation of the assassination, still had no knowledge of the existence—and the meal—of Bonnie Ray Williams. In any case, while Fritz talks of "the other window above there," he does not specify which window, and his doleful reference to bad publicity brought by the chicken bones cannot be used to support the Commission's new thesis.

The first person who discovered the assassin's nook in the southeast corner was Deputy Sheriff Luke Mooney.

Luke Mooney was questioned by the Commission a day after

it had heard Williams' testimony. Mooney told the panel he had noticed the barricade of boxes, worked his way through them, seen the shells on the floor, and spotted near the window sill a box that seemed to have been used as a gun rest, and which, he had even noticed, had a slight crease on top. When Assistant Counsel Ball asked him if he had seen anything else in the corner, Mooney immediately mentioned "a partially eaten piece of fried chicken," and added later that this was on top of one of the boxes used as a shield in front of the window. He also said a small grocery bag was on the same box.

Senator John Sherman Cooper, another Commission member, then intervened:

> *Senator Cooper.*   How far was the chicken, the piece of chicken you saw, and the paper bag from the boxes near the window, and particularly the box that had the crease in it?
>
> *Mr. Mooney.*   I would say they might have been 5 feet or something like that. He wouldn't have had to leave the location. He could just maybe take one step and lay it over there, if he was the one that put it there.
>
> *Senator Cooper.*   You mean if someone had been standing near the box with the crease in it?
>
> *Mr. Mooney.*   Yes, sir.

Even more explicit was the testimony of two policemen questioned by David W. Belin in Dallas.

Motorcycle Officers Clyde Haygood and E. D. Brewer had been in the motorcade and later returned to the Depository to help search the building. They were on the sixth floor when Mooney noticed the three shells on the floor.

Following is part of Haygood's testimony (he had just told how he had gone to the southeast corner after hearing someone say he had found the shells) :

> *Mr. Belin.*   See any paper bags or anything around there?
>
> *Mr. Haygood.*   Yes; there was a lunch bag there. You could call it a lunch bag.

Mr. Belin.   Where was that?

Mr. Haygood.   There at the same location where the shells were.

Mr. Belin.   Was there a coke bottle or anything with it?

Mr. Haygood.   Dr. Pepper bottle.

Next, part of Brewer's testimony (he also was searching the floor when the shells were found) :

Mr. Belin.   Did you go and take a look at the cartridge cases?

Mr. Brewer.   Yes, sir.

Mr. Belin.   How many cartridge cases did you see?

Mr. Brewer.   Three.

Mr. Belin.   Where were they?

Mr. Brewer.   They were there under, by the window.

Mr. Belin.   What window?

Mr. Brewer.   In the southeast corner of the building, facing south.

Mr. Belin.   See anything else there at the time by the window?

Mr. Brewer.   Paper lunch sack and some chicken bones or partially eaten piece of chicken, or a piece of chicken.

Mr. Belin.   Anything else?

Mr. Brewer.   A drink bottle.

Mr. Belin.   What bottle?

Mr. Brewer.   A cold drink bottle, soda pop bottle.

A third policeman searching the storage room, who also went to the southeast corner when the shells were found, was Sergeant Gerald L. Hill. He confirmed Luke Mooney's story: "On top of the larger stack of boxes that would have been used for conceal-ment, there was a chicken leg bone and a paper sack which ap-peared to have been about the size normally used for a lunch sack."

Two detectives of the homicide bureau arrived shortly after the discovery of the shells and before the rifle was found. They were ordered by Fritz to guard the southeast corner until the arrival of Lieutenant J. C. Day and his assistant, Robert Lee Studebaker,

the police laboratory technicians assigned to look for fingerprints
and take pictures. Detectives L. D. Montgomery and Marvin Johnson were questioned in Dallas, one by Ball and the other by Belin.

Montgomery's deposition seems particularly convincing and
informative, even though the witness hesitated between a box
and the floor.

> *Mr. Ball.*   Did you see anything else over in the south-
> east corner of that sixth floor?
>
> *Mr. Montgomery.*   Well, sir, as I say, there was a lot of
> boxes and there was a sack and there was this pieces of
> chicken.
>
> *Mr. Ball.*   Was there a piece of chicken over there?
>
> *Mr. Montgomery.*   Yes, sir—there was chicken bones and
> what not—it looked like somebody had been eating
> chicken there.
>
> *Mr. Ball.*   Where was that?
>
> *Mr. Montgomery.*   It was right there with the boxes—
> right there on the floor.
>
> *Mr. Ball.*   On the floor?
>
> *Mr. Montgomery.*   Yes, sir.
>
> *Mr. Ball.*   All right.
>
> *Mr. Montgomery.*   Well, let me see, there was one piece
> of chicken on a box and there was a piece on the floor—
> just kind of scattered around right there.
>
> *Mr. Ball.*   Where was the paper sack?
>
> *Mr. Montgomery.*   Let's see—the paper sack—I don't re-
> call for sure if it was on the floor or on the box, but I
> know it was just there—one of those pictures might show
> exactly where it was.
>
> *Mr. Ball.*   I don't have a picture of the paper sack.
>
> *Mr. Montgomery.*   You don't? Well, it was there—I can't
> recall for sure if it was on one of the boxes or on the floor
> there.
>
> *Mr. Ball.*   It was over in what corner?
>
> *Mr. Montgomery.*   It would be in the southeast corner of
> the building there where the shooting was.

Marvin Johnson, Montgomery's partner, was less certain of this last point than his colleague. He told Belin that "over to the right, which would be back toward the west of the window, there was a lunch sack—a brown paper bag—and some remnants of fried chicken, and a pop bottle." When Belin pounced on his reference to the "west side," Johnson admitted the items he had seen could have been near the second pair of windows. But he refused to place them beyond that point when Belin tried to make him say the bones could have been between the second and third set of windows. Since the Report locates the meal between the third and fourth set, we are still far from any confirmation of the audacious thesis of the Commission, presented in the Report as a statement of fact.

But on the same day Ball came up with Robert Lee Studebaker. Detective Studebaker worked in the Dallas police laboratory under Lieutenant Day; both had arrived on the sixth floor after all the others mentioned above. We learn in the course of his testimony that Studebaker collected important items of evidence without photographing them first, and that while he took a number of pictures of the boxes near the window, only two of these were taken before the boxes were moved. It seems, however, that Studebaker did photograph a grocery bag and a bottle of Dr. Pepper, and said this was done in front of the third set of windows.

> *Mr. Ball.* Now, did you see a chicken bone over near the boxes in the southeast corner, over near where you found the cartridges and the paper sack? [*Studebaker had found nothing at all, and the paper sack mentioned by Ball is the wrapping in which Oswald was said to have carried the rifle but which Studebaker did not bother to photograph before picking it up*—L. S.]
>
> *Mr. Studebaker.* I don't believe there was one there.
>
> *Mr. Ball.* You didn't see any. One witness, a deputy sheriff named Luke Looney [*Ball means Mooney*—L. S.] said he found a piece of chicken partly eaten up on top of one of the boxes; did you see anything like that?
>
> *Mr. Studebaker.* No.

There never was a confrontation between Mooney and Studebaker, or between Studebaker and Detectives Montgomery and Johnson, although Studebaker said "they were with me all the time over in that one corner" (the southeast corner). They were with him all the time, yet Studebaker did not see what they saw near one window, and they did not see what Studebaker claims to have seen near another. The Commission deemed it unnecessary to explore the contradictions. It was content to choose from the seven depositions the one that suited its purpose, and ignored the six others.

Deputy Sheriff Mooney, the first to find the remnants of the meal; Sergeant Hill and Motorcycle Officers Haygood and Brewer, early arrivals on the scene; and Detectives Montgomery and Johnson, who guarded the southeast corner—the testimony of each of these six men clearly ought to have carried more weight, however, than the word of Studebaker, the last to appear on the sixth floor. If during the utterly incompetent search of the sixth floor the remnants of the meal were moved, the testimony of the first to arrive obviously should count for more than the statements of the latecomer, even if they weren't six to one.

There is another reason for believing that if evidence was moved, the direction was from the first window to the third, not vice versa. All the officers before Studebaker agreed—even when they were not sure whether the bag and bones were on the floor or on a box—that there was a piece of chicken, or bones, outside the bag. But Studebaker said the bones "were all inside the sack, wrapped up and put right back in." It seems logical to assume that the bones were outside the bag *before* being inside, rather than believe they were scattered around *after* having been "wrapped up and put right back in."

The decision of the Commission to accept Studebaker's version in the face of all these contradictions finally appears to have been as arbitrary as its conclusion that the timing tests foreclosed the possibility of an alibi for Oswald. And this mystery of the chicken bones is by no means petty or insignificant. Because of the way it sets out to reconstruct the events, the Commission's entire case may ultimately depend on where Bonnie Ray Williams had lunch on November 22, 1963.

3

THE ITALIAN RIFLE
MYSTERY

THE CONTROVERSY OVER THE MANNLICHER-CARCANO 1940, said to have been the murder weapon, was followed closely throughout the world and is still a subject of international dispute.

A number of European experts—including engineers of the Beretta firm, which manufactured the rifle, and instructors in the Italian Army, which used it in World War II—said a gunman armed with this weapon could not fire three shots with such accuracy, from such an angle, at a moving target, in five or six seconds. Other experts, European as well as American, said the opposite— as might be expected whenever experts are brought into a case. But even those who said the performance was possible were nearly unanimous in adding that it required an expert marksman who was thoroughly familiar with the rifle and who practiced regularly.

Austrian Olympic champion Hubert Hammerer considered such an exploit "highly improbable." To minimize the unfavorable effect of statements such as this the Dallas authorities at first sought to cast doubt on the testimony relating to the rapidity of the shots.

Assistant District Attorney Jim Bowie, for example, carefully explained to me how mistaken the human ear can be and that the shots that reportedly lasted five or six seconds could well have taken four times as long. Sheriff Bill Decker, stating that Oswald had "plenty of time to fire the three shots which killed President Kennedy and wounded Governor John Connally," announced on his own that the shots were fired "probably within 20 seconds."

49

Then on November 27, Dr. Kemp Clark, who had operated on the President at Parkland Memorial Hospital, let it be known that the first bullet had struck Kennedy "just below the Adam's apple, at about the necktie knot." His statement was released to the press by the local officials, along with comments to the effect that the medical opinion confirmed that the duration of the shots had been closer to 20 seconds than 5.

Thus, according to the November 27 theory, Kennedy was first hit when his car was still on Houston Street, slowing for the sharp turn into Elm Street. When the motorcade then went on to the triple railroad underpass leading to the Stemmons Freeway, the assassin traced a 90-degree arc with his rifle, still keeping his target in the telescopic sight, and fired two more times. He therefore had at least 10 or 15 seconds between the first and the second shot, it was said, and the wire services quickly dispatched this reassuring news to Austria, Italy, and everywhere else where doubts had been raised as to the capability of the Mannlicher-Carcano 1940.

The same day, however, Connally denied this theory in his first interview at Parkland Memorial Hospital. Here is Connally's description of the attack:

> We had just turned the corner. We heard a shot. I turned to my left. I was sitting in the jump seat. I turned to my left and looked in the back seat. The President had slumped. He had said nothing. Almost simultaneously, as I turned, I was hit, and I knew I'd been hit badly, and I said—I knew the President had been hit—and I said, "My God, they're going to kill us all." And then there was a third shot, and the President was hit again. . . .

Finally, a film taken by a local amateur proved the Presidential car had passed the Depository at the time of the shooting. On the basis of the film speed, it was officially determined that the interval between the first and last shots was five and a half seconds.

For the investigators who seemed to consider their first duty not to seek the truth but to convict Oswald, this was a double catastrophe.

They had enthusiastically seized on Dr. Clark's statement because, linked to the theory that the first shot had been fired
when Kennedy was on Houston Street, it tended to extend the
estimated duration of the shots and thus smooth over the question
of the rifle's capability. When they had to abandon the shot before
the turn, Clark's statement placed them in a most embarrassing
situation. As Richard Dudman asked in the *St. Louis Post-Dispatch*
December 1, "How could the President have been shot in the
front from the back?"

The answer came on December 18, again in the hypocritical
form of one of those deliberate leaks that played such a large role
in the Oswald affair. It was solemnly attributed this time to "a
source fully acquainted with results of a post-mortem examination
conducted at the Bethesda, Maryland, Naval Hospital."

In their first statements on the day of the assassination, the
Parkland doctors, including Dr. Clark, had confessed they were
puzzled by the President's throat wound. The wound, they said,
could have been caused by the exit of the bullet that had struck
the back of the President's head, but it could also have been
caused by the entrance of another bullet that lodged in the body.
I don't know how these doubts were transformed five days later
into Dr. Clark's certainty that the throat wound marked the entrance and not the exit of a bullet. Yet the opposite version is
given in the December 18 autopsy report.

According to that report—which the American press, knowing
the method by which it was made public, considered to be official
—the first bullet had struck the President in the back some five or
six inches below the collar line, and had lodged in the flesh without damaging any vital organ. The Parkland doctors had not seen
this wound because the President was lying on his back and there
was no time to turn him over for a general examination. The
urgent thing was to remedy, if possible, the effects of another
wound immediately recognized as critical. This second wound
came from a bullet that had gone through the head from back
to front, exiting just under the Adam's apple, the December 18
autopsy report said.

Dallas thus had been saved by Washington, so far as Dudman's question was concerned. But in return it had lost the "evidence" that the shots could have lasted 20 seconds, and it still was necessary to prove Oswald's skill as a marksman. In the Marines, Oswald's scores had varied between a mediocre 191 and a 212, which is about average. Furthermore, it was the general opinion that even a champion would require regular practice to be able to fire with the accuracy of Kennedy's assassin. Oswald, the police told us, had received the weapon on March 20. To hit his target three times in five and a half seconds with a bolt-action rifle he had never touched before March 20, he would have needed intensive practice up to the day before the assassination. Where? How?

Oswald's family life, especially after October 7, hardly lent itself to secret rifle practice.

Such practice was out of the question when Oswald was in Dallas looking for a job or working at the Depository, for the simple reason that according to the authorities themselves the rifle was kept in the garage of the Paine house in Irving. But it was no easier during the weekends Oswald spent in Irving—with his wife, children, and Mrs. Paine's television set. He would have had to sneak out of the small four-room house with his rifle and remain away for hours at a time without explaining his absence.

Two weeks after the assassination, however, on December 6, the *Dallas Morning News* reported that the police had found witnesses who said they had seen Oswald practicing on a local rifle range with his Italian weapon.

Floyd Davis, owner of the Grand Prairie Sportsdrome, was soon located by reporters. He told them that he himself had seen nothing, but that four of his customers had mentioned a visitor who had acted strangely. Quite an expert with his foreign rifle equipped with telescopic sight, he had caused some annoyance among those around him by nonchalantly firing at their targets. According to Davis, these customers viewed Lee Oswald on television and recognized him as the man they had seen on the rifle range; it was only because they never considered it important enough that nobody told the police or the FBI for 15 days.

An interesting point about the "testimony" of the witnesses

who said they recognized Oswald was that they had seen him arrive at the wheel of a car. Oswald had no car, and Mrs. Paine—who had tried to teach him, without much success—said he did not know how to drive.

The Warren Report does not retain the testimony of the Sportsdrome customers. It comments that on one of the dates Oswald was supposed to have been there, September 28, 1963, he was actually in Mexico. Concerning another date, November 10, the Report says "there is persuasive evidence that on November 10 Oswald was at the Paines' home in Irving and did not leave to go to the rifle range." It notes finally the allusions to "an old car, possibly a 1940 or 1941 Ford," driven to the Sportsdrome by the mysterious rifleman, and remarks that as of the date it was seen, September 28, "there is evidence that Oswald could not drive"; besides, it adds, "there is no indication that Oswald ever had access to such a car."

There are two major "revelations" by the Warren Commission that belong in this chapter. Its Report completely overturns what had been published before—and accepted as fact up to then—regarding the bullet wounds. It also upsets the rules of logic by trying to prove, against its own evidence, that Oswald had the skill required to fire the shots.

Unlike other critics of the Dallas inquiry, I have not been involved in the medical dispute over the wounds of Kennedy and Connally. But while I do not feel like questioning or even scrutinizing the horrible scientific descriptions of the doctors, I expect them to agree among themselves about their conclusions before presenting them to the public. Above all, I believe the Commission has no excuse for having allowed a false autopsy report to be circulated as official findings. The Commission never challenged the authenticity of that report, and then compounded the irresponsibility of its behavior by publishing a new autopsy report without even acknowledging that there had been a completely different one before.

I am still waiting for someone to give me a good reason why the Bethesda autopsy report was not made public as soon as it was completed.

While doing nothing to prevent leaks, and indeed committing them itself, the Commission said of its inquiry in general that it had to complete all of its studies before publishing any results. But it hardly could have made new discoveries about the President's wounds after he was buried, and the public had indeed the right to expect that there would be no change in the autopsy report once it was finished and signed. It is impossible to imagine any valid reason to withhold such a report, and that is why even those who deplored the lack of dignity in the leak never doubted the authenticity of the document publicized on December 18.

This document was attributed to "a source fully acquainted with results of a post-mortem examination conducted at the Bethesda, Maryland, Naval Hospital." It was carried as such throughout the world by all the press services and remained the official truth until September 27, 1964. Then suddenly, on the date the Warren Report was published, it became "non-existent," as George Orwell would have said.

According to the Warren Report, the first bullet that hit the President "entered the base of the back of his neck slightly to the right of the spine. It traveled downward and exited from the front of the neck, causing a nick in the left lower portion of the knot in the President's necktie." The second bullet—the only fatal one —was now described by the Bethesda doctors as having "entered the skull above and to the right of the external occipital protuberance." This bullet apparently fragmented in passing through the cranial cavity from back to front, and "a portion of the projectile made its exit through the parietal bone on the right carrying with it portions of cerebrum, skull and scalp." Here finally is the summary given by the Report concerning Connally's wound: "The Governor had been hit by a bullet which entered at the extreme right side of his back at a point below his right armpit. The bullet traveled through his chest in a downward and forward direction, exited below his right nipple, passed through his right wrist which had been in his lap, and then caused a wound to his left thigh." A more detailed description elsewhere in the Report adds that "a small metallic fragment remained in the Governor's leg."

While confirming that a total of three shots were fired, the Report suggests that one of the three bullets may have gone astray completely and that the Governor's wounds in this case were caused by the bullet that had passed through Kennedy's neck without striking any bone.

This hypothesis was categorically rejected by Connally himself, and not only in his statement before the Commission. In the course of a two-hour CBS telecast on the occasion of the Report's publication on September 27, 1964, the Governor said flatly: "I understand there's some question in the minds of the experts about whether or not we could both have been hit by the same bullet, and that was the first bullet. I just don't happen to believe that. I won't believe it, never will believe, because, again, I heard the first shot, I recognized it for what I thought it was. I had time to turn to try to see what had happened. I was in the process of turning again before I felt the impact of a bullet."

Even though the Report's general summary recognizes that the theory of two bullets causing all the wounds gave rise to "some difference of opinion" among Commission members, it maintains elsewhere that "there is persuasive evidence from the experts that one of these two bullets [which struck Kennedy] also struck Governor Connally." And the Report does not refrain from referring to a lost bullet—and thus to a wild shot—when it seeks to prove "Oswald's Rifle Capability" (the title of the last section of Chapter IV, "The Assassin").

The next-to-last section of Chapter III, devoted to a study of the shots, has the positive title "The Shot That Missed." The Commission starts by giving the reasons why it cannot decide whether the assassin missed on the first, second, or third shot, and the last sentence of the section openly admits: "The wide range of possibilities and the existence of conflicting testimony, when coupled with the impossibility of scientific verification, precludes a conclusive finding by the Commission as to which shot missed." The Commission also describes the futile efforts to recover traces of a possible stray bullet. But at the end of the chapter, before proceeding to "The Assassin," it considerably lengthens its estimate of the time required for the shots, which now becomes "approximately 4.8 to in excess of 7 seconds." The technical reasoning follows:

(a) "The time span between the shot entering the back of the President's neck and the bullet which shattered his skull was 4.8 to 5.6 seconds"; this would be the total time span of the shots not only if none of the shots missed but also if the second one missed.

(b) If the "missed shot" was the first or third, "then a minimum of 2.3 seconds (necessary to operate the rifle) must be added to the time span of the shots which hit, giving a minimum time of 7.1 to 7.9 seconds for the three shots."

Then comes an extraordinary argument in which, to establish that Oswald was perfectly capable of such a feat, the Report begins by affirming that it did not amount to feat at all; then demonstrates by tests that it was in fact an exceptional one; and finally concludes that it has proved its point.

To begin with, the Report disregards completely the opinions of the Olympic champion Hubert Hammerer and the Italian Army instructors, as well as those of many other experts (including some in the United States) who had stated that accuracy with such a rifle was conceivable only after intensive training with the weapon. The Commission knows of only four competent experts in the world: a major and a sergeant of the Marines, an FBI specialist, and a civilian ballistics expert heading the "Army Infantry Weapons Evaluation Branch." The major said the shots were "not particularly difficult"; the sergeant considered them "easy"; the FBI man did not see "any difficulty" in hitting the target; and the ballistics expert believed the job would not require "an exceptional shot" but merely "a proficient man with this weapon." The Commission, therefore, happily concludes that the whole thing was "easy."

Later, however, the Commission—in a daring display of independence—conducted some tests under the supervision of Ronald Simmons, the ballistics expert.

Using Oswald's Mannlicher-Carcano, three expert riflemen, all "rated as master by the National Rifle Association," fired two series of three shots from the top of a tower at three targets placed at distances and positions corresponding to the Elm Street locations. The Report says the targets were in the shape of "silhouettes" but does not define what it means by "hitting the target." I suppose, out of respect for the Commission, that it did not mean *any* part of the silhouette but only the area of the head and neck. The Report, however, fails to make this explicit.

Now we come to the results. The time spans of the three masters of the National Rifle Association were 4.6, 6.75, and 8.25 seconds for the first series, and 5.15, 6.45, and 7 seconds for the second. Of six shots fired at each target all hit the first, four missed the second "by several inches," and one missed the third.

It is astonishing, then, to read in the Report: "On the basis of these results, Simmons testified that in his opinion the probability of hitting the targets at the relatively short range at which they were hit was very high." *Very high!* These words close page 193 of the Report, where the test results are recorded. Of three champions rated as masters by the National Rifle Association— among the best riflemen in the country—only one succeeded in keeping within the time span generally attributed to Oswald (4.8 to 5.6 seconds). Even if we accept the hypothesis of the missed shot—never proved and not accepted unanimously by the Commission—and add 2.3 seconds to Oswald's time, that would still leave one of the three champions who did not do as well as the suspect. To the normal human mind this signifies that, contrary to the claim of Ronald Simmons, which has become the Commission's theory, the "probability of hitting the targets" was in fact very low.

In the course of another test with the Mannlicher-Carcano conducted by FBI experts, a "defect in the scope" was discovered that, according to Agent Robert A. Frazier, "would cause a slight miss to the right." Frazier adds, however, that "a person familiar with the weapon could compensate for it."

Was Oswald familiar with the weapon? The Report, as we have seen, rejects the possibility that Oswald trained at the Sportsdrome in Grand Prairie. In another section, where fibers taken from the butt plate are offered as evidence that Oswald used the rifle on November 22, the Report even declares there was "no reliable evidence that Oswald used the rifle at any time between September

23, when it was transported from New Orleans, and November 22, the day of the assassination." What then remains? "Marina Oswald testified that in New Orleans in May of 1963, she observed Oswald sitting with the rifle on their screened porch at night, sighting with the telescopic lens and operating the bolt." One need not be an expert to know that you cannot find a defect in a telescopic sight, much less get used to compensating for it, without firing the rifle. But the Report can mention only a single "occasion" (sometime in March or April) when, according to Marina and one of her Russian friends, Oswald went off with the Mannlicher-Carcano, saying he was going to do some target shooting.

The Commission, however, takes note of each time Oswald is believed to have gone hunting in Texas or in the Soviet Union. It does not mention the statement given by Marina Oswald on December 10, 1963, to the FBI concerning her husband's Russian hunting experience. She recalled, the FBI quoted her as saying, "only one occasion when he went hunting," and on that occasion he was "unsuccessful in bagging any game." As its final proof that Oswald was the kind of rifleman who easily could have done better than a master of the National Rifle Association, the Commission produces Oswald's record in the Marines.

The Report confirms Oswald's scores given earlier in this chapter. "Oswald was tested in December of 1956, and obtained a score of 212, which was 2 points above the minimum for qualification as a 'sharpshooter' in a scale of marksman—sharpshooter—expert. In May 1959, on another range, Oswald scored 191, which was 1 point over the minimum for ranking as a 'marksman.'" To the uninformed reader the words "marksman" and "sharpshooter" both suggest some kind of a crack shot, but the Report simply omits the fact that the Marine Corps has no lesser categories. The classification in three categories, based on a system of points running from 190 to 250, applies to all of the men and not to an elite group; a score of 190 is equivalent to zero. In other words, in May 1959, shortly before leaving the service, Oswald scored just one point more than the minimum required of each of the 175,571 officers and men then in the Marines.

If there were any doubts left about Oswald's *lack* of "rifle capability," we have the deposition of Lieutenant Colonel Allison G. Folsom, Marine Corps personnel records chief. His testimony is transcribed in Volume VIII of the Hearings.

Questioning Folsom in the name of the Commission, John H. Ely informed the officer that the panel counted on him—"because of your position"—to "interpret" the scores, abbreviations, and other notations in Oswald's military records. Folsom explained a number of technical points relating to the documents and finally talked about Oswald's rifle scorebook. He pointed out, for instance, that at the time Oswald shot his best score (the 212 that edged him into the middle class, sharpshooter), his results were poorer than what was considered the norm.

Folsom even gave the impression that, in the context of the scorebook, Oswald's 1956 classification as sharpshooter might have been due largely to chance.

> *Mr. Ely.*   I just wonder, after having looked through the whole scorebook, if we could fairly say that all that it proves is that at this stage of his career he was not a particularly outstanding shot.
>
> *Colonel Folsom.*   No, no, he was not. His scorebook indicates—as a matter of fact—that he did well at one or two ranges in order to achieve the two points over the minimum score for sharpshooter.
>
> *Mr. Ely.*   In other words, he had a good day the day he fired for qualification?
>
> *Colonel Folsom.*   I would say so.

The 26-volume record gives us several other depositions, all attesting that, contrary to the Commission's claim, Oswald was not even close to being a crack shot when he left the Marines nearly four years before the assassination. In Volume XI, for instance, there is the testimony of Kerry W. Thornley, a corporal in Oswald's unit at the base in El Toro, California, during Oswald's last year in the Marines.

> *Mr. Jenner [assistant counsel].*   . . . While you were based

at El Toro, did the unit engage with any regularity in
rifle practice?

Mr. Thornley.   None whatsoever. At that time, the whole
time we were there, we did not engage in rifle practice.

Thornley explained that the unit was part of the Marine air
wing, where the accent was on technical specialties rather than
rifle ability. The Commission, having studied all of these depositions, nevertheless concludes that "Oswald's Marine training in
marksmanship, his other rifle experience and his established
familiarity with this particular weapon show that he possessed
ample capability to commit the assassination."

Evidently determined to pound this conclusion into every
reader's brain, the Report repeats it in even more dogmatic terms
in the "Speculations and Rumors." The statements of Hubert
Hammerer, the Italian experts, and dozens of other specialists
around the world are reduced there to an anonymous "speculation" of one and a half lines: "Oswald did not have the marksmanship ability demonstrated by the rifleman who fired the shots."

The Commission's response, word for word:

> Oswald qualified as a sharpshooter and a marksman with
> the M-1 rifle in the Marine Corps. Marina Oswald testified
> that in New Orleans her husband practiced operating the
> bolt of the rifle. Moreover, experts stated that the scope
> was a substantial aid for rapid, accurate firing. The Com-
> mission concluded that Oswald had the capability with a
> rifle to commit the assassination.

4

BULLETS, EXPERTS, AND THE MYSTERY OF THE IRVING GUNSMITH

How MANY SHOTS WERE FIRED from the sixth floor of the Texas School Book Depository at President Kennedy's car?

In a rare instance of agreement among the investigators, they adopted a precise, uniform, and apparently definitive position: There were three, they said, basing this figure primarily on the number of shells found near the window. But vague, incomplete, or contradictory statements set in again, not only about the wounds but also about the bullets that caused them. Following Richard Dudman in the *St. Louis Post-Dispatch,* reporters thus counted on their fingers and discovered that the three shots apparently had produced four bullets: one in Kennedy's back, one found on a stretcher, one in fragments on the floor of the car, and one in Connally's thigh.

Underlying this arithmetic problem was a confusion lasting several weeks as to what happened to the bullet that hit Connally.

For days, and without taking into account what had been said the day before or would be said the day after, assorted doctors and detectives who supposedly were qualified spoke with equal assurance and incompetence about the bullet that "pierced" Connally's thigh and about the bullet that "lodged" in it. Reporter Dudman's reasoning was based on the second version, an understandable choice since it was the one offered by Connally's physician, Dr. Robert Shaw, on November 23. But those who accepted the other version also appeared to have access to official

61

information, and I could not see why such a simple problem could not be settled.

I therefore called the Executive Mansion at Austin, Texas, reached one of the Governor's aides, and asked him to tell me, unless it involved a state secret, whether the bullet had lodged in Connally's thigh or passed through. I had to wait a few minutes, while consultations probably were held, and then the reply: "The bullet came apart; only a fragment was left in the thigh, and it was removed."

My call to Austin may have solved the enigma of the four bullets produced by three shots, but it led to a new puzzle concerning the conclusions based on examination of the bullets.

Chief Curry as well as Gordon Shanklin, FBI Dallas agent, had declared that laboratory tests in Washington had shown that the three bullets had come from the Mannlicher-Carcano found in the Depository. How could valid observations be made about a bullet as fragmented as the one that struck Connally? If we take the word of Söderman and O'Connell (John J. O'Connell had been chief inspector in the New York Police Department), ballistic identification is possible only "if the bullet has retained its shape or is only partly deformed."

When the question was asked on November 24 at the historic press conference of District Attorney Wade, the following exchange took place:

> *Reporter.*   How about ballistics tests?
> *Wade.*   Well, I said this was the gun that . . .
> *Reporter.*   Killed the President?
> *Wade.*   Yes.

Was this Wade's subtle way of limiting the results of the ballistics tests to the two bullets that hit Kennedy, while not mentioning the one that struck Connally?

Subtlety of that sort would be surprising in Henry Wade, whose other answers that night combined ignorance with a total lack of restraint. In any case, the public made no such distinction. It had already been informed that afternoon, by a no less official spokesman, that the laboratory tests proved the three bullets had come from "Oswald's rifle."

To determine whether the authorities still were undecided on a definitive interpretation of these tests, I telephoned the Justice Department in January 1964. This was not as easy as my call to Austin.

Again, there was a long wait during which I suppose a discussion went on; then I was told that all of the documents had been turned over to the Warren Commission and that the Justice Department had nothing to say to the press. But my question concerned what had been said previously, I insisted. The reply was that there had never been any official statements on the ballistics tests. Did that mean, I wanted to know, that the statements made in Dallas connecting the three bullets to Oswald's rifle were unfounded? There was a moment of panic on the other end of the wire, followed by: "No, not at all, but you have to use your own judgment." Finally the press officer of the Justice Department gave me the phone number of his counterpart in the FBI, who might have more to tell me.

The FBI press officer was expecting my call, but first recited the couplet about the documents turned over to the Commission and the impossibility of saying anything to the press. He hastily added that, as far as the ballistics tests were concerned, they had been conducted in the FBI laboratories at the request of the local authorities in Dallas and the results forwarded to those officials. The FBI was not responsible for anything said after that by the Dallas authorities, and I had to use my own judgment. The FBI itself could neither confirm nor deny; that would be against its policy.

Having no other choice than to use my own judgment, by invitation of the Justice Department and the FBI, I decided that the Dallas authorities could not have obtained positive identification of a bullet that had left a fragment in Connally's thigh and the rest in bits on the floor of the car.

The Warren Report modifies considerably the data given above, starting with the retroactive obliteration of the December 18 autopsy report. It had been believed, until publicaton of the Warren Report, that the bullet that had hit Kennedy in the back lodged in the flesh and was recovered in the autopsy, giving the FBI an intact bullet to work on. The same conclusion, it can be noted, applied to the "information" issued from Dallas before the December 18 "revelations" of Bethesda: The theory about a bullet penetrating "just under the Adam's apple" presumed that this bullet had remained in the back. Since a second bullet, almost whole, was said to have been found on a stretcher, the FBI would have had two usable bullets for its ballistics tests, and my objections concerned only the scattered fragments then generally attributed to the bullet that wounded Connally.

But now the new and only official "truth," as proclaimed on September 27, 1964, is that no bullet was recovered from the President's body. Here is the Warren Report's summary of what the autopsy produced: "The surgeons observed, through X-ray analysis, 30 or 40 tiny dustlike fragments of metal running in a line from the wound in the rear of the President's head toward the front part of the skull, with a sizeable metal fragment lying just above the right eye. From this head wound two small irregularly shaped fragments of metal were recovered and turned over to the FBI."

The only whole or almost whole bullet examined in the FBI laboratories thus was the one found, according to the Report, "on Governor Connally's stretcher at Parkland Hospital after the assassination."

Apart from this bullet and the two fragments recovered in the autopsy, some more fragments were discovered later. On the night of the assassination, after the Presidential car had been brought back to Washington, "Secret Service agents found two bullet fragments in the front seat": one weighed 44.6 grains and "consisted of the nose portion of a bullet," and the other weighed 21 grains and "consisted of the base portion of a bullet." On November 23, FBI agents found "three small lead particles" on the rug under the left jump seat that had been occupied by Mrs. Connally. They noticed at the same time (a mere journalist, Richard Dudman, had noticed it the day before) a pattern of cracks in the windshield and a dent in the chrome strip across the top of the windshield. Robert Frazier, the FBI expert, certified that the dent had been caused by "some projectile which struck the chrome on the inside surface." Frazier believed that this projectile could have been either of the fragments found on the front seat.

According to the Report, "it was the unanimous opinion of the experts that the nearly whole bullet, the two largest bullet fragments and the three cartridge cases were definitely fired in the rifle found on the sixth floor of the Depository Building to the exclusion of all other weapons."

Contrary to what the Commission has done, one must make a distinction between the shells found near the window and the bullets or fragments recovered in or near the victims. Since the purpose of the ballistics tests was to identify the murder weapon —that is, to show that the Mannlicher-Carcano had actually been used to commit the crime—identification of the shells could prove nothing: If the rifle had been placed on the sixth floor to implicate Oswald, it would not be difficult to place there at the same time some cartridge cases fired by the rifle. It is only the evidence concerning the bullets that counts.

The "nearly whole bullet," the Report says, was "slightly flattened, but otherwise unmutilated." This was the bullet, according to the Commission, that caused all of Connally's wounds after passing through Kennedy's neck; it is therefore surprising that the Report should not take into account here the fragment that remained in the Governor's leg. But the whole story of this "nearly whole bullet" is so extraordinary that I prefer to leave it aside for the moment, in order to return to it in the proper context.

With regard to the two fragments of 44.6 and 21 grains (one less than a third, the other hardly an eighth of a whole bullet), the Report first cites Frazier's general explanations concerning the methods of ballistic identification and then observes: "Under some circumstances, as where the bullet or cartridge is seriously mutilated, there are not sufficient individual characteristics to enable the expert to make a firm identification." Now in the case of the two fragments we are dealing with here, they were mutilated enough for the Report to state that "it was not possible to determine from the fragments themselves whether they com-

prised the base and nose of one bullet or of two separate bullets."
The conclusion of the Commission experts was nevertheless that
"each had sufficient unmutilated area to provide the basis of an
identification."

I have no intention of questioning the technical competence of
Frazier or of Joseph D. Nicol, superintendent of the Illinois
bureau of criminal identification and investigation, who was the
second expert resorted to by the Commission. I do have the right
to remind them, however, that none of the police manuals I have
checked seems inclined to admit the possibility of positive identification in conditions comparable to those indicated above.

It is time now to take up one of the strangest episodes of the
whole affair.

On November 28, Dial D. Ryder, a gunsmith at the Irving
Sports Shop, said he had mounted a telescopic sight on a rifle a
few weeks earlier for a customer named Oswald. He remembered
neither the man nor the rifle. He had simply found in his records
a repair tag for the work showing a charge of $6.00 (drilling $4.50,
bore sighting $1.50) , and the tag bore the name Oswald. This
was given out as sensational news until someone remembered that
the Mannlicher-Carcano ordered by Oswald from a Chicago mail-
order firm was supposed to have been equipped with a telescopic
sight. So the Dallas police quickly advised the reporters, to whom
they had triumphantly announced Ryder's discovery, to forget
the entire incident. It was all a "mistake," they said without
further explanation.

There had been from the start some doubt about the Italian
rifle with the telescopic sight, because of the price Oswald was
said to have paid for it.

The press of the whole world had already made much of the
"$12.78 second-hand rifle" that had killed John F. Kennedy when
the *New York Times* reproduced the advertisement that was supposed to have seduced the assassin. It can be seen from the ad,
however, that $12.78 (item No. C20-1196) was the price of the
"6.5 Italian carbine" without the scope. The same rifle "with
brand new 4X scope" was priced at $19.95. Were the police
wrong about the price or were they wrong about the rifle? A

statement by Milton P. Klein, president of Klein's Sporting Goods in Chicago, straightened it out: The rifle sent to Oswald's post-office box in Dallas under the name A. Hidell was, he said, the $19.95 item with mounted telescopic sight. And since everyone, by this time, had become used to the fact that the men responsible for the investigation of the assassination of the President of the United States rarely knew what they were talking about, nobody paid much attention to the error.

The story of the Irving gunsmith suddenly put back on the table not only the initial contradiction about the price but the entire question of the assassination weapon that the police, after some ballistic juggling, claimed to have resolved once and for all.

The Dallas police tried to get out of it at first by telling reporters a theory according to which Oswald might have had a second rifle. But they soon realized that the cure was worse than the disease, since it demanded some explanations that they could not provide. Where had Oswald bought the second rifle? Where had he bought the second telescopic sight? Where was the scope-equipped rifle now? It clearly was wiser to suggest a "misunderstanding," and the main concern of the investigators became not to explain what was in Pandora's box but to put the lid back on it: The Irving gunsmith was never mentioned again.

There was something disturbing in this episode, however, which no serious inquiry could overlook.

Unlike so many witnesses in the case, Dial D. Ryder did not say he had met Lee Oswald or that he remembered him, but only that he had a record of his name. Was he sure of that? Perhaps the police, after examining the repair tag and comparing it with Ryder's handwriting, had reached the conclusion that the name on it was not Oswald; this would constitute a valid reason for disregarding the matter. I therefore called Ryder at the Irving Sports Shop and asked him what exactly was the "mistake" or "misunderstanding" referred to by the Dallas authorities.

"Well," he replied, "you know that the rifle Oswald got from Chicago was already equipped with a telescopic sight. This couldn't have been the rifle he brought to me. Either it was another rifle or another Oswald. . . ."

"Are you absolutely sure, Mr. Ryder, that the name is really Oswald? You couldn't have misread it?"

"The repair tag is still here. It's Oswald, no doubt about that. No first name or initial, just Oswald."

Just Oswald! But Oswald is not Smith, Jones, or Brown. If there was an Oswald, other than Lee Harvey, in Irving or in the area, he should not have been hard to find. Is it possible that no one in Dallas or Washington realized how imperative it was to find him? For if a man went to a gunsmith in Irving a few weeks before the assassination to have a scope mounted on a rifle, and if the man gave the name Oswald when he was not Lee Harvey or any other real Oswald, it could mean only one thing: that the stage was being set to frame Lee Harvey Oswald as the assassin of the President, and that his rifle was to play a part in putting the finger on the ex-turncoat whose defection to the Soviet Union had brought him wide and unfavorable publicity throughout the region. Not knowing how easy it would be to trace Oswald through the pseudonym A. Hidell, under which he had purchased the rifle, the plotters might have tried to do the trick by placing his name in the records of the Irving gunsmith.

The Warren Commission carefully avoids considering such a possibility, although it was aware of it: I had suggested the hypothesis in March 1964, in my *Commentary* article, which the Commission knew of, since it is mentioned elsewhere in the Report. The gunsmith incident is discussed in the Report, but the question is deliberately reduced to whether Oswald owned a second rifle, or whether—as the Report phrases it in the "Speculations and Rumors" appendix, and as the only speculation on the subject—"there was a second Mannlicher-Carcano rifle involved in the assassination." As a matter of fact, the Warren Report officially confirms its intention of dodging the question by coolly titling the four pages devoted to the gunsmith episode, "Ownership of a Second Rifle."

The notion of a second rifle, briefly considered by the Dallas police as a way out of the repair-tag dilemma, had been a dead issue well before the commission began working on its Report.

It is this dead issue that the Commission zealously labors: "All of the evidence developed proves that Oswald owned only the one rifle—the Mannlicher-Carcano—and that he did not bring it or a second rifle to the Irving Sports Shop." As if to emphasize its refusal to consider any other conceivable interpretation, the Report even explains that "the possession of a second rifle warranted investigation because it would indicate that a possibly important part of Oswald's life had not been uncovered."

More than half of the space is devoted to the testimony of two elderly women who claimed that Oswald, at the time mentioned by Ryder, had dropped in at the furniture store operated by one of them to get information about work he wanted done on a rifle.

Since they also claimed that Oswald was accompanied by his wife and two children, and that they drove up in a 1957 Ford, perhaps the evidence given by the two ladies was of special interest precisely because the man çould *not* have been Lee Oswald. It is a pity nobody tried to find out more about the visiting family. But the Warren Commission looks the other way, happy to conclude that, in eliminating the idea that the man described by Mrs. Edith Whitworth and Mrs. Gertrude Hunter was Lee Oswald, it has destroyed a "possible corroboration for Ryder's story."

How does the Commission finally explain "Ryder's story," and how does it justify its decision to consign the episode to oblivion?

The Report announces in passing, without further comment, that "no other person by the name of Oswald in the Dallas-Fort Worth area has been found who had a rifle repaired at the Irving Sports Shop." It then proceeds to comment on various considerations that seem to "reflect on Ryder's credibility," and adds: "Investigation has revealed that the authenticity of the repair tag bearing Oswald's name is indeed subject to grave doubts."

I do not know Ryder personally, and my only contact with him was a brief telephone conversation. But, in view of the extraordinary faith of the Commission in certain witnesses plainly unworthy of such confidence, it seems to me difficult to accept the Commission's standards for determining the credibility of a witness. In this case, the Commission was unfavorably impressed by the fact that Ryder was one of the few witnesses who did not proclaim that he had "recognized" or "identified" Oswald. To me, this would seem to speak in his favor. The Commission appears particularly displeased by his response when shown a photo of the suspect. He knew, he said, that it was a photo of Oswald because he had seen his pictures in the newspapers, "but as far as seeing the guy personally, I don't think I ever have." I rather like that attitude.

The Commission vainly tried to obtain testimony that would damage Ryder's credibility. Since it did not succeed, there is no mention of those attempts in the Report. But Volume XI of the Hearings recounts the questioning of Charles W. Greener, owner of the Irving Sports Shop, by Assistant Counsel Wesley J. Liebeler:

> *Mr. Liebeler.*   Do you have any opinion as to what the real situation is?
>
> *Mr. Greener.*   Nothing more than I have confidence in the boy, or I wouldn't have him working for me.
>
> *Mr. Liebeler.*   You don't think he would make this tag up to cause a lot of commotion?
>
> *Mr. Greener.*   I don't think so. He doesn't seem like that type boy. I have lots of confidence in him or I wouldn't have him working for me and handling money. Especially times I am going off. He—if he wasn't the right kind of boy, and he pretty well proved he is by dependability and in all the relations that we have together, and I just don't figure that is possible. Now I say I don't figure that. Of course, there is always possibilities of everything, but I don't feel that way.
>
> *Mr. Liebeler.*   You don't feel Ryder would do that?
>
> *Mr. Greener.*   Not at all; no.

Even more astonishing—since this is given as a reason to drop the matter—is the second argument of the Commission, casting doubt on the authenticity of the repair tag turned up by Ryder. If Ryder, contrary to the opinion of his boss, fabricated a false tag in order to gain the limelight, it is hard to see why he didn't make himself even more interesting by telling about "seeing the guy personally" and inventing a conversation to top it off. If, on the other hand, he fabricated a tag for reasons other than a desire for publicity, we are led back to the starting point of this discussion: Ryder himself, in this case, could well have been mixed up in a scheme to channel the investigation in Oswald's direction. If the Commission wanted to insinuate that Ryder perpetrated a fraud, shouldn't it have brought him to justice to prove it in court?

But it is not at all certain that this is really what the Report wants to insinuate, for one sentence seems to imply something else: "On November 25, 1963, Dial D. Ryder, an employe of the Irving Sports Shop, presented this tag to agents of the FBI, claiming that the tag was in his handwriting."

Claiming? If the Commission means that it suspects Ryder of having lied, why didn't it ask for the opinion of a handwriting expert? If an expert confirmed that Ryder had lied in "claiming" the handwriting was his, we would again be led back to our disturbing point of departure. The Commission would then have established that a false repair tag had been made up by unknown persons to be placed later—with or without Ryder's complicity— where Ryder would find it or pretend to find it.

Since the only possible reason for such a scheme would be to furnish "evidence" against the chosen scapegoat, the Commission's hypothesis would lead to a conclusion similar to the one it did not mention, namely, that a real customer may have gone to the shop with a real rifle to have Ryder make out a real repair tag— in Oswald's name.

But this is precisely a conclusion the Commission wants to avoid at any price.

When Wesley J. Liebeler questioned Ryder, he thus took care to define—and limit—the Commission's objective in such a manner as to prevent any expedition into forbidden territory: "We want to examine you briefly concerning the possibility that you did some work on a rifle for a man by the name of Oswald who may in fact have been Lee Harvey Oswald."

When he questioned Greener a week later, Liebeler demonstrated in an even more startling way the Commission's stubborn insistence on ignoring whatever did not conform with its aims.

Enumerating the possibilities suggested by the discovery of the repair tag, Liebeler deliberately reduced these to three, and pretended never to have heard of any other alternative:

> As we discussed briefly off the record before we started, it appears that there are three possibilities concerning this tag. One, in view of the fact that Mr. Ryder is quite clear in his own mind that he never worked on an Italian rifle similar to the one that was found in the Texas School Book Depository, we can conclude either that the Oswald on the tag was Lee Oswald and he brought a different rifle in here, or it was a different Oswald who brought another rifle in here, or that the tag is not a genuine tag, and that there never was a man who came in here with any gun at all. Can you think of any other possibilities?

Duly prepared by the discussion "off the record" (the Commission never deigned to explain the countless discussions "off the record" mentioned in the Hearings, though it is often impossible, as in this case, to imagine any justification for them in terms of national security, or morals, or even manners), Greener hastened to reply: "That about covers the situation, it looks to me like." May I raise my hand to remark respectfully to the zealous assistant counsel for the Commission that I, for one, can think of another possibility: that a man came into the Irving shop with a gun, that he was neither Lee Oswald nor a different Oswald, but that he gave Oswald's name in order to help build a case against him.

It is difficult to understand how such evident subterfuges can be practiced and officially condoned in a free country without provoking indignation, criticism, or even disagreement. But it is difficult also to believe that the last word has been said about the mystery of the Irving gunsmith. The Commission does not soothe us when it declares, apparently to question Ryder's credibility: "Moreover, the FBI had been directed to the Irving Sports Shop by anonymous telephone calls received by its Dallas office and by a local television station."

5

FINGERPRINTS, WITNESSES, AND THE MYSTERY OF THE OAK CLIFF POLICEMAN

MILLIONS OF AMERICANS believe that the fingerprints of Lee Oswald were on the rifle used to kill John F. Kennedy; they heard it on television or read it in their newspapers. Such evidence would be impressive. But it is not true. And in the final analysis, it might not be so impressive either.

Here is what we find on the subject in the tape recording of Wade's press conference, which was supposed to establish definitively the guilt of the suspect executed a few hours earlier by Jack Ruby.

> *Reporter.*   What other evidence is there?
> *Wade.*   Let's see. . . . His fingerprints were found on the gun, have I said that?
> *Reporter.*   Which gun?
> *Wade.*   On the rifle.
> *Reporter.*   You didn't say that. . . .
> *Reporter.*   The rifle fingerprints were his, were Oswald's?
> *Wade.*   Yes.
> *Reporter.*   Were there any fingerprints——
> *Wade.*   Palm prints, rather than fingerprints.
> *Reporter.*   Were there any fingerprints at the window?
> *Reporter.*   Palm prints on the what?
> *Wade.*   Yes, on——
> *Reporter.*   On the rifle?
> *Wade.*   Yes, sir.

Reporter.   Where are they on the rifle?
Wade.   Under—on part of the metal—under the gun.

A palm print is not a fingerprint, and Wade, a former FBI official, certainly knows the difference. But the public does not. Still, if only by elimination, the Dallas District Attorney, contrary to what most people understood, confirmed that there were *no* fingerprints on the rifle. But there should have been.

If Henry Wade has read Sherlock Holmes, does he remember the "curious incident" of the dog who "did nothing in the nighttime" and whose very silence was the significant clue?

Since we are told the Mannlicher-Carcano belonged to Oswald, it would be natural to find his fingerprints on it, although their presence would not prove in any way that he used the rifle to assassinate the President. Nothing could be *less* natural, on the other hand, than to find no fingerprints when Oswald was supposed to have fired his rifle at Kennedy that day.

Did he wear gloves? No, since Wade tells us he left a palm print "on part of the metal."

Before hiding the rifle behind the book cartons, did he take out a handkerchief to wipe it off carefully, missing only a small place underneath? Someone, in this case, should explain why this amazing assassin suddenly became preoccupied with fingerprints when he made no other effort whatever to avoid identification. Wouldn't he have taken the elementary precaution, for example, of destroying the cards in the name of A. Hidell that he carried in his wallet, and which would permit the police—with or without fingerprints—to track him down quickly as the owner of the rifle?

Furthermore, the time necessary to clean the rifle would then have to be added to the time Oswald needed to get down to the second floor, thus strengthening his alibi.

It would all seem less implausible, of course, if the assassin was someone else. This other person, in fact, would have the greatest interest in getting rid of his fingerprints even if in so doing he erased Oswald's as well. Just as the silence of the dog intrigued Sherlock Holmes, the absence of fingerprints—if Oswald was the murderer—should have been a sufficiently "curious incident" to warrant the interest even of a Henry Wade.

But Henry Wade had other things to do, and so did his colleagues; they were busy trying to convince the world that the case was "a cinch." The fact is that until Oswald's murder the Dallas "investigators," aided by the immense, frightening resources of American television, succeeded in brainwashing the public so completely that the most gratuitous statements were accepted as incontrovertible truth.

Simply because Chief Curry or Captain Fritz said so on television, it was taken as an established fact, for example, that Oswald went from the Depository to his room on North Beckley Avenue to get his jacket and a revolver. But Mrs. Earlene Roberts, the housekeeper who saw Oswald "come in running like the dickens," said he "just ran in his room, got a short tan coat and ran back out"; she did not mention any revolver. She indeed had never seen a revolver in his room, which measured about six by nine feet; nor had she seen a holster, though the police said they found an empty holster when they searched the room Friday afternoon.

There is not the slightest proof, of course, that Oswald picked up a revolver in his room, and one might wonder why the Dallas police did not simply decide that he had it in his pocket when he went to work in the morning.

Perhaps they were afraid that some evidence might turn up to show that if Oswald had carried the .38 the whole day before, and during the evening at the Paine house in Irving, and again for four hours at the Depository that Friday morning, it would have been noticed. The authorities no doubt also saw in the revolver the necessary explanation for the "assassin's" hurrying home after the shooting instead of heading for the Mexican border: Even if it had not been such a sunny Texas autumn day, the jacket alone would not have been reason enough. It was indispensable, in any case, that Oswald be armed with a revolver—since Officer Tippit was killed by a man with a revolver.

The personality of this "$490-a-month city policeman" who was "shot down by Oswald while attempting to question the assassination suspect on an Oak Cliff street," as the *Dallas Morning News* summed up the story the day after his funeral, has been the subject of much comment.

I certainly do not intend to back up the statements made by Mark Lane on February 18, 1964, at a meeting in New York's Town Hall and repeated by him on March 4 before the Warren Commission in its first public session in Washington. Lane, an attorney, had been hired by Mrs. Marguerite Oswald, according to her statement to the press, "to represent my son Lee Harvey Oswald before the Warren Commission." Chief Justice Earl Warren took it upon himself to reject Lane's request when the lawyer asked to defend the interests of the deceased Oswald before the Commission. The Chief Justice, however, allowed Lane to appear as a "witness," eagerly granting Lane's special wish for a public hearing. Thus it came about that Mark Lane, attorney for Marguerite Oswald but witness to nothing, contributed to the Warren Commission some additional fiction instead of the necessary cross-examination of the Commission's own spurious witnesses.

Lane said he had heard, through "sources who could not be identified," of a "secret meeting" held on November 14 at Jack Ruby's Carousel Club. Three men, according to these "sources" and Lane, were present. The first was Bernard Weissman, an unemployed salesman whose name appeared as the only signature on a full-page ad in the *Dallas Morning News* on November 22 (cost: $1,484) denouncing Kennedy as practically an agent of Moscow. The second man, said Lane and his "sources," was Officer J. D. Tippit. As to the third, Lane said he could not name him in public. Warren ordered the hearing closed so that the third man's name could be whispered into the ears of the Commission members. It was none other than Jack Ruby himself, as we were to learn from the transcript.

The story is hard to believe. If there was a plot, it was certainly not likely that Ruby's club would be the place to hatch it; nor was it likely that it would be concocted by a character like Ruby, with the complicity of a "$490-a-month city policeman" and the pitiful Bernard Weissman, the obvious front man of an anonymous right-wing group that found it useful to hide behind a Jewish name. Lane never produced any evidence for his affirmations, and his tale, which would seem to have been invented to discredit serious criticism of the Dallas investigation, is at about the same intellectual level as the brainstorms of Professor Revilo P. Oliver in the "private" John Birch Society publication *American Opinion:* "You, who read these lines, may owe your life or at least your liberty to the vigilance and sagacity of Officer J. D. Tippit, the policeman who stopped Oswald on the street and was murdered by the [Communist] conspiracy's well-trained but not infallible agent. . . ."

Whoever the murderer was, the cause as well as the circumstances of the Tippit murder remain unexplained. Even granting that the man with the .38 was Oswald, it is completely incredible that Tippit could have spotted him on the basis of a vague police broadcast that did not describe any outstanding detail fitting Oswald's appearance, an alarm that, for example, did not—and could not—include the most conspicuous detail: the beige zipper jacket he had donned in the interval. Did Tippit stop Oswald without suspecting who he was? This is what Wade suggested in the *Dallas Morning News* of November 23: "Tippit may never have known that he had accosted the assassin who killed the President." But why then did he stop Oswald? And why then should Oswald have shot him? Above all, how do we know it was Oswald?

In a summary of the case published December 1, 1963, in the *New York Times,* even such a careful reporter as Donald Janson wrote without hesitation, though under the headline "The Dallas Mystery," that Oswald "killed the policeman, another mass of evidence shows. . . ." What mass of evidence? The police said three witnesses had seen the murder. Wade confirmed this in his press conference and undertook to relate what had happened, while admitting that he did not know *where* it had happened: "I don't have it exact. It's more than a block [from Oswald's room]. It's a block or two." According to Wade's interpretation of the testimony of the "three witnesses," Oswald "shot him [Tippit] three times and killed him." But when the reporters finally caught up with one of these witnesses, a Mrs. Helen Louise Markham, they discovered that the man she had described to the police as Tippit's assassin was "about 30 years old, with bushy hair, and wearing a white jacket." Oswald, as we know, was 24, his hair was rather thin, and he wore a beige or tan zipper jacket easy to notice and describe.

District Attorney Wade never explained how he could say that three witnesses had seen Oswald kill Tippit when one of the three apparently had seen another man. Neither did he explain how he could describe Oswald's actions after the murder in two short sentences loaded with categorical statements, all of which are inaccurate or misleading: "He then walked across a vacant lot. Witnesses saw him eject the shells from a revolver and place—reload—the gun."

The witness who had seen someone "eject the shells from a re-volver" was one Mrs. Barbara Davis, who lived at the corner of Tenth Street and Patton Avenue (Tippit was shot on Tenth Street a short distance from this intersection). Reporters asked her what she had told the police. She confirmed that she had seen "a man" ejecting the shells from a revolver, but added that she had been unable to describe the man to the police because she had seen him only from behind and was too upset to pay attention even to his size or clothing. This did not prevent her, however—according to the Warren Report—from "identifying" Oswald in a lineup.

Out of the "mass of evidence" available on December 1 against Oswald in the Tippit murder, I know of only one witness whose testimony, when checked, proved the same as reported by the authorities.

Ted Callaway, who ran a used-car lot at Patton and Jefferson avenues, said that he had seen a man walking along the sidewalk with revolver in hand and that he had identified him later. "I got a real good look at him," he told a *Life* reporter. "It was Oswald. I picked him out of a police lineup that night." When I questioned Callaway myself, by telephone, he repeated this and added some details:

"He had just turned the corner of Tenth Street, walking south on Patton Avenue toward me but on the opposite sidewalk. When I saw the revolver in his hand, as if he were ready to shoot, I thought right away that he must be the assassin. I had heard the shots, and then screams, and somebody told me a man had just been shot on Tenth Street. That's why my first idea was, 'This man is the assassin.' I shouted 'Hey!' . . ."

"You were not afraid," I asked, "face to face with an assassin ready to shoot?"

"No, but I didn't try to stop him. He mumbled something I didn't get, and went on walking. Then he turned west on Jefferson Avenue."

"Are you absolutely sure it was Oswald? Had you heard any description on the radio?"

"No, sir. I'm the one who gave the description to the police. First I tried to find him along Jefferson Avenue, riding up and down in a taxi. He must have hidden somewhere before he went into the theater. But when the police showed me half a dozen men lined up that night and asked if I recognized the one with the revolver, I said yes and pointed to Oswald."

The testimony of Callaway, at first glance, may appear convincing. But if there had been a chance of defense for Oswald, even posthumously, his lawyer certainly would have asked to see, first of all, the notebook of the officer who took down Callaway's description. And he would have reminded the jury—or the "fact-finding" Commission—that identification of Oswald in a lineup did not mean much because of his black eye and the bruises on his face, and the "arrogant sneering expression" that, it seems, provoked Jack Ruby's psychomotor epilepsy.

There is also the odd episode reported by Bob Considine in the *New York Journal-American*. An "ordinary shooting"—that was the way Captain Fritz had described the shooting in Dallas of "a car dealer who identified Lee Oswald in a police lineup after the assassination," Considine wrote on March 3, 1964. "The dealer witnessed Oswald running away from the site of the murder of Officer J. D. Tippit, reloading the gun as he ran. The dealer was shot in the head by an unknown assailant early in January."

Despite some discrepancies, I thought at first the man referred to by Considine was Ted Callaway. Callaway, however, told me: "No, it wasn't me, but I know about it. It was Warren Reynolds who was shot in the head. . . ." (I later learned that Considine had given Reynolds' name in an earlier story that I had not seen.) As Callaway told me, Reynolds was another used-car salesman who was a witness in the Tippit case: "He saw the assassin, but from a distance; I was the one who gave the identification to the police, not him." Had there been some confusion between the two car salesmen? Did the unknown assailant of Reynolds intend to kill the one who had identified Oswald?

But both Ted Callaway and Warren Reynolds had already given whatever evidence they had against Oswald before January 1964. Thus, paradoxically, if someone had an interest in getting rid of a prosecution witness, it was the prosecution. For the only way such a witness could change the situation after having testified would be in favor of Oswald: by talking too much and contradicting himself, or even by retracting his statements.

Even if one were to disregard this "ordinary shooting" as a meaningless coincidence, one could not help noticing, after a quick glance at a map of the Oak Cliff section of Dallas, the bizarre behavior attributed to Oswald after the murder of Tippit.

The expression used by Considine (the witness had seen Oswald reload "as he ran") reflected the official Dallas statements of November 23 and 24, including the two sentences of District Attorney Wade in his November 24 press conference; the "vacant lot" Wade mentioned would seem to have been the next place Oswald turned to after killing Tippit, and where he proceeded to eject the shells and reload.

But the definitive version that began to take shape on November 25 located the "vacant lot" somewhere behind the stores on Jefferson Avenue, and the only activity Oswald was said to have carried out there was to reload.

The revolver sequence thus passed through three unconnected and therefore utterly incomprehensible stages: (1) Oswald ejects the shells at the corner of Tenth Street and Patton Avenue; (2) keeping the revolver in his hand without reloading, Oswald walks along Patton Avenue; (3) Oswald reloads the revolver at a vacant lot near Jefferson Avenue.

There were other significant discrepancies that marked the

utterances of the Dallas authorities. One is particularly obvious.

The first reports of the Tippit killing said that Tippit had been struck by two bullets, and Captain Fritz drew a unanimous and conclusive "Ah!" when he told newsmen Friday night there were "two empty chambers in the .38 taken from Oswald at the Texas Theater." But how could there have been two empty chambers in Oswald's revolver if he had been seen in the vacant lot reloading the gun?

For the Warren Commission, however, there is not the slightest question left about Tippit's murder. It's all quite plain: "Two eyewitnesses saw the Tippit shooting and seven eyewitnesses heard the shots and saw the gunman leave the scene with revolver in hand. These nine eyewitnesses positively identified Lee Harvey Oswald as the man they saw."

Witness Number 1 is Mrs. Helen Louise Markham. Mrs. Markham, a waitress, was about to cross Tenth Street at Patton Avenue when, the Report says, she saw a police car

> slowly approach the man [walking on Tenth Street] from the rear and stop alongside of him. She saw the man come to the right window of the police car. As he talked, he leaned on the edge of the right window with his arms. The man appeared to step back as the policeman "calmly opened the car door" and very slowly got out and walked toward the front of the car. The man pulled a gun. Mrs. Markham heard three shots and saw the policeman fall to the ground near the left front wheel. . . .

In the CBS television program mentioned earlier, Mrs. Markham showed the manner in which "the man" leaned on the edge of the window, then described what happened next: "The policeman calmly opened the door, he calmly got out. And me, I didn't pay no attention because I thought they were talking friendly. And the policeman walked—got to—the front wheel on the driver's side, and this man shot him in the wink of the eye. Just bang, bang, bang."

Now who was "the man" whose three shots—and, according to the Report, four bullets—ended such a friendly chat? Here is the Commission's answer: "At about 4:30 p.m., Mrs. Markham, who had been greatly upset by her experience, was able to view a lineup of four men handcuffed together at the police station. She identified Lee Harvey Oswald as the man who shot the police-man."

I cited earlier Mrs. Markham's description of the man as she gave it to reporters: "About 30 years old, with bushy hair, and wearing a white jacket." In front of the CBS cameras, when asked if the man was big or small, she replied: "No, he wasn't a very big man. He was short, kind of short as well as I can remember." Mark Lane, who questioned her by telephone and tape-recorded her statements, said she had described the killer as "short, a little on the heavy side," with "somewhat bushy" hair. The Commission examined the transcript of the Lane recording. Its Report tells us that, in her talk with Lane, "Mrs. Markham strongly re-affirmed her positive identification of Oswald and denied having described the killer as short, stocky and having bushy hair."

One would like to be able to take the Commission's word and forget about Mark Lane, but this, unfortunately, soon appears impossible.

Seven lines after declaring that the Commission was "satisfied" that Mrs. Markham had denied ever describing the assassin as "short," the Report states without any qualms: "Although in the phone conversation she described the man as 'short,' on Novem-ber 22, within minutes of the shooting and before the lineup, Mrs. Markham described the man to police as 5'8" tall." Two lines after declaring the Commission was "satisfied" that Mrs. Markham had denied ever speaking of "bushy" hair, the Report admits that she used the words "a little bit bushy," but offers an explanation of this. And what an explanation! "The transcript establishes that she was referring to the uncombed state of his hair, a description fully supported by a photograph taken at the time of his arrest." It is embarrassing to have to remind the Presidential Commission that the description given by Mrs. Markham was of a man walking quietly on the sidewalk, while the photo was taken after the struggle in the Texas Theater.

The Report further recognizes that in her deposition "Mrs.

Markham initially denied that she ever had the above phone conversation." Confronted with the tape, Mrs. Markham admitted she had lied, but the Commission is not disturbed by that. It is content to tell us, without even bothering to elaborate, that Mrs. Markham "offered an explanation for her denial." After all this, how much of Mrs. Markham's testimony could be retained? In my opinion, none of it. In the Commission's opinion: "Addressing itself solely to the probative value of Mrs. Markham's contemporaneous description of the gunman and her positive identification of Oswald at a police lineup, the Commission considers her testimony reliable."

The seventh volume of Hearings contains eight pages that confirm once and for all not only that Mrs. Markham's testimony is clearly and beyond doubt unreliable, but also—and equally as certain—that an investigative body that accepts such testimony is hardly more reliable than the witness.

These eight pages contain the unexplained "explanation" that led the Commission to accept Mrs. Markham's testimony even though she had been caught lying. "During her testimony," the Report says, "Mrs. Markham initially denied that she ever had the above. phone conversation. She has subsequently admitted the existence of the conversation and offered an explanation for her denial." The readers of the Report are never told what the explanation was, and are supposed to be satisfied with the knowledge that the Commission found that explanation satisfactory.

Those who are interested enough to consult the 26-volume set will find in Volume VII, pages 499–506, an account of the pitiful exhibition that the Report, with appalling casualness, calls "an explanation."

Mrs. Markham was questioned on July 23, 1964, in the U.S. Attorney's office in Dallas, by Assistant Counsel Wesley J. Liebeler. Liebeler explained first to Mrs. Markham that he wanted to ask her about statements she had made to the Commission four months earlier.

> *Mr. Liebeler.*   Do you remember at that time that Mr.
> Ball [*who had questioned her at the March 26 Commis-*

sion hearing—L.S.] asked you the question, "Did you ever talk to a New York lawyer who said he was from New York?" And that you answered, "No, sir." Mr. Ball then asked you, "Did you ever talk to a lawyer who was investigating the case on behalf of the deceased man, Lee Oswald?" Your answer was, "No, sir." Mr. Ball asked, "Did you ever talk to a man who said he was representing the mother of Lee Oswald?" And you answered, "No, sir." And then Mr. Ball asked you, "You don't remember ever talking to a man named Mark Lane?" And then you answered, "No, sir."

Mrs. Markham.   Right.

Mr. Liebeler.   Do you remember giving that testimony at that time?

Mrs. Markham.   Yes, sir.

Mr. Liebeler.   Have you ever talked to Mark Lane?

Mrs. Markham.   No; I haven't—I haven't never seen the man in my life.

Mr. Liebeler.   Have you ever talked to Mark Lane on the telephone?

Mrs. Markham.   No.

Mr. Liebeler.   And you remember that Congressman Ford specifically, and Mr. Dulles, asked you whether or not you had talked to Mark Lane on the telephone and you told them at that time that you had not talked to Mark Lane?

Mrs. Markham.   No, sir; I have never seen the man. If he was to come in here, I wouldn't know who he was.

Mr. Liebeler.   Now, aside from the fact you have never seen the man, you also told the Commission when you were in Washington that you had never talked to him over the telephone?

Mrs. Markham.   Right.

Mr. Liebeler.   Have you talked to Mark Lane over the telephone since you were in Washington, before today?

Mrs. Markham.   No, sir.

> *Mr. Liebeler.*   You have never talked to Mark Lane over
> the telephone?
> *Mrs. Markham.*   No, sir; no, sir. Now, the old lady, and
> they told me they were reporters, came to my house.
> *Mr. Liebeler.*   Right, but you have no recollection of ever
> talking to him yourself?
> *Mrs. Markham.*   I never even talked to her even.

Having established the foundation with irreproachable precision and patience, Liebeler announced that he had a tape of the
conversation in question, and a transcript of it. Suddenly the
memory of the witness was stirred:

> *Mrs. Markham.*   I am going to tell you this, now, there
> was someone—let me tell you this—there was someone
> one day—this was all to me—I was scared, and I was,
> you know, frightened, and one day—now, this brings
> me back—the memories. . . . One day on my job there
> was someone that called, but he told me he was from
> the city.
> *Mr. Liebeler.*   From here in Dallas?
> *Mrs. Markham.*   That's right; the city hall down here,
> and this man told me he was—now, I can tell you what
> he told me he was—he said he was Captain Fritz—over
> this telephone—Captain Will Fritz and I know you are
> familiar with him, maybe. Now, he said he was Captain
> Fritz with the police department of the city of Dallas.

After a short discussion concerning telephone numbers, Liebeler
declared he would have a tape recorder brought in, and Mrs.
Markham repeated: "Sure, and this man—what this man told me
—he told me he was from the Dallas police department. . . ."

Secret Service Agent John Joe Howlett brought in the tape recorder, and the tape was played after Liebeler had given Mrs.
Markham a copy of the transcript to follow. But the transcript
does not record the start of the phone conversation. A parenthetical note explains that the verbatim record begins "at the time
Mrs. Markham began indicating her reactions." It is necessary

to refer to the 20th volume, containing a facsimile reproduction of the transcript prepared by the FBI a week earlier, to find the beginning of the tape.

Here is the first passage following the telephone preliminaries:

> *Mark Lane (L):*   My name is Mr. Lane. I'm an attorney investigating the Oswald case.
> *Helen Markham (M):*   Yes.
> *L:*   And, uh, I'm going to testify, I don't know if you've heard it on the radio yet, in Washington on this Wednesday before the Warren Commission
> *M:*   Yes.
> *L:*   about the result of the investigation that I've conducted,
> *M:*   Yes.
> *L:*   which is being concluded now, and I know that you were an eye witness to a portion of the case not relating directly to the assassination but the shooting of Officer Tippit.
> *M:*   That's right.

This entire passage, which is quite plain and leaves no room for ambiguity, does not appear in Volume VII, together with Mrs. Markham's "explanation." The Commission thus imposes on the persevering reader the added task of finding the photocopy of the FBI transcript in Volume XX (page 572). The portion of the tape quoted in the record of Mrs. Markham's testimony begins with Lane's telling her he has read her affidavit and would like to talk with her. After a few sentences, Liebeler interrupted:

> *Mr. Liebeler.*   You are shaking your head, as you listen to this tape recorder, Mrs. Markham. John Joe, let's stop the recorder for a moment. What do you mean to indicate by that?
> *Mrs. Markham.*   I never talked to that man.
> *Mr. Liebeler.*   Is that not your voice on the tape?
> *Mrs. Markham.*   I can't tell about my voice, but that man—I never talked to no woman or no man like that.

> *Mr. Liebeler.*   Well, we will play the recording some
> more, and are you following it along, Mrs. Markham?
> *Mrs. Markham.*   Yes; I am right here.
> *Mr. Liebeler.*   And does this memorandum appear to be
> an accurate and exact transcript of the recording?
> *Mrs. Markham.*   That man—whoever that man is—I
> don't know, but it says, "Mark Lane." No, sir—I'll tell
> the truth (raising right hand) and those words that he's
> saying—that's nothing like the telephone call I got—
> nothing.

After Mrs. Markham, already under oath, thus compounded
the perjury, Liebeler continued to run the tape. There is the
passage where she confirms that the man she saw was short, and
where Lane mentions the "rather bushy hair"; at this moment
she interrupted to say "Yes; that's my voice." We then have
another page and a half of transcription from the tape, until
Liebeler interrupted:

> *Mr. Liebeler.*   Now, at this point you were shaking your
> head, what do you mean by that?
> *Mrs. Markham.*   This man—I have never talked with.
> This lady was never on the telephone. This man that
> called me like I told you, he told me he was from the
> city hall, the police department, the police department
> of the city hall.
> *Mr. Liebeler.*   Well, now, do you remember having this
> conversation with somebody?
> *Mrs. Markham.*   Yes; I do, but he told me he was from
> the police department of city hall. . . .

We have next a brief digression about Mrs. Markham's boss as
well as a woman who called her on behalf of Tippit's sister. Then
the "witness" (the reader will no doubt have to be reminded at
this point that Mrs. Markham is a key witness against Oswald)
returns to her leitmotif:

> *Mrs. Markham.*   That man—I have never talked to that
> man. I talked to a man that was supposed to have been
> from the police department of the city hall.

Mr. Liebeler.   Do you recognize this as the voice of the man you talked to?

Mrs. Markham.   No; it is not.

Mr. Liebeler.   This is not the same voice?

Mrs. Markham.   No.

Mr. Liebeler.   How do you explain the fact that the woman's voice on this tape recording is your voice?

Mrs. Markham.   I never heard that.

Mr. Liebeler.   You never heard the man's voice before?

Mrs. Markham.   And I never heard this lady's voice before—this is the first time.

Mr. Liebeler.   Do you have any doubt in your mind at all that the lady's voice on the tape now is your voice?

Mrs. Markham.   It is my voice, but this man told me he was from the city police.

A similar scene occurs twice more, and again Mrs. Markham raises her right hand to swear she never spoke to Mark Lane because the man she never talked to told her he was from the police.

Mr. Liebeler.   . . . In fact, your testimony is that you had never had anybody introduce themselves to you as Mark Lane?

Mrs. Markham.   No, sir.

Mr. Liebeler.   And you haven't talked to him over the telephone?

Mrs. Markham.   No, sir; and so help me (raising right hand) I did not.

Mr. Liebeler.   You don't have any doubt, however, that you did engage in this particular conversation, except that you are having trouble at the beginning and end of it because you said that the man told you that he was from the police department when he called?

Mrs. Markham.   Yes, sir; he certainly did. I know he did.

And this is the explanation that satisfied the Warren Commission—even though it had the FBI transcript showing that Lane had clearly identified himself, and even though Liebeler had been led to remark several times that Lane's comments confirmed that he could not have been claiming any connection with the police.

Toward the end of that memorable deposition, Liebeler had even given the impression that Mrs. Markham would not get away with her "explanation," and when he stated that "we will have to do further investigation into this," Mrs. Markham did not conceal her worry. She first tried to get Liebeler's sympathy by telling him that she never thought the man could be Mark Lane because she was in a hurry to get off the phone and back to work: "I was going to get fired if I didn't get back." Then came the crowning touch in the form of that strange exchange between the witness caught in the act of perjury and the representative of the Presidential Commission:

> *Mrs. Markham.*   That was dirty in that man doing that.
> *Mr. Liebeler.*   Pardon?
> *Mrs. Markham.*   That was dirty in that man doing that.
> *Mr. Liebeler.*   Well, I would think that's right.
> *Mrs. Markham.*   Well, he's not no better than Oswald— that's right.
> *Mr. Liebeler.*   Thank you, Mrs. Markham, very much.

Apart from the Markham affair, the Commission has the Davis case on its hands. Barbara Davis, as I said earlier, had told reporters she did not remember the appearance of the man who had ejected shells from a revolver while passing her house; but according to the Report, Barbara Davis and her stepsister, Virginia Davis —who had not been mentioned before—picked Oswald out of a lineup of four men "on the evening of November 22." Though the Report says also "she was not sure whether she had seen his picture in a newspaper on the afternoon or evening of November 22 prior to the lineup," the Commission sees no reason not to count Barbara Davis among the "nine eyewitnesses."

Concerning the mysterious shooting of Warren Reynolds, the Report gives its opinion at the end of a short note in the "Speculations and Rumors" appendix: "The Commission has found no evidence that the shooting of Warren Reynolds was related in any way to the assassination of President Kennedy or the murder of Patrolman Tippit."

Even if we grant this—since the contrary cannot be proved—
the Commission had not found the slightest explanation or motive
for this "ordinary shooting" in which Reynolds received a bullet
wound in the head. The Report, moreover, in the 11 lines devoted
to this "rumor," confirms another troubling aspect of it. A stripper
named Betty MacDonald, whose testimony freed one suspect in
the Reynolds case, was arrested on February 13, 1964, for disturbing the peace. The Report calmly admits that "after being placed
in a cell at the Dallas city jail, she hanged herself," but it has an
answer ready for Bob Considine: "Investigation revealed no
evidence that she had ever worked at [Jack Ruby's] Carousel
Club."

Warren Reynolds himself appears in the Report as one of the
"nine eyewitnesses"—six more than Wade had counted—aligned
against Oswald in the Tippit murder.

Was Ted Callaway mistaken in telling me that Reynolds had
seen the assassin only "from a distance" and could not identify
him? No, Callaway was right, since the Report confirms that
"Reynolds did not make a positive identification when interviewed by the FBI." If the Commission considers him an "eyewitness" anyway, it is because "he subsequently testified before a
Commission staff member [*during the summer of 1964, after
recovering from his head wound*—L. S.], and when shown two
photographs of Oswald, stated that they were photographs of the
man he saw."

I shall have occasion to discuss other "eyewitnesses" who were
led to the desired identification under even more astonishing
conditions. Meanwhile, Ted Callaway remains the only one of
the "nine" who had no need to be coaxed, or who did not contradict himself, or whose identification of the accused did not take
place after the press and television had already superimposed
Oswald's features over those of all other potential suspects.

One should keep in mind, nevertheless, the argument mentioned
before concerning the bruises—and the sneer—on Oswald's face.
The Report itself stresses this involuntarily in the section titled
"Oswald's Legal Rights," aimed only at showing that Oswald was
not mistreated while in jail: "Oswald received a slight cut over

his right eye and a bruise under his left eye during the scuffle in the Texas Theatre with the arresting officers, three of whom were injured and required medical treatment. *These marks were visible to all who saw him during the 2 days of his detention* and to millions of television viewers." (Italics mine.)

The testimony of Ted Callaway, on one point, contradicts the initial statements of the authorities.

On the basis of these declarations—themselves based, it seems, on the statements of Mrs. Markham—it had been assumed that Tippit was not on guard when he got out of his car and had not even unsnapped his holster. Here is Callaway's account, as he gave it on the CBS telecast of September 27, 1964: "He was laying on his pistol. The strap on his holster was unsnapped, and I imagine that he had drawn his pistol while he was falling, because it was laying under his left side."

The Commission seems to agree with this: "Apparently," the Report states, "he had reached for his gun; it lay beneath him outside of the holster." But the Commission never confronted Mrs. Markham or Callaway with each other's testimony, to clear up this point.

This was not the only gap left by the Commission. Two young research assistants at Columbia University's Bureau of Applied Social Research, George and Patricia Nash, conducted their own inquiry in Dallas and named a number of essential witnesses—especially in the Tippit case—who were never "questioned or even contacted by the Commission."

By far the most amazing negligence, as revealed by the Nashes in their study published in *The New Leader,* was the absence of any effort on the part of the FBI or the Commission to question Clayton Butler, the ambulance driver, and Eddie Kinsley, his assistant, who arrived on the scene of the Tippit murder minutes after it had happened. Since they took him away before the police arrived, they could have provided such indispensable details as the exact position of the body. The FBI and the Commission similarly neglected to question Frank Wright, who lived in a ground-floor apartment on Tenth Street, heard the shots half a block away, and said he was "the first person out." It was Frank

Wright's wife who saw from her window that "there was a man lying on the street" and immediately dialed the telephone operator. The ambulance call slip bore the address of the Wrights, which had been taken down by the dispatcher.

It is not irrelevant, of course, to notice that all of these "potential witnesses" (including the manager of the apartment house facing the murder site) had information that, according to the Nashes, was "in direct contradiction" to some of Mrs. Markham's statements, such as her recollection about the lapse of time between the shooting and the arrival of the ambulance.

George and Patricia Nash also talked to Helen Markham. "I'm the witness," she proudly told them. "I'm the one he was talking to when he died. . . . I couldn't understand what Tippit said. I guess he wanted me to call on the car radio and get some help. . . ." The Warren Report says the "four bullets" that hit Tippit "killed him instantly." Mrs. Markham thus contradicted not only the witnesses the Commission chose not to hear but the Commission itself. That was not news to the Commission, although its Report does not pass the word along. The Report says only that "Helen Markham was screaming as she leaned over the body." In Volume III of the Hearings we learn from Mrs. Markham that, while she was "screaming and hollering," Tippit "tried" to talk to her. Later we have this exchange between Assistant Counsel Joseph Ball and the Commission's "reliable" witness:

> *Mr. Ball.*   Was he alive?
> *Mrs. Markham.*   Yes, sir.
> *Mr. Ball.*   Did he say anything?
> *Mrs. Markham.*   He was trying to, but he just couldn't. I just couldn't make out what he was trying to say.

The main failure of the Warren Report, however, is the fact that it gives no valid indication of why Tippit stopped Oswald and why Oswald shot Tippit.

All the Report can offer is a theory—summed up, appropriately, in the "Speculations and Rumors" appendix—that runs as follows: "It is conceivable, even probable, that Tippit stopped Oswald because of the description broadcast by the police radio." The

Commission accepts Mrs. Markham's testimony according to which Tippit came "from the rear"; it repeats twice that Tippit and "the man" were going "in the same direction." But the Report quickly adds: "The man's general description was similar to the one broadcast over the police radio. Tippit stopped the man and called him to his car."

Contrary to the official version accepted until the Report was published, the description broadcast by the police radio was not the one Truly had given on noticing the absence of the employee seen earlier on the second floor.

Strange though it may seem, the Commission never made a final determination as to the origin of the broadcast information, which it says described the suspect as "white, slender, weighing about 165 pounds, about 5'10" tall, and in his early thirties." The Report notes that Oswald was 5'9" tall and 24 years old. As to his weight, Oswald gave it as 140 pounds at the time of his arrest, but the autopsy report estimated it at about 150.

This is not a question of haggling over a mere inch, a dozen pounds, or a half-dozen years. What matters is that the broadcast contained no information (hair, ears, bearing, clothing, etc.) that would permit the recognition of a man from behind. No less important is the fact that the scene was several miles from the downtown location of the assassination, in a neighborhood where there was no reason to look for the assassin. If the Dallas police had picked up all white men about 30 years old, 5'9" or 5'10" tall, and weighing between 140 and 165 pounds, all over the city, there would not have been enough stadiums, convention halls, and theaters to hold them all.

But not a single arrest based on the broadcast was reported on November 22, not even in the area of the Depository, where the police might have been especially zealous, nor in the neighborhood of the bus and railroad stations or of the airport, where the police should have been especially watchful. Unless we were dealing with a kind of "supersleuth" of unparalleled perspicacity, it is *improbable, even inconceivable,* that it was the police broadcast that incited Tippit to pull up to the curb behind a man walking quietly on Tenth Street in Oak Cliff.

There is one point at least where the Commission, alone in having the technical means to verify it, made sure it had the last word. This concerns the curious absence of fingerprints on the rifle.

According to the Report, an FBI expert named Sebastian F. Latona declared that "the poor quality of the wood and the metal would cause the rifle to absorb moisture from the skin, thereby making a clear print unlikely." This explanation is repeated to refute the "speculation" that Oswald "would not have had time to wipe the prints off the rifle after he had fired it." The Commission's reply, apart from citing Latona's finding, is: "There is no evidence that Oswald wore gloves or that he wiped prints off the rifle."

Once again, obviously, I will not attempt to build a technical case against the conclusions of an expert.

Nevertheless, I regret that the Commission did not produce, along with Latona's expertise, a statement from the Beretta firm to the effect that its Mannlicher-Carcano 1940 was made of wood and metal of a special nature making them fingerprint-resistant. Or perhaps the Commission might have asked Klein's Sporting Goods of Chicago to certify that the Mannlicher-Carcano Number C2766, sent to A. Hidell in Dallas, had particularly suffered from age or exposure to the elements. For if this rifle was made of the same wood and metal that rifles generally are made of, why is it that police can find fingerprints on other rifles provided they are not cleaned and gloves are not worn?

Regarding, finally, the statement of Captain Fritz that Oswald's reloaded revolver had two empty chambers, the Warren Commission has chosen an even easier way out. It just ignores the statement.

6

THE MYSTERY OF THE TEXAS THEATER

IN ITS ISSUE OF FEBRUARY 21, 1964, *Life* magazine published 12 illustrated pages on Oswald under a title—"The Evolution of an Assassin"—leaving no doubt that, without waiting for the conclusions of the Warren Commission, *Life* had returned its own verdict.

The *Life* article begins: "Ever since the assassination of President Kennedy, two questions have haunted the nation and the world: What was the President's killer really like? How did he grow up to commit this terrible act?" I don't know whether the editors of *Life* are qualified to say what haunts the United States. As for the world, I can state that the question that haunts it is a third one ignored by *Life:* Was it really Oswald who killed the President?

The cover of the issue shows the famous photo portraying Oswald with all the paraphernalia of the perfect assassin: rifle with telescopic sight, revolver, Trotskyite newspaper (an official Communist paper might have led to complications with the Soviet Union).

The photo is reproduced again on an inside page, with a detailed caption.

I suppose the enlargements established without question that the newspaper Oswald was "proudly holding" was *The Militant,* as *Life* declares. A close examination of the rifle, which the captions says Oswald "used to shoot President Kennedy," shows that the telescopic sight has been retouched, if not entirely added by an artist. But *Life* at least feels the need to justify itself, noting

95

that "Dallas police have confirmed that this is the rifle found in
the Texas Book Depository."

Looking at the revolver, we see only the butt emerging from
the holster (some photographers believe this, too, shows the re-
toucher's hand). But *Life's* magic eye identifies the weapon inside its holster, for the caption states flatly, without further
comment: "On Oswald's hip is revolver which killed Dallas policeman J. D. Tippit."

A strange revolver, this . . . While detailed, though often inaccurate, information was lavished on the press about the
Mannlicher-Carcano, nothing or virtually nothing had been published by that time about the Smith and Wesson. No identification
of the Los Angeles mail-order firm that sold it. No mention, true
or false, of fingerprints or palm prints. In fact, when Oswald was
officially charged with Tippit's murder, it had not even been
proved that he owned a revolver.

On November 26, however, Will Fritz suddenly revealed to
newsmen, who were waiting for him as usual in the corridor, that
Oswald had admitted the revolver was his.

This admission had never been mentioned before, not even by
District Attorney Wade when he recited his proofs on the night
of Oswald's death. Why did the homicide chief wait until two
days later to disclose the alleged admission, and why hadn't
Wade mentioned it before? It all seemed a bit too fishy even for
Dallas and raised the question of how the admission had been
obtained, since Oswald had been questioned for two days without
a lawyer. Some newspapers passed the information along, but
with unaccustomed prudence (smaller headlines, conditional
verbs). Others telephoned the Dallas police for verification. They
were told that the news was not confirmed, that it probably was all
a misunderstanding, and that it was better to wait. There was to
be no further mention of it until the Warren Report came out.

Meanwhile the "evidence" concerning the revolver consisted of
the photo published in *Life*, which if authentic could prove only
that Oswald had a revolver the preceding spring; the testimony of
Ted Callaway; and the statements of the officers who arrested
Oswald at the Texas Theater.

The story of this arrest, as told in the unforgettable Wade press conference, seems to have been borrowed from the theater of the absurd:

> *Wade.*   Someone saw him go in the Texas Theater. A search was made of that later by a number of police officers. At the time an officer of the Dallas police spotted him and asked him to come out. He struck at the officer, put the gun against his head and snapped it, but did not —the bullet did not—go off. We have the snapped bullet there. Officers—officers apprehended him at that time.
>
> *Reporter.*   Was that an attempted suicide, sir?
>
> *Wade.*   Against the officer's head.
>
> *Reporter.*   Do you know why the gun . . .
>
> *Reporter.*   Which officer?
>
> *Wade.*   McDonald was his name.
>
> *Reporter.*   Why didn't it go off?
>
> *Wade.*   It snapped. It was a misfire. Then officers subdued him—some six officers—subdued him there in the theater, and he was brought to the police station here.
>
> *Reporter.*   Mr. Wade, why didn't the gun fire?
>
> *Wade.*   It misfired, being on the—the shell didn't explode. We have where it hit it, but it didn't explode. It didn't fire the shell.
>
> *Reporter.*   There was one officer who said that he pulled the trigger, but he managed to put his thumb in the part before the firing pin. It didn't . . .
>
> *Wade.*   Well . . .
>
> *Reporter.*   . . . strike the—the bullet didn't explode. Is that . . .
>
> *Wade.*   I don't know whether it's that or not. I know he didn't snap the gun is all I know about it.
>
> *Reporter.*   You would say it was a misfire?
>
> *Wade.*   It didn't fire.
>
> *Reporter.*   Let's get the story again. . . .

They did not get the story again, and it is hard to see what miracle could have clarified this account. It must be said that the officers cited by Wade had not made the job any easier for him.

According to the account given the same day by Officer Mc-
Donald to the *Dallas Morning News,* Oswald pointed himself out
by getting up as the policeman approached and shouting: "This
is it!" Here is the rest of the story, as reported by the local paper:

> McDonald, when he ran to Oswald, was struck with a
> fist. Then Oswald made a grab for a gun. McDonald said
> he rammed his hand into the top of the man's trousers and
> grabbed the revolver. He said Oswald pulled the trigger,
> but apparently the officer's finger jammed the action and
> kept the gun from firing. Other officers came to McDonald's
> aid and Detective Bob K. Carroll got possession of the
> pistol. Detective Paul Bentley sprained an ankle during the
> fracas.

The next day some papers published a story under M. N.
McDonald's byline with the notation, "Written for the Associated
Press." After stating that he had been sent to the scene following
a telephone call that informed police "a man acting funny was
holed up on the balcony of the Texas Theater," McDonald gave
the following account:

> I went in from the rear and came out through the cur-
> tains on the side of the screen. I noticed about 10 or 15
> people sitting in the theater and they were spread out good.
> A man sitting near the front, and I still don't know who it
> was, tipped me the man I wanted was sitting in the third
> row from the rear on the ground floor and not in the
> balcony.
>
> I went up the aisle, and talked to two people sitting about
> in the middle. I was crouching low and holding my gun
> in case any trouble came. I wanted to be ready for it. I
> walked up the aisle and turned in Oswald's row. We were
> no more than a foot from each other when he suddenly
> stood up and raised both hands. "It's all over now," he told
> me.
>
> Then he hit me a pretty good one in the face with his

fist. I saw him going for his gun and I grabbed him around the waist. We struggled and fell around the seats for a few seconds and I got my hand on the butt of his pistol. But he had his hand on the trigger. I was pulling the gun toward me and I heard the hammer click.

The primer (which detonates the bullet) was dented and it didn't fire. This might have saved me. I got the pistol out of his hand and another officer, Bob Carroll, reached me and took the pistol from me. I held Oswald. As we took him out of the show, he calmed down. . . .

The story is a graphic one, but I wish the man from A.P. who took it down had asked the officer a few questions. Why, for example, on his way to the suspect did McDonald pause for a conversation with two spectators? And what did he do with the revolver he was holding in his hand "in case any trouble came"? This revolver must have been in his way when he was wrestling Oswald. Why didn't he use it? I admit I was quite astonished— and puzzled—by the restraint of this Dallas policeman who, with gun in hand, approached a man suspected of killing one of his colleagues, let himself be punched in the face, and watched the suspect "going for his gun" without even shooting him in the arm.

And what about Oswald's behavior? We are told he was the assassin of the President of the United States and that he had just slain a policeman who, according to a "reliable" witness, had made no threatening move against him. How does he react now when he sees another officer coming at him with a revolver? He gets up, raises his hands, and says "It's all over now," which seems to mean either that he is ready to give up or that he is determined to seek a high price for his life. But he does neither: He punches the armed policeman in the face, which in Texas as well as in New York is usually an efficient method to commit suicide. Why didn't Oswald already have his gun in his hand? McDonald gave him plenty of time by stopping to speak with the two spectators. And why didn't he fire as soon as the officer came close?

I shall only note in passing that when Henry Wade spoke of

Oswald's putting his revolver against McDonald's head, this apparently was a purely personal invention of the Dallas District Attorney; McDonald himself said nothing of the kind.

But there remains the man "sitting near the front," who knew immediately, according to McDonald, not only why the police were rushing in but which man they were looking for and where he was seated. In fact, McDonald's informer was not a spectator but Johnny Brewer, the manager of a shoe store near the theater, who had seen a terrified Oswald flatten himself against his store window when a police car went by. Brewer followed Oswald and saw him enter the theater. He asked the cashier, Julie Postal, to call the police, waited for the officers at the back door, and stepped in front of the screen with them when the lights were turned on, to point out the suspect.

McDonald may have some excuse for not recalling, in his excitement, that the man who pointed out Oswald was standing on the stage, not sitting in the audience. But what excuse could there be for his superiors, who read his report and did nothing to track down McDonald's mysterious informer? What was the FBI's excuse for not questioning Brewer until, as he told me himself, "a week later, after the papers printed my story"?

Earlier there had been a great variety of explanations of why the police had gone to the theater. McDonald believed the cashier was the one who had called to report a man acting in a suspicious manner, hiding in the balcony. On November 27, my conversation with Assistant District Attorney Jim Bowie took an unexpected turn when we arrived at this point:

"What led the police to the Texas Theater, Mr. Bowie? A telephone call?"

"Half a dozen calls! Everybody was calling at the time. But I think that somebody had seen him go into the theater. In any case, there was a call from the cashier. There was a man in the theater acting in a strange manner, she said."

"What was he doing?"

"I think she saw him change his seat several times, shift around in the seat, I don't know what else . . ."

"How could she have seen him? Did she leave the ticket booth to watch him? By the way, did Oswald buy a ticket before going in?"

Bowie looked at me for a moment, saying nothing, and then grumbled:

"Maybe an employee came to tell her, what difference does it make?" For the first and only time in our talk there was a note of irritation in his voice.

He added: "As to the ticket, I don't know if Oswald bought one or not. The cashier was too upset to remember; she had been listening to the news about the President over her transistor radio."

In February, when I returned to Oak Cliff to ask Brewer some questions, I recognized Julie Postal at the ticket window as I passed the Texas Theater. Introducing myself, I asked her if she remembered now whether Oswald had paid for a ticket, hoping that her memory might have been refreshed by the passage of time.

"No comment," she said, with a wide smile.

"Was there a ticket-taker at the door, and would he have let Oswald go through without a ticket?"

The same smile and the same answer, a little more insistent: "No comment."

"Do you remember how many people were in the audience? You said there were 20, I believe, at the time."

"No comment."

"Can you tell me how many rows there are in the orchestra?"

"No comment."

"Is that what you were told to say to newsmen, especially when they have a foreign accent? Or is it your own decision?"

"No com—— I mean, it's my own decision."

The question I wanted to ask Brewer had to do with the number of spectators in the theater at the time of the arrest.

I doubted that there could have been many, so early on a weekday afternoon in a neighborhood of working people. "About 20," Julie Postal had told reporters who questioned her that day. McDonald had noticed "about 10 or 15 people" who were "spread out good." Johnny Brewer was in a good position to give a correct estimate, since he had been on the stage when the lights went on, searching the house for the man he had seen outside his store.

"I would say 15 or 20 people," Brewer answered.

He went on:

"A few of them were sitting toward the back, not far from where Oswald was."

Thus some 15 or 20 people attended the arrest of Lee Harvey Oswald. But despite the incoherent television accounts of what Oswald had done with his revolver or what the police had done with it, none of these 15 or 20 people had yet been asked to tell what he had seen.

Even more disturbing, none had appeared voluntarily. It is hard to believe that 15 or 20 movie fans, privileged to have ringside seats at the capture of the assassin of the President of the United States, would not have rushed forward to give their personal accounts of how he had tried to shoot his way out of the theater. It is easier to imagine that 15 or 20 Oak Cliff residents, having seen no revolver in Oswald's hands, preferred to keep quiet rather than contradict the Dallas police.

The mystery of the vanished spectators was one of the points I discussed in my *Commentary* article of March 1964. The Report deals with it in the course of opposing its "true facts" to the "Speculations and Rumors":

> *Speculation.*—Not a single one of the people in the Texas Theatre at the time of Oswald's arrest has come forward or been brought forward to give an eyewitness account of the arrest.
>
> *Commission finding.*—Johnny C. Brewer, the shoe store manager, and two patrons of the theatre—John Gibson and George Jefferson Applin, Jr.—were present in the theatre and testified before the Commission on the circumstances of Oswald's arrest at the Texas Theatre. Only 6 or 7 people were seated on the main floor of the theatre.

What was said by these two patrons—found by the Commission after publication of the *Commentary* article?

"George Jefferson Applin, Jr. confirmed that Oswald fought with four or five officers before he was handcuffed. He added that

one officer grabbed the muzzle of a shotgun, drew back, and hit
Oswald with the butt end of the gun in the back."

Obviously Applin's testimony solves nothing: Instead of telling
about Oswald's revolver, he offers a story about a shotgun and a
blow in the back, which the Report suggests is sheer invention.

I am ready to believe it—to believe the Commission in this instance, and not George Jefferson Applin, Jr.—but what then remains of Applin's testimony?

"No other theatre patron or officer has testified that Oswald was
hit by a gun," the Report goes on, refuting its first witness. Here
is where the second one comes in: "John Gibson, another patron
in the theatre, saw an officer grab Oswald, and he claims he heard
the click of a gun misfiring. He saw no shotgun in the possession
of any policeman near Oswald." Nobody has ever questioned
the fact that a policeman grabbed Oswald. The click that Gibson
"claimed" to have heard is denied by the experts who established,
says the Commission on the same page, that "the hammer of the
revolver never touched the shell." In short, nothing remains of
John Gibson's testimony either, except to the extent that it can be
used against the testimony of George Jefferson Applin, Jr.

How can the Commission declare in spite of this that two
patrons testified on the circumstances of the arrest? Why did it
give up the search for other patrons, when it recognized that this
pair had given absolutely no valid information on the arrest? The
Commission does not answer these questions.

According to the Report there were only "6 or 7 people" in the
orchestra. The cashier had said "about 20," McDonald "about 10
or 15," and Brewer "15 or 20." The Report fails to say where it
obtained its figures. But even if we assume there were only six or
seven, what happened to the missing four or five patrons?

The Hearings contain nothing to explain this or even to indicate that any effort was made to fill in the gap.

At first, though—judging from the questioning of Captain
W. R. Westbrook, the highest-ranking officer at the scene—the
Commission appeared eager to find out more. When Westbrook
said he had given orders to take down the names of everyone in

the theater, Assistant Counsel Joseph A. Ball showed a keen interest:

> *Mr. Ball.*   We have asked for the names of people in the
> theater and we have only come up with the name of
> George Applin. Do you know of any others?
> *Mr. Westbrook.*   He possibly might have been the only
> one in there at the time—the rest of them might have
> been working there, because I'm sure at that time of day
> you would have more employees than you would have
> patrons.
> *Mr. Ball.*   You didn't take the names of any of the
> patrons?
> *Mr. Westbrook.*   No, sir.

A little later in the same interrogation, John H. Ely, a Commission staff member, came back to the question.

> *Mr. Ely.*   Captain, you mentioned that you had left orders
> for somebody to take the names of everybody in the
> theater, and you also stated you did not have this list;
> do you know who has it?
> *Mr. Westbrook.*   No; possibly Lieutenant Cunningham
> will know, but I don't know who has the list.
> *Mr. Ely.*   That's all.

That was all indeed. Even though Lieutenant Cunningham was mentioned again (as we will see in Chapter 10, in connection with the Walker case), he was never questioned by the Commission. As to the seriousness with which orders are given or carried out in the Dallas Police Department, one gets an idea from this passage in the interrogation of John Gibson:

> *Mr. Ball.*   Well, did any officers talk to you afterwards
> and get your name and address?
> *Mr. Gibson.*   No.
> *Mr. Ball.*   Did you see them take the name and address
> of anybody else?
> *Mr. Gibson.*   No, sir. . . .

On this point, however, Johnny Brewer contradicts Gibson. The police, he said, "got everybody that was in the theater and set them aside, and another officer was taking their names and addresses. . . ." If the Commission had really wanted to get to the bottom of this, it could have done so. But, as I said, it saw no reason to question Lieutenant Cunningham and neglected to ask the many officers who did testify if one of them was, by any chance, the "other policeman" mentioned by Brewer. Brewer himself, who said he had given his name and address to this officer, was turned up by the press and not by the police.

In general, the Warren Report's description of the events at the Texas Theater matches the exotic nature of the earlier accounts that emerged from the Dallas inquiry.

Brewer, bitter because the FBI had ignored him so long when he was the person most instrumental in Oswald's arrest, tried to regain some stature before the Commission. But Julie Postal, having decided she had some comment to make after all, did not intend to fade into the background. So while Brewer told the Commission that he "knew from radio broadcasts that the President had been shot," Julie Postal said she was the one who had told Brewer about the assassination. She had seen a man "duck into" the theater lobby; though she left the box office, it was not to go after him but to walk to the curb because she was "attracted by the sound of the sirens."

The Report goes on: "Shortly thereafter, Johnny Brewer, who had come in from the nearby shoestore, asked Mrs. Postal whether the fellow that had ducked in had bought a ticket. She said, 'No; by golly, he didn't' and turned around, but the man was nowhere in sight." If we are to believe her, and the Report, she then took charge and "sent Brewer into the theatre to find the man and check the exits," while she called the police.

Brewer gets his revenge with the revolver; Julie Postal, whether or not she went back to her glass booth, did not go up on the stage with the police, but Brewer "testified he saw Oswald pull the revolver and the officers struggle with him to take it away. . . ."

He also declared, however, that "while fists were flying he heard one of the officers say 'Kill the President, will you.'" The

Report admits it was "unlikely" that any of the officers could have alluded to the President's assassination, since they believed they were capturing only Tippit's killer. Even more striking was Officer McDonald's performance before the CBS cameras, in which he acted out with his interviewer the scene of Oswald's arrest. According to McDonald, Oswald's revolver was "tucked in his belt on the right side" and "of course he had the shirt over it." From his re-enactment as well as from his words, it appears not only that the struggle for the revolver was centered on the belt, but also that before Oswald had time to take out the gun McDonald was standing between him and the stage. In other words, it was totally impossible for Brewer to have seen the revolver from the stage, and very unlikely that he could have seen it even if he had followed McDonald up the aisle.

But again, this is not a problem for the Commission. *"Specula-tion.*—There is no independent witness aside from the police who testified that Oswald was carrying a gun when arrested by the police. *Commission finding.*—Johnny Brewer testified before the Commission that he saw Oswald pull a gun and that he saw it taken away from him by a policeman."

As far as I'm concerned, the testimony of Johnny Brewer must be considered null and void, inasmuch as there was no cross-examination—and no direct examination, either—to establish where he stood at the time he claimed to have seen the revolver and no re-enactment to determine whether he could have seen it from such a position.

Contrary, however, to the impression given by the Report, and contrary to the impression I myself have given on the basis of the Report's statements and silences, Brewer was not the only "civilian" who testified he had seen a revolver in Oswald's hand. For when John Gibson, one of the two patrons in the theater cited by the Commission in opposition to my "speculation" or "rumor" in *Commentary,* testified on April 8, 1964, in Dallas, he said that he had watched the police go down the two center aisles "and then the next thing was—Oswald was standing in the aisle with a gun in his hand."

Mr. Ball. That's the next thing you saw?

Mr. Gibson. Yes, sir.

Mr. Ball. Was there anybody with him—near him?

Mr. Gibson. I couldn't swear to that—I don't know—you mean other policemen?

Mr. Ball. That's what I mean—was he in the aisles?

Mr. Gibson. Well, he was in the aisle when I saw him.

Mr. Ball. What was he doing?

Mr. Gibson. Well, he had this pistol in his hand.

Mr. Ball. Was anybody near him?

Mr. Gibson. Just the officers.

Mr. Ball. What was the officer doing—did you say officers or police officer?

Mr. Gibson. Officers.

Mr. Ball. Plural, officers?

Mr. Gibson. Yes; there were more than one.

Mr. Ball. What were they doing?

Mr. Gibson. Well, they were going toward him.

Mr. Ball. Did they have ahold of him at the time?

Mr. Gibson. No; I don't believe so.

Mr. Ball. Did anyone have ahold of him at that time?

Mr. Gibson. I don't think so.

I had stressed the necessity of establishing, with the help of the theater patrons, the exact circumstances of Oswald's arrest, which had been described in an improbable and contradictory manner by the police who had taken part in it. The Commission triumphantly produced John Gibson and George Jefferson Applin, Jr., only to recognize that Gibson and Applin did no more than contribute additional improbabilities and contradictions. And when Gibson finally came up with an unexpected but much sought confirmation of the existence of Oswald's revolver, his testimony was so opposed to the official account that the Commission plainly would have preferred never to have heard of him, and in fact does not mention this confirmation in its Report.

The Commission of course wants no part of an Oswald standing up in the theater with gun in hand, before any policeman grabbed him: It has enough troubles already in making it seem plausible that Oswald did not fire at the police and that the police did not fire at him.

Still, Gibson is absolutely positive in his statement. "He was standing in the aisle with a gun in his hand," he repeated obstinately, perhaps hoping to please Ball. And again: "When I saw him he was facing the police with a gun in his hand." I have no intention of endorsing Gibson's version, but neither can I approve of the way the Warren Report conjures away his testimony without justifying this sleight of hand.

It is quite possible that Gibson imagined the whole scene. It is also possible that he actually did see a man standing in the aisle holding a revolver, but that it was a plain-clothes officer; this would not be any more helpful to the Commission.

In its "Narrative of Events" at the beginning of Chapter I, the Report gives us this apparently positive and definitive account of what happened at the theater: "McDonald ordered the man to his feet and heard him say, 'Well, it's all over now.' The man drew a gun from his waist with one hand and struck the officer with the other. McDonald struck out with his right hand and grabbed the gun with his left hand. . . ." The account ends with this conclusion: "Within 80 minutes of the assassination and 35 minutes of the Tippit killing Oswald resisted arrest at the theatre by attempting to shoot another Dallas police officer."

But the categorical statements quoted above are presented in a slightly different manner in Chapter IV:

' "The other officers who helped subdue Oswald corroborated McDonald in his testimony except that they did not hear Oswald say, 'It's all over now.' Deputy Sheriff Eddy R. Walthers recalled such a remark but he did not reach the scene of the struggle until Oswald had been knocked to the floor by McDonald and the others."

I do not attach excessive significance to the words attributed to Oswald, but why are they included in the official narrative of the events when the Commission itself later admits their doubtful character?

As to Oswald's attempt to "shoot another Dallas police officer," the Report notes that most of the police said they heard a click that they believed was caused by the hammer of the revolver. But it goes on to cite the experts' view that "the hammer of the revolver never touched the shell in the chamber." It follows—and the Report admits this—that the witnesses had not heard the sound of a misfire. The Report speculates (outside of its appendix devoted to "Speculations and Rumors," since this appendix is reserved for the speculations of others) that the witnesses "might have heard a snapping noise resulting from the police officer grabbing the cylinder of the revolver and pulling it away from Oswald while he was attempting to pull the trigger."

Finally, the Report runs up against the simple anatomical fact that McDonald had only two hands.

I cited earlier the A.P. story under McDonald's byline: "I was crouching low and holding my gun in case any trouble came," he related, adding again for emphasis, "I wanted to be ready for it." Reading his account, I wondered what he had done with his own revolver while he was desperately struggling to disarm Oswald. But the Commission never asks such questions. "McDonald struck back with his right hand and grabbed the gun with his left hand." The riddle: In which hand did he hold his own revolver?

Again in his signed story, which he never denied but which the Commission totally ignores, there is the episode of the two spectators—never located, by the way—to whom McDonald talked before he went to the suspect pointed out to him.

In the Report this incident becomes another interlude reminiscent of the theater of the absurd. The Report confirms that Brewer, on stage, pointed out the suspect to McDonald. (I don't believe the Commission intentionally minimizes the suspicions about Oswald by defining him at this point as "the man who had come into the theatre without paying.") The Report goes on to say that McDonald, going toward Oswald, "first searched two men in the center of the main floor, about 10 rows from the front." It is left to the reader to inquire, since the Report says nothing about it, why this strange policeman, who has been shown the exact place where the suspect is sitting, wastes time by *searching* two others (in the A.P. story he was content to *talk* to

them, but even that is odd enough) at the risk of giving the suspect
time to escape or at least get ready to resist.

The transcript of the Hearings shows that in this case, as in
several others, some members of the Commission had trouble
swallowing the incongruities they were served—though nothing in
the Report reflects the trouble.

McDonald had told how he had arrived with three other officers
at the rear exit of the theater, where they were met by Johnny
Brewer. We know already that Brewer was waiting there to let
them in, since the door opened only from inside, but there was a
bad moment for him at first; Patrolman C. T. Walker had drawn
his gun and Brewer had a difficult time explaining to them who
he was and why he was there. Finally they went inside and
climbed up to the stage next to the screen.

> *Mr. McDonald.*   . . . I looked into the audience. I saw
> the person that the shoe store salesman had pointed
> out to us.
>
> *Mr. Ball.*   Were the lights on or off?
>
> *Mr. McDonald.*   The lights were up, and the movie was
> playing at this time.
>
> *Mr. Ball.*   And could you see to the rear of the theater?
>
> *Mr. McDonald.*   Yes, sir.
>
> *Mr. Ball.*   You could see the man. Did the civilian point
> out to you the man in one of the rear seats?
>
> *Mr. McDonald.*   He didn't point out personally. He was
> pointing out the suspect to another officer with him on
> the right side of the stage, just right of the movie screen.
>
> *Mr. Ball.*   What did you do then?
>
> *Mr. McDonald.*   Well, after seeing him, I noticed the
> other people in the theater—there was approximately
> 10 or 15 other people seated throughout the theater.
> There were two men sitting in the center, about 10
> rows from the front.
>
> I walked up the left center aisle into the row behind
> these two men, and Officer C. T. Walker was behind
> me. When I got to these two men, I told them to get on

their feet. They got up. I searched them for a weapon.
I looked over my shoulder and the suspect that had
been pointed out to me. He remained seated without
moving, just looking at me.

Mr. Ball.   Why did you frisk these two men in the center
of the theater?

Mr. McDonald.   I wanted to make sure that I didn't
pass anything or miss anybody. I wanted to make sure I
didn't overlook anybody or anything.

Mr. Ball.   And you still kept your eye on the suspect?

Mr. McDonald.   Yes, sir. He was to my back. I was looking over my shoulder at him.

For Ball, apparently, that sufficed. But when he said he had no
more questions, Senator John Sherman Cooper of Kentucky
stepped in:

Senator Cooper.   May I ask—if the suspect was pointed
out to you, why was it you did not go directly to him,
but you searched other persons?

Mr. McDonald.   Well, usually on information of that
sort, you have to weigh it a little bit to make sure you
get the right person. He could have been mistaken. If a
suspect was in that theater, I wanted to make sure I got
him, and not overlook him.

Senator Cooper.   You said, though, that before you went
into the theater, where the seats were located, that a man
pointed out to you a person who he claimed was the
suspect.

Mr. McDonald.   Yes, sir; he said that that was the man
that had acted suspiciously in running into the theater.

Senator Cooper.   That was the man that was identified
to you?

Mr. McDonald.   Yes, sir.

Senator Cooper.   Then, if he was the man identified to
you, why did you stop and search these two men before
you got to the man you later arrested?

> *Mr. McDonald.* Well, I wanted to make sure he was right.

The questioning continued with some exchanges in which the officer assured the Senator that while he searched the men, keeping the suspect in the corner of his eye, the suspect "just sat in his seat, with his hands in his lap, watching me." Is this what the Report means by "attempting to shoot" another officer? The following question by Cooper was to further weaken the Commission's thesis:

> *Senator Cooper.* Then when you told the man you arrested to stand up did he immediately pull his pistol out?
>
> *Mr. McDonald.* No, sir; he stood up and starting raising his hands, "Well, it is all over now." But in my opinion it was an act of giving up or surrendering. . . .

In McDonald's interrogation and in the testimony of other policemen who took part in the arrest, we find some interesting revelations on the method used by the police to identify the revolver said to have been taken from Oswald.

The original identification was made by Marina Oswald. It was on February 6 that John M. Thorne, the lawyer chosen to represent the widow (under circumstances we will take up later), introduced as an exhibit against the husband the Smith and Wesson .38 sent on March 20, 1963, by Seaport Traders of Los Angeles to A. J. Hidell, Post Office Box 2915, Dallas.

> *Mr. Thorne.* Exhibit 143 is a pistol.
> *Mrs. Oswald.* Lee Oswald's.
> *Mr. Rankin.* You recognize that as a pistol of your husband?
> *Mrs. Oswald.* Yes.
> *Mr. Rankin.* I offer in evidence Exhibit 143.
> *The Chairman.* It may be admitted.

Just as in the case of the Mannlicher-Carcano, I do not question the purchase of the Smith and Wesson by Oswald, in view of the convincing documents produced by the Commission without need of Marina Oswald's ridiculous affidavit, so unblushingly accepted by General Counsel Rankin. But the Commission has not proved that Oswald used it against Tippit, nor that he tried to use it against McDonald. The Hearings finally reveal that there isn't even any proof that Exhibit 143 was taken from Oswald at the theater.

> *Mr. Ball.* We have here Exhibit 143 for identification. Do you know whether or not this is the revolver that you took from the man that you arrested?
>
> *Mr. McDonald.* Yes, sir; this is it. I found the mark here.
>
> *Mr. Ball.* You found your mark?
>
> *Mr. McDonald.* Yes, sir.
>
> *Mr. Ball.* What mark is it?
>
> *Mr. McDonald.* I marked the initial "M."
>
> *Mr. Ball.* Where?
>
> *Mr. McDonald.* Right here, on this steel plate.
>
> *Mr. Ball.* Of the butt?
>
> *Mr. McDonald.* Yes, sir.
>
> *Mr. Belin [another assistant counsel].* Let the record show the witness is pointing to a point on the steel plate directly below the screw on the butt.

This is very impressive, but there is something wrong with it. McDonald said himself that the struggle for the gun had centered on the belt, then on the floor, in the dark between rows of seats. He added that he had given the revolver to Detective Bob Carroll *during* the fight. He therefore had no time to examine the weapon, let alone put his initial on it. When did he mark the gun? How did he determine that the revolver he marked was indeed the one he says he took from Oswald?

The two Commission attorneys who took part in questioning McDonald did not ask him these questions. Senator Cooper, at least, showed some interest in the first one:

> *Senator Cooper.* To whom did you turn over the possession of the pistol?
>
> *Mr. McDonald.* Detective Bob Carroll. He had come

        into the aisle. Whenever I hollered, "I got him" imme-
        diately I was swarmed by officers.
    Senator Cooper.   Did you mark the pistol at that time
        before you turned it over?
    Mr. McDonald.   No, sir; I marked it at the police
        station.
    Senator Cooper.   But you recognized it then as the same
        pistol you had identified today?
    Mr. McDonald.   Yes, sir.
    Senator Cooper.   That is all.

It is too bad that Senator Cooper, who displayed more curiosity
than the Commission's lawyer, did not venture further in the
questioning. If we take McDonald's word, he touched the gun but
did not see it. Exhibit 143, which he identifies under oath, is thus
from all the evidence a revolver about which he knows only what
he was told at the police station.

The Smith and Wesson .38 had still another mark, placed there
by Sergeant Gerald Hill, who received the weapon from Carroll.

Questioned by David W. Belin on April 8, 1964 (McDonald
had appeared two weeks earlier, March 25), Hill said first that he
had marked the revolver at 4 P.M., or more than two hours after
the arrest. The interrogation continued:

    Mr. Belin.   Did you keep that gun in your possession
        until you scratched your name on it?
    Mr. Hill.   Yes, sir; I did.
    Mr. Belin.   Was this gun the gun that Officer Carroll
        handed to you?
    Mr. Hill.   And identified to me as the suspect's weapon.
    Mr. Belin.   This is what has now been marked as Com-
        mission Exhibit 143, is that correct?
    Mr. Hill.   Yes, sir; that is what it says.

Completing the cycle is the deposition of Bob Carroll, questioned by Ball on April 3. Carroll, with other policemen, had
rushed to where Oswald and McDonald were wrestling:

    Mr. Carroll.   When I got up close enough, I saw a pistol

> pointing at me so I reached and grabbed the pistol and jerked the pistol away and stuck it in my belt, and then I grabbed Oswald.
>
> *Mr. Ball.*   Who had hold of that pistol at that time?
>
> *Mr. Carroll.*   I don't know, sir. I just saw the pistol pointing at me and I grabbed it and jerked it away from whoever had it and that's all, and by that time then the handcuffs were put on Oswald.

The cycle is indeed complete, and here is where we stand: On April 8 Sergeant Hill told David W. Belin that Exhibit 143 had been "identified" by Detective Carroll "as the suspect's weapon." But on April 3 Carroll had told Joseph A. Ball that he did not know "who had hold of that pistol" when he grabbed it. Hill and Carroll were never confronted with this discrepancy. The fact that McDonald stated that he had given the pistol to Carroll is utterly meaningless. Though neither Ball nor Belin saw fit to ask any question to this effect, it is quite obvious that McDonald, fighting with Oswald and "swarmed" by officers, could not have seen which one took the pistol, if he did give a pistol to someone. To sum up, the testimony of the three policemen directly involved does not support the conclusion that a gun was taken from Oswald at the Texas Theater, and the identification of Exhibit 143 as such is without foundation.

The mystery of the revolver becomes impenetrable when we finally go back to the admission Oswald is supposed to have made on the subject. I refer to the statement by Captain Fritz on November 26, 1963, that Oswald had admitted he owned the .38.

This alleged admission was tucked away for 10 months in the thick file of false news out of Dallas, and from the way it is approached by the Report one might wonder if the Commission really intended to bring it out on September 27, 1964.

In the part of the Report attempting to sketch a psychological portrait of the man it proclaims the assassin, the Commission notes that Oswald "admitted nothing that would damage him but discussed other matters quite freely." The fact of owning a revolver that the police said had killed Tippit would certainly tend to damage him. It would seem from the Report, therefore, that Oswald did not admit that.

Considering Oswald's "statements during the interrogation," the Report furthermore comments that he "provided little information." Since an admission about the revolver would in fact amount to much information, it would again seem there was no such admission. And yet . . .

And yet there is a section of the Report, titled "The Revolver," composed of a single paragraph of six lines, reprinted here in full:

> At the first interrogation, Oswald claimed that his only crime was carrying a gun and resisting arrest. When Captain Fritz asked him why he carried the revolver, he answered, "Well, you know about a pistol. I just carried it." He falsely alleged that he bought the revolver in Fort Worth, when in fact he purchased it from a mail-order house in Los Angeles.

According to the reminiscences of the Dallas homicide chief, reproduced in the Report to compensate for the absence of any stenographic transcript of Oswald's interrogation, the suspect denied owning a rifle but admitted spontaneously that he not only possessed a revolver but brought it to the theater: "I asked him where he went to when he left work," Fritz stated, "and he told me that he had a room on 1026 North Beckley, that he went over there and changed his trousers and got his pistol and went to the picture show."

We can skip over the fact that, according to the authorities, Oswald did not change his trousers but put on a jacket, although it would be interesting to know if this error resulted from a lack of attention on the part of Fritz or a lack of truth on the part of Oswald. The Commission, in any case, should have explained why Oswald so willingly told Fritz about getting his revolver at Beckley Avenue when he was continuing to deny to the very end, even when confronted with photos and documents, that he had ever ordered or owned the Mannlicher-Carcano.

Why, incidentally, did the compulsive talkers of Dallas keep so quiet for days concerning the alleged admission about the revolver? Why did Fritz suddenly decide to refer to it late in the evening on November 26, when the admission was supposed to have been made on the afternoon of November 22? Why were the local officials so reluctant to confirm the revelations of Captain Fritz, to the point that their reluctance was interpreted as a virtual retraction?

And why, finally, did the Warren Commission show in its turn such unwillingness to mention the admission of Oswald, to the point of referring to it only in passing, in a slight interpretive paragraph of six lines, without making it the subject of one of its categorical statements so numerous in the Report, without even mentioning it in its "Conclusions"?

7

THE MYSTERY OF THE USELESS CROSSES

ON THE NIGHT OF NOVEMBER 23, Police Chief Jesse Curry told the world his men had discovered that very morning an "entirely new" piece of evidence against Oswald. This proof, he said, was *startling*. But he refused to say more about it, except that it did not concern the rifle.

Wade, however, made no reference to any new evidence in his press conference the following day. This was an important conference; the assassination of Oswald, in the midst of the police responsible for guarding him and at the hands of a dubious character well known to the department, had shaken Americans out of their complacency. The haste with which the investigation had been declared closed was beginning to convince a few that something was rotten in the State of Texas. Wade therefore sought to nip in the bud the rising irritation by listing, "piece by piece," the reasons that permitted him to conclude: "There is no doubt that Oswald was the assassin of President Kennedy." How could the D.A. have omitted the "startling" evidence mentioned by the Chief?

The newsmen asked him:

> *Reporter.* Mr. Wade, what was the evidence that we were told was startling evidence that could not be told to the press . . .?
> *Another reporter.* Saturday morning.
> *First reporter.* Saturday morning. They said it came in Saturday morning, and it could not be revealed. It was . . .

Wade.   I don't know. That wasn't me that said that, I
don't think.

The same night, the early edition of the *Dallas Morning News*
revealed the "startling" discovery: The police had found a map of
Dallas in Oswald's room. On it, various intersections where the
Presidential motorcade was to pass were marked by a cross; the
corner at the Texas School Book Depository was marked not only
by a cross but also by a line corresponding to the trajectory of
the bullets.

This was too good to be true. Yet it was too specific to be
ignored, forgotten, or intentionally put aside by Wade in his
press conference shortly before. Reporters rushed to the phones.
They were unable to reach the D.A. but his first assistant, Jim
Bowie, told them he knew nothing about it.

"The police had more urgent things to do than to phone us
every time they found something," he told me three days later,
when I expressed surprise that Wade had not been immediately
informed of such a discovery.

On November 25, in any case, without referring to his silence
of the preceding day, Wade officially confirmed the story. Although he had not seen the map himself, he said, the police had
found it in Oswald's room—a map with a line showing the trajectory of the assassin's bullets. Besides the Elm-Houston intersection,
two other points on the route were indicated by crosses, apparently
"locations the assassin considered as possibilities," he said.

The presence of a map of Dallas in the North Beckley Avenue
room had been noticed by Mrs. Earlene Roberts, the housekeeper,
when the police first went there Friday afternoon. She mentioned
it when reporters asked her what the police had taken from the
room.

There was nothing unusual, of course, in Oswald's having a
map of the city. Mrs. Ruth Paine said later that she had given it to
him when he left his pregnant wife and his daughter with her in
Irving to look for a job in Dallas. What was strange, though, was
that the police—who found the map among the suspect's belongings Friday afternoon—should have waited until the following day

to open and examine it. Where was it between the time the police took it from the room and the time they made the "startling" discovery?

This question is not necessarily an insinuation, since it is quite evident that the Dallas notions of how to conduct an investigation differed considerably from those of the rest of the world.

Typical of the Dallas approach was the treatment accorded the most important of all the evidence, the Mannlicher-Carcano said to have been the murder weapon.

This rifle, it was announced, was to be sent to Washington to be examined in the FBI laboratories in the most minute detail that modern criminological methods would permit. One might suppose that Captain Fritz and his men, after taking the necessary precautions in completing their own work, would place the rifle in a box carefully guarded from any foreign contact so that not the slightest microscopic trace could be erased, or modified. Yet millions of Americans watching their television screens saw a Dallas detective brandishing this piece of evidence in his ungloved hands as he showed it to reporters in the third-floor corridor of police headquarters. And in the Saturday morning papers there was a photo (see Illustrations) showing a Dallas detective carelessly holding the rifle by the top of the sling while the butt rubbed against his trousers.

The Warren Report has revealed some more instances of gross professional negligence, but without drawing any conclusions from them as to the competence of the Dallas investigators and as to the validity of their investigation.

For example, the four cartons—two large and two small—that the assassin apparently had set up in front of the sixth-floor window as a gun support were sent to the FBI in Washington so that the special service headed by Sebastian Latona could try to obtain latent fingerprints not found in Dallas. Using the action of silver nitrate on sodium chloride, Latona was able to bring out 20 fingerprints and 8 palm prints sufficiently complete to be identified. Of these 28 prints, 24 were those of R. L. Studebaker and F. L. Lucy. Studebaker was the detective who handled the cartons at the scene. Lucy was a local FBI employee who shipped them to

Washington. Neither apparently had ever heard of the methods perfected to protect pieces of evidence against accidental alteration.

Of the remaining four prints, three—one fingerprint and two palm prints—were attributed to Oswald. The Report then tells us with the greatest calm that "one identifiable palm print was not identified." Obviously this identifiable but unidentified print never kept anyone awake in Washington or in Dallas.

Nor did anyone in Dallas or in Washington seem to have wondered about the absence of fingerprints of the workmen who, that same morning, had carried the same boxes from one place to another on the sixth floor. And nowhere in the Report is there any mention that prints were found—or even sought—on the massive "shield" of 50-pound boxes piled up behind the assassin (see Illustrations). Piling up those boxes in the few minutes available *must* have caused some sweat, which would have left prints.

But this was an investigation conducted with appalling disregard for the most elementary rules and methods of modern criminal investigation, as well as with a disarming informality.

The first foreign correspondents who settled down at Dallas police headquarters Friday night related with retrospective amazement how they had been able to walk practically anywhere they liked, sit down on the tables, use the phones, open the drawers to look for paper or pencil—imitating their American colleagues. Nobody checked press credentials. The mere fact of having some visible connection with television, even if only a cable looped around a shoulder, sufficed to open all doors. Not to mention Jack Ruby, who needed nothing at all.

I myself walked into the office of Jim Bowie without an appointment and without being announced in advance. The D.A.'s offices and those of the Sheriff, as well as the courtrooms and the county jail, are located in a modern building almost directly opposite the Depository Building. It was late in the day, employees had gone, and nobody was around except a young woman putting on makeup. I asked if I could see Mr. Bowie. She told me he had a visitor and pointed to an office where I could see two men talking, then closed her bag and left. I waited for the visitor to leave, walked in, introduced myself, and told Bowie I would like to ask some questions. He stretched out his hand, offered me a chair, and said, "Go ahead."

Reporters welcome such informality, and I certainly appreciated Jim Bowie's friendly reception. But the fact remains that for some 20 minutes I had the offices of the Dallas District Attorney all to myself and could have opened any drawer, including Henry Wade's very own, picking the lock if necessary.

It is quite improbable, in any case, that anyone guarded with particular care a map of the city that nobody had been curious enough to open. Since no "expert" could claim to be able to identify the author of three crosses and a small straight line, those marks could have been added by anyone for any reason between Friday afternoon and Saturday morning.

There is an even more important point, however, and it was for this no doubt that the Dallas investigators, when the public had been sufficiently impressed by the "startling" proof of Curry, preferred to dump the map entirely.

From the beginning, much had been made of the fact that President Kennedy's visit to Dallas had been announced in the *Dallas Morning News* of September 26, well before Oswald had begun working at the Depository. This tended to show premeditation, some said, and the marked map reinforced this theory. Didn't it signify, as Wade suggested, that the assassin had considered various possible locations for his crime before choosing the building on Elm Street?

After this, though, it was established that Oswald's job was not due to any premeditation or even any initiative of his own: A neighbor in Irving had told Mrs. Paine about the job opportunity, and she immediately passed the word to Oswald and telephoned Truly about him.

The mystery of the useless crosses lies in the fact that, according to the now official theory, Oswald, the unbalanced and solitary assassin, conceived his crime only after having started to work at the Depository and because of the very temptation that the building's location offered to his sick mind. We might imagine him, in these conditions, tracing on a map the trajectory of the bullets he planned to fire from the window; but why would he have placed crosses at two other positions?

Before examining whether the Warren Report can illuminate this mystery, I would like to cite here the Commission's general attitude toward the "errors" of the investigators:

> Insinuations that Dallas police officials and District Attorney Henry M. Wade fabricated or altered evidence to establish the guilt of Oswald were baseless. It is true that police officials and the District Attorney made errors in giving evidential information to the press, but these were clearly the result of misapprehensions or ignorance rather than intent, and at the worst represent bad judgment.

In regard to the useless crosses, however, the Report itself shows that the mistake was intentional, and not the result of any misapprehension on the part of the Dallas authorities or even of their habitual ignorance.

The Report confirms that the marked map cannot be retained as proof against Oswald. It does not do so openly, but eliminates it indirectly by listing it among the "errors" for which the local officials are mildly rebuked: "It was also reported that the map found in Oswald's room contained a marked route of the Presidential motorcade when it actually contained markings of places where Oswald may have applied for jobs, including, of course, the Texas School Book Depository." The Commission goes no further than this.

But the Report does publish facsimiles of the statements given by the various law enforcement officials who attended the interrogations of Oswald and who later tried to remember what had been said. The marked map appears in three of these accounts, which confirm that the question was taken up in the last interrogation of Oswald on Sunday morning, before the suspect was led to Jack Ruby's revolver.

Statement of Will Fritz, chief of the Dallas homicide bureau (undated):

> At 9:30 on the morning of November 24, I asked that Oswald be brought to the office. At that time I showed

him a map of the City of Dallas which had been recovered in the search of his room on North Beckley. This map had some markings on it, one of which was about where the President was shot. He said that the map had nothing to do with the President's shooting and again, as he had done in the previous interviews, denied knowing anything of the shooting of the President, or of the shooting of Officer Tippit. He said the map had been used to locate buildings where he had gone to talk to people about employment.

Statement of U.S. Postal Inspector H. D. Holmes, who was present at the interview that took place, he says, "Sunday morning, November 24, 1963, between the approximate hours of 9:25 a.m. to 11:10 a.m." (This "informal memorandum" is dated December 17, 1963) :

Captain Fritz advised him that among his effects in his room, there was found a map of the City of Dallas that had some marks on it and asked him to explain this map. Oswald said he presumed he had reference to an old City map which he had on which he had made some X's denoting location of firms that had advertised job vacancies. He stated that he had no transportation and either walked or rode a bus and that as he was constantly looking for work, in fact had registered for employment at the Texas Employment Bureau, and that as he would receive leads either from newspaper ads or from the Bureau or from neighbors, he would chart these places on the map to save time in his traveling. He said to the best of his recollection, most of them were out Industrial, presumably meaning Industrial Blvd. When asked as to why the X at the location of the Texas School Book Depository at Elm and Houston, he stated that "Well, I interviewed there for a job, in fact, got the job, therefore the X."

Statement of Inspector Thomas J Kelley of the Secret Service, dated November 29, noting that "this interview started at approximately 9:30 a.m. on Sunday, November 24, 1963":

Captain Fritz displayed an Esso street map of Dallas which had been found among Oswald's effects at the rooming house. Oswald was asked whether the map was his and whether he had put some marks on it. He said it was his and remarked "My God don't tell me there's a mark near where this thing happened." The mark was pointed out to him and he said "What about the other marks on the map? I put a number of marks on it. I was looking for work and marked the places where I went for jobs or where I heard there were jobs." Since it was obvious to Captain Fritz that Oswald was not going to be cooperative, he terminated the interview at that time.

It seems to me no less obvious that though Curry may have sinned by "misapprehension" or "ignorance" in announcing his "startling discovery" on Saturday, the police officials who gave the mistaken information to the *Dallas Morning News* Sunday night, and District Attorney Wade who made it official Monday morning, knew perfectly well what they were doing. They spread throughout the world a "discovery"—damning Oswald—about which the suspect had given a completely satisfactory explanation, accepted without reservation by the Warren Commission.

Thus it is technically true that the police and Wade did not "fabricate or alter evidence," since they did not put the crosses on the map themselves. But they did alter and fabricate the significance of the crosses by giving them a meaning that they knew to be false.

8

THE PROBLEM OF THE BROWN PAPER BAG

Mysteries cloud the Oswald affair to such a degree that the prosecution's brief contains more gaps than evidence. Among these mysteries, however, is one that if not enough to condemn the accused is certainly of a nature to embarrass the defense. I refer to the package Oswald carried with him that Friday morning after spending the night in Irving, contrary to his usual routine.

Wesley Frazier was a 19-year-old youth who worked at the Depository and lived with his sister, Linnie Mae (Mrs. William E. Randle), in Irving. The Randle home on West 5th Street was only about a hundred yards from Ruth Paine's house. It was Mrs. Randle who told Mrs. Paine about the job open at the Depository; Lee Oswald began his temporary work as a $50-a-week stock clerk there on October 16, four days before the birth of his second daughter.

A bus line runs between Dallas and Irving, and the fare is not high, but Oswald did not like to pay when he could avoid it. Wesley Frazier, who like many Texans drove to work, gave Oswald a ride to Irving each Friday night for the weekend, and picked him up each Monday morning.

On November 21, during the morning, Oswald asked Frazier if he could ride with him to Irving that night. "Some curtain rods to bring back," was the vague explanation mumbled by Oswald, never known for his affability. Frazier shrugged his shoulders. It made little difference to him if Oswald wanted a lift on Thursday this time instead of Friday. He had nothing in common with this distant and taciturn man, but one doesn't refuse to do such a simple favor for a fellow worker who also is a neighbor. "Okay," Frazier said.

I talked to Wesley Frazier, as well as to Mrs. Paine and Mrs. Randle, who were, besides Marina Oswald, the two witnesses directly involved in this crucial episode.

Ruth Paine does not know if there were any curtain rods among Oswald's things in the garage. There was no mention of them that evening, nor was the Kennedys' visit discussed, she told me. Lee Oswald had been the first to go to bed, at about 9 o'clock. He must have gone to the garage before, since Mrs. Paine found the light on when she went there a little later to paint some blocks for the children. What had surprised her was Oswald's impromptu midweek visit. "He was never one for good manners," she said, "but he only came on weekends before and always called me to let me know. Why the sudden change?" A good question at the time, and certainly something to worry about until Marina Oswald herself gave the answer to Chief Justice Warren.

About 7:20 A.M. on Friday Mrs. Randle, looking out the kitchen window, saw Oswald walk across the lawn toward Wesley's car. Mrs. Paine, who had gone to bed at 11 o'clock the night before, was still sleeping when Oswald left.

Until now Mrs. Randle had hardly glimpsed the bizarre young man who had been to Russia and come back with a Russian wife. She therefore looked him over with curiosity, she told me. "He carried a brown paper bag, the heavy kind, you know, like a grocery bag but bigger. I would say maybe two and a half feet long. He was holding it at the top, where it was folded, and the bottom almost touched the ground because he was not very tall, you know, at least by Texan standards. I saw him put the bag on the back seat of the car. Pretty soon Wes was ready and they left."

Frazier didn't see the package until he got behind the wheel. "What's that?" he asked without much interest. Oswald answered with like indifference: "The curtain rods I told you about." There was no further talk of the package during the trip.

When the two men arrived at the employee parking lot, behind an annex about 200 yards from the main building, Oswald picked up his "curtain rods" and went toward the Depository without waiting for Frazier, who remained behind for a minute or two and reached the loading platform at the rear of the building only after Oswald had already entered. Frazier had a second glance at the package as Oswald was walking away from the car: "No, not very long, maybe two or three feet. It was a brown paper bag, or at least it looked to me like a paper bag. . . ."

Official statements at the beginning referred to witnesses, including a policeman, who supposedly had seen Oswald enter the Depository with a package, had asked him what was inside, and had been told by him that it contained curtain rods. But none of these witnesses was ever produced or identified, or even mentioned again. It is quite probable that this testimony, if not entirely invented, amounted to embellishments of Wesley Frazier's story.

In fact, the Dallas investigation did not turn up a single witness who had seen Oswald either entering the Depository with the package or inside the Depository with it. The Warren Report was to confirm this later: "When Frazier entered the building, he did not see Oswald. One employee, Jack Dougherty, believed that he saw Oswald coming to work, but he does not remember that Oswald had anything in his hands as he entered the door. No other employee has been found who saw Oswald enter that morning."

What the investigators did claim to find was the wrapping of his package. In their usual style, they even added that there was a print of Oswald on the paper, and it took turns (like the one on the rifle) as a fingerprint and a palm print. But they carefully and constantly omitted any mention of where the wrapping had been found.

Logically, it should have been near the southeast window on the sixth floor or behind some cartons in that area. But Captain Fritz had not mentioned it, neither at the time he announced the discovery of the chicken leftovers nor later, when he told about the rifle. If Oswald, before going down to the second-floor lunchroom, had hidden the wrapping with such care that it took the police 24 hours to find it, then the time this would have taken, added to the delay involved in the other operations mentioned earlier, would end by making his alibi absolutely airtight. But it was even less plausible that Oswald would have hidden the wrapping before going to the sixth floor, since he thus risked being caught on the stairway not with a package but with a rifle in his hands.

The Warren Commission answers the question in the Dallas style: Its Report tells us at the outset, without hesitation or side-stepping and even with the aid of sketches, *where* the paper bag was found, but it refuses to say *when* the discovery was made.

No mystery, then, about the location. In the "Narrative of Events" we are told that "a handmade paper sack" was found "in the southeast corner of the building within a few feet of the cartridge cases." There is even an entire section in the Report titled "Location of Bag," which begins: "A handmade bag of wrapping paper and tape was found in the southeast corner of the sixth floor alongside the window from which the shots were fired." At the end of the section the Report says that "at the time the bag was found, Lieutenant Day of the Dallas police wrote on it, 'Found next to the sixth floor window gun fired from. May have been used to carry gun. Lt. J. C. Day.'" But why not tell us exactly when it was found?

The question becomes all the more pertinent in that the Report publishes a photograph (see Illustrations) that shows the spot on the floor, traced with a dotted line, where the bag was found. The position is not hidden by boxes, books, or anything else, and the bag measured 38 inches long, according to the Commission. Even by the eyes of a Dallas policeman an object of that size, plainly visible in the very area where the search was concentrated, could hardly have gone unnoticed. The investigators were quick to proclaim all their discoveries the minute they made them or thought they made them, without even waiting to look at them carefully: the chicken bones, the shells, the rifle. Why nothing, for 24 hours, about the paper bag?

Improving on Frazier's statements to fit their own requirements, the probers built up the mysterious package as a major item of evidence against Oswald. It seems odd that they did not top it off by immediately trumpeting the discovery of the wrapping. Yet it is impossible to believe they had not seen the bag if it was left in the spot indicated in the Report. How can we avoid the conclusion that it was *not* there?

When the full transcript of the Hearings was published on November 23, 1964, I searched them for some answer to the question.

I started, naturally, with the deposition of Deputy Sheriff Luke Mooney, since it was he who had found the assassin's nook at the southeast window. While returning several times to the chicken leftovers he had seen near that window (and not 10 yards away, as the Commission would like to have it), Mooney made no allusion to a paper bag in the corner. Nor was he questioned about it. "Now, was there anything you saw over in the corner?" Ball had asked him. But when Mooney answered no and went on to the piece of fried chicken that had caught his attention at the other side of the window, Ball changed the subject and the bag was not mentioned again.

I also looked up the testimony of the man who was supposed to be in charge of the investigation, Captain Fritz.

> *Mr. Dulles.*   When was the paper bag covering that he apparently brought the rifle in, was that discovered in the sixth floor about the same time?
>
> *Mr. Fritz.*   No, sir; that was recovered a little later. I wasn't down there when that was found.
>
> *Mr. Dulles.*   It was recovered on the sixth floor, was it not?
>
> *Mr. Fritz.*   Yes, sir; I believe so. We can check here and see. I believe it was. But I wasn't there when that was recovered.

It seemed appropriate to examine the statements of the two Dallas police technicians, Lieutenant J. C. Day and Detective Robert L. Studebaker, since their work consisted of recording the locations of each item of evidence and taking pictures.

Questioned by David W. Belin, Lieutenant Day identified in two photos (one is reproduced in the Illustrations) "the sack found on the sixth floor in the southeast corner of the building on November 22, 1963." This is something: Now we at least know the day. Will we also learn the hour? No. Belin asked when he had written his identifying note on the sack, but Day wouldn't budge: "I wrote that at the time the sack was found before it left our possession." And Belin responded to this: "All right. . . ."

Detective Studebaker, Day's assistant, drew the dotted lines in the photo showing the bag's location. "I drew a diagram in there for the FBI, somebody from the FBI called me down—I can't think of his name, and he wanted an approximate location of where the paper was found," he told Joseph A. Ball.

> *Mr. Ball.*   Where was that with reference to those pipes —the paper wrapping?
>
> *Mr. Studebaker.*   Laying right beside it—right here.
>
> *Mr. Ball.*   Was it folded over?
>
> *Mr. Studebaker.*   It was doubled—it was a piece of paper about this long and it was doubled over.
>
> *Mr. Ball.*   How long was it, approximately?
>
> *Mr. Studebaker.*   I don't know—I picked it up and dusted it and they took it down there and sent it to Washington and that's the last I have seen of it, and I don't know.
>
> *Mr. Ball.*   Did you take a picture of it before you picked it up?
>
> *Mr. Studebaker.*   No.
>
> *Mr. Ball.*   Does that sack show in any of the pictures you took?
>
> *Mr. Studebaker.*   No; it doesn't show in any of the pictures.

My talks with Mrs. Paine, Mrs. Randle, and Wesley Frazier show, moreover, that it is by no means certain that this bag was in fact the wrapping of Oswald's package.

Two or three weeks after the assassination, Mrs. Paine told me, some FBI men had dropped in and shown her a brown paper wrapper. "It was a large sheet of wrapping paper rolled into a kind of sack, held together lengthwise by tape. One of the ends was folded with another piece of tape holding it closed, and the other end was open." The FBI wanted to know if she had paper or tape like that in her house. When I asked what her answer had been, she opened a chest drawer and took out some pieces of brown wrapping paper. "I had the paper, but as far as I know it's still here. And I never used such wide tape."

Roy Truly, whom the FBI had shown the same wrapping before going to Mrs. Paine, informed me that the tape as well as the paper seemed to be of the same kind used for wrapping books at the Depository. Why then did the FBI agents ask Mrs. Paine about it?

In any case, what the Dallas authorities found in the Depository was a wrapper held together by tape, while the only two witnesses who had seen Oswald talked of a "bag." I questioned both of them closely on this point. When I asked Frazier if the bag was taped or tied with string, he answered: "I didn't see anything like that. It looked to me more like a bag than a package." His sister, Linnie Mae Randle, told me the FBI had shown her, too, the taped wrapping paper. Was this the package Oswald carried across her lawn? "It's possible," she replied, "but I can't say for sure. I really don't remember seeing any tape on the bag he was carrying. . . ."

The Report does not bother much about this; it mentions the tape but not the fact that neither of the two witnesses recalled having seen it. In fact, the Report dodges everything those two witnesses said about the differences between the package of Friday morning and the wrapping said to have been found on the sixth floor. It notes with satisfaction that Linnie Mae Randle thought the color of the bag Oswald carried "was similar to that of the bag found on the sixth floor of the School Book Depository after the assassination." But when she and her brother give some details that contradict its conclusions, the Commission either omits them or, if the contradiction is too flagrant, rejects the testimony rather than re-examine the facts.

Linnie Mae Randle, as well as Wesley Frazier, had referred to the object as a bag, not a package, and Mrs. Randle had described it to me as "a grocery bag but bigger."

The Commission admits that the handmade bag found on the sixth floor "was not a standard type bag which could be obtained

in a store and it was presumably made for a particular purpose."
The word "presumably" here is one of the Report's linguistic
niceties; it is hard to imagine that a sheet of paper would have
been taped into the form of a bag for anything but "a particular
purpose." Still, the Commission has confirmed that the wrapping
left in the open near the window—but noticed only later, at a
moment not determined—was nothing like a "grocery bag." The
photo published in the Report (see Illustrations) allows the
reader to see this with his own eyes.

According to the Report, analysis by an FBI expert named
James C. Cadigan showed that the paper and the tape used in the
handmade bag were "identical in all respects" to the paper and
tape used in the Depository shipping room.

If Oswald is to be presumed guilty, and if, as Cadigan's other
findings would suggest, the bag was made within the three days
before the assassination, Oswald thus would have had to take it
with him to Irving on the night of November 21. How did he
carry it? The photo shows that the bag had been folded to one
eighth of its length. Were the folds there when it was found or
had they been added in the course of handling by the investigators, federal and local? The Report states that Oswald "could have
concealed it in the jacket or shirt which he was wearing." But
folded several times, the bag would become quite bulky and
awkward, and not easily kept in place under a shirt or jacket.

The most serious obstacle presented by Mrs. Randle and Wesley
Frazier to the Commission's conclusions, however, lies in their
testimony concerning the length of the package.

In their statements to me, the two witnesses estimated the
length, as we have seen, at a maximum of 3 feet. They were even
more affirmative in their statements before the Commission; Mrs.
Randle estimated the package was "approximately 28 inches long"
and her brother spoke of it as 2 feet long "give and take a few
inches." The Report tells us these estimates matched some practical tests given the witnesses. Frazier, for example, was asked
by the FBI to mark on the rear seat of his car the width occupied
by the package. The FBI measured this distance as 27 inches. Mrs.
Randle, having maintained that the bag she saw in Oswald's

hands "definitely wasn't" as long as the bag shown to her, folded the bag to indicate the size of the one she remembered. "And she folded the bag to a length of about 28½ inches," the Report says with understandable regret, since this test confirmed the figure she had given earlier, with a mere half-inch difference.

The advertisement of Klein's Sporting Goods, in describing the rifle that attracted Oswald's attention, specified that it was "only 40 inches long."

This matter must have disturbed some highly placed person well before the Report came out; in fact, about three weeks after the assassination, word began to circulate in Washington—I repeat: Washington, not Dallas—that the rifle had been dismantled when Oswald brought it to the Depository. From whom did this report come? Most of the newspapers cited "qualified" or "reliable" sources, but the *New York Herald Tribune,* on December 12, 1963, spoke directly of "government sources" and referred to "the FBI report."

But we know from Will Fritz that Oswald was still in the company of witnesses shortly before the motorcade arrived. We have learned from Roy Truly that he behaved normally in the morning and carried out his duties. Where and when would he have had the chance to assemble his rifle with the necessary care and precision?

The Commission has no answer to this double question, but that does not prevent it from giving official status to the "rumor," by then half forgotten, of the dismantled rifle.

As we have seen in connection with the chicken bones, the Report prefers to ignore the statement by Captain Fritz that "no less than six witnesses" had seen Oswald on the sixth floor shortly before the assassination, so that the assassin had no time to assemble the rifle, just as he had no time to eat the chicken. But, according to the Commission, Oswald had 35 minutes to make his preparations. I shall have occasion, in Chapter 24, to examine closely all the possible uses of those 35 minutes. Meanwhile, the first fact blocking the Commission's path is that, according to the two existing witnesses, the bag Oswald carried to work in the morning was not long enough to carry a rifle, *even dismantled.*

"The rifle," says the Report at the beginning of its first chapter, "was about 40 inches long and when disassembled it could fit into a handmade paper sack which, after the assassination, was found in the southeast corner of the building within a few feet of the cartridge cases." Elsewhere it does not hesitate to emphasize with laudable objectivity: "Only if disassembled could the rifle fit into the paper bag found near the window from which the shots were fired."

But the Commission's objectivity stops there. If the rifle, once disassembled, fits into the bag found by the police, it still fails to fit into the one seen by the witnesses in the hands of the suspect. This is graphically shown by the Report in the photo of the disassembled rifle that accompanies the picture of the handmade bag in Exhibit 1304, and in the explanation on the opposite page:

> In deciding whether Oswald carried the assassination weapon in the bag which Frazier and Mrs. Randle saw, the Commission has carefully considered the testimony of these two witnesses with regard to the length of the bag. Frazier and Mrs. Randle testified that the bag which Oswald was carrying was approximately 27 or 28 inches long, whereas the wooden stock of the rifle, which is its largest component, measured 34.8 inches. The bag found on the sixth floor was 38 inches long.

And now the decision: "The Commission has weighed the visual recollection of Frazier and Mrs. Randle against the evidence here presented that the bag Oswald carried contained the assassination weapon and has concluded that Frazier and [Mrs.] Randle are mistaken as to the length of the bag."

A subheading on the following page perfectly illustrates the spirit in which "the evidence here presented" was approached. The evidence concerning the bag obviously should have related to the rifle, not to Oswald, but the subheading—and the section it introduces—mixes the two: "Scientific Evidence Linking Rifle and Oswald to Paper Bag." This allows the Report to go into great detail about "Oswald's fingerprint and palmprint found on bag" or about "Materials used to make bag," all of which remains totally irrelevant because it proves nothing about whether the package contained a rifle.

The Report, true enough, insidiously stresses that the palm print is at the bottom of the bag; that the palm print suggests the bag contained "a heavy or bulky object," since "a light object is usually held by the fingers"; and also that the print in question was that of the right hand "in which he carried the long package as he walked from Frazier's car to the building." But I don't think the Commission can claim it has proved there was a rifle in the bag simply because it was "heavy or bulky" or carried in the right hand. In addition, I would draw the Commission's attention here to the fact that while on page 135 it accepts Frazier's testimony on the manner in which Oswald held the package, it has rejected his testimony on exactly the same point on page 134, because "the disassembled rifle was too long to be carried in this manner."

The Commission would like to convince us that the presence of the rifle was indicated by fibers in the bag; these could have come from the blanket in which the rifle was wrapped at the Paine garage, it suggests.

But here is exactly what FBI expert Paul M. Stombaugh found inside the bag, according to the Report: ". . . a tiny wood fragment which was too minute for comparison purposes, and may have come from the woodpulp from which the paper was made; a particle of a waxy substance, like candle wax; and a single brown delustered viscose fiber and several light-green cotton fibers." There is no comment anywhere in the Report on the waxy substance. As to the fibers, the Report admits that "Stombaugh was unable to render an opinion that the fibers which he found in the bag had probably come from the blanket, because other types of fibers present in the blanket were not found in the bag."

Oddly enough, the expert found no trace of powder and no oil stains. J. Edgar Hoover, in a letter to the Commission providing some technical information, noted in passing that the rifle had been in "well-oiled condition" when received by the FBI. Hoover's letter is reprinted in Volume XXVI of the 26-volume set, but it is not mentioned in the Report. The Commission thus avoids the necessity of explaining why Oswald's "well-oiled" rifle left no oil stains inside the paper bag.

If in spite of all these considerations the mystery of the brown paper bag remains a major problem for those who want the truth, as well as for those who want to dispose of the affair, it is because we have difficulty imagining what Oswald could have brought with him that morning from Irving. For as to what Oswald himself said about it we know only what the Dallas police —and the FBI and Secret Service—have left for us to know: that is, nothing.

Oswald had been questioned for two days without an attorney. Was there at least a stenographer and, if so, were the questions as well as the answers taken down? This point was raised on a CBS television program by Percy Foreman, a Texan (from Houston, though, not Dallas) who headed the National Association of Defense Lawyers. "Usually," he said, "you get only the answers in our state, and frequently, without the question, it doesn't carry the effect—tenor of the conversation."

Up to the publication of the Report we did not even know whether an impartial and competent person had recorded Oswald's answers, let alone the questions.

Judging from the atmosphere that prevailed in Fritz's homicide bureau, there was good reason to doubt that any transcript had been taken in the 12 hours of Oswald's questioning. The Report gives us a definitive answer on this point, one that does not contribute to erasing the impression that the investigation constitutes a scandal without precedent in the judicial history of the modern world: "There were no stenographic or tape recordings of these interviews," we read on page 598 of the Report.

One would search in vain, in the 888 pages of the Report, for a hint of any condemnation or even criticism of this state of affairs.

One does find, however, scattered here and there, some suggestive details: "Captain Fritz of the homicide and robbery bureau did most of the questioning, but he kept no notes and there were no stenographic or tape recordings." (Page 180.) Even more astonishing is the 13-page personal "report" of Captain Fritz with the final paragraph, full of complaints and excuses: "Inasmuch as this report was made from rough notes and memory, it is entirely possible that one of these questions could be in a separate interview from the one indicated in this report. . . . I have no recorder in this office and was unable to record the interview. . . ."

Fritz does not say what he did to remedy this unfortunate situation. He could not, of course, improve his memory. I am not sure, either, that less rough notes would have been more reliable. But was it really impossible to obtain a tape recorder?

It seems unlikely that the city would have refused permission to buy the machine if Fritz had asked for it. Many private firms or individuals would have been happy to lend him one if he had expressed the desire. As a final resort, he might have tried to secure the money needed for a tape recorder by passing his Stetson hat around among the reporters stationed in the corridor.

It would be unjust, however, to aim all our sarcasm at Captain Fritz when Washington was as much to blame as Dallas.

Representatives of the FBI and Secret Service attended the questioning from the start; the interrogations were conducted over a period of 48 hours; and nobody said a word about the lack of a transcript all that time. The Justice Department had announced it was closely following the conduct of the investigation, but apparently did not feel this required, to begin with, an exact transcript of the statements made by the man suspected of having assassinated the President of the United States. Or else the Justice Department was afraid to encroach on the prerogatives of the State of Texas by offering Fritz a stenographer or a tape recorder. Whatever its reasons, Washington did nothing to correct the situation, and the Warren Commission finds everything perfectly normal.

To get back to the problem of the paper bag: I have carefully studied the "recollections" about Oswald's interrogations that the Report reproduces in its Appendix XI (pages 598–636) .

Besides the "report" of Fritz, Appendix XI gives us the statements of FBI Agents James P. Hosty, James W. Bookhout, and Manning C. Clements, Secret Service Inspector Thomas J. Kelley, and Postal Inspector H. D. Holmes, who attended the session Sunday morning. I found a brief allusion to the package in the statements of Fritz and Bookhout. Both say merely that Oswald denied having carried a long package and that he denied having mentioned any curtain rods to Wesley Frazier. I found nothing to show that the question was followed up later, or even to indicate in what way it was approached the first time.

The comic extravagance of the whole situation is perhaps best illustrated in the following exchange between Captain Fritz and Assistant Counsel Ball, as recorded in Volume IV of the Hearings:

> *Mr. Ball.*   On the curtain rods story, do you remember whether you ever asked him if he told Frazier that he had curtain rods in the package?
>
> *Mr. Fritz.*   If I asked him what, please, sir?
>
> *Mr. Ball.*   Did you ever ask Oswald whether or not he had told Frazier that he had curtain rods in the package?
>
> *Mr. Fritz.*   I am sure I did but I can't remember that right now. But I am sure I asked him that because I must have asked him that because I asked him a lot of questions, I asked him if he was fixing his house, I remember asking about that, and he said he was not.
>
> *Mr. Ball.*   He said he was what?
>
> *Mr. Fritz.*   He was not.
>
> *Mr. Ball.*   He said he was not fixing it?
>
> *Mr. Fritz.*   Yes.
>
> *Mr. Ball.*   Do you know what he said in reply to your question?
>
> *Mr. Fritz.*   No, sir; I don't remember what he said about that.

Task Number 1 for the Commission should have been to reconstruct some kind of acceptable substitute for the missing transcript of Oswald's interrogation by questioning, without delay, each of the officers who had attended the sessions with Oswald.

Since the above exchange, however, did not take place until April 22, 1964—the Commission having opened its hearings on February 3—it appears that the Commission's idea of Task Number 1 was quite different. It was, in fact, to give Marina Oswald, who could not have been admitted legally as a witness before Judge Brown in Dallas, the opportunity to accuse her husband before the Chief Justice of the United States.

9

MARINA OSWALD IDENTIFIES A RIFLE

MARINA NIKOLAEVNA OSWALD was introduced to the public by District Attorney Wade on the afternoon of November 22, 1963.

The young Russian woman, who was then still the wife and not the widow of Lee Harvey Oswald, had been questioned at police headquarters earlier in the afternoon, but the public knew only that the interrogation was hampered by the fact that Mrs. Oswald did not speak English. Even the personality of Marina Nikolaevna was rather enigmatic. Dressed in black, with long straight hair, without lipstick or makeup, she would have been almost beautiful if her eyes were not so hard and her mouth so firmly set. There was something incongruous about the presence in Texas of this little pharmacist's assistant from Minsk whom the Soviet authorities, departing from custom, had promptly authorized to follow an American husband to the United States along with a baby born in the Soviet Union.

But until Henry Wade named her (though she could not testify) as one of the witnesses who would help him send Oswald to the electric chair, the mystery of the Russian widow did not necessarily constitute an integral part of the strange circumstances that surrounded the assassination.

Wade, unlike Chief Justice Warren two and a half months later in Washington, did not declare that Mrs. Oswald had identified the rifle found by the police in the Elm Street building. Mrs. Oswald, he said, had admitted that her husband owned "a rifle similar in appearance to the murder weapon." What he preferred to stress was that, identical or similar, Marina Oswald had told the police she had seen a rifle Thursday night in the Paine garage, but that it was not there Friday morning. Wade repeated this in his press conference Sunday night. With all the carefree innocence and clear conscience of a man not directly involved, who feels he need not know all the details of the business at hand, Wade began by mentioning that Oswald "had a package under his arm that he said was window curtains, I believe, or window shades." Then he added, "The wife had said he had the gun the night before, and it was missing that morning after he left."

The D.A. would have had a hard time proving in a courtroom that the package—which Oswald told Frazier contained not curtains or shades but curtain rods—concealed instead the murder weapon. This, however, had been the impression given to the public. In announcing now that, according to the suspect's own wife, the rifle had disappeared from the garage the very morning that Oswald had left with the package, Wade transformed the impression into a certainty.

But Mrs. Oswald could not have made any such statements. Was Wade misinformed by the police? Did he misunderstand them? The fact is that Mrs. Oswald had not seen the rifle "the night before," and the Dallas police knew it. The first time Marina had occasion to comment on this point was not when she was brought to police headquarters but while she was still in Irving. The first police to arrive there shortly after the assassination questioned Marina through her Russian-speaking friend, Mrs. Paine. Three months later, as we stood in the garage where Oswald had kept his things, Mrs. Paine told me about that initial meeting with the police.

> They started with me. They wanted to know if I had ever seen a rifle in the garage or elsewhere in the house. I said no. I added that being a Quaker, I would never have allowed a weapon in my house. Then they asked me to translate the question for Marina. I thought it was ridiculous but I asked the question anyway. To my surprise, Marina nodded yes, and said that her husband had a rifle which he kept in a blanket over there, near the power saw.

Mrs. Paine pointed toward a corner of the garage where there was still a power saw but no blanket.

She then told me how everyone started looking for the blanket as soon as she had translated Mrs. Oswald's reply. They quickly discovered it, rolled up and tied with a string, but empty. I wanted to know what Marina had said next about the rifle, and whether she had explained how she had become aware of its existence. I was thinking of the statements she had made less than two weeks earlier at her press conference in Washington, and Mrs. Paine's answer showed that she guessed my thoughts:

> She didn't say that she had seen her husband play with it, no. She said only that one day, in the garage, she glanced inside the blanket, and it was then that she saw there was a rifle in it. She also said she hadn't taken the rifle out of the blanket, and since this had taken place a week or two earlier she did not feel able to describe what it looked like.

I was taking down this point, which hardly supported the Commission's faith in the "identification" it attributed to Mrs. Oswald, when the importance of what Mrs. Paine had just said struck me suddenly:

"She said that happened one or two weeks before, not the night before? She didn't say Thursday night?"

"Marina never said anything about Thursday night," Ruth Paine replied categorically. "The police insisted on asking what day it was that she looked inside the blanket and saw the rifle. But she answered that she couldn't remember exactly, that it was maybe one or two weeks before. . . ."

On February 3, when Marina Oswald went to Washington to testify before the Commission, nobody asked her when she had last seen her husband's rifle. Chief Justice Warren himself, in his official statement of February 6, made no allusion to it. He had something better to report: "Mrs. Oswald has identified the rifle that was found on the sixth floor of the Texas School Book Depository Building in Dallas immediately after the assassination as the one which her husband kept at their home prior to the assassination."

This identification did not surprise the Chief Justice. He had announced two days earlier that the witness would be asked to identify the Mannlicher-Carcano, and added in the manner of a Curry or a Fritz: "We haven't shown her the gun yet. I have an idea that she'll say that is the gun."

And so she did. Earl Warren's prophesy, however, might have been more impressive if his February 6 statement had revealed the method of identification. Neither Wade nor the Dallas police, who were not likely to play down evidence putting the finger on Oswald, had gone so far as to say that Marina Oswald had actually identified the rifle. By what miracle did the former pharmacist's assistant, never said to be an expert on firearms, recognize her husband's rifle in February when in November she had found the weapon at most "similar in appearance"?

"Marina Oswald testified that the rifle found on the sixth floor of the Depository Building was the 'fateful rifle of Lee Oswald,' " the Report declares.

I confess I cannot imagine Marina convincing objective judges that she could identify a given rifle. It is even harder to imagine her—Slavic soul or not—talking about the "fateful rifle." The Commission, however, seems to have been greatly impressed by the phrase, since it quotes it again in discussing the "identification" in the "Speculations and Rumors" appendix: "When Marina Oswald appeared before the Commission she was shown the Mannlicher-Carcano 6.5 rifle found on the sixth floor of the Depository and identified it as the 'fateful rifle of Lee Oswald.' "

There was an odd misunderstanding during Marina's February 7 press conference in a Washington TV studio.

Some months before the assassination, Marina said in reply to a question, her husband had "practiced" with the rifle. Recalling the story of Floyd Davis' Sportsdrome at Grand Prairie, and forgetting (among other things) the fact that Mrs. Oswald had said "some months" and not "some weeks," the wire services signaled the world: "The President's alleged assassin was practicing with his rifle before the assassination, the Russian-born widow says."

Later, however, the attorney John M. Thorne, who did not understand Russian but obviously knew what his client was supposed to say, corrected this sensational revelation. In speaking of "practice," he explained, Mrs. Oswald did not mean she had seen her husband firing at a target. She meant only that she had seen him "handling it at home, sighting it, taking aim, and things like that."

In relation to this statement of Marina Oswald, the Commission reveals on page 128 of its Report some hesitations that it no longer shows on page 192 and that totally evaporate by page 645.

Page 128: "It *appears* from his wife's testimony that Oswald *may have* sat on the screened-in porch at night practicing with the rifle by looking through the telescopic sight and operating the bolt." (Italics mine.) Page 192: "Marina Oswald testified that in New Orleans in May of 1963, she observed Oswald sitting," etc. Finally, page 645: "Marina Oswald testified that in New Orleans her husband practiced operating the bolt of the rifle." The Commission does not specify what happened between those pages to allow its total acceptance of a fact that at first seemed only a possibility.

More important, because it tends to lead the reader to conclusions that the Commission knows and recognizes to be false, is the statement that "From September 24, 1963, when Marina Oswald arrived in Irving from New Orleans, *until the morning of the assassination,* the rifle was, according to the evidence, stored in a green and brown blanket in the Paines' garage among the Oswalds' other possessions." (Italics mine.)

In the eight pages of the Report criticizing (with remarkable moderation) not the methods of the investigators but their lack of discretion, the Commission takes up Wade's statement to the press Friday night to the effect that "Oswald's wife had told the police that her husband had a rifle in the garage at the house in Irving and that it was missing the morning of the assassination." This summary of Wade's statement follows a preamble in which Wade is reproached merely for having talked too much, and it is possible therefore that the Commission does not wish to deny the truth in what he said, only criticize his indiscretion. But the

Report's reference to Wade's remarks is followed by several examples of inaccurate statements, such as "the error that the murder rifle had been a Mauser." It is thus also possible that the Commission intended to place the D.A.'s statement among the "many details that proved to be erroneous" resulting from the "running commentary on the investigation by the police."

In short, the Report is sufficiently ambiguous so that one cannot be sure whether it intends to criticize the basis as well as the form of Wade's statement. In declaring, however, that the rifle was in the Paine garage "until the morning of the assassination," the Commission implicitly makes this statement its own. For the Commission, in effect, makes two assumptions: that the rifle disappeared from the garage only that morning, and that it had been there the night before. The two assumptions are unsupported by evidence.

According to Ruth Paine, Marina had told the Secret Service she had seen the rifle for the last time in the blanket "one or two weeks earlier." Mrs. Paine later gave the same account to the Commission, which does not contest it in the Report. On the contrary, the Report brings out some new information that helps destroy its own double assumption. In the "Narrative of Events" we thus learn that Mrs. Paine translated for Marina as the TV reports on the assassination came in. When she told Marina the shots apparently had been fired from the building where Lee worked, Marina "went quietly to the Paines' garage where the rifle had been concealed in a blanket among their other belongings. It appeared to her that the rifle was still there, although she did not actually open the blanket."

This information, unreported before, is related in greater detail in another section of the Report, with direct quotations:

> On the day of the assassination, Marina Oswald was watching television when she learned of the shooting. A short time later Mrs. Paine told her that someone had shot the President "from the building in which Lee is working." Marina Oswald testified that at that time "My heart dropped. I then went to the garage to see whether

the rifle was there and I saw that the blanket was still there and I said 'Thank God.' " She did not unroll the blanket. She saw that it was in its usual position and it appeared to have something inside.

This means that, according to the testimony of Marina Oswald as presented by the Commission, there is no evidence whatsoever to show when the rifle disappeared from the garage. The absence of the rifle was not discovered until the police arrived at about 3 P.M. on the afternoon of the assassination. As to its presence in the garage "the night before" (Wade's press conference) or "until the morning of the assassination" (Warren Report), it certainly is not implied in Marina Oswald's testimony. Marina believed the rifle was still wrapped in its blanket after the crime, at a time when, according to the Commission, it was already "partially hidden" behind some boxes in the Depository Building. Since Marina admitted she could not judge from looking at the blanket whether the rifle was still in it, the Commission in fact confirms that the weapon could have disappeared from the garage at any time in the days or even weeks before the assassination.

Concerning the miraculous "identification" of the rifle, the Commission adds little to what its Chairman had already told the press.

The Report does give us the testimony of Captain Fritz: "I showed the rifle to Marina Oswald, and she could not positively identify it, but said that it looked like the rifle that her husband had. . . ." In the "Speculations and Rumors" appendix, the Report confirms as a "Commission finding" that on November 22, at Dallas police headquarters, Marina "said that she could not identify as her husband's the rifle shown her by policemen." But this leads without transition or explanation to: "When Marina Oswald appeared before the Commission she was shown the Mannlicher-Carcano 6.5 rifle found on the sixth floor of the Depository and identified it as the 'fateful rifle of Lee Oswald.' "

How did Chief Justice Warren—no firearms expert himself— arrive at the conclusion that Marina had really identified the rifle? Did he show her the weapon along with five or six others of a similar type, and did she choose the right one? In the absence of any cross-examination, this method would at least show that an effort was made to obtain a credible identification. But while the reporters noticed that the Mannlicher-Carcano was brought into the Commission hearing room two days in a row, they saw nobody enter with other rifles.

It was therefore possible that Earl Warren had simply asked Marina, "Do you recognize this rifle?" It was also possible that Marina, after 20 years under the protection of Stalin and Khrushchev and 10 weeks under the protection of the Secret Service, had answered with like simplicity: "Yes, your honor." And it was even quite possible, though profoundly depressing to contemplate, that the Chief Justice of the United States had judged this sufficient to announce: "Mrs. Oswald has identified the rifle."

The publication of the Hearings late in 1964 finally revealed the exact conditions under which the identification had been made. It was even worse than I had reluctantly imagined. Here is the entire passage (Volume I, page 119) to which the Warren Report refers:

> *Mr. Thorne* [Marina Oswald's lawyer, chosen by the business adviser selected for her by the Secret Service— L.S.].   Exhibit 139.
> *Mrs. Oswald.*   That is the fateful rifle of Lee Oswald.
> *Mr. Rankin* [general counsel of the Commission].   Is that the scope that it had on it, as far as you know?
> *Mrs. Oswald.*   Yes.
> *Mr. Rankin.*   I offer in evidence Exhibit 139.
> *The Chairman.*   It may be admitted.

That's all there is. Not the slightest question inviting the widow to elaborate on how she now recognized her husband's rifle at first glance, when Exhibit 139 had before appeared only "similar in appearance." Not the slightest question about possible spots or scratches or other distinctive marks that she might have recalled in the meantime. There is nothing more before the Commission goes on to the next exhibit, other than the parenthetical note: "The article referred to was marked Commission Exhibit No. 139, and received in evidence."

10

MARINA OSWALD
IDENTIFIES A GENERAL

FOR TEN DAYS after the speedy and semisecret burial of Oswald in a Fort Worth cemetery there was no further word about the widow. It was known that the Secret Service was keeping her isolated, if not imprisoned, in a motel in the area. But everyone understood that this very young woman, whose distress could easily be imagined, had to be guarded against possible attack by a fanatic and even against the crowds of reporters. What annoyed newsmen most was that the brush-offs came from neither Mrs. Oswald nor the Secret Service but from one James H. Martin, manager of the Six Flags Inn.

Then suddenly, on December 6, two weeks after the assassination, the name of Marina Nikolaevna Oswald arose anew in the investigation. She was said to have disclosed that it was her husband who had tried to kill Major General Edwin A. Walker on April 10, 1963.

I had visited General Walker on November 30 and spent over an hour with him at his house on Turtle Creek Boulevard, recognizable by its three flags—American, Texan, and Confederate—flying above the front lawn. A few weeks earlier the flags had been flown upside down. This was the general's way of protesting the official apology offered by the City of Dallas to Adlai Stevenson after he had been insulted and spat upon during his visit to the city. Now, after the assassination of President Kennedy, Walker's flags were again right-side up.

"The European press seems more free than ours," Walker said in greeting me. "I've had German, Italian, Scandinavian reporters
148

here in the last few days, and now you, a Frenchman. No American reporters dared to come and ask my views."

The ex-commander of the 24th Infantry Division at Augsburg, Germany, who had cheered on the racist shock troops at Oxford, Mississippi, in 1962, told me that "99 per cent of Americans are against the assassination" and that "the American concept of an orderly and constitutional system of government is shared by all who are right of center and by a majority on the left."

"When you speak of those who are right of center," I asked, "would that include organizations like the Ku Klux Klan?"

The cold stare of the general—an influential member of the John Birch Society and the leader of the Association of Friends of General Walker—bored into me as he detached his syllables for emphasis: "The Ku Klux Klan is a movement which supports the principles of constitutional government."

Then, pointing accusingly at me, he added without raising his voice but in the tone of a man who knows whom he is dealing with: "You, I see, you are completely to the left, an out-and-out leftist, a socialist. . . ."

I nevertheless asked the general what he thought of the Commission created by the President:

"An investigation is necessary," he said, "but any investigation that follows the slanderous line of the Party and *Pravda* against the so-called right-wing extremists, when it's obvious that Oswald was a Marxist Communist and that Rubenstein is connected with the underworld, would be a complete and inconceivable distortion of reality."

The sentence is long, but faithfully copied from my notes. The general, in fact, was not speaking to me; he was dictating his answers, keeping a suspicious eye on my notebook to make sure the lines were no shorter than the ones he had delivered, and stopping for me to write some more if he thought I had put down the pencil too soon.

"Do you mean, general, that in your opinion the Warren Commission will follow the *Pravda* line?"

Since Warren had been denounced by the Birch Society and the Friends of General Walker as a traitor and the top agent of Communist subversion in the United States, my question was reasonable. I waited for the answer with pencil poised.

But the general changed his tactics: "I have no other statement to make to you," he said icily, and stood up.

Walker did have something more to say. I had already stepped outside and was heading toward the frontier marked by the three flags when he called me back with an imperious gesture and a brief command: "Come on, I want to show you something."

I obeyed. The general led me to a rear room that looked like a kind of study. He pointed to a small hole in a window, apparently caused by a bullet. Still without talking, he showed me the wall opposite, where a large map hung above a table. On the map, at the level where the head of a man seated at the table would be, there was a black hole. Then the general began to speak, pointing to a chair at the table.

"I was sitting here on the night of April 10, about 9 o'clock, preparing my income tax return. I had just moved my head, and the bullet missed by an inch."

"Did the police catch the man?" I asked politely. Again politely, but I fear with a note of impertinence, I added: "They say that Dallas has a highly efficient police department."

A hoarseness came into the general's throat:

"The Dallas police. . . . It's a mistake to think that Dallas is a conservative town. . . ."

The haste with which he replied gave me the impression he had brought me there only to give me the chance to ask that question, or more accurately to give himself the chance to answer it.

"Dallas is under the control of liberals, don't forget it," he said. "They bow down before the U.N. and apologize to Adlai Stevenson. Look at them. . . . Not one of the city officials goes around today without a bodyguard, at city expense. But me—did you see anyone on guard near here, when there are so many Oswalds running around loose?"

He shook his head bitterly, then gestured toward the hole in the wall: "The police came, stuck their noses here and there, and that was all. They could have found the man who tried to kill me if they really wanted to find him."

On December 6, less than a week after our talk, the man had been found, or so they said: He was Lee Harvey Oswald.

True, the Dallas police were not in on it. The news was published first in a Chicago newspaper that said it had come from Washington, implying a new leak from the "secret" FBI report. At Dallas police headquarters, an official spokesman—Captain Glenn King—amazed the reporters by replying "No comment," a phrase seldom heard in those precincts. D.A. Wade also was unusually silent but recalled that Oswald's file had been sent to the FBI, thus giving the local authorities a chance to get any eventual credit. The discovery was soon trumpeted from the rooftops: Lee Oswald, returning to his home on the night of April 10, had admitted to his wife that he had just shot at Walker, and Marina had confessed it in turn (the reports did not indicate in what language) to the Secret Service men "protecting" her.

General Walker spoke to a group of journalists the next day, and had the satisfaction of finding some American reporters there this time. He offered an opinion somewhat different from the one he had given me a week earlier. The Dallas police, he now said, would have solved his case rapidly if they had not been held back by instructions from Attorney General Robert Kennedy. He strongly implied that if Robert Kennedy had not "prevented" the arrest of Oswald in the days after April 10, there would have been no November 22.

What was the truth about the charge that Oswald had tried to kill Walker?

A virtually official version was soon provided by the "government sources" already invoked in regard to other FBI leaks. According to these sources, the federal agents had obtained a note in Russian, which Oswald supposedly left for his wife on the night of April 10. The note, it was hinted, displayed Oswald's intention to kill Walker, and it was also "confirmed" that he had told his wife on his return that he had just shot at the general.

Details rounding out the story were soon made available. The *Houston Chronicle* on December 30 said it had the exact text of the note. And on the next day the *New York Times* carried a story headed: "Widow Says Oswald Admitted Firing at Walker." The *Times* subhead went on to say: "She Tells Agents Investigating Assassination of Statement About Shot at General."

The text under these headlines cited neither Mrs. Oswald nor the agents involved. "The disclosures, which confirm earlier reports that Oswald had told his wife about trying to kill Mr. Walker, came today from Jim Martin, speaking for Mrs. Oswald," the article declared. As to Martin's qualifications, the *Times* defined them in a paragraph of expressive brevity: "Mr. Martin, a motel executive who met Mrs. Oswald when the Secret Service secluded her at his motel, has become her agent and spokesman while she remains in the protective custody of the Government."

To believe this "agent and spokesman," the note found by Marina in the bedroom of their apartment consisted mainly of practical instructions on what to do in case he was arrested: information about his post-office box and key; reference to a check due from a former employer; explanations about the gas and electric bills; and addresses, including that of the Soviet Embassy in Washington as well as the Dallas jail.

Martin did not say that Walker was mentioned in the note. He did describe Oswald's behavior when he returned that night (I quote the *Times* quoting Martin quoting the "protected" widow) : " 'She said he was trembling,' Mr. Martin said." He also described Marina's reaction: " 'She told him if he ever did that again, she would turn his note over to the police,' Mr. Martin said." Is this what happened, then? That would certainly fit nicely into the picture, but Marina—contrary to the general impression—did not give the note to the authorities, even after they had told her that her husband had killed the President.

I learned from Ruth Paine how the authorities had found out about the note.

Between the time of the "disappearance" of Marina and the first revelations of December 6, Mrs. Paine had on several occasions brought Mrs. Oswald's mail to the Irving police to be turned over to her friend. She included a short note each time, but they never were answered. Early in December she also sent two books that Marina liked to leaf through, "books of a practical sort, you know, on how to keep house and bring up children," Mrs. Paine that Marina liked to leaf through, "books of a practical sort, you know, on how to keep house and bring up children," Mrs. Paine said. When Secret Service agents came to her later with a note in Russian and asked her where she had found it, she did not understand at first what they were talking about. She was told at last that the note had been discovered between the pages of one of the books she had sent to Marina; the federal agents, considering censorship of the mail to be one of their "protective" duties, had taken the liberty of removing it.

Mrs. Paine was not given time to read the entire note carefully, but she nevertheless gave me a certain number of details about it.

She remembered quite well, for example, that the first sentence had to do not with any plans of Oswald but with the key to the post-office box. The author of the note, she told me, had apparently forgotten the word for "key" in Russian and had simply written "key" in Cyrillic characters. It was this that led Mrs. Paine to believe the note had been written by Oswald, since she would not have recognized his handwriting. As for the rest, she remembered only some practical instructions that might be useful if he were arrested.

"Useful in general?" I asked.

"Yes," said Mrs. Paine. "But I only was able to give a quick look at the note."

"Was it dated?"

"I don't think so."

"Was the name of Walker mentioned in it?"

"I'm sure it wasn't, at least not in the part I saw. I certainly would have remembered if Walker had been mentioned."

Thus I was quite surprised to read in the papers that on March 20, after her second day of questioning by the Commission, Ruth Paine had declared she was "convinced now that Lee had tried to kill Walker." According to the Washington stories, she even conveyed the impression that Oswald may have driven to Turtle Creek Boulevard, mentioning the fact that she had given him some driving lessons. During our last conversation in February, Mrs. Paine had not seemed convinced at all about the Walker attempt. What had changed her mind? I called her to find out, and reminded her what she had told me in connection with the Grand Prairie rifle range: that she did not see how Oswald could have driven there. How then could he have driven on the much busier streets of Dallas between Oak Cliff and Turtle Creek Boulevard?

Mrs. Paine said she knew nothing more than what she had told me before concerning Oswald's alleged attempt on Walker's life; she had simply thought about it in the meantime and now it seemed plausible to her.

As to Oswald's ability not as an assassin but as a driver, she said the reporters had misunderstood her.

> As you know, I gave him three lessons in all. He knew how to start and stop and turn, but he wasn't able to park, and I haven't the slightest idea how he might have gotten along on a busy street. The difference, for me, is that at Irving I don't see where he could have gotten a car to go to Grand Prairie, since I certainly wouldn't have allowed him to take mine. At Oak Cliff, I think he could have found one more easily. He also could have gone by bus, and even walked a couple of hours to Turtle Creek Boulevard and back.

At the time of the shooting, on April 10, the police had found only one witness, a 14-year-old boy who lived nearby and said he had heard a shot and seen two men make their getaway in separate cars, one of them carrying what appeared to be a rifle. This was published at the time without further comment, but as soon as Oswald was brought into the case the *Dallas Morning News* let it be known that the police had never believed that account. It didn't match, of course, the conception of a solitary fiend who did not drive. This is why the police preferred to say nothing (not even through the *Morning News*) about what they had been told on April 10 by Bob Surrey, Walker's assistant, secretary, and bodyguard. Surrey had declared that two days earlier, at nightfall, he had seen two men prowling behind the house. They ran off when he approached, he said, and fled in a car without license plates.

To pin the Walker shooting on Oswald it would therefore be

necessary either to admit that he had an accomplice, which would upset the entire official thesis on the assassination of President Kennedy, or to furnish proof on a number of points regarding which no evidence was ever obtained.

While inducing public opinion to accept the story (after all, he admitted it to his wife!), the Dallas authorities never bothered to explain how Oswald got to Walker's house at 4011 Turtle Creek Boulevard. Let's say he felt capable of driving a car at night without fear of an accident; but what car? He couldn't rent one, since he had no driver's license to show; he would also have been unable to put up a deposit. If he borrowed a car, we have not been told who lent it; if he stole one, no police record has been produced concerning a car stolen and recovered the night of April 10 in Oak Cliff (where the Oswalds had an apartment at the time). A taxi, perhaps? Mrs. Paine, when I suggested this, burst out laughing: "Lee would never spend several dollars for a taxi under any circumstances." Besides, the police would have been able to find the cab driver, especially since—with few enough cabs cruising in downtown Dallas and none likely to appear on Turtle Creek Boulevard—he would have been obliged to have the taxi wait for him, with meter ticking, while he committed his assassination attempt.

In the final analysis, there remained only the possibility that Oswald walked all or part of the way, or took a bus, or used a combination of buses.

Imagine Oswald with his rifle (another brown paper bag?) under his arm, marching off to slay the general, and planning to return home the same way. And what did he do with the rifle before returning that night? Marina said through her agent, James Martin, that Oswald had come back "white and shaking." She did not say that he had carried a rifle in his trembling hands.

This still does not worry the Commission, which knows how to make use of Marina Oswald.

"Marina Oswald also testified that her husband had used a bus to return home," the Report says, and "a study of the bus routes" convinced the Commission that "it would have been possible for him to take different routes in approaching and leaving the scene of the shooting." Witnesses? None. The rifle? "Marina Oswald stated that when she asked her husband what he had done with the rifle, he replied that he had buried it in the ground or hidden it in some bushes, and that he also mentioned a railroad track in this connection. She testified that several days later Oswald recovered his rifle and brought it back to their apartment."

The major document used here by the Commission is an FBI report dated June 10, 1964, published as Commission Exhibit No. 1953 in Volume XXIII of the 26-volume set. It contains "information concerning buses available to passengers inbound towards the downtown area of Dallas, Texas, from the general area in and around 4011 Turtle Creek Boulevard, Dallas Texas," as given to the FBI on June 3 by V. C. Snider, Dallas Transit Company schedule engineer. Snider also informed the FBI that "any passenger, after paying his fare on any bus, can obtain a transfer coupon which entitles him to board any other bus in the downtown area."

I am as firmly convinced as the Commission is that there are indeed buses and transfer coupons in Dallas, but I doubt very much that a Lee Harvey Oswald, before reaching home "white and shaking," could make use of those buses and transfers, walk to and from the bus stops, wait at the bus stops for some time (the buses in Dallas, as elsewhere, do not run frequently at night), and do all this without being noticed by anyone.

The FBI, however, was not interested in looking for witnesses; it had waited until June 3, 1964, to ask Schedule Engineer Snider for the bus routes Oswald might have used. Nor was the Commission curious about it; at no time did it seek out witnesses who might have noticed Oswald that April night. If Oswald had acted as the Commission would have us believe, there would almost certainly have been some witnesses. Remember (though the Report does not) that Oswald is supposed to have carried his 40-inch-long Mannlicher-Carcano on his bus ride to Turtle Creek Boulevard. Could this have been overlooked by the driver and the few passengers of a late bus, even if the Commission were to suggest that Oswald dismantled the rifle for the bus trip and reassembled it in the dark behind Walker's house? Furthermore, on his way back Oswald showed none of the nervousness that attracted Johnny Brewer's attention on November 22; but he suddenly became "white and shaking" when he arrived home.

Marina's explanations, as recorded by the FBI in Commission Exhibit No. 1953, explain nothing at all. If anything, they make the situation even more implausible. This is what the FBI document states:

> On June 4, 1964, Marina Oswald was interviewed. . . . She said she had asked Oswald how he had arrived at the Walker home on the night he attempted to kill Walker by shooting him. Oswald replied that he had walked up to the house. Marina said she later learned Oswald had taken a bus to the vicinity of the Walker home and she presumes that he had gotten off the bus a distance from the Walker home and had traversed the remaining distance on foot. She said Oswald had said also he had returned to their home by bus after the attempted assassination. Marina advised she was not aware of what buses Oswald took to arrive in the vicinity of the Walker home or to leave the vicinity of the Walker home en route back to their home.
>
> Marina said she remembers Oswald telling her he had run away from the Walker house after the attempted assassination and that he could run very fast. She said she does not recall that Oswald told her how far he ran or what bus he boarded or where he boarded the bus.
>
> She does remember Oswald told her he came home on the bus after the attempted assassination.
>
> Marina said she does not recall Oswald telling her what he did with his rifle after he made the first trip to the Walker home for the purpose of assassinating General Walker. She said he did not bring the rifle into their home upon his return to her knowledge. She said she did not ask him what he had done with the rifle on this first visit of Oswald to the Walker home for the purpose of assassinating Walker. She does recall she had asked Oswald when

he returned home and confessed he had attempted to assassinate General Walker that night what he had done with the rifle because she was afraid the rifle might be found and traced to Oswald. In answer to her query, Oswald told her he had buried the rifle in the ground or in the bushes far away from the actual spot of the shooting. . . .

According to Marina, Oswald went twice to the Walker house "for the purpose of assassinating Walker," which means there should have been twice as many chances for witnesses to have seen him riding the buses or walking the streets with a rifle. But leaving this aside, there is one suggestion that must be brought up again because it is so ridiculous that it amounts to utter contempt for the public.

The Report mentions "a point near the railroad tracks where he may have concealed the rifle," and practically endorses Marina's statement that Oswald "buried the rifle in the ground or in the bushes," though it prefers to drop Marina's observation that this took place "far away from the actual spot of the shooting." The Commission does not consider the possibility that Lee might have lied to Marina, or that Marina might have lied to the FBI. Shouldn't it then explain how it came to believe that Oswald could have "buried" or "hidden" the rifle? If he buried it, with what tool? A "point near the railroad tracks" is generally not made of soft earth, or was this an exception? Admitting that Oswald dug a hole with his hands, a hole deep enough and long enough, had he thought of bringing along any material such as oilcloth to protect the rifle during the "several days" it remained buried? The laboratory reports on the Mannlicher-Carcano did not mention the discovery of any soil particles. And if the rifle was only hidden "in some bushes," why did nobody see it before Oswald went back "several days later"? The FBI does not say the "point near the railroad tracks" was in a secluded area; in fact it mentions photographs of the area showing various buildings and even "a multi-story building under construction in the background." Finally, how did a man of such erratic mind, who did not know the city well enough to get around without a street map, manage to find his way back to the exact spot where he had hidden the rifle several nights—*nights*—before?

There is still much more to the Walker story. I am referring not only to the fact that we are not advised how the Elm Street champion could miss a man sitting under a lamp less than 40 yards away, or why he did not fire a second time, inasmuch as nobody was around to interfere. I am thinking also of the bullet that Oswald's clumsy shot left behind.

The day after the attack on Walker, the Dallas police reported the bullet had "flattened" in penetrating the thick wall, thus preventing eventual identification through ballistics tests. When Oswald's name was linked to the attempt, the word went out nevertheless that the bullet of Turtle Creek Boulevard was similar to those of Elm Street. But the rumor was based on nothing, and on December 20 Chief Jesse Curry admitted that the laboratory tests in Washington had produced no results: The condition of the bullet, he explained, was too poor. Some kind of scientific police work was urgently needed, however, to corroborate the widow's statements; so Curry came back on February 18 with his own "ballistic report." The author of this report, Chief of Detectives M. W. Stevenson, took the precaution of warning that his discoveries could not be considered "final or conclusive," but he stressed that "generally the comparison points of the slugs were good." And the police chief, forgetting his statement of December 20, quickly announced that the same rifle "probably" had been used against Walker and against Kennedy.

The Curry-Stevenson report did not correct the earlier calculations—based on weight—as to the caliber of the Walker bullet. The Dallas police had called it a .30-caliber slug, which is 7.65 mm. in the continental rating. Oswald's Mannlicher-Carcano was, as we know, a 6.5 mm. rifle. A 6.5 mm. rifle cannot fire 7.65 bullets.

In spite of all this, the Commission displays no hesitation in convicting Oswald on the Walker count, too. The "Narrative of Events," in the opening pages of the Report, tells us that "on April 10, he [Oswald] attempted to kill Maj. Gen. Edwin A. Walker (Resigned, U.S. Army), using a rifle which he had ordered by mail 1 month previously under an assumed name." A few pages later, among the conclusions of the "Summary," the same affirmation is accompanied by an indication of the use the Commission finds for it: "Oswald had attempted to kill Maj. Gen. Edwin A. Walker (Resigned, U.S. Army) on April 10, 1963, thereby demonstrating his disposition to take human life."

Since the alleged attack on Walker is one of the eight arguments invoked by the Commission in calling Lee Harvey Oswald the assassin of President Kennedy, I shall return to it in the concluding chapter of this book, devoted to the Commission's eight "proofs." Here I will only review the reasoning that led the Commission, despite the improbabilities and even impossibilities mentioned above, to call Lee Harvey Oswald the would-be assassin of General Walker.

The Report completely ignores the initial Dallas police statement giving the caliber of the Walker bullet as 7.65 mm., which excluded the possibility of its being fired from Oswald's 6.5 mm. rifle. The Report simply states that "it was a 6.5 millimeter bullet," and that's all. At least the Report admits that the bullet was "badly mutilated" and that because of its "battered condition" it was impossible at first to "determine the type of weapon which fired the bullet." But this statement is followed by an entire page of quibbling about the opinions of two firearms experts who examined the bullet at the Commission's request.

Robert A. Frazier of the FBI said he was "unable to reach a conclusion," but the Commission still manages to incriminate Oswald: "Frazier testified, however, that he found no microscopic characteristics or other evidence which would indicate that the bullet was not fired from the Mannlicher-Carcano owned by Lee Harvey Oswald."

Joseph D. Nicol, the other expert, believed the bullet showed enough characteristics "to say that it could have come, and even perhaps a little stronger, to say that it probably came from this, without going so far as to say to the exclusion of all other guns." But to identify a person or an object is to distinguish one from all others, and Nicol flatly says that "this I could not do." Conclusion of the Commission: "Although the Commission recognizes that neither expert was able to state that the bullet which missed General Walker was fired from Oswald's rifle to the exclusion of all others, this testimony was considered probative when combined with the other testimony linking Oswald to the shooting."

The transcript of the Hearings shows that the Commission never sought to clarify the contradictions between the December investigation and the one in April or even tried to learn the circumstances that had led the Dallas police to their initial statements about the Walker case.

Chief Jesse Curry, for example, was questioned three times. His three appearances occupy a total of 78 pages in Volumes IV, XII, and XV of the Hearings. I found no mention of the Walker case and no mention of Curry's earlier statements about the incident. Volumes XII and XV also contain the testimony of Deputy Chief M. W. Stevenson, who as Chief of Detectives was in charge of all criminal investigation work of the Dallas police. It was Stevenson who had signed the "ballistic report" published on February 18. But his interrogation included no questions about Walker, no inquiry about the caliber of the bullet fired at the general, no effort to find out why a 6.5 mm. bullet should have been described at first as a .30 caliber one.

The only policeman who the Commission believed had something useful to say on the Walker case was Will Fritz.

> *Mr. McCloy.* Captain Fritz, did you have charge of the attempted shooting of General Walker?
>
> *Mr. Fritz.* No; that wasn't homicide, it would be handled by Captain Jones, it would have been the other bureau.
>
> *Mr. McCloy.* Captain Jones. Have we examined Captain Jones?
>
> *Mr. Hubert* [assistant counsel]. A deposition has been taken.
>
> *Mr. Dulles.* You had nothing to do with the investigation of the Walker case?
>
> *Mr. Fritz.* Not at all. That happened to be Captain Jones and Lieutenant Cunningham.
>
> *Mr. Dulles.* Did that case come up at all in any of your

interrogations of Oswald? Did you ever ask him whether
he was involved or anything of that sort?

Mr. Fritz.   I don't think that I ever asked him about that.
If I did, I don't remember it. I don't remember asking
about that, asking him about that at all. We had a little
information on it but I didn't want to mix it up in that
other case and I didn't want to mix it up.

The Walker case did not come up again while Fritz was being
questioned, and no one showed any curiosity about the "little
information" that Fritz said he had been aware of at the time of
Oswald's interrogation. The theory of the Dallas police was then—
and remains now—that until the "revelations" of Marina Oswald
there was not the slightest suspicion of Oswald in regard to the
Walker shooting. If Will Fritz did not want to "mix it up" with
"that other case," the assassination of President Kennedy, the
Commission itself did not hesitate to mix up the two. It thus
might have asked about the "information" that Fritz had.

But the Commission showed no more interest in this than in
all the other aspects of the matter.

Fritz had mentioned Captain O. A. Jones, whose deposition is
contained in Volume XII of the Hearings. But there is no question
in that deposition relating to the Walker assassination attempt.
Perhaps Leon D. Hubert, Jr., when he questioned Jones in Dallas
on March 24, did not know that Jones had been the officer in
charge of the Walker investigation. But when he informed McCloy
in the above exchange that a deposition had been taken from
Jones, he must have recalled that it contained nothing about the
questions raised by McCloy. Captain Jones, nevertheless, was not
brought back to testify. As to Lieutenant Cunningham, mentioned
by Fritz as a participant in the Walker investigation, and a possibly useful witness in connection with the questioning of the
patrons in the Texas Theater, his name does not appear among
the 552 witnesses the Commission chose to hear.

Volume V of the Hearings adds to these instances of selective
indifference the disclosure of a truly remarkable episode that
suggests some fascinating possibilities concerning the Walker

shooting, as well as some intriguing questions concerning the attitude of the Commission's assistant counsel, Albert E. Jenner, Jr.

On June 16, 1964, Jenner was questioning Robert Alan Surrey. I well remember the nervous and suspicious aide to Walker, who had opened the door at the Turtle Creek Boulevard house and kept an eye on me all the while, from a distance but not very discreetly. It was he, the Commission established, who had arranged for the printing of the *Wanted for Treason* pamphlets distributed before Kennedy's arrival in Dallas.

I don't know what led Jenner to start pressing Surrey about a dog in the home of Mrs. Ruth Jackson, a woman doctor who lived next door to Walker. I know even less what led him to drop abruptly this interesting line of questioning.

> *Mr. Jenner.*   Does she [Dr. Ruth Jackson] have a dog that is sometimes obstreperous, does a lot of barking?
>
> *Mr. Surrey.*   Yes; she does.
>
> *Mr. Jenner.*   You are quite familiar with that fact, are you?
>
> *Mr. Surrey,*   Yes, sir; I am.
>
> *Mr. Jenner.*   How and why did you become familiar with that fact?
>
> *Mr. Surrey.*   Anyone approaching the house, generally her house or General Walker's house, would be barked at, in the middle of the night noises.
>
> *Mr. Jenner.*   And you have approached General Walker's house, I assume, at night, have you?
>
> *Mr. Surrey.*   Yes.
>
> *Mr. Jenner.*   If the dog is out in Dr. Jackson's yard, the dog is alerted and barks?
>
> *Mr. Surrey.*   Not so much any more. Evidently he knows who I am now.
>
> *Mr. Jenner.*   I see. But before the dog became familiar with you, he did bark?
>
> *Mr. Surrey.*   Yes, sir.
>
> *Mr. Jenner.*   What kind of a dog is it, by the way?

> *Mr. Surrey.*   A small Collie, I guess—shaggy, brownish dog.
>
> *Mr. Jenner.*   Do you recall whether or not at or about the time of the attempt on General Walker's life that dog became or was ill?
>
> *Mr. Surrey.*   Yes; it was. This was reported to me. I do not know of firsthand knowledge.
>
> *Mr. Jenner.*   I would prefer not to have your hearsay. You have no knowledge firsthand, however?
>
> *Mr. Surrey.*   No; I do not.
>
> *Mr. Jenner.*   Unless, Mr. Chairman, you desire to pursue the hearsay——
>
> *The Chairman.*   No, no.

Thus a new mystery is introduced. When Jenner launches his offensive against Surrey to make him describe the peculiarities of Mrs. Jackson's dog, it seems obvious that he has something in mind. One begins to guess what that may be when the witness confirms that the dog "became or was ill" at the time of the attempt on Walker's life. Did someone poison the dog to carry out the shooting? We follow Jenner's line of attack with rising interest, since it suggests an entirely new direction in the investigation. Did Oswald have an opportunity to poison the neighbor's dog? Otherwise, who might have been able to do it?

And then, suddenly, without explanation, almost as if someone in the room had cut him off with a meaningful glance, a gesture, or a scribbled note, Jenner swings around and goes off in another direction.

A lawyer's scruple against hearsay testimony? But the Warren Commission had officially declared that it did not feel bound by such rules, and besides the transcript crawls with hearsay evidence. Nothing, moreover, prevented the Commission from obtaining direct testimony if it had a sudden desire to make an exception this time. All it had to do was question Dr. Ruth Jackson, but it didn't.

The tale of the sick dog thus enriches the long list of inconsistencies that mark the Dallas events and the Washington probe.

The FBI report of June 10 (Commission Exhibit No. 1953) informed the Commission that the dog did not belong to Dr. Jackson but to one of her employees, Mrs. Ross Bouve. The report nevertheless confirmed the sickness:

> Mrs. Bouve stated she was of the opinion someone had given him something to quiet him or drug him or poison him, because he did become sick and vomited extensively on April 11 and 12, 1963. She did not take him to a veterinarian. She stated she based her belief that the dog had been given something because of the shooting incident and the dog's habit of barking at anyone or anything in the alley area. She stated she had no other basis for this belief or any proof whatsoever, and this was only opinion on her part.

The Commission, in any case, was not interested. It preferred to stay with Marina Oswald: "The admissions made to Marina Oswald by her husband are an important element in the evidence that Lee Harvey Oswald fired the shot at General Walker."

The Report gives us "additional corroboration" based on the irreplaceable Russian widow.

She told the Commission that three days after the shooting Oswald showed her a notebook containing photographs of Walker's house and a map of the area. The Report announces triumphantly: "Although Oswald destroyed the notebook, three photographs found among Oswald's possessions after the assassination were identified by Marina Oswald as photographs of General Walker's house." Two pages earlier, at the start of this section titled "Prior Attempt to Kill," we were informed that "until December 3, 1963, the Walker shooting remained unsolved." The three photographs must have been found "among Oswald's possessions" on November 22 or November 23 at the latest. Wasn't it strange that the federal and local investigators who examined the pictures failed to identify them when they could have checked with the tourist bureau, the Chamber of Commerce, cab drivers, or Boy Scouts, and when they could have published the pictures in the local papers and asked the public to provide the information?

But the Commission deems it quite natural that the investigators had to wait until December 3 for Marina Nikolaevna, who surely knew the streets of Minsk better than she knew Turtle Creek Boulevard, to identify the photos as pictures of Walker's house.

There remains, finally, the famous "note" found in a Russian book when "Mrs. Ruth Paine turned over to the police some of the Oswalds' belongings." I should like to point out again that Mrs. Paine, according to what she told me, did not "turn over" anything to the police but gave it to them only to be delivered to Marina. Next, and above all, I should remind the Commission that if the text of the note as published in the Report shows that Lee Oswald really expected to be arrested, or even that he really intended to commit some criminal feat, there is nothing in it to indicate what it would be. The note is undated, no mention is made of General Walker, and we are left only with the word of Marina Oswald to link the note with the Walker shooting.

I have only one more comment on this curious interlude born in a motel near Dallas where Marina Oswald was kept under the "protection" of the Secret Service, with the motel manager as sole and mandatory spokesman. Marina did not speak English, and her husband, we are told, systematically kept her from having much to do with life around her. It is quite probable that the name of Edwin A. Walker meant nothing to her in April; I wonder whether she would have remembered it in December unless someone whispered it to her.

This notion is supported by a picturesque episode that takes up a page and a half in the Report under the title "Richard M. Nixon Incident."

According to the Report: "In January 1964, Marina Oswald and her business manager, James Martin, told Robert Oswald, Lee Harvey Oswald's brother, that Oswald had once threatened to shoot former Vice President Richard M. Nixon." Robert Oswald repeated this to the FBI and then to the Commission, which noticed that Marina had not mentioned it when she testified in February 1964. She was called back on June 11, 1964. Meanwhile, naturally, the usual "leaks" had disclosed under banner headlines that Oswald had tried to kill not only Walker but also Nixon before going after Kennedy.

From the account given by Marina on June 11, it appears that several days before going to New Orleans on April 24, 1963, Lee Oswald finished reading the morning paper, put on a good suit, took his revolver, and prepared to leave. When his wife asked where he was going, he replied that Nixon was coming to town and that "he would use the pistol if the opportunity arose." Marina told the Commission she called Oswald into the bathroom and "we actually struggled for several minutes." Then she shut him in the bathroom to keep him from going out with the gun.

When questioned about this, the Report notes, Marina "said she might have been confused about shutting him in the bathroom, but that 'there is no doubt that he got dressed and got a gun.' "

Perhaps J. Lee Rankin should be congratulated for having reminded Marina that bathroom doors generally don't lock from the outside. More serious, however, is the fact that neither of the two Dallas newspapers mentioned any forthcoming visit by Nixon between January 1 and May 15, 1963. Nixon himself told the Commission that his only visit to Dallas in 1963 was on November 20 and 21.

The Commission tried to convince Marina that her husband may have been threatening not Nixon but Lyndon Johnson, then Vice President, who had been in Dallas on April 23 and whose visit had been discussed in the local papers for weeks before. At first Marina replied, "There is no question that in this incident it was a question of Mr. Nixon." When asked again if Oswald might have meant Johnson, she answered: "Yes, no. I am getting a little confused with so many questions. I was absolutely convinced it was Nixon and now after all these questions I wonder if I am right in my mind."

Without further ado the Warren Commission, which never imagined that Marina might have been mistaken about Walker, admits she may have "misunderstood her husband" in regard to Nixon. And the same Commission, which could not imagine that Oswald might have been simply bragging when he said he had shot at Walker, admits that "regardless of what Oswald may have said to his wife he was not actually planning to shoot Mr. Nixon at that time in Dallas."

The Commission resigns itself to ending the section on the "Richard M. Nixon Incident" with these wise words: "In the absence of other evidence that Oswald actually intended to shoot someone at this time, the Commission concluded that the incident, as described by Mrs. Oswald, was of no probative value in the Commission's decision concerning the identity of the assassin of President Kennedy."

On February 6, 1964, commenting on Marina's testimony, Chief Justice Warren abstained from any discussion of the Walker aspect of the case—even though he had confirmed on February 4 that the question had been examined on the second day of Marina's testimony. The Chief Justice may have been in a hurry to get to his main point: "She stated that while she did not like to believe her husband killed President Kennedy, the facts presented to her since the assassination would not permit her to reach any other conclusion."

What facts, Mr. Chief Justice? And presented to her by whom?

11

MARINA OSWALD ACCUSES HER HUSBAND

FIRST REDUCED TO A MISERABLE LIFE at the side of a bitter and sullen misfit, then alone at the age of 22 with two small daughters to care for, Marina Nikolaevna Oswald deserved a sympathetic understanding. But the role she agreed to play in the macabre farce that followed the assassination of the President helped turn one of the most tragic dramas of our time into one of its most outrageous scandals.

For weeks the world waited for the United States to account for the Dallas investigation, demanding that the repeated statements about the man held responsible for the crime be replaced by acceptable proof or that an entirely new inquiry be started.

The response came on January 8, 1964, from the mouth of a motel manager whom the authorities were not ashamed to push forward, or who at least stepped forward with their consent. That morning the Associated Press sent out a story datelined Dallas that began: "The young widow of Lee Oswald has accepted as a fact that her husband killed President John F. Kennedy, her business adviser said today." The business adviser had not spoken only to A.P.; Jack Langguth wrote in the *New York Times* under a Grand Prairie dateline: "Mrs. Lee H. Oswald is convinced that her husband assassinated President Kennedy, her business adviser said today. James H. Martin, the adviser, said her conviction was so strong that even if a jury could find Oswald not guilty her opinion would be unchanged."

On January 26, flanked by her democratic guardians of the Secret Service, Mrs. Oswald herself went to a Dallas TV studio

169

to confirm in person the statements made by her agent. "Do you
believe that your husband killed President Kennedy?" she was
asked. And the widow—"in simple and touching phrases of
broken English," the *Times* commented—replied, "I don't want
to believe, but I have to watch facts, and facts tell me that Lee
shot Kennedy."

Thus, abandoning all pretense of having valid arguments to
submit to a doubting world, the United States offered instead
a crude exhibition of Soviet-style propaganda, made all the more
intolerable by a dash of Hollywood syrup.

The subjective views of the widow certainly could not close the
gaps of the inquiry, even if we were sure she had not been brainwashed in her two months with Secret Service agents. And can
we be sure of that? "I have to watch facts," says Marina Nikolaevna. In the Soviet Union she might have said, "It is well
known. . . ." Were the statements of Wade and Curry and Fritz
translated for her, and if so, were they followed also by all the
variations, corrections, denials, and deletions? Did the FBI provide a special Russian version of its leaks? Was she allowed to
decode the American newspapers herself and, if so, which ones?
Did she have access to publications containing articles that questioned some of the alleged "proofs"?

In fact, despite all the official denials, Mrs. Oswald was not
protected but isolated by the authorities.

"The Justice Department and Secret Service spokesmen say that
the guard is solely for Mrs. Oswald's protection from anyone who
might want to harm her, and that she may see anyone she likes,"
Donald Janson wrote in the *Times* in a December 20 dispatch.
A month later, in her televised interview, Mrs. Oswald was asked
whether she feared for herself and her children. "No," she replied, "I'm not afraid because everyone pity me and help me."
Why then such strict security measures, not relaxed until after
Marina had appeared before the Warren Commission?

The answers to this question can be found in the same story
by Donald Janson, and I don't believe they have ever been denied.
Based on imprudent comments made to Janson by James H.
Martin, the story redefines Martin's situation in one of those

exquisite understatements that the *Times* correspondents carry
off so well: "Recently the Secret Service became the intermediary
through which she acquired a representative to handle her business and personal affairs." A little further on, Janson shows himself to be less delicate: Martin, he states, took charge of Marina's
financial and personal affairs "at the suggestion of the Secret
Service."

It should be kept in mind that the Secret Service, while "help-
ing" Mrs. Oswald find a business adviser, "protected" her not only
against reporters, lawyers, and assassins, but also against her
mother-in-law, Mrs. Marguerite Oswald (who after all was the
grandmother of her children) and against Ruth Paine, one of the
few friends who could converse with her in her own language.

Mrs. Paine, we know, had made Marina welcome in her home,
and had even made the necessary arrangements for the birth of
the Oswalds' second baby, since Lee was not around. She told me
that, having received no reply to her notes other than the visit
by Secret Service agents concerning the Walker incident, she had
written Marina to ask if she really wanted no visitors. This went
unanswered, too, although Mrs. Paine received a Christmas card
from Marina.

Donald Janson's interview with James H. Martin took place in
Dallas, after the "business adviser" had just returned from a trip
to Washington:

> Mr. Martin spoke with the Deputy Attorney General,
> Nicholas deB. Katzenbach, and with J. Lee Rankin, gen-
> eral counsel for the Presidential commission investigating
> the assassination. Before that, he said, Justice Department
> instructions had been relayed to him through the Secret
> Service agents here. Mr. Katzenbach asserts that technically
> Mrs. Oswald is free to see and talk with anyone she likes,
> including the press, but that the Justice Department has
> recommended that she talk to nobody but Federal investi-
> gators.

In other words, Katzenbach, borrowing the definition of freedom current behind the Iron Curtain, said that Marina was free

to do what she liked so long as she did only what she was told.

Janson's article, an important addition to the record of the affair, also contains a clear indication of the type of pressure applied to Marina: "Mr. Martin said he would not permit her to alter this arrangement without Justice Department approval because informal custody was more comfortable for her than incarceration as a material witness in the assassination might be." According to Janson, Martin came back to this point, repeating that he feared "Mrs. Oswald might be arrested as a material witness if he or she permitted any breach in the secrecy that now surrounds her."

Marina Nikolaevna, by the way, had good personal reasons for heeding the Justice Department instructions.

Even though her existence appears to have been no happier in the United States than it had been in the Soviet Union, she had learned what life in America could offer her and the children, and she had no desire to be sent back to the Soviet paradise—indeed, she was very much afraid of that. She often spoke to Ruth Paine about her dream of becoming "an American like the others"; she did not miss a commercial on television, and she learned avidly about the material comforts of American life.

The transcript of Marina's interrogation provides not only an interesting insight into her personality but also precise facts showing that the authorities—those of Washington, not Dallas—knew her mental state perfectly well and tried to take advantage of it.

This interrogation, with which the Commission began its work on Monday, February 3, 1964, takes up 126 pages in Volume I of the Hearings. A sometimes disconcerting light is thrown on Marina in those pages. She obviously had decided to cooperate, but television must have taught her there is more to the United States than washing machines. She knew there were certain rights, and that one did not have to accept everything. Under the guise of the helpless child-wife unable to make her way through life without the protection of others, she allows us to see the cold calculation, the methodical will of a woman who knows what she wants and is ready to do whatever is required to get it—but will not be stepped on when it is not necessary.

The tone is established at the start, when J. Lee Rankin, general counsel of the Commission, mentions the "more than 46" FBI and Secret Service interviews she had already undergone and asks if she has anything to say about them:

> *Mr. Rankin.*   As far as you can recall now, do you know of anything that is not true in those interviews that you would like to correct or add to?
>
> *Mrs. Oswald.*   Yes, I would like to correct some things because not everything was true.
>
> *Mr. Rankin.*   Will you tell us——
>
> *Mrs. Oswald.*   It is not just that it wasn't true, but not quite exact.

She did not change any of her earlier statements except to reinforce them in the way the Commission wanted, as in the case of the rifle identification or the story about the Walker shooting. But she balked, with perceptible irritation, when someone tried to put words in her mouth.

In her second day of testimony, for example, she was questioned by Rankin about the possibility that Oswald might have practiced with the rifle during his weekends at Irving.

> *Mr. Rankin.*   On these weekends, did you ever observe your husband going to the garage, practicing with the rifle in any way?
>
> *Mrs. Oswald.*   No.
>
> *Mr. Rankin.*   Did you see him leave the house when he could have been going to the garage and practicing with the rifle?
>
> *Mrs. Oswald.*   No, he couldn't have practiced while we were at the Paines', because Ruth was there. But whenever she was not at home, he tried to spend as much time as he could with me—he would watch television in the house. But he did go to the garage to look at our things that were there.
>
> *Mr. Rankin.*   And you don't know when he went there what he might have done with the rifle? Is that what you mean?

> *Mrs. Oswald.*   At least I didn't notice anything.
>
> *Mr. Rankin.*   Now, you have described your hus-
> band's——
>
> *Mrs. Oswald.*   Excuse me. I think that it takes consider-
> able time to practice with a rifle. He never spent any
> great deal of time in the garage.

In reply to Rankin's questions, Marina gave assurances that she had no objections to her Secret Service guard, that it was arranged with her consent, and that she had never been "forced to do any-thing that I did not want to do." But when Rankin, on Wednes-day afternoon, imprudently returned to the question of the pre-vious interviews, a definite resentment can be felt in her reply:

> *Mrs. Oswald.*   In the police station there was a routine
> regular questioning, as always happens. And then after
> I was with the agents of the Secret Service and the FBI,
> they asked me many questions, of course—many ques-
> tions. Sometimes the FBI agents asked me questions
> which had no bearing or relationship, and if I didn't
> want to answer they told me that if I wanted to live in
> this country, I would have to help in this matter, even
> though they were often irrelevant. That is the FBI.
>
> *Mr. Rankin.*   Do you know who said that to you?
>
> *Mrs. Oswald.*   Mr. Heitman and Bogoslav, who was an
> interpreter for the FBI.

The index in Volume XV of the Hearings lists the name of Boguslav, Anton, with only one reference—the one where he is mentioned by Mrs. Oswald. Thus he was never questioned by the Commission. The name of Heitman, Wallace R., appears with two additional references, but neither relates to Mrs. Oswald's accusations, and he too was never called before the Commission.

The only result of those accusations, in fact, was a hasty effort by Rankin to make sure the witness would not come up with similar complaints about the Commission itself:

> *Mr. Rankin.*   You understand that you do not have to tell

this Commission in order to stay in this country, don't you, now?

Mrs. Oswald.   Yes.

Mr. Rankin.   You are not under any compulsion to tell the Commission here in order to be able to stay in the country.

Mrs. Oswald.   I understand that.

Mr. Rankin.   And you have come here because you want to tell us what you could about this matter, is that right?

Mrs. Oswald.   This is my voluntary wish, and no one forced me to do this.

That same afternoon, however, on February 5, Marina disclosed that she had been exposed to still other pressures, in the person of a representative of the Immigration Service, whose title is enough to define his role.

Mr. Rankin.   What did he say to you?

Mrs. Oswald.   That if I was not guilty of anything, if I had not committed any crime against this Government, then I had every right to live in this country. This was a type of introduction before the questioning by the FBI. He even said that it would be better for me if I were to help them.

Mr. Rankin.   Did he explain to you what he meant by being better for you?

Mrs. Oswald.   In the sense that I would have more rights in this country. I understood it that way.

Mr. Rankin.   Did you understand that you were being threatened with deportation if you didn't answer these questions?

Mrs. Oswald.   No, I did not understand it that way. You see, it was presented in such a delicate form, but there was a clear implication that it would be better if I were to help.

Mr. Rankin.   Did you——

Mrs. Oswald.   This was only felt. It wasn't said in actual words.

> *Mr. Rankin.*   Did you feel that it was a threat?
>
> *Mrs. Oswald.*   This was not quite a threat—it was not a threat. But it was their great desire that I be in contact, in touch with the FBI. I sensed that.

The situation could not be summed up better than Marina herself described it in this reply, which the Report does not touch on:

> *Mrs. Oswald.*   I think that the FBI agents knew that I was afraid that after everything that had happened I could not remain to live in this country, and they somewhat exploited that for their own purposes, in a very polite form, so that you could not say anything after that. They cannot be accused of anything. They approached it in a very clever, contrived way.

The words are the interpreter's, but the spirit is certainly Marina's. She had understood the warning. And when we arrive at the "facts" that led her to become the flag-bearer in the parade of witnesses against her husband, it is not difficult to see that the only fact that mattered to her was her desire to prove herself a good American.

> *Mr. Rankin.*   Recently you said that you thought your husband did kill President Kennedy.
>
> *Mrs. Oswald.*   I now have enough facts to say that.
>
> *Mr. Rankin.*   Can you give us or the Commission an idea generally about when you came to this latter conclusion, that he did kill President Kennedy?
>
> *Mrs. Oswald.*   Perhaps a week after it all happened, perhaps a little more. The more facts came out, the more convinced I was.

How the facts changed her mind was well described in the deposition of "Business Adviser" Martin, though the Report says nothing about it.

> *Representative Ford.*   Marina testified here, and she has said elsewhere, that based on the facts as she now knows

them, she believes that Lee was guilty of the assassination of President Kennedy.

Mr. Martin. Yes.

Representative Ford. Was that her attitude when you first met her?

Mr. Martin. Well, when I first met her, we didn't converse very well at all. There was lack of communication because of the language barrier, and I didn't discuss it with her probably until the latter part of December, although she was speaking fairly good English by the 15th of December.

Representative Ford. When you first discussed it with her, what was her attitude?

Mr. Martin. Well, she said she thought he was crazy.

Representative Ford. But did she indicate when you first discussed the question of guilt or not being guilty, what was her attitude?

Mr. Martin. She thought he was guilty.

Representative Ford. The first time you discussed the matter?

Mr. Martin. Yes.

Representative Ford. Did she indicate why?

Mr. Martin. No. I asked her why, and she said it was just a feeling.

Representative Ford. At that point had she——

Mr. Martin. A woman's feeling.

Representative Ford. At that point had she been given or shown the evidence that had been accumulated by various agencies of the Federal Government?

Mr. Martin. I don't know. I assume she had through the FBI. The FBI were showing her pictures and numerous things. I was not in on any of the questioning at all.

Marina's haste in dispensing with the services of her "adviser" as soon as she was allowed to do so suggests that the "Americanization" of the Russian widow had begun with her acquisition of a sound American sense of business.

Everything we know about the break between Marina and Martin, as well as her break with John M. Thorne, the lawyer chosen for her by Martin, shows that the essential disagreement was over money. Marina's husband—stingy by nature, no doubt, as well as by necessity—had taught her the value of a penny. She had no intention of allowing herself to be exploited at a time when contract offers for publishing rights or film adaptations led her to foresee a return in thousands of dollars. In fact, her day-to-day troubles had ended with the assassination of her husband. In her television interview on January 26 it was revealed that donations she had received up to then amounted to $35,000. That was far from the $600,000 contributed to Mrs. Tippit, but for the wife of a misfit like Oswald, used to getting along on unemployment payments or temporary wages as unskilled help, it was a fortune.

The official pretext for Marina's appearance before the TV cameras was her desire to thank the public. "I want to thank much, but my bad English does not give me to say much. I want to say thank you American people, thank you for me and my children. And now I am happy. American people help me and support me. And American people have very big heart. . . ." It must not have been too difficult for her, in view of these feelings, to recite the declaration that seems to have favorably impressed Chief Justice Earl Warren but that brought back to European minds the moral degradation of denunciations in Stalin's courts: "I don't want to believe, but I have to watch facts, and facts tell me that Lee shot Kennedy. . . ."

Hoping to find some expression of outrage at such a shameful exhibition, I checked the editorial pages of many American newspapers.

I found only one editorial that could pass for a protest, though it was inspired by strictly professional considerations. The editorial, in the *New York Post*, even began with congratulations: "We congratulate the CBS network on its exclusive interview with Mrs. Lee Oswald. It is hard to understand, however, why she should not have been available to the rest of the press through these many long weeks." As to the other aspects of the problem, the liberal daily was not overly upset: "We are not seeking to cast doubt on the substance of her replies to CBS, but there are too many unanswered questions hovering about the whole Oswald affair to which the public is entitled to have answers, if there are answers. Naturally this primarily is a job for the Warren Commission, one which it is doing. It is reassuring to know that the commission plans to call Mrs. Oswald as the first witness."

The *Post* may have felt reassured, but the choice of Marina as the first witness obviously remains open to discussion. In the meantime, her appearance before the Commission is the basis for a choral work in three movements (with prelude by J. H. Martin) on the theme "Lee Harvey Oswald accused by his widow." We already have the first movement, in the CBS interview: "I don't want to believe, but I have to watch facts, and facts tell me that Lee shot Kennedy." The second movement, employing the brasses as well as the strings, culminates in the solemn affirmation of the Chief Justice: "She stated that while she did not like to believe her husband killed President Kennedy, the facts presented to her since the assassination would not permit her to reach any other conclusion." The third movement was to be played, *adagio sostenuto*, in another TV interview, in Washington, when Marina declared: "I feel very sorry for Lee Oswald. You know, this is my husband. I don't want if Lee shot Kennedy."

For on February 7, the day after Earl Warren had distributed his own appreciation of what he deemed relevant in Marina's testimony, the widow responded to the *Post*'s complaint by agreeing to hold an open press conference televised by all three networks. William Blair, in the February 8 *New York Times*, reported its major aspects better than I could:

> Mrs. Oswald wore a chartreuse jumper over a long-sleeved white blouse with silver cufflinks, buttoned at the neck. Her shoes were brown and black, with medium heels, and she carried a two-toned brown handbag.
>
> She had a gold band on the third finger of her left hand and a ring of an Alexandrite semi-precious gem, set in silver, on the third finger of her right hand.

She smoked a cigarette as she talked with newsmen before and after the conference. As she left the studio she
said, "Now I go to church."

She was accompanied by Secret Service agents, who
brought her from Texas last Sunday. . . .

12

THE MYSTERY OF THE RUSSIAN WIDOW

THE COMMISSION'S CHOICE OF MARINA OSWALD as its first witness, rather than Jesse Curry or Will Fritz, was symbolic of its basic assumption that the accused was guilty and of its view that an examination of Oswald's life and character took priority over any consideration of the evidence against him.

In summoning the widow on the day after her TV exhibition, the Commission nevertheless would have been justified had its objectives been:

(1) To bring to light immediately the "facts" upon which Mrs. Oswald claimed to base her conviction, and either release to the public any new evidence that might be provided by her or report that her opinion was a purely subjective one arrived at without proof, and

(2) To determine without delay the conditions under which Mrs. Oswald had been led to make her televised statement, and either release to the public convincing proof that she was not detained to be brainwashed, or report—and protest—the illegality of her detention.

Neither of these two purposes was taken into consideration by the Commission, though Warren touched on the second question in his talk with reporters on February 4. He did not say, however, that he was troubled by the question, nor even that it had been raised at any time in the first two days of interrogation. But when he was asked about the status of this extraordinary witness who moved only behind a wall of Secret Service agents, Warren replied casually that she was a "free agent." Forgetting that there could be skepticism about "free agents" on this as well as the other side of the Iron Curtain, he added: "Whatever the Secret Service and others are doing for her is what she wants. There is no compulsion of any kind."

The word of the Chief Justice cannot be put aside lightly, and the question might have been considered settled if he had approached it in a different way. Gentlemen, he might have said, I know there has been some question abroad, and perhaps even here in the United States, about the apparently excessive protection given to Mrs. Oswald. I can assure you that I am not unconcerned about the matter. I have closely studied the reasons why this protection was provided, and why it has been continued for such a long time, as well as the way it has been carried out, including the manner in which Mrs. Oswald was provided with an attorney and a business agent. I also had a long private conversation with Mrs. Oswald, far from any kind of policemen who might have intimidated her. This is why, gentlemen, I think I am right in stating that whatever the Secret Service and others are doing for her is what she wants . . .

But Earl Warren did not say that. According to William Blair in the *Times,* "He said that he assumed her lawyer, John Thorne of Grand Prairie, Texas, had requested the Secret Service aid and had asked her not to talk to newsmen because he might have wished to prevent 'harassment.' " Other correspondents confirmed that Warren had said the protective guard had been requested by her lawyer. Mentioning the possibility of "harassment," the *Times* account added that Warren had "said he was inclined to agree with this position 'until we have finished with our job.' "

Apparently no one asked the Chief Justice—and the Chief Justice did not ask himself—how Thorne could have requested the Secret Service guard when the agents were already there at the time Thorne was picked by Martin as Marina's lawyer. I had hoped to find an acceptable explanation somewhere in the Report, or at least an effort to convince the public that there was such an explanation. The Commission did not take the trouble. And the Report disposes of all questions and doubts in a four-line note among the "Speculations and Rumors":

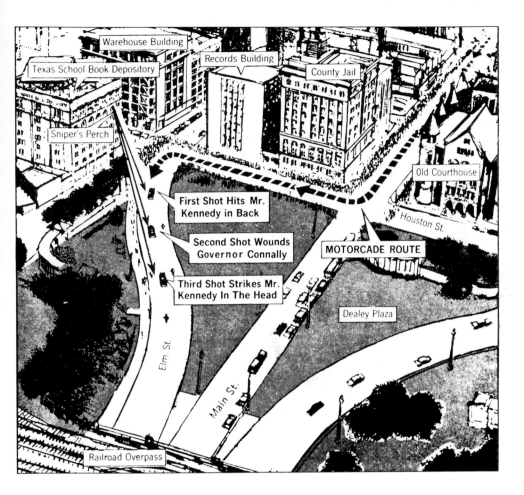

Warehouse Building

Texas School Book Depository

Records Building

County Jail

Sniper's Perch

Old Courthouse

First Shot Hits Mr. Kennedy in Back

Second Shot Wounds Governor Connally

Houston St.

MOTORCADE ROUTE

Third Shot Strikes Mr. Kennedy In The Head

Dealey Plaza

Elm. St.

Main St.

Railroad Overpass

1. This official document, issued by the United States Information Service before publication of the Warren Report, gives a general view of the assassination scene and shows the location of the President's car at the moment each of the shots was fired. Notice that the sequence of shots does not correspond to the final theory of the Warren Commission: that one of the shots missed the car and that Governor Connally was hit by one of the bullets that struck Kennedy.

AERIAL VIEW (500 FT. ALTITUDE)
OF FREEWAY CONVERGENCE WEST OF
TRIPLE UNDERPASS, DALLAS, TEXAS

2. Aerial view showing the freeway convergence beyond the triple underpass and the barrier dividing the Main and Elm extensions, with its "No Turns" sign. The Trade Mart, where the President was headed, is on Stemmons Freeway, which is normally—and legally—reached via Elm Street *(Commission Exhibit No. 2116).*

3. View of the Texas School Book Depository, taken by the Commission on March
20, 1964, and showing where witness Howard L. Brennan was sitting at the time
of the assassination. The letters A and B were written on the photo by Brennan
when he was being questioned. A marked the spot where he had seen the assassin
(correct) and B the place where he had seen two Negroes (false: they were directly
beneath window A). The name of the building is plainly visible over the door
(Commission Exhibit No. 477).

4. Enlargement of picture taken by Thomas C. Dillard a few seconds after the assassination. The two employees on the fifth floor who were watching the motorcade have not yet realized what happened. Above, the assassin's window behind which Howard L. Brennan claims to have recognized Lee Oswald (*Commission Dillard Exhibit C*).

5. The southeast corner of the sixth floor of the Depository Building, with the "shield of cartons" piled in front of the window. Each of the boxes weighed about 50 pounds, according to the Report *(Commission Exhibit No. 723)*.

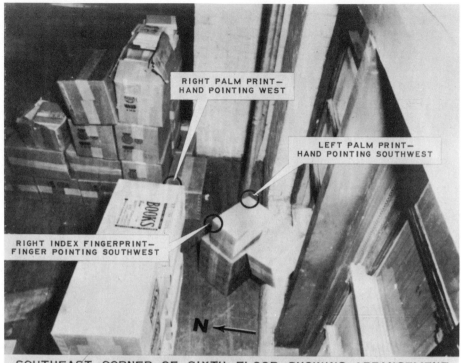

RIGHT PALM PRINT—
HAND POINTING WEST

LEFT PALM PRINT—
HAND POINTING SOUTHWEST

RIGHT INDEX FINGERPRINT—
FINGER POINTING SOUTHWEST

N ←

SOUTHEAST CORNER OF SIXTH FLOOR SHOWING ARRANGEMENT
OF CARTONS SHORTLY AFTER SHOTS WERE FIRED.

6. The gunman's position at the southeast corner window indicating the three prints of Oswald found on the boxes. Oswald's prints were not found on the other cartons he must have handled in setting up the "shield." The photo also shows the distance between the window and the fourth carton Oswald was said to have used as a seat *(Commission Exhibit No. 1301)*.

APPROXIMATE LOCATION OF WRAPPING-PAPER BAG AND LOCATION OF PALM PRINT ON CARTON NEAR WINDOW IN SOUTHEAST CORNER. (HAND POSITION SHOWN BY DOTTED LINE ON BOX)

7. Detail of the southeast corner, with the dotted rectangle at right showing the location where, according to Detective Studebaker, the wrapping-paper bag was found. No pictures were taken of the bag at the time of its discovery or at the place where it was discovered (*Commission Exhibit No. 1302*).

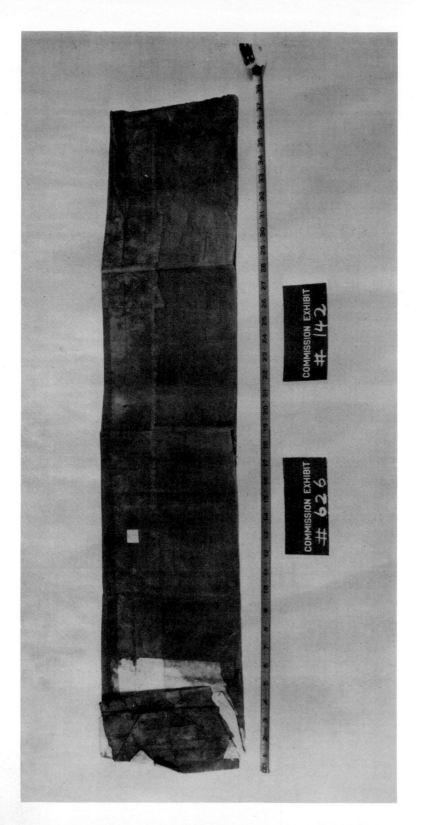

8. The brown wrapping paper that the Commission contends was the "grocery bag" described by the two witnesses (*Commission Exhibits 626 and 142*).

9. The dismantled rifle, which the Commission states Oswald carried to the Depository in the wrapping shown in Illustration 8 (*Commission Exhibit No. 139*).

10. A Dallas detective carries the "murder weapon" to police headquarters, to be sent to the FBI laboratories in Washington for detection of fingerprints, traces of fibers, etc. (*U.S. Information Service document*).

TEXAS SCHOOL BOOK DEPOSITORY
DIAGRAM OF SECOND FLOOR
SHOWING ROUTE OF OSWALD

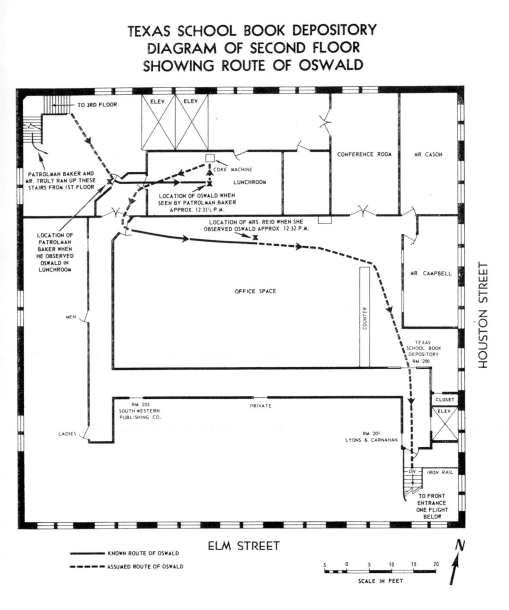

ELM STREET

KNOWN ROUTE OF OSWALD
ASSUMED ROUTE OF OSWALD

N

SCALE IN FEET

11. Diagram of second floor of Depository Building, showing the "known" and "assumed" routes of Oswald. Notice the arrow pointing to "location of Patrolman Baker when he observed Oswald in lunchroom." It can easily be seen that a man running from one stairway to another to reach the roof as quickly as possible had no reason to make the detour that would place him in the indicated position. It can also be seen that, because of the angle formed by the vestibule and lunchroom doors, Baker could not have glimpsed Oswald unless Oswald had remained just inside the vestibule, near the window in the door. The second cross in the large "office space" shows where Oswald, carrying his Coke, was seen by an employee who spoke to him about the assassination but did not remember what he did after that *(Commission Exhibit No. 1118)*.

LOCATION OF EYEWITNESSES TO THE MOVEMENTS OF
LEE HARVEY OSWALD IN THE VICINITY OF THE
TIPPIT KILLING

12. Aerial view of section of Oak Cliff showing the site of the Tippit murder and the location of the various "eyewitnesses". Counting the names listed on the picture, we find that the 9 "eyewitnesses" of the Report have become 13 instead. To surround Helen Markham and her eight co-witnesses with better protection (five of them had seen Oswald on television or in the newspapers *before* identifying him) the Commission added four more it had not counted at first. Example: L. J. Lewis who, says the Report, declared that "because of the distance from which he observed the gunman he would hesitate to state whether the man was identical with Oswald" *(Commission Exhibit No. 1968).*

13. Picture of Oswald posing with the rifle, not retouched here *(Commission Exhibit No. 134)*.

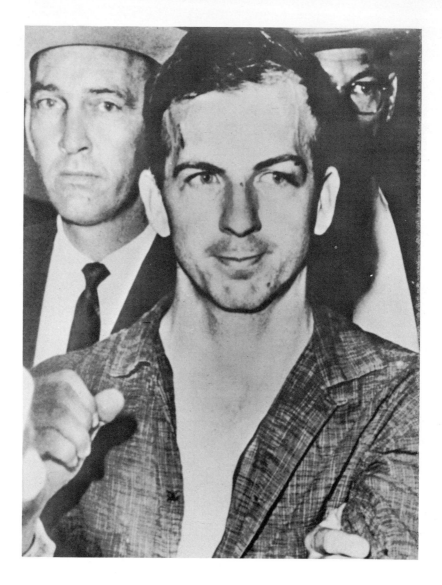

14. Photo, distributed by U.S. Information Service, showing Oswald shortly after his arrest, with his twisted little smile . . . and the "white" shirt mentioned in the police broadcast on Tippit's killer *(USIS document)*.

15. The murder of Lee Harvey Oswald *(Commission Pappas Exhibit 1)*.

16. Marina Oswald as she was interviewed on television *(USIS document).*

Speculation. The Secret Service incarcerated Marina Oswald immediately after the assassination.

Commission finding. Marina Oswald was given protection by the Secret Service for a period of time after the assassination. She had freedom to communicate with others at any time she desired, to go where she pleased, or to terminate the protection at any time.

The Commission believes there is no need to prove its "finding." It wants us to take its word for it. Since it devotes pages and pages to the psychology not only of Lee but also of Marina Oswald, the Commission at least could have suggested a theory to explain why the widow, if she was free to "communicate with others at any time she desired," preferred the company of federal agents to the companionship of Ruth Paine, for example.

This is what the Report has to say about the relations between the two women before Marina—who said she never feared any physical harm to herself or her children—entered the hermetic "protection" of the Secret Service.

Marina Oswald and Ruth Paine subsequently became quite friendly, and Mrs. Paine provided considerable assistance to the Oswalds. Marina Oswald and her child resided with Ruth Paine for a little over 2 weeks while Oswald sought a job in New Orleans in late April and early May 1963. In May, she transported Marina Oswald to New Orleans, paying all of the traveling and other expenses. While the Oswalds were in New Orleans, the two women corresponded. Mrs. Paine came to New Orleans in late September and took Marina Oswald and her child to her home in Irving. . . . Marina Oswald lived with Ruth Paine through the birth of her second daughter on October 20, 1963, and until the assassination of President Kennedy.

Since it is not impossible that the young widow, in her distress, may have thought the Secret Service would offer more moral support than she could obtain from a friend, I will not insist further on this point.

I prefer to direct the Commission's attention to James H. Martin's statements as reported in the December 20, 1963, *New York Times* story. Does Warren accuse Donald Janson, who wrote it, of having fabricated the account? Or does he think the business manager imagined the instructions from the Justice Department? No doubt Martin was not too smart in letting the story out, but I must say that between the peremptory statement of the Warren Report on the "freedom" of Mrs. Oswald and the Janson article describing what that freedom amounted to, I consider the article to be more reliable.

The choice is made easier by a revealing passage closing the 126 pages of Marina Oswald's testimony in Volume I of the Hearings. This is the embarrassed statement by John M. Thorne, in behalf of his client, at the end of her four-day interrogation on February 6, 1964.

After Warren had thanked him for his spirit of cooperation, Thorne announced that during the lunch recess Marina had made four requests.

First, he said, she had asked him to express to the Chairman and the Commission members her "extreme gratitude" for the manner in which she had been treated. Second, she wished to inform the Commission that she would be ready to assist at any time her services might be needed. The third request had to do with copies of letters and documents that Marina, thinking no doubt of her future literary activities, wanted returned. And the fourth:

> *Mr. Thorne.* . . . And the final point was this. She has been, as you know, under protective custody of the Secret Service from shortly after the assassination. She has been most grateful for this protection. The Secret Service have shown her every courtesy, as everyone has in this matter. She is extremely grateful for this protection they have given her.
>
> I haven't had personally enough time to think this thing out myself. I don't know. It is her request, however, that, at this point she feels the protection is no

longer necessary. She feels that at this time she can walk among people with her head held high. She has nothing to hide. She is not afraid.

She feels that the Secret Service has performed a noble service to her. And this is not meant by way of saying for some action on their part she wants to get rid of them.

I have noticed that since we have been in Washington she resents being guided. She feels she can find her way by herself.

And, if the Commission would give this matter consideration—we don't know whom to go to. I haven't thought about it. I don't know who has suggested the Secret Service continue protecting her. It is a matter, of course, that ought to be considered.

But it is her request that as soon as it is practical, she would like to be a free agent and out of the confines of this protection. . . .

From the following passage of the transcript it appears that Warren was even more embarrassed than Thorne:

The Chairman. Mr. Thorne, we can understand Mrs. Oswald's desire to live a perfectly normal life with her children. Whatever has been done, as you recognize, has been done for her protection, and for her help during these terrible days that she has been going through.

But she may feel from this moment on that she is under no protection, except what she might ask for. And so you are perfectly free, Mrs. Oswald, to live your normal life without any interference from anyone. And should anyone interfere with you, I hope you would call it to the attention of the Commission.

Mrs. Oswald. Thank you very much.

Warren's promise seems to have been kept, and Marina Oswald, as we know, lost no time in getting rid of not only the Secret Service men but Thorne and Martin as well.

Yet the Chief Justice, in granting Mrs. Oswald's freedom "from this moment on," was implicitly admitting that this freedom had not existed until then. Such an admission surely warranted investigation. It also should have led the Commission to take another, more critical, look at the statements, identifications, and other revelations of the overprotected widow. The Commission did nothing of the kind. Its attitude is all the more regrettable in that its Report contains some new information tending to increase, rather than dispel, the mystery of the Russian widow.

When Marina Oswald finished testifying on February 6, Warren felt completely free to divulge immediately, contrary to the rule of secrecy he and the Commission were said to have imposed on themselves, a summary of her deposition.

What was in that summary? First, above all, the rifle identification; I have already commented on that. There is also mention of some information given by Mrs. Oswald "about her childhood and schooling, and life in the Soviet Union up to the time she met Lee Oswald." All right. Marina, Warren added, "filled in and elaborated on many things which she had previously described in interviews." Well and good. Warren's official leak presents only one new fact gleaned from the questioning of Mrs. Oswald, aside from the rifle identification. "She also testified that while they lived in New Orleans, during the summer of 1963, in some of his activities he used the fictitious name of A. Hidell, which was the same as that under which the rifle was purchased from a mail-order house in Chicago."

This disclosure would have had some significance if the Hidell alias had ever been seriously in doubt. But at the time, as today, this was one of the least disputed points in the case. The childish way Oswald hid behind false names would be laughed at by 10-year-olds who play cops and robbers. We need only recall, for instance, how Oswald used the name O. H. Lee at his rooming house on North Beckley Avenue, giving the phone number to his wife so she could call in an emergency but not telling her whom to ask for. Oswald, furthermore, did not rent a post-office box under the name A. Hidell, as it was first believed. He rented the box in his *own* name, and gave A. Hidell as another person authorized to use the *same* box!

The Report does tell us something new that Warren's selection did not include. Oswald's Fair Play for Cuba membership card is signed, for the nonexistent New Orleans chapter, by A. J. Hidell. What Warren did not say was that, according to the Report, "Marina Oswald herself wrote the name 'Hidell' on the membership card at her husband's insistence."

Was this the resigned complicity of a wife who did not dare say no to her husband? Judging from the way Marina treated him in front of friends, as described in the Report, she was more of a nagging pest than a submissive wife. There are two or three pages on the intimate relations between them, pages that were gobbled up by the Sunday supplements and that go so far that the Commission feels obliged to add that it "does not believe that the relations between Oswald and his wife caused him to assassinate the President."

No, indeed, as the Report notes, "it is unlikely that the motivation was that simple," even though Hollywood might be tempted to accept it. Meanwhile we can meditate on the fascinating evidence of Marina's double game, as revealed by the Warren Report.

Until the Report was published, it had been believed that when Lee Oswald went to Mexico in September 1963 he told his wife only that he was going to Houston to look for a job. When he telephoned her on October 3, Marina and Mrs. Paine were understood to have assumed that he had just returned from Houston after failing to find employment. And then suddenly, lost in the middle of a long paragraph, a single sentence of the Warren Report completely changes the story: "Though Marina Oswald knew this to be false, she testified that she joined in this deception."

An attentive reading of the Report allows us to pick up here and there some other odds and ends along the same line. For example: "Marina Oswald testified that Oswald had told her that the purpose of the trip was to evade the American prohibition on travel to Cuba and to reach that country. . . . She testified that he had earlier laid plans to reach Cuba by hijacking an airliner flying out of New Orleans, but she refused to cooperate and urged him to give it up, which he finally did." Or again: "Marina Oswald testified that when she first saw him after his return to the United States he was disappointed and discouraged at his failure to reach Cuba."

Finally, in the 50 pages the Report devotes to a psychological portrait of Oswald and his "possible motives," we are given an 18-line recapitulation of Marina's testimony about her husband's interest in Cuba in connection with his travel plans.

Marina told the Commission that Oswald had become involved in activities of the Fair Play for Cuba Committee "primarily for purposes of self-advertising. He wanted to be arrested. I think he wanted to get into the newspapers, so that he would be known." Was Marina practicing psychoanalysis here? No, there were practical reasons: "According to Marina Oswald, he thought that would help him when he got to Cuba. He asked his wife to help him hijack an airplane to get there, but gave up that scheme when she refused." Marina Nikolaevna, however, did not refuse to help her husband go to Cuba by other means; the Report repeats at this point how she lied to Mrs. Paine when the latter arrived in New Orleans on September 20: "While Marina Oswald knew of her husband's plan to go to Mexico and thence to Cuba if possible, Mrs. Paine was told that Oswald was going to Houston and possibly to Philadelphia to look for work."

The Commission leaves aside, without trying to probe further and without even taking it into account in judging the credibility of such a witness, all that its own Report divulges about the equivocal role played by Marina in her husband's Cuban plans.

Was Lee departing as the advance guard, with the intention of bringing his family later, and if so, had this plan been passively accepted or actively approved by his wife? Or was Oswald going alone and for good, after a break between them? In either case, whether she lied out of loyalty to her husband or for her own personal reasons, the confidence we can have in Marina's word is hardly reinforced. But this was not Earl Warren's view.

The most striking element in the encounter of the Russian widow and the U.S. Chief Justice was Warren's solicitude regarding her.

His statements to the press during Marina's four days before the Commission are studded with phrases of grateful appreciation. She "fully cooperated," Warren said on February 3, adding "It's going well." He repeated it the next day: "She is a witness full of good will." On February 5, he showed a fatherly interest in Marina's fatigue (she had slept only two hours because June Lee had kept her awake). And he insisted a third time: "She is very cooperative, and willing to help." On February 6, it was an avalanche: "Cooperative . . . serious . . . very composed . . . very tired . . . . She is a very brave little woman."

The communiqué issued on February 6 in the name of Earl Warren tried hard to show the virtually idyllic conditions under which the questioning had taken place.

"Mrs. Marina Oswald," it began, "has appeared and testified voluntarily for four days before the Commission. Her attorney, John M. Thorne of Grand Prairie, Texas, has sat with her and been available to her for advice at all times. He was offered an opportunity to ask any questions he desired of Mrs. Oswald. On occasions he did participate in the questioning. He has fully cooperated with the Commission."

Thus were the rights of Marina Oswald protected, at least during the hours she spent before the Commission headed by the Chief Justice of the United States . . .

With the exception that she arrived each time escorted "voluntarily" by four Secret Service men, and departed each time "voluntarily" in the same way. And with the exception that the lawyer "available to her for advice at all times" had been chosen for her "voluntarily" by her business agent, who had also been "voluntarily" picked for her by the Secret Service . . .

But above all, with the exception that the rights crying out to be upheld in this case were not the rights of the widow who had come to accuse her husband, but those of Lee Harvey Oswald, condemned and executed without trial.

13

THE ASSASSINATION OF LEE OSWALD

THE ACCUSATIONS LEVELED AGAINST THE CITY OF DALLAS for failing to prevent the assassination of President Kennedy were totally unjustified.

Leaders in a democracy will always be exposed to possible attack by an assassin hiding in the shadows, such as the one who put an end to the life and dreams of John F. Kennedy. The President could have been protected against the two bullets that hit him: It would have been easy enough to surround him with a human shield of Secret Service men or, better still, to let him ride in a closed, bulletproof car; the best method of all would have been to drive to the Trade Mart at top speed, by a circuitous route, and at a time not announced in advance. But if John F. Kennedy had accepted any of these measures, he would not have been John F. Kennedy; and besides, why in this case should he have bothered to go to Dallas at all?

The trip to Dallas was a traditional political jaunt, for the purpose of making friends and gathering future votes. This purpose could be served only if the visit progressed as it did: with the President riding in an open car for all to see, waving to the crowds along the route, with the car moving slowly enough so that everyone could get a good look at the President and his charming wife, and with the Secret Service men making themselves as inconspicuous as possible. Under such conditions, the President could have been assassinated anywhere.

True enough, the fact is that Kennedy was killed in Dallas

190

and not anywhere else. But the local authorities cannot be blamed for it.

The protection of the President of the United States is primarily the responsibility of the Secret Service. This agency can request the cooperation of local police in prevention measures, such as surveillance of strategically located buildings. But did the Secret Service ask the Dallas police to post a man at the Depository Building? It is also the duty of the Secret Service, together with the FBI, to check not only the buildings but also the individuals who might be inclined to make use of them. If Lee Oswald was to be counted among such persons, Jesse Curry is completely exonerated: Right or wrong, the FBI had not tipped him off about Oswald's presence in the Elm Street building. Apparently the FBI also considered it unnecessary to warn the Secret Service about him. Whatever the argument might be between the two federal agencies, the Dallas police had nothing to do with that.

The crime of the Dallas police begins with the investigation of the assassination, with its frightening neglect of constitutional rights and professional standards, condoned by Washington's fear of treading on "states' rights." The final disgrace was Oswald's murder at police headquarters, while he walked between two Dallas detectives and was handcuffed to one of them.

Naturally the uproar caused by the presence of newsmen and TV crews made Oswald's murder easier. The prisoner's transfer to the county jail was announced in advance and was to be a major TV spectacle. There was no room for security precautions in the basement jammed with broadcasting equipment and newsmen. Reporters who were there told me that Curry even changed some arrangements at the last minute after a TV crew had protested that its view was blocked.

But none of this reduces the responsibility of the local authorities or changes the fact that Jack Ruby was able to kill Oswald literally in their arms.

Initially the police claimed that Ruby had tricked them by giving the impression that he was with one of the television crews. This line was taken up semiofficially by Mayor Earle Cabell, who at the same time expressed full confidence in Chief Curry. Perhaps vaguely realizing that in most other cities where such an event had taken place there would have been at least two resignations—those of the mayor and the police chief—Cabell (who did resign later, but to maneuver for a seat in Congress) even felt the need to say he would not accept Curry's resignation if it were offered. Curry, however, had no intention of quitting; as he was to confide later to Scripps-Howard columnist Inez Robb, "I thought every precaution had been taken."

It was hardly likely that Ruby could have passed for a TV technician or for anyone else but Ruby. He was well known to all the Dallas police; the detectives who grabbed him identified their prisoner immediately. A police sergeant, questioned a few minutes later by reporters, admitted that he not only knew Ruby but would have made him leave if he had noticed his presence.

Finally, through his first lawyer, Tom Howard, Ruby gave his own explanation: He had succeeded in slipping into the basement that Sunday morning because the two officers guarding the ramp entrance were talking and did not see him.

The ramp is just wide enough for a car to pass with a few inches on each side. It would have been physically impossible for two men standing at the entrance to miss someone trying to sneak through. Howard must have realized this, since he quickly modified the story: The conversation that gave Ruby his chance took place not at the ramp entrance but near the sidewalk. One of the men on duty, Howard said, was speaking to an officer who was in a patrol car. But two men had been posted to guard each of the two ramp entrances. Either the second policeman, not taking part in the conversation, did not see Ruby or else there was only one guard, and this one had left his post to chat with a colleague without keeping an eye on the entrance as he talked.

It really appears more likely that the officers recognized Ruby but shrugged him off as a familiar figure around police headquarters.

This would not have been the first time. During Ruby's trial, reporter John Rutledge of the *Dallas Morning News* testified that he had seen Oswald's future assassin at headquarters at least three times on the night of November 22. Other reporters who were there that night told me the same, and added that they saw him again the next day. They remembered him perfectly, and many still carried the Carousel Club business cards—decorated with a stripper in black stockings—that Ruby had passed around. Later Jack Ruby would cry at will whenever the name of Kennedy was mentioned, but at that time he did not seem at all depressed by the assassination. Obliging and eager around the newsmen, he made himself quite useful to foreign correspondents by explaining the organization of the Police Department, giving the names and functions of officers who made statements, and so on.

Those officers saw nothing wrong in the fact that the strip-joint owner thus played the part of a public relations man for the Police Department.

One of them testified that at 10:30 P.M. on November 22, when he and others were questioning Oswald, he received a phone call: It was Ruby, who wanted to know whether the officer would like some sandwiches. He declined the offer. Another policeman said he recognized Ruby an hour later among the newsmen waiting on the third floor for Oswald to pass by. When asked what he was doing there, Ruby replied, "I brought some sandwiches." Neither the prosecution nor the defense at Ruby's trial sought to find out what happened next. Apparently nothing happened, which means that Ruby, though recognized, was allowed to stay and get his first look at Oswald that very night.

In the interview with Inez Robb that appeared in the *New York World-Telegram* on February 29, Jesse Curry said he "couldn't reveal" how Ruby had been able to get into the basement. Then he complained about his troubles, while pleading not guilty: "It is the worst thing that ever happened to all of us. But I want to say now that it is not true, as reported, that a great many Dallas policemen knew Ruby. Out of a force of 1,150 men, probably less than 50 knew him and only because they worked in his district or inspected his place under the licensing laws."

The 50 must have passed the word to the 1,100 others, because Ruby obviously felt at home at headquarters. He was enough of an insider to arrange a local radio station's telephone interview with District Attorney Wade. A member of the station staff, Glenn Duncan, testified that Ruby had called him on the night of November 22 and asked if he wanted an interview with Wade, who he said was with him at headquarters. Duncan naturally leaped at the chance; Ruby handed the phone to Wade, and the interview was taped and broadcast soon afterward. John Rutledge, the *Morning News* reporter, was standing near Ruby and Wade. In reply to a question from Melvin Belli, Ruby's lawyer, Rutledge confirmed that he had seen Ruby dial a number, talk into the phone, and then call out to the D.A.: "Hey, Henry, I have Duncan on the line. . . ." At the prosecution table, Henry, who now was asking the electric chair for Jack, did not look embarrassed.

Perhaps it was only just, after this, that no disciplinary measures were taken against ordinary cops who had let Jack Ruby walk into the basement Sunday morning without inviting him (as in the more demanding Westerns) to check his revolver at the door. Chief Curry, launching a personal investigation of the case, had certified at the beginning of January that his men were not to blame. And Wade had let it be known that Curry was not to blame either: "There is no indication of collusion, in any form, between Ruby and and Dallas police," he stated with all the legal authority of his office.

During his press conference on November 24, the *incident* that had taken place that morning prompted this exchange:

> *Reporter.*   Do you think it was unusual for Jack Ruby to be in that crowd?
> *Wade.*   I won't pass on that—unusual to be in that crowd?
> *Reporter.*   There are reports that he had planned to——
> *Wade.*   I haven't been here since last night, so I don't know anything about it.

I don't believe that the petty third-rate gangster who killed Oswald yielded to an "irresistible patriotic impulse," as Tom Howard wanted us to believe. Nor do I believe, as Melvin Belli contended, that the helpful headquarters hanger-on suffered a sudden attack of "psychomotor epilepsy" coupled with "temporary insanity." But is there any more truth in the theory, popular in Europe and accepted by some in the United States, that the Sunday-morning shot was the consequence and proof of an earlier tie between Ruby and Oswald, and that the two men were accomplices in the assassination of the President?

Nothing in the lives, characters, interests, or neuroses of Ruby and Oswald predisposed the two even to meet, let alone conspire together.

Those who persist in seeing them as a team automatically turn the pitiful Ruby into a kind of hardened, calm, and determined conspirator, thinking out every step in advance, including the elimination of his accomplice. I leave aside the claims of certain French and Italian reporters, carried away by the spirit of Hollywood and better informed about Al Capone than about John F. Kennedy, who solved the problem in two seconds: the time it takes to say "Cosa Nostra" in suitably dramatic tones. But there were also some serious journalists who commented on possible links. Richard Dudman—the first, I believe, to launch the theory of a second gunman on the railroad bridge—suggested in *The New Republic* that this second assassin was Ruby: "The south end of the viaduct is four short blocks from the office of the *Dallas Morning News,* where Jack Ruby was seen before and after the shooting. . . . No one remembered for sure seeing Ruby between 12:15 and 12:45. The shooting was at 12:30. . . ."

I wonder whether Dudman, after attending Ruby's trial and observing the man for several days, could still view him in such a role: galloping (with or without a rifle?) from the *Morning News* office to the railroad overpass and back again, to shoot the President from the front, after first stationing Oswald at the sixth-floor window to shoot him from behind. Now, really . . .

It was not at all necessary for Ruby to have known Oswald before killing him, nor was it essential for him to have played any role in the assassination.

If Jack Ruby acted not for some psychopathological reason but simply because Oswald had to be eliminated, it would be more in keeping with what we know of him to assign him no role higher than executioner. The best executioners—as the annals of crime in the United States have shown many times—are those who never had any contact with the victim and have only a vague idea of the reasons for the assignment; all they have to know is where to find their man and how to get him. Ruby, true enough, was hardly more a professional killer than a political conspirator. But his past, added to his present, exposed him to all kinds of blackmail and corruption. It would not have been very hard to persuade him, moreover, that far from risking the electric chair he had a good chance of being hailed a hero.

The arguments put forward to link Ruby with Oswald in any way other than killer and victim are plainly childish.

A mountain was made of the fact that Ruby's apartment was only a few minutes' walk from the spot where Tippit was shot. But there are hundreds of other apartments in Oak Cliff even closer, and absolutely nothing proves that Oswald—assuming he knew where he was going, which I doubt—was headed for Ruby's place. Theories also were built around the Y.M.C.A. where Oswald had spent a night after his return from Mexico, because a stripper from Ruby's club said her boss frequently worked out in the Y.M.C.A. gym. But Oswald could not have found a cheaper place to stay in Dallas, and that was reason enough to explain his choice. Some reporters even believed they had made a major discovery in finding that the windows of the *Dallas Morning News* advertising office (where Ruby was revising an ad for his strip show at noon on November 22, rather than standing on the street to acclaim his "idols" John and Jacqueline Kennedy) provided an excellent view of the sixth floor of the Depository Building. And what is that supposed to prove? That Ruby and Oswald were exchanging signals?

In the midst of all this fantasy, the trial of Jack Ruby opened in the court of Judge Joe Brown in Dallas, on February 17, 1964.

14

THE TRIAL OF JACK RUBY

I CAN THINK OF ONLY THREE REASONS why so many reporters flocked to Dallas on February 17, 1964: (1) the expectation of some Texas-size excitement (a prisoner's brief escape from a jail in the courthouse should have satisfied these demands); (2) the promise of spectacular courtroom drama (Melvin Belli supplied this); and (3) the prospect of seeing one or more of Ruby's strippers demonstrating their seductive talents on the witness stand (here they were disappointed, since the main "exotic dancer" who appeared was eight months pregnant).

I learned however that for certain newspapermen, or rather for certain newspapers, there was a fourth reason: not to miss the execution of the accused.

They did not mean the official execution, decided by the Dallas jury in 2 hours and 19 minutes but probably never to be carried out. What they meant and what they expected was the "private" execution of Jack Ruby by some other Jack Ruby. Judge Brown's courtroom, they thought, would do as well as the basement of police headquarters.

The New York correspondent of a large European newspaper told me, while Belli was asking his familiar questions to the 13th or 14th prospective juror, that she had orders to attend even the preliminary sessions. Her assignment was not to report on these proceedings but to stand by and be ready to cable an eyewitness account of how Jack Ruby was shot down between two tall Texan deputy sheriffs wearing ten-gallon hats.

The reasoning behind this expectation was hardly more solid than the gratuitous theory of collusion between Ruby and Oswald.

197

It again assumed that Ruby, in any conspiracy, could have been more than a minor wheel. Ruby probably would not have known the structure of the plot and certainly would not have known the leaders of it; if he had been encouraged to give free rein to his patriotic indignation, he might not have even comprehended the reason for such prompting. What he surely must have understood from the start, however, was that if he dropped the slightest hint indicating he had killed by order of someone else, he would be signing his own death sentence. Not so much because he would become the target for reprisal, but he simply would have no defense left in court.

The fact that the jury condemned him to death anyway could give him a reason to change his attitude, one might assume. But he knew that appeals would take years and that if he were not sent to an institution in the meantime, the sentence would eventually be set aside. It was absolutely vital for Ruby to stick to his story in order not to jeopardize his chances in a future trial.

No serious plotters, in any case, would consider getting rid of Ruby in the same way that Oswald had been disposed of. They would know that even the most credulous American would have trouble swallowing the story of a third "solitary crackpot." I am even inclined to think that if there was a conspiracy, its authors prayed for Ruby's health; they knew well enough that if Ruby were to die of a heart attack, nobody would believe it, and then nobody would believe the rest of the story either.

Nor would such plotters have anything to fear: Because of the way the trial was conducted, it would have taken a totally unlikely combination of circumstances for the truth to come out of those proceedings.

I have mentioned four reasons for the world interest in this trial. I did not cite the main one, since most of the press, afraid to appear ridiculous, did not put it forward. Against all logic, nevertheless, those newspapers did not rule out completely the chance that something in the trial might throw light on the real case, the assassination of President Kennedy. The simple fact that Henry Wade was Ruby's prosecutor, however, prevented any such development.

Although American opinion was not shocked by this, it seems inconceivable to me, legally as well as morally, that the D.A. charged with presenting the case against Ruby should be the same one who "solved" the assassination of President Kennedy by declaring Oswald the sole assassin and closing the case with Oswald's death.

The dilemma was glaringly evident. If Wade succeeded too well in his case against Ruby, that is, if he led him to betray himself and admit that he had not acted spontaneously, he would destroy in the same blow all that he had said and done as prosecutor of Oswald. He therefore was obliged to refrain from asking any questions in the trial that might have reopened the Oswald case, and the fact is that he was even more cautious than the defense in avoiding any suggestion that Ruby might have acted for reasons not related exclusively to his personal psyche.

Under banner headlines in the *New York Journal-American* of February 21, 1964, four days after the trial had begun, the late Dorothy Kilgallen revealed that this preoccupation was shared not only by the local prosecution and the defense but also by the Justice Department in Washington.

Miss Kilgallen stated that in January an "arrangement" had been made between the Justice Department and Ruby's lawyers. The defense would be given "reams of helpful information" by the FBI "on the condition they do not ask for anything at all about Ruby's alleged victim, Lee Harvey Oswald." Miss Kilgallen referred to a letter, dated January 28, from Assistant Attorney General Herbert J. Miller to Joe Tonahill, in reply to a request made by the lawyer. The letter informed Tonahill that the FBI had been instructed to provide names and addresses of various persons who might be useful to the defense, but contained the following restriction, Miss Kilgallen reported: ". . . information concerning Oswald's assassination of the President will not be available as it does not appear to be relevant."

This letter, whose authenticity has never been questioned and in which Miss Kilgallen rightly detected "an Orwellian note," thus blessed the unanimous agreement not to discuss the assassination of the President at the trial of the man accused of killing the "assassin" (Miller showed no more restraint than Wade in thus describing Oswald). I do not know on what rules or precedents the Justice Department jurists based their opinion that information about the victim's crime was not relevant, when the victim's murder was a direct result of that crime. But the fact is that the Justice Department opinion was scrupulously followed throughout the Ruby trial.

From beginning to end, the duel between prosecution and defense was voluntarily limited to the confrontation of two equally subjective explanations. According to the defense, Jack Ruby killed Oswald because he was in a state of temporary insanity. According to the prosecution, he knew perfectly well what he was doing. On this point, squads of psychiatrists were placed on the stand to neutralize one another. Logically, it would seem that to convince the jury that Ruby knew what he was doing the prosecution would have to explain persuasively at the same time *why* he did it. At most Wade suggested, without being very explicit, that Ruby acted out of a desire for publicity. This was more reasonable than Belli's theory of a sudden (though delayed) patriotic-sentimental shock, with psychomotor epilepsy triggering a literally automatic pistol. Belli, however, could have reminded Wade and the jury that a man who kills for publicity is not normal, either; he did not do so.

Is it that he did not want to challenge the prosecution to furnish a different explanation? He abstained from pressing the issue of motive and never asked Wade to describe his conception of the mental process that had led Ruby to kill Oswald. Belli knew, of course, that Wade was in a delicate position: He had to prove that Ruby's act was premeditated while avoiding at all costs any suggestion that it could have been premeditated in any mind other than Ruby's. Belli, on the other hand, had to avoid suggesting that the state was holding its fire, since an insinuation of that kind could have led the jury to suppose the defendant was even more guilty than Wade wanted to say.

Did the jurors have their minds made up, their verdict decided, even before the first witness was called? This is what Melvin Belli declared on March 14, after the jury had convicted Ruby, as he denounced the outcome with a virulence that for once did not seem to be mere histrionics. Perhaps the outburst betrayed not only the disappointment of a famous lawyer not accustomed to losing, but also the fury of a man who agrees to a compromise and then finds he has been "taken." Melvin Belli clearly was stunned by the sentence; only he could say whether he had some grounds for believing it would be different. The death sentence was in fact the only surprise of the trial. It shocked many of the correspondents who had gone to Dallas convinced that Ruby would get off lightly, and were ready to attack the jury for it; but while they thought Ruby deserved the chair, the sentence did not seem justified by the trial they had attended.

The decisive moment, I believe, and one that best illustrates how the scales of justice were tipped, occurred on March 4 during the testimony of one Doyle Lane.

An employee of the Western Union main office near the Dallas municipal building, Lane testified that Ruby had gone into the office on Sunday morning to wire $25 to Fort Worth, where one of his strip-tease girls (Karen Lynn Bennett, known as Little Lynn, 19 and pregnant) was behind in her rent. Little Lynn had telephoned Ruby to ask his help at about 10 A.M. that morning, and Ruby was then at his Oak Cliff apartment. The money, the Western Union records showed, was sent at 11:17. Lee Oswald was shot at 11:21, as a basement clock visible in the videotape recorded it. Wasn't this the proof that, as the defense claimed, only an unlucky coincidence had brought Ruby to the basement a minute before Oswald?

Wade said nothing. Was he caught short by an unexpected disclosure? Not at all; Doyle Lane as well as Little Lynn had already testified in a pretrial hearing on December 23. Belli at that time had leaned on the testimony of these two witnesses in demanding that his client be freed on bail. The importance of their statements was perhaps a bit overshadowed in the press by the fact that Little Lynn, before going to court, had forgotten to remove the revolver she carried in her handbag along with her lipstick. (The gun wasn't loaded.) But Wade had time to study the Western Union records, asked whether he knew Ruby personally (Lane said no), and then proceeded to the next witness. Thus Lane's significant testimony was not refuted, explained, or otherwise neutralized, and the jury condemned to death—for premeditated murder—a man who was miles away at the time Oswald's transfer had been scheduled to take place and who only four minutes before the move did occur was involved in the peaceable business of sending a money order to a stripper in distress.

There was, of course, an answer to this. Wade might have recalled the excellent relations between Ruby and the Dallas police to conclude that he could easily have learned from some friendly detective that the transfer announced for 10 A.M. would not be carried out before 11:20. Thus it was a smart tactic for Ruby to show himself at the Western Union office as late as possible, and not appear in the basement too early. After all, even if 1,100 members of the department did not know him, as Curry said, one of the 50 others might take some unexpected action after watching him stand around for over an hour in a place where Curry had ordered strict security measures. Such an officer, for example, might have felt the right pocket of this suspicious person whose record included two arrests for carrying concealed weapons.

Wade would have had no trouble establishing, if he had wanted to do so, that a fairly large number of policemen knew the actual time that Oswald would be transferred and that they did not keep it secret. I later learned that some of the reporters who showed up dutifully at 10 knew the operation would not take place for another hour. But if the D.A. had attempted a rebuttal along these lines, he would have dragged out from under the carpet the question of police negligence, if not even collusion, and he had already absolved the Police Department of all responsibility. So he kept quiet.

Artificial at its inception, since both sides had tacitly agreed to limit their examination of motive, the trial of Jack Ruby thus was unjust in its result; the defendant was condemned to death under circumstances that did not justify such a penalty. But Wade limit their examination of motive, the trial of Jack Ruby thus was unjust in its result; the defendant was condemned to death under circumstances that did not justify such a penalty. But Wade had gathered new laurels—24 death sentences out of 25 he had sought in his career—and he was now talked of as a likely U.S. Senate candidate.

"Mr. Wade," a reporter had asked him toward the end of his November 24 press conference, "how do you feel about not being able to try Oswald as the killer of the President?" It was only on the night of March 14 that one could appreciate the full meaning of his reply: "Well, we will try Ruby and ask the death penalty on him, about the same time."

15

OSWALD AND THE LAW

FROM THE MOMENT THE SHOTS WERE FIRED by an assassin I consider unidentified, John F. Kennedy was subjected, in death, to the same conflict that had plagued him before in Mississippi or Alabama: the struggle over states' rights.

In the days after November 22, many American newspapers pointed out the anomaly of a system that made it a federal crime to assault a national park guard but left the assassination of the President of the United States to local authorities. These papers, however, generally failed to mention that nothing prevented the local authorities from waiving their rights in such an exceptional case. Futhermore, even if the Texans were not ready to withdraw graciously and spontaneously, they would have been hard put to turn down the idea if someone in Washington had suggested it. But nobody in Washington had the slightest desire to embarrass Texas.

Proof of this was provided quickly in the Justice Department's diplomatic precautions designed to minimize the importance of the federal investigation ordered by the new President.

Appalled by what went on in Dallas in the 48 hours after President Kennedy's murder, I had first mistaken my wishes for reality in interpreting too literally the forceful statements released by the White House Sunday night. President Johnson, it was said, had summoned J. Edgar Hoover and ordered him to move the FBI into the case immediately. A Justice Department spokesman, it seemed, had unequivocally rejected the indecent attitude of the Dallas police chief, who believed the slaying of his prisoner had put an end to the investigation of President Kennedy's assassination. The spokesman had told newsmen: "The

case will not be closed until all the facts are known and all paths
are explored thoroughly." He had also announced that Nicholas
deB. Katzenbach, then Deputy Attorney General, had assigned the
head of the Department's criminal division, Assistant Attorney
General Herbert J. Miller, to go directly to Dallas. I therefore
cabled my newspaper, before boarding a plane for Dallas myself:
"The Justice Department, as shown by the attitude of Mr. Katzenbach, which is believed to reflect the view of Mr. Robert
Kennedy, clearly does not intend to be pushed aside in a case
affecting it so directly, so profoundly, and so personally." But I
nevertheless went on to explain the "delicate" problem of states'
rights.

The first thing I learned when I arrived in Dallas the next
day was that Herbert J. Miller had left for Austin to confer with
Texas Attorney General Waggoner Carr, after having met with
federal officials in Dallas for a few hours.

On Tuesday night, Miller appeared at a press conference in
Austin with Carr. Carr had announced on Monday, in Washington, that the state was setting up its own "court of inquiry." At
Miller's side, he now said he foresaw no conflict with federal
authorities, and added that his office would turn over information to the FBI "and vice versa." Miller, for his part, stressed
that the objectives of Austin and Washington were "identical."
President Johnson in the meantime had officially directed "a
prompt and thorough investigation of all the circumstances surrounding the brutal assassination of President Kennedy and
the murder of his alleged assassin." Assistant Attorney General
Miller, speaking in the Texas capital, interpreted this order as
just a service rendered to the local authorities: "We want to get
all the facts and to lay to rest the speculation and rumors that
are abounding."

The Washington correspondent of the *Dallas Morning News*
added his personal contribution to the desired ambiguity after a
visit to the Justice Department: "The FBI has promised full cooperation with State of Texas officials into the state's court of
inquiry. . . . The meeting between Miller and Carr in Austin
was cited as evidence of cooperation into the separate investiga-

tions." Then came the following two sentences: "Justice Department officials here believe the state wants to look closely into the handling of the case in Dallas. Carr said here Monday the call of the probe was no reflection on the Dallas police department."

An extremely interesting point was raised by Telford Taylor in a letter that appeared in the *New York Times* of December 3, 1963.

Taylor, chief prosecutor for the U.S. at the Nuremberg war crimes trials, began by drawing attention to the need for new federal laws, "both to strengthen the legal basis for federal investigation and to insure creditable treatment of apprehended suspects." But he emphasized that until such laws were enacted, existing laws provided adequate grounds for federal authorities to take charge of the Dallas investigation. Referring to the possibility that the assassin might have acted "in concert with others," he wrote: "Although it is not a federal crime for an individual acting alone to kill the President, it is such a crime for two or more persons to conspire to injure any officer of the United States engaged in discharging the duties of his office."

The former Nuremberg prosecutor drew no conclusions from this except that "If such a sinister combination is in existence, it may be a continuing threat to the lives of Government officers and to national security."

It is tempting to consider this legal point in the light of the Dallas authorities' haste and insistence in proclaiming not only that Oswald was guilty but that he had acted alone. Assuming that in 24 hours the Dallas investigation could have conclusively established Oswald's guilt, it was impossible in such a short time to have foreclosed the possibility that accomplices were involved. Yet Wade and Curry had done exactly that; were they in a hurry to get around the law mentioned by Taylor?

When he appeared before the Warren Commission on June 8, 1964, District Attorney Wade gave some rather astonishing information on this subject.

J. Lee Rankin asked him what he had done when he had first learned of the President's death. "The first thing that I did," said Wade, "was go check the law to see whether it was a Federal offense or mine. I thought it was a Federal offense when I first heard about it. We checked the law, and were satisfied that was no serious Federal offense, or not a capital case, anyhow. There might be some lesser offense. . . ."

This was only the beginning. The District Attorney then said that he had discussed the possible "lesser offense" with his colleague, U.S. Attorney Barefoot Sanders. Then came the revelation: Both of them had agreed, Wade declared, that "it was going to be our case rather than his."

But we know Henry Wade by now, and are aware that accuracy is not one of his strong points. When Rankin asked where he had discussed the matter with the U.S. Attorney, Wade replied: "On the telephone as I recall, in his office from my office. I am not even sure I talked with him, somebody from my office talked to him. . . ."

Was this major decision, determining who had the responsibility for investigating the assassination of the President of the United States, made in Dallas "in his office from my office" by the obscure Barefoot Sanders? We have only Wade's uncertain word and hazy memory on this point. As for Sanders, a glance at the list of witnesses heard by the Commission shows he was never called to testify.

Regardless of who made the decision, the fact remains that the Justice Department had a ready legal basis to take over the investigation, as Taylor suggested. The Department had only to assert its responsibility and point out that it was reasonable to suppose this political assassination might have been committed "in concert with others." If that risked creating some ill will toward Lyndon Johnson in his home state, no one would have dared to speak out against such a decision.

The Warren Report relates an episode at the Parkland Hospital that shows there was at least one instance when federal authorities disregarded the "rights" of Texas without causing any argument later on.

> After the President was pronounced dead, [Kenneth] O'Donnell [special assistant to the President] tried to per-

suade Mrs. Kennedy to leave the area, but she refused. She said that she intended to stay with her husband. A casket was obtained and the President's body was prepared for removal. Before the body could be taken from the hospital, two Dallas officials informed members of the President's staff that the body could not be removed from the city until an autopsy was performed. Despite the protests of these officials, the casket was wheeled out of the hospital, placed in an ambulance, and transported to the airport shortly after 2 p.m.

The Report even tells us that O'Donnell was "concerned that the local officials might try to prevent the plane's departure" and therefore "asked that the pilot take off immediately." The take-off was delayed only long enough for a judge to arrive and swear in the new President.

In Volume VII of the Hearings we find O'Donnell's testimony, which illustrates the curious problems created by the principle of states' rights. Grief-stricken by Kennedy's death, O'Donnell had been courageous enough to challenge those "rights." In his deposition, given on May 18, 1964, while he was still a White House aide, O'Donnell tried to play down the political significance of his action and to reduce the incident to a gesture of sympathy for Jacqueline Kennedy.

"I realized," he said, "that she was going to stay with her husband, no matter what anybody did, and there was no possible way of in any way getting her to leave. And so, therefore, the only alternative I could see was that we move the President. It is an assumption I probably would have arrived at anyway, but I arrived at it in this manner."

O'Donnell went on to say that when the casket containing the President's body was being pushed to the exit, "a gentleman arrived who said that we would not be allowed to remove the body from the hospital until the necessary papers had been signed." Ten or 15 minutes went by, while this gentleman telephoned some unknown person and while O'Donnell wondered whether the red tape would take "a week or an hour." Then another man arrived who was identified to him as "a Judge Brown" (apparently Judge Joe Brown, who presided at the Ruby trial, though no first name is given). "Very calm and cool and collected," Brown or one of the other Texans present declared that this was "just a homicide case," that there were certain formalities to be carried out, that an autopsy had to be performed, and that "the law must be met."

When he heard the word "autopsy," O'Donnell realized "we were talking not about hours, but perhaps even days, which was an impossible situation for Mrs. Kennedy." He suggested that Dallas send a doctor to accompany the body and take charge of the autopsy. The Texans refused to do so. Then O'Donnell made his historic decision:

> We pushed the casket out through the hall. This first gentleman that had come in, who, I presume, was from the coroner's office, shouted very loudly, "You can't do that, you can't leave here now." Nobody paid any attention to him. We pushed out through another set of swinging doors. I remember a Catholic priest was between this and the doorway, and was praying. It was most disconcerting because we were concerned at all times that some moment they would say stop, and I hated to think what might happen to Mrs. Kennedy if she had to go back and go through this all over again.

O'Donnell's resolute attitude had intimidated the Dallas officials and they did nothing about it. O'Donnell added, however, that he "was in a highly desperate strait to get that airplane in the air and back to Washington." He was anxious about the possibility that the police might try to block the takeoff; "the difficulty of that to Mrs. Kennedy was incalculable," he hastened to explain.

There never was any complaint by the Texans, who kept quiet about their attempt to keep the body and their failure in that attempt. The episode thus attains the value of an example. Wasn't there a single person in the Justice Department willing to face Wade or Curry or Fritz as O'Donnell had faced Judge Brown?

Why didn't the Justice Department publicly demand that the Dallas authorities step aside and let federal justice take over?

Except for Telford Taylor's important contribution showing that Washington had legal as well as moral justification for making such a move, the question was hardly raised in the United States.

The American Civil Liberties Union, in a statement issued on December 5, 1963, brought up a number of points concerning Lee Harvey Oswald's rights. Much of the ACLU "white paper" dealt with "trial by television" and more generally with the responsibility of the press in the Dallas scandal. But the ACLU, most of whose leaders are lawyers, also asked some questions of immediate legal interest: "How much time elapsed before he was advised of his right to counsel? How much time elapsed before he was permitted access to a telephone to call his family and an attorney? During what periods and for how long was Oswald interrogated? What methods of interrogation were used? Was he advised of his right to remain silent?"

The crucial point, obviously, is that Oswald, at the time of his death two days after his arrest, still had no lawyer.

Passing in front of the TV cameras on Friday night, in the third-floor corridor of police headquarters, Oswald yelled that he wanted a lawyer and gave the name of John Abt of New York. After this incident (TV sometimes can be useful) a delegation of three lawyers from the Dallas chapter of the ACLU went the same night to the jail on the fourth floor of police headquarters. But the lawyers, the ACLU statement reported, "were informed by police officers and the justice of the peace before whom Oswald had been first arraigned that Oswald had been advised of his right to counsel and that he had declined to request counsel. Since the attorneys had not been retained by either Oswald or his family, they had no right to see the prisoner nor to give him legal advice."

A highly instructive discussion on the legal questions was broadcast over the CBS network on December 29, 1963. Several eminent jurists were on the program, including Paul Freund, a Harvard law professor specializing in constitutional law; Leon Douglas, state prosecutor in the Texas Court of Criminal Appeals; and Percy Foreman, president of the National Association of Defense Lawyers.

At the start of the program, moderator Dan Rather showed a photocopy of the official affidavit filed Friday night by Justice of the Peace David Johnston under the heading "The State of Texas vs. Lee Harvey Oswald." Everything was properly filled in: the charge ("Murder"); the name of the District Attorney ("Henry Wade"); even "Defendant's Address, City Jail." But next to the words "Defendant's Attorney" the line was blank.

None of the three legal experts (nor the fourth participant, Newton Minow, former chairman of the Federal Communications Commission, himself a lawyer) wondered whether, in a democracy, jail guards were qualified to say what a prisoner does or does not want.

Percy Foreman, however, did allude to the justice of the peace mentioned in the ACLU statement. "I wonder," he said, "if the justice of the peace didn't come down, if he did come at all, and walk in where the man was being questioned by some 15, 20, or 30 officers behind bars . . . suppose a justice of the peace is going to advise a man of his rights to have a lawyer, and there are around him 15 or 20 booted and hatted and pistoled officers, and that they constitute the audience, what effect is that going to have on the average man in such a condition?"

Foreman went further. He implied that even if Oswald had been duly informed of his right to legal assistance, and even if he really had "declined to request counsel," this was not a reason for questioning him without the presence of a lawyer. After all, Foreman remarked, the man might have been insane. Was he to be allowed to deprive himself of legal protection when his life was at stake?

The Warren Report devotes a page and a half to "Oswald's Legal Rights," attempting to persuade us that those rights were fully respected. Oswald, we are told, had only himself to blame if he had no lawyer with him from the time of his arrest and during the interrogations. The Commission rejects as "speculations" and "rumors" the accusations made against the Dallas police on this subject and offers its own "finding": "On November 23, Oswald was visited by the president of the Dallas Bar Association, H. Louis Nichols, who offered him help in getting a lawyer; Oswald refused the offer."

Did Oswald then believe he could get along without a lawyer? Not at all. One need only read the official text of Oswald's statement in what the Commission describes as "the Friday midnight press conference in the basement assembly room":

> *Oswald.*   Well, I was questioned by Judge——[Johnston]. However, I protested at that time that I was not allowed legal representation during that very short and sweet hearing. I really don't know what the situation is about. Nobody has told me anything except that I am accused of, of, murdering a policeman. I know nothing more than that and I do request someone to come forward to give me legal assistance.
>
> *Reporter.*   Did you kill the President?
>
> *Oswald.*   No. I have not been charged with that. In fact nobody has said that to me yet. The first thing I heard about it was when the newspaper reporters in the hall asked me that question.

All the Report finds to say about the last point is: "At this time Oswald had been arraigned only for the murder of Patrolman Tippit, but questioning by Captain Fritz and others had been substantially concerned with Oswald's connection with the assassination."

The Commission thus admits that at the time the Dallas authorities told the world that Oswald was officially accused of the assassination of President Kennedy, the accused himself had not been informed of the charges publicly leveled against him. None of the seven members of the Commission appeared disturbed by the irregularity of this procedure. They probably considered it a detail of no importance, a trifle of interest only to hair-splitters. To the practical minds of the Commission, "Oswald's legal rights" had been respected even though, contrary to law, he had not been informed of the charges made against him; after all, he should have guessed what he was suspected of from the questions he was asked.

The Commission makes no comment, either, on the strange timetable followed by the authorities that night.

Here is the statement of Captain Fritz as reproduced in the Report:

> After reviewing all of the evidence pertaining to the killing of President Kennedy . . . I signed a complaint before the District Attorney charging Oswald with the murder of President Kennedy. This was at 11:26 p.m. He was arraigned before Judge David Johnston at 1:35 a.m., November 23, 1963. Oswald was placed in jail about 12:00 midnight and brought from the jail for arraignment before Judge David Johnston at 1:36 a.m.

I will not quibble with Fritz about the arraignment that took place at 1:35, one minute before Oswald was taken before the judge; perhaps this was only a typing error and, besides, such a slight contradiction involving a difference of only one minute amounts to a rather favorable showing by Dallas criminological standards. But the Report, confirming that "Oswald was arraigned for the murder of President Kennedy before Justice of the Peace David Johnston on the fourth floor of the Police Department building at 1:35 a.m., November 23," also confirms the "midnight press conference." Here, then is the schedule of events: At 11:26, Fritz signs the complaint; around midnight, press conference in the basement, after which Oswald is taken to his cell; at 1:35, he is led from the cell to the justice of the peace. Wouldn't it have been more normal to arraign Oswald immediately after the complaint was signed—before presenting him to the press—and then leave him alone in his cell when the reporters were through with him?

It never occurred to the Commission, apparently, that the authorities might have deliberately set up the arraignment after the press conference so there would be no danger of his making too much of a protest in front of the newsmen. And the Commission is not concerned with a matter that troubled legal experts such as Percy Foreman: the conditions under which Oswald had been arraigned "on the fourth floor of the Police Department building at 1:35 a.m., November 23."

But what about the fundamental problem that the prisoner was deprived of legal assistance? The Commission, headed by the Chief Justice of the United States, considered itself free to dispose of it in a few lines. Yet the Report quotes from the midnight press conference, in which Oswald complained twice about his lack of counsel; it furthermore allows us to learn that he had constantly raised this question during his interrogation sessions.

Summing up his recollections for the Commission, FBI Agent James W. Bookhout wrote, for example, that Oswald "stated that he would not discuss the photograph [the one showing him holding a rifle—L.S.] without advice of an attorney." The statement by Secret Service Inspector Thomas J. Kelley, who attended the interrogation Saturday morning, is even more significant. The question of an attorney, in fact, comes up no less than three times. "He refused to answer any questions concerning the pistol or a gun until he talked to a lawyer," Kelley wrote. A few lines further he noted another statement by Oswald announcing that he would not answer questions "until he had been given counsel." Finally, Kelley told how he himself had asked Oswald if he had shot President Kennedy, then if he had shot Governor Connally. Oswald answered "no" to both questions and the Secret Service Inspector summed up the rest of Oswald's reply as follows: "He did not intend to answer further questions without counsel and that if he could not get Abt, then he would hope that the Civil Liberties Union would give him an attorney to represent him."

It seems unlikely, after all this, that any serious and respectable person could suggest that Oswald had no lawyer because he did not want one. But here is the final paragraph of the Report's section on "Oswald's Legal Rights":

> On Friday evening, representatives of the American Civil Liberties Union visited the police department to determine whether Oswald was being deprived of counsel. They were assured by police officials and Justice of the

Peace Johnston that Oswald had been informed of his rights and was being allowed to seek a lawyer. On Saturday Oswald attempted several times to reach John Abt, a New York lawyer, by telephone, but with no success. In the afternoon, he called Ruth Paine and asked her to try to reach Abt for him, but she too failed. Later in the afternoon, H. Louis Nichols, president of the Dallas Bar Association, visited Oswald in his cell and asked him whether he wanted the association to obtain a lawyer for him. Oswald declined the offer, stating a first preference for Abt and a second preference for a lawyer from the American Civil Liberties Union. As late as Sunday morning, according to Postal Inspector Harry D. Holmes, Oswald said that he preferred to get his own lawyer.

All the Commission finds relevant is that Oswald had rejected the offer made by Nichols. But that proved only that Oswald did not want an attorney picked by the Dallas bar. At the same time, it is quite evident that Oswald did want a lawyer, but *one of his own choice,* in accord with the right granted by law to any defendant.

The Dallas authorities denied Oswald this right, but the Commission has no criticism about that. It even rewrites, to make things easier, the "assurances" given by these authorities Friday night to the ACLU delegation. According to the Report, the explanation given to the delegation was that Lee Oswald, duly informed of his rights, "was being allowed to seek a lawyer." According to the ACLU statement of December 5, the delegation had been told that Oswald, duly informed of his rights, "had declined to request counsel." The Warren Commission thus covers up for the lie told by the Dallas police to the ACLU group.

In the absence of Abt, Oswald wanted a lawyer from the ACLU. The members of the ACLU delegation were not allowed to see Oswald, on the pretext that Oswald had not retained them. But Oswald could not retain them since they were prevented from seeing him. This is one of those artificial vicious circles that leave no doubt as to the bad faith of those who invent them.

Certainly the ACLU ought to have persisted that night and come back the following day. The way the local ACLU representatives allowed themselves to be intimidated by Captain Fritz, stepping aside without a protest, hardly inspires admiration. The fact is, however, that the Dallas authorities clearly did all they could to prevent Oswald from obtaining an ACLU lawyer as he desired. Saturday evening, for example, when the prisoner stated to the head of the Dallas bar his "second preference for a lawyer from the American Civil Liberties Union," the least the authorities could have done was to inform the local ACLU chapter—whose representatives they had thrown out the day before because Oswald "had declined to request counsel."

As early as December 5, the authors of the ACLU "white paper" were concerned with the question of whether the Commission under the chairmanship of Chief Justice Warren was going to grant Oswald—at least posthumously—the rights denied him in Dallas.

The ACLU document approved "wholeheartedly" the creation of the Commission, on the assumption that it "undoubtedly will concentrate on the facts of the assassination." It would also be in the public interest, the ACLU added, if the Commission were to undertake a "thorough examination of the treatment accorded Oswald." But the ACLU at the same time did not hide its reservations about the possibility of a completely fair "judicial or quasi-judicial inquiry" involving a dead defendant: "To hold an inquiry into the facts of the assassination in the absence of the individual charged with the crime presents the major objection that he is unable to provide his counsel with information bearing on his defense and the evidence against him. Evidence damaging on its face has, in other cases, been explained satisfactorily to jurors. No matter how scrupulously fair an inquiry now might be, there can be no substitute for the presence of the accused."

After this it might seem surprising that the ACLU did not formally insist that the Commission at least permit a representative of the accused to cross-examine witnesses and put forward whatever arguments might weaken the prosecution's case.

In stressing the "major objection" resulting from the absence of the accused without thereby opposing the Commission's existence, the ACLU seems to have expected that steps would be taken to remedy the situation as far as possible. Its statement clearly implies that it was better to have a lawyer as substitute for the accused than to have no defense at all. It is regrettable that the ACLU did not see fit to proclaim its opinion loudly instead of implying it.

The president of the National Association of Defense Lawyers was more explicit. Following is a transcript of his comments in the discussion televised on December 29, 1963:

> *Foreman.*   Actually, I think somebody should, in the interest of the public, not in the interest of Lee Oswald, but in the interest of the people of the United States, defend Lee Oswald before this commission.
>
> *Rather.*   You mean the Warren Commission?
>
> *Foreman.*   Right. The President has appointed, and properly, a group of men of unimpeachable integrity, who hold the respect of all of America because the President, as we all know, is concerned about—that the public know and have confidence in whatever facts are behind or applicable to this homicide.
>
> *Rather.*   What you're suggesting, then, is that Lee Oswald, the late Lee Oswald, have some sort of defense before the Commission?
>
> *Foreman.*   Absolutely. There's no other way, in my opinion, that the evidence in this case can be properly evaluated.

After Foreman made his proposal, Dan H. McCullough, former president of the Association, had the organization's board of directors adopt a resolution commending to the Commission the "wisdom" of appointing a lawyer to represent the late Lee Harvey Oswald. The resolution stated: "We believe the interests of justice will best be served if J. Lee Rankin appear as a Prosecutor or as a Postulator of the Cause and the counsel for Lee Harvey Oswald appear as Defense Counsel to the end that all evidence be submitted under the rules of evidence and that all evidence and witnesses be given the severest scrutiny in accordance with those rules which have found acceptance in our legal system. . . ."

In April 1964 I telephoned McCullough at his home in Toledo, Ohio, to ask how the Commission had reacted to this resolution of the National Association of Defense Lawyers. He replied that the appointment on February 25 of Walter Craig, president of the American Bar Association, as an "independent attorney" charged with defending Oswald's interests, appeared to be a direct reaction and the best possible response. "Our impression," he said, "is that the Commission in choosing Craig has done exactly what we had in mind. Obviously, since the hearings are secret, we have no way of knowing if the proceedings are now being conducted in a contradictory manner as we suggested. But we assume that was the reason for appointing Craig."

Professor Paul Freund, the teacher of many lawyers now in government service, had made a similar "assumption" in the course of the TV discussion, and this too eventually proved to have been wishful thinking.

Rather had asked him whether he agreed with Percy Foreman's idea that an attorney representing Oswald's interest should be appointed. Freund did not deny the importance of adversary proceedings, but he explained that in his opinion Rankin himself could fulfill the defense role: "I assume," he declared, "that the counsel and his staff who have been designated by the Warren Commission will have this very much in mind, and without the appointment of a so-called formal counsel for a deceased defendant, I would surely assume that what Mr. Foreman has in mind will actually be done, and done very conscientiously."

One month later, Earl Warren assured the world (in a handout from the U.S. Information Service) that the hearings were being conducted "as nearly like a judicial proceeding as possible, in decorum and for protection of the rights of witnesses."

Nobody wondered then why he insisted specifically on the rights of witnesses. How could anyone imagine that the Chief Justice meant to exclude from his "protection," if not from his "decorum," the rights of the accused? Apparently that indeed was his intention.

16

OSWALD AND THE TRUTH

I ASKED A NUMBER OF AMERICAN LAWYERS which of the rules of judicial procedure they considered most precious in the search for truth, and thus most indispensable for the administration of justice. They answered unanimously: the right of cross-examination or, more precisely, the right to put accusers on the spot. According to John Henry Wigmore, American authority on evidence, cross-examination is "beyond any doubt the greatest legal engine ever invented for the discovery of truth." Wigmore even added: "If we omit political considerations of broader range, then cross-examination, not trial by jury, is the great and permanent contribution of the Anglo-American system of law to improved methods of trial procedure." And yet a commission of inquiry, whose assignment was "to satisfy itself that the truth is known as far as it can be discovered," and whose chairman, the Chief Justice of the United States, had promised that hearings would be conducted "as nearly like a judicial proceeding as possible," took upon itself to banish cross-examination from its search as well as from its proceedings.

On January 14, 1964, Mrs. Marguerite Oswald announced that she was retaining New York attorney Mark Lane to represent her late son's interests before the Warren Commission.

For those who may not have noticed, I will now formally declare that I have nothing in common with either Mrs. Oswald or Mark Lane. As far as the latter is concerned, it soon became obvious that his unsupported statements, like the "scientific" arguments of Thomas Buchanan to which I will return later, offered exactly the kind of samples needed by Dallas to discredit the critics of its police and its District Attorney. One can get an idea of the

kind of "truth" Lane was after by noting that he asked the help
of the International Association of Democratic Jurists in Prague.
This organization, which is "democratic" in the same sense as
the East German Republic of Walter Ulbricht, had established
its own concept of "truth" by lending its support to Communist
charges such as the allegations about use of bacteriological weapons during the Korean War. I might add that Lane, who meanwhile had founded a "Citizen's Committee of Inquiry," furnished
with the usual "progressive" names, was dismissed by Mrs. Oswald
on April 1, 1964.

Still, for better or worse, Lane, in January, was the lawyer
chosen by Oswald's mother to defend her son's interests, and whatever personal objections there may have been regarding him, he
had a right to a place in the planned "quasi-judicial" proceedings.
But when he informed the Commission of the task he had been
given by Mrs. Oswald, he received the following reply from J. Lee
Rankin:

"The Commission does not believe that it would be useful or
desirable to permit an attorney representing Lee Harvey Oswald
to have access to the investigative materials within the possession
of the Commission or to participate in any hearings to be conducted by the Commission."

If Rankin really wrote this (the text was made public by Lane
in February 1964 and was never questioned), one can only recognize in it a statement of principle that does away with any vestige
of the confidence originally placed in the Commission's inquiry.
The Commission not only rejects any possibility of cross-examination; it contends that it would not be "useful or desirable" to
have a representative of the accused poking his nose into its files
or listening to its discussions. Did the Commission foresee that
it would have something to hide? Here it is, in any case, declaring
it useless and undesirable for a lawyer representing Oswald to
have a chance to examine critically the evidence on which it will
base its verdict. For it certainly is a verdict we are dealing with; in
the absence of a trial, we are expected—and invited—to take the
Commission's conclusions as the final word on the case.

Actually, J. Lee Rankin was reflecting the position adopted by

Warren himself on February 10, 1964, during Marguerite Oswald's appearance in Washington. The Chief Justice's stand can be seen in the following exchange, recorded in the Hearings:

"I implore you, I implore you in the name of my son, Lee Harvey Oswald, who is accused of assassinating the President, and I, the mother of this man, who is the accused's mother, be repre-sented by counsel," Marguerite Oswald pleaded. Warren replied that "the Commission is not here to prosecute your dead son," that "if Mr. Lane has any evidence of his own knowledge or has any accumulation of affidavits from others . . . he will have an opportunity to come here," but that "so far as his being here at all times before the Commission to cross-examine or to be present when all witnesses are testifying—that is not in accordance with the procedures of the Commission."

The Warren Commission thus adopted a much more extreme position than that envisaged at the beginning for the Texas "court of inquiry." Commenting on the investigation the state had planned (but later abandoned), Texas Attorney General Waggoner Carr had specified that if Oswald's wife or his mother chose a lawyer to defend his interests, this lawyer would be allowed to attend the hearings but would not automatically have the right of cross-examination; the decision on this would be left in each case to the presiding judge, Carr said.

In Washington, the presiding Chief Justice seemed to have settled the question at the very outset, once and for all. There was to be no lawyer for the defense, he decreed on January 27, when he announced the first witness. As we have seen, this first witness was Marina Oswald, who the day before had proclaimed on television: "I don't want to believe, but I have to watch facts, and facts tell me that Lee shot Kennedy." It was this witness whom Earl Warren intended to shelter from all cross-examination: Marina Oswald, whose credibility was nil as long as certain questions—such as the Secret Service "protection," for example— were not fully answered.

Then came the turning point of February 25, when, without giving the slightest explanation for this change of policy, Warren announced that he had asked Walter E. Craig to assume the functions of "independent lawyer" whose duty would be "examining every facet of the case pointing toward the involvement of Lee H. Oswald, in his absence, and in fairness to his family advise the Commission in that regard."

Had the chances improved for getting at the truth? This was the opinion of the *New York Post*, expressed in an editorial two days later:

> The only question that may be properly raised is whether the Commission should have initially refused to assign counsel to the accused dead man. But its readiness to admit and rectify an apparent error is another sign that Justice Warren will vindicate the country's confidence. We believe the inquiry he is conducting will unfold as much of the truth as conscientious men can obtain in circumstances of almost unprecedented complexity.

Nothing, however, could have authorized the *Post* to write that the Commission had shown "readiness to admit and rectify an apparent error." The definition of Craig's role as an "independent lawyer" attached to the Commission was rather vague and did not include any mention of cross-examination. The name of Walter E. Craig was heard no more, in the months that followed, in connection with the Commission's work—though it made news in a noisy dispute with Melvin Belli after the Ruby trial.

Even supposing that the Commission really wanted to "admit" some error, it was too late to "rectify" the most scandalous one of all: the interrogation of Marina Oswald without cross-examination. One could not imagine any other aspect of the case pointing more directly "toward the involvement of Lee H. Oswald, in his absence." If an "independent lawyer's" services were considered necessary on February 25, why not on February 3?

> In fairness to the alleged assassin and his family, the Commission on February 25, 1964, requested Walter E. Craig, president of the American Bar Association, to participate in the investigation and to advise the Commission whether in his opinion the proceedings conformed to the

basic principles of American justice. Mr. Craig accepted
this assignment and participated fully and without limi-
tation. He attended Commission hearings in person or
through his appointed assistants. All working papers, reports, and other data in Commission files were made available, and Mr. Craig and his associates were given
the opportunity to cross-examine witnesses, to recall any
witness heard prior to his appointment, and to suggest
witnesses whose testimony they would like to have the
Commission hear. This procedure was agreeable to counsel for Oswald's widow.

These few lines in the Foreword to the Report intend to give
the impression that the wrong had been atoned for, at least after
February 25. The impression is an illusion, and the intention a
fraud.

To begin with, this passage constitutes the one and only allusion in the Report to the person, mission, or activities of Walter
E. Craig. His activities, if not his person or mission, were so
negligible that the name of Craig, Walter E., does not even appear
in the index of the Report.

The reference, moreover, to Craig's "opportunity" to recall
witnesses heard before his appointment seemed designed to
counter the argument cited earlier that Marina Oswald was able
to identify, accuse, and condemn while guarded against any threat
—even a theoretical one—of cross-examination.

The widow-witness was called back to Washington later; but
this was only because the Commission wanted to hear her added
accusations against Oswald concerning Richard Nixon, and to
see if she could be made to replace the name of Nixon with that
of Johnson. If Marina had been recalled at Craig's request—to
give him a chance to ask her, for example, how she had recognized
the Mannlicher-Carcano in February—why would the Report
hide it?

The distressing conclusion that the paragraph in question is
there only to pull the wool over the reader's eyes is reinforced,
alas, by the brazen impudence of the final sentence.

For the casual reader, on whom the Report obviously relies, the fact that the Commission's methods were "agreeable to counsel for Oswald's widow" may represent a kind of moral assurance of impartiality and fairness concerning the accused. But the attentive reader knows that John M. Thorne was assigned to Marina Oswald, at least indirectly, by the Secret Service. He above all knows that by no stretch of the imagination could Marina be considered to represent the interests of her late husband. She was the star witness for the prosecution. Congressman Gerald R. Ford, Republican minority leader in the House, who was one of the seven members of the Commission, is certainly the only person in the world who would dare to write, as he did in his *Portrait of the Assassin:* "If anyone had a right to designate an attorney to represent Lee Oswald, it would not have been Marguerite but Lee's widow, Marina."

There is also, however, Louis Nizer. "One would think so!" he exclaimed in commenting on the statement that "this procedure was agreeable to counsel for Oswald's widow."

The renowned American lawyer was not trying to be sarcastic. He did not mean that any decision by the Commission must have been "agreeable" to Marina and her lawyer because they were in no position to refuse their agreement. Nizer's point was that the decision was so favorable to Oswald, so marvelously generous, that even those most attached to the moral interests of Lee Oswald could only be profoundly grateful to the Commission.

Louis Nizer, in fact, in the preface to one of the paperback editions of the Report, saw in Craig's appointment "an exquisite blend of thorough probing and preservation of the rights of the individual (including even the reputation of the accused slayer) in accordance with the great traditions of Anglo-American jurisprudence."

This opinion apparently was shared by the *New York Herald Tribune,* since this newspaper reprinted Nizer's incredible eulogy in full. My own opinion is that the Craig episode provided glaring proof of the Commission's lack of principles, if not of honesty.

In discovering three weeks after the start of the hearings the necessity for "fairness to the alleged assassin and his family," the

Commission abandoned its excuse that Oswald was not accused, was not the "alleged assassin," and therefore had no need to be defended. The Commission's effusive description of Craig's supposed functions reveals, furthermore, that it was perfectly aware there is no such thing as "fairness" without cross-examination of witnesses and contradictory examination of all items of evidence. Finally, if this passage of the Report, which seems to repudiate the previous statements of Earl Warren and J. Lee Rankin, represents a commitment of the Commission, the fact is this commitment was never fulfilled. So what is left of Nizer's "exquisite blend"?

I do not mean, of course, to question the personal integrity of the Commission members, above all that of its chairman, the Chief Justice. It is even particularly unpleasant for me to criticize an Earl Warren, who has played such an eminent role in the historic decisions against racial injustice, and who remains today the butt of the vilest attacks by American right-wingers. But as Marina Nikolaevna said from behind four Secret Service men: "I have to watch facts. . . ."

The Commission's press office had kindly furnished me, before publication of the Report, with a list of the witnesses who appeared during the first two months of the hearings, and the dates of their appearances. It is a document that points accusingly at the Commission, for it confirms that the Commission set out to learn not about the assassination but about Lee Oswald.

The first three witnesses were Marina Oswald (February 3–6), Marguerite Oswald (February 10–12), and Robert Oswald (February 20–22). None of these witnesses could possibly have given any significant direct information about the assassination of President Kennedy, nor helped to retrace the steps of the Dallas investigation or to draw the outline of a different line of inquiry. By devoting its first three weeks to listening to the widow, the mother, and the brother of Lee Oswald—that is, to witnesses whose essential contribution had to bear on the past, the habits, and the psychology of the alleged assassin—the Commission demonstrated that it took Oswald's guilt for granted and wanted to find out only why he had done it.

The corollary of this attitude was the secondary place given to the witnesses who could have provided information of value in establishing *who* had done it.

After devoting another full day (February 27) to James H. Martin, whose only link with the assassination was his Secret-Service-endorsed role as Marina's "business adviser," the Commission sat back and waited until March 11 to hear Wesley Frazier and his sister, Linnie Mae Randle, the only witnesses to have seen Oswald carrying the package on the morning of the assassination. It waited until March 24 to question Roy S. Truly, manager of the Texas School Book Depository, and the famous Bonnie Ray Williams, who held the key, it seemed, to the mystery of the chicken bones. Marrion L. Baker, the motorcycle officer who was the first policeman to enter the Depository Building and who had seen Oswald in the lunchroom, was finally interrogated on March 25, seven weeks after Marina. The Commission, in a hurry by this time, gave him only a minimum amount of time, since it had four other witnesses before it the same day. One of these four, also speedily dispatched, was M. N. McDonald, the patrolman who had arrested Oswald at the Texas Theater and had given several contradictory accounts of that episode.

The Commission's own official statements confirmed the deductions suggested by a mere glance at the witness list.

On February 12, at the end of the third and last day of Mrs. Marguerite Oswald's testimony, newsmen heard Earl Warren (some didn't believe their ears, but their notebooks attest to it) publicly evaluate the significance of the officially secret testimony: "She has not given us any facts that would change the picture as we knew it up to the time she testified." And who had painted the picture that Warren knew as of February 12? Marina Oswald was the only witness he had heard before the mother; he could not have meant that her deposition, prepared under the auspices of the Secret Service and necessarily limited to certain aspects of the case, had given even an approximate picture of the events.

According to the U.S. Information Service, Warren had declared earlier that he was "concerned with developing the facts as best we can." But, according to his declaration of February 12, he accepted as established fact the conglomeration of contradictory information whose unconvincing "picture" had made the Commission necessary.

The Commission's state of mind was to be definitively displayed less than two weeks later, in the official announcement of Craig's appointment. Apparently afraid this might be interpreted as a reflection of possible doubts about Oswald's guilt, the Commission hastened to emphasize that it did not question "the reasonableness of the action of the authorities in charging Oswald." This is why I did not feel the need to wait for the Report before commenting on "the Oswald affair" as early as March of 1964.

There is one incident in particular that I wish could be ignored, in view of Earl Warren's major role as Chief Justice of the United States.

During Marina's second day of questioning on February 4, Warren made a statement to newsmen, which the A.P. summed up as follows: "All of the testimony will be preserved for the public, but if there is anything that touches on national security, it may remain secret for decades, 'and I say that seriously.' " The A.P. story contained another quotation: "The secret deposition of Mrs. Marina Oswald on events preceding the assassination of President Kennedy 'might not be made public in your lifetime,' Justice Warren revealed. The White House declined comment on his statement."

The idea had apparently preoccupied Warren since the day before. A *New York Times* story dated February 3 said that the Chief Justice, "in discussing the general point of whether the testimony received by the Commission will be made public," had replied, "Yes, the time will come, but it may not be in your lifetime. I am not referring to anything in particular, but there could be certain things touching on security matters. These would be preserved but not published."

On February 5, after his remarks had stirred some concern (commentators concluded that Marina had given evidence of Oswald's involvement in espionage, a logical deduction but one that did not please the authorities), Warren called the reporters together and explained politely that in using the phrase "not in your lifetime" he was only being "a little facetious." But he repeated that some findings might very well remain secret: "Oswald's trips to Russia and more recently to Mexico could involve security questions, and in this case we might not make these matters public in our Report."

One can only deduce from this that Warren did not rule out the possibility that Oswald had been an American agent, or a Soviet agent, or both, and that if such evidence were to come out in the inquiry, the Commission would carefully keep such findings from the public. In other words, we were warned officially on February 5 that the Warren Commission could not be counted on to tell the whole truth.

The White House had announced on November 29, 1963, that President Johnson had instructed the Commission to "report its findings and conclusions to him, to the American people and to the world." There was no mention of two different reports, one for President Johnson and the other for the American people and the world. When the Chief Justice himself, moreover, formally promised, according to the USIS, that "whatever is said and done before the Commission will be preserved for the public," he did not give the impression of reserving the right to distinguish between "preserve for" and "communicate to." But the National Archives in Washington confirmed in December 1964 that some of the Commission records deposited in its vaults would not be opened to the public for 75 years.

As to the sense of humor that Earl Warren said he was trying to display at the time, it would be better not to discuss that lest we be led to wonder, with the *New York Daily News,* "what there is in the Oswald case to be facetious about."

17

OSWALD AND THE PRESS

THE LANGUAGE OF AMERICAN JOURNALISM includes an assortment of adjectives and adverbs whose function, legally and morally, is to protect the American journalist against both legal action and his own conscience. Murderer, swindler, sex fiend, anyone charged with a crime, even if he is caught in the act, has the right to the adjective "alleged" until he has been duly convicted. The use of such additional terms as "reportedly" allows the newspapers to show they take no responsibility for the statements but limit themselves to printing what the authorities allege or report.

These are alibi terms, of course, a hypocritical way of alleging and reporting without assuming responsibility. But hypocrisy, we all know, is the tribute paid by vice to virtue. Taught in the journalism schools, drilled into beginning reporters, these solidly rooted formulas make up part of the professional tradition of the American press. When they disappeared almost entirely in the accounts of the Oswald case, it was all the more significant.

The mass of police statements on November 22 and 23 had conditioned journalistic minds to the point that, as early as Sunday morning, many papers had dropped the "alleged" before "assassin" when naming Oswald. On the day after Jack Ruby fired his shot, it became the rule. The *Columbia Journalism Review,* which devoted an entire issue to the role of the press in Dallas, gave a particularly good example in two headlines of the *Fort Worth Star-Telegram.* The early-edition headline, "SUSPECT OSWALD SLAIN IN DALLAS," became in later editions "JFK ASSASSIN SLAIN."

The *New York Times* was led into this practice along with the others, but I believe it was the only newspaper to recognize its mistake. It did so, however, in a way that tended to reduce the significance of the correction and thereby diminished the elegance of the gesture.

The *Times* on that Monday found itself in an embarrassing position. "PRESIDENT'S ASSASSIN SHOT TO DEATH," an eight-column banner on page one declared. Inside, a lead editorial admonished the Dallas authorities for having declared Oswald guilty of a crime he was only "alleged" to have committed, without waiting for the verdict of a jury. A Brooklyn reader soon pointed out the contradiction, in a letter to the editor: "Unfortunately, your editorial was outflanked by your front-page headline which accepted as fact the Dallas officials' allegations, screaming across the entire front page, 'President's Assassin Shot to Death.' At least 10 times as many viewers see your headlines and it is to be hoped that the lesson of your editorial will be reflected in future headlines."

The Brooklyn reader's letter, in the November 27 issue, was followed in the same column by another letter signed by Turner Catledge, managing editor of the *Times:* "The *New York Times* erred, in news reports published on Monday, in referring to Lee Harvey Oswald as 'President Kennedy's Assassin.' Although Oswald was accused of the assassination and the Dallas police thought they had an air-tight case against him, he was never tried and convicted. Under the American system of justice, he is innocent until proved guilty. Future articles and headlines will reflect that fact."

Such a rectification, a credit to the managing editor, would also have been a credit to his newspaper if the *Times* had printed his statement as an editorial or at least as an editor's note attached to the Brooklyn reader's letter. But in spite of the fact that the last sentence obviously committed the newspaper to the position of the man who had signed it, the Catledge letter was presented not as an editor's note but as just another letter from a reader; in fact it was even addressed (and mailed?) "To the Editor of The New York Times."

The *Times*, in any case, kept the promise of its managing editor. It even pushed this principle to the point of referring to Ruby, whose crime was witnessed by millions, as the "alleged" assassin of Lee Harvey Oswald until the time Ruby was convicted.

Other newspapers and newsmen did not feel the need for such restraint. I mentioned earlier the arrogant style of *Life* magazine, but one could find a similar arrogance in the liberal *New York Post*. On November 29, for instance, the usually gentle and modest Harry Golden wrote in his column: "The assassin, Lee Harvey Oswald, killed the President to satisfy his own sense of importance, and the man who killed Oswald was jealous and wanted to make himself an equally important figure." Thus all is explained, and it does not occur to Golden, who speaks with such certainty about others' sense of importance, that in offering his theory as absolute truth he does not show much humility himself. Another *Post* columnist, Max Lerner—who previously had ridiculed the "fantasy world" of the "amateur investigators"—wondered on February 7 "how a mind worked that directed a shot equally at Gen. Walker and at John F. Kennedy." Given the stature of the author of *America as a Civilization,* it is regrettable to be forced to ask in turn how a mind works that accepts and repeats, without qualms or reluctance, such an unproved and unbelievable affirmation.

It was the *Daily News,* with which the *Post* would not like to be identified, that added the final touch to the lamentable exhibition offered by the American press. The *Daily News,* in a February 1964 editorial, sneered because "Oswald is still delicately called by some the 'accused assassin.' " It's too bad that so few newspapers deserved such a sneer.

While most newspapers and all television news programs were carried away by the tide and transformed it into a torrent, the source of it was neither press nor television. Their fault, essentially, was in leaving out the qualifying elements and failing to ask questions when they published statements of authorities considered responsible. This may indeed represent a kind of complicity or at least negligence on their part, but the real culprits were the authorities themselves. Where TV was concerned, if Oswald's rights and American dignity were to be preserved, it would have been necessary to take the microphones away from Curry and Fritz and cut off the power two minutes after Wade began his Sunday-night press conference. It seems to me that there is something wrong in a situation—and in a country—when press and television can respect the law only by censuring the authorities responsible for applying it.

The Dallas police chief and the District Attorney tried to justify the turmoil later by talking about the crowds of reporters, and it is true that more than once in those tragic days the phrase "mob of newsmen" meant just that. But it would be false to contend, as some did, that the authorities' eagerness to submit to the mob's requirements was the price paid for freedom of the press.

There were some who talked of a "dilemma" and learnedly weighed the constitutional pros and cons of individual rights versus freedom of the press. The dilemma is artificial. No serious journalist in Washington believes freedom of the press is infringed when the Pentagon spokesman says "no comment" in reply to an indiscreet question, or when the Secretary of State does not invite him to sit in on his talks with the Soviet ambassador. Nor, I believe, would anyone have talked seriously about freedom of the press in Dallas if Oswald had been moved from one jail to another in secrecy, or even if Jesse Curry had refused to allow reporters and TV crews to station themselves permanently outside his door. The Dallas authorities are in the position of the lady of easy virtue who complains of rape and is asked by the judge, "Did you try to say no?"

While the "officers of the law" tried to evade responsibility for their irresponsibility by making charges against the press, no one in Texas ever thought of making any charges against the "officers of the law."

The Dallas County Criminal Bar Association issued a statement on November 27 expressing "full confidence in the integrity and devotion to duty of Chief Curry and the men who serve under him." One might have believed for a moment, at the beginning of December, that things were going to change; suddenly we learned that a grievance committee of the Texas State Bar had summoned Tom Howard, Ruby's first lawyer, and District Attorney Wade, requesting their appearance on December 5. According to the *Times*, "the grievance committee planned to discuss the propriety of public statements made by the lawyers, particularly Mr. Wade." The session lasted three hours. When it ended, the committee chairman read a statement that first of all emphasized that "District Attorney Henry Wade was before the committee only as an invited witness." After which the guardians of Texas legal ethics hastened to proclaim: "The committee has no charges against Mr. Wade and in no manner criticizes any conduct or action on his part."

To help define the respective contributions of newsmen and public officials toward the establishment of the truth, it might be useful to cite here a specific example of what happened when reporters were able to check on some statements made by the Dallas D.A.

In the course of his press conference summing up the "proofs" against Oswald, Wade made the following statements, as recorded on tape and transcribed by the *Times:*

> *Wade.*   The next we hear of him is on a bus where he got on a bus at Lamar Street, told the bus driver the President had been shot, the President. (He) told the lady—all this was verified by statements—told the lady on the bus that the President had been shot. He said, "How did he know." He said a man back there told him. The defendant said, "Yes, he's been shot," and laughed very loud.
>
> *Reporter.*   This was to a lady?
>
> *Wade.*   A lady. He then—the bus, he asked the bus driver to stop, got off at a stop, caught a taxicab driver, Darryl Click. . . .

The D.A. had said enough to allow reporters to follow up his lead. Several did so, including two from the *Dallas Morning News,* who found their information contrary to Wade's statements and tried to smooth it over by making veiled allusions to "sketchy reports released by law enforcement sources earlier." But they were able to establish the true facts, which were as follows:

(1) Oswald took the bus at Griffin Street, not Lamar Street.
(2) He said nothing to the bus driver, C. J. McWatters, nor to

any woman on the bus. (3) The driver learned of the assassination from a passerby in the street when the bus was held up in the traffic jam near the Depository Building. (4) Oswald did not laugh, "very loud" or otherwise. (5) He got off the bus together with another passenger, not at a bus stop but when the bus was halted in traffic. (6) Before getting off, he asked the driver for a transfer ticket, a detail strangely omitted by Wade; it was the transfer with its distinctive punch mark that enabled the police to trace McWatters and his bus. (7) The taxi driver who picked up Oswald was Bill Whaley, not Darryl Click.

The Warren Report, criticizing Wade's "lengthy formal press conference," stresses in an equally formal and lengthy manner— two quotations with narrative and comment, then some repetition and related remarks—that Wade was innocent of the seventh error above: The Commission had found after listening to the tape that Wade had said "Oak Cliff," not "Darryl Click."

Concerning the other errors, the Report admits there was little to praise in the D.A.'s press conference: "Unfortunately, at that time, as he subsequently testified, he lacked a thorough grasp of the evidence and made a number of errors." But the Commission rejects all "insinuations that Dallas police officials and District Attorney Henry M. Wade fabricated or altered evidence to establish the guilt of Oswald." Such insinuations were "baseless," it declares.

The Commission's brief annoyance with the Dallas investigators is due mainly to the fact that they contributed to the doubts the Commission is trying to dispel.

> Though many of the inaccuracies were subsequently corrected by the police and are negated by findings of the Commission included elsewhere in this report, the publicizing of unchecked information provided much of the basis for the myths and rumors that came into being soon after the President's death. The erroneous disclosures became the basis for distorted reconstructions and interpretations of the assassination. The necessity for the Dallas authorities to correct themselves or to be corrected by other sources gave rise not only to criticism of the police department's

competence but also to doubts regarding the veracity of
the police. Skeptics sought to cast doubt on much of the
correct evidence later developed and to find support for
their own theories in these early police statements.

Since the Commission's criticism is aimed less at the "inaccuracies" (to use the Report's indulgent term) than at the fact they
were publicized and at the interpretations to which they led, the
Report does not spare press and television, responsible for the
publicity and the interpretations.

The first sentence of the section "Responsibility of News Media"
still blames the authorities: "While appreciating the heavy and
unique pressures with which the Dallas Police Department was
confronted by reason of the assassination of President Kennedy,
primary responsibility for having failed to control the press and
to check the flow of undigested evidence to the public must be
borne by the police department." But the next paragraph begins
to re-establish the equilibrium: "The Commission believes, however, that a part of the responsibility for the unfortunate circumstances following the President's death must be borne by the news
media." When the Report arrives at a discussion of what happened
Sunday morning in the basement of police headquarters, press and
police are rebuked equally: "The Commission believes that the
news media, as well as the police authorities, who failed to impose
conditions more in keeping with the orderly process of justice,
must share responsibility for the failure of law enforcement which
occurred in connection with the death of Oswald."

Taking everything into account, the truth is that most reporters
performed their job better than the District Attorney did his. If
the American press nevertheless disconcerted foreign observers, it
was probably for two main, related reasons.

One reason was a consequence of the "split personality" imposed on the reporter by American journalistic tradition, demanding that he separate himself into the man who observes and reports
and the man who thinks and evaluates. A European reader—a
French one above all—could not help taking this discipline, which
requires the exclusion of personal reactions, as a kind of indiffer-

ence if not stupidity. Personally, I don't see why it should be necessary for a reporter to limit himself to reproducing dispassionately everything said or done as if nothing affected him, leaving all comment to the editorial writers. In the Dallas affair especially —and this was the second reason for European disappointment— the editorial writers were always behind the news. There were some who never caught up.

Having reduced themselves to the level of distributing machines and amplifiers and failing to question, analyze, and criticize that which they distributed and amplified, the American press and television rapidly created a situation that, the American Civil Liberties Union said in its December 5 statement, "made it simply impossible for Oswald to have received a fair trial on any of the charges against him."

The ACLU statement referred to a Supreme Court decision handed down six months earlier, reversing a murder conviction in Louisiana because a local TV station had broadcast an "interview" before the trial, between the defendant and the sheriff, in which the accused killer had admitted the crime. The Supreme Court had ruled: "Any subsequent court proceedings in a community so pervasively exposed to such a spectacle could be but a hollow formality." And a hollow formality is what the Oswald trial would have been, the ACLU declared: "Where in Dallas, or anywhere in the state or nation for that matter, could there be found twelve citizens who had not formed a firm and fixed opinion that he was guilty?"

The ACLU even saw an "ironic note" in the likely consequences of the "vast publicity in which the law enforcement officers participated": "If Oswald had lived to stand trial and were convicted, the courts would very likely have reversed the conviction because of the prejudicial pre-trial publicity. Thus, the spectacular publicity in which the officials took part would likely have defeated them in the end."

In their television discussion of December 29, Percy Foreman and Professor Freund expressed similar preoccupations and conclusions. Foreman said that Oswald, because of the "undue publicity," would not have been able to obtain more than a "mock

trial" that would have "degraded" the court. Freund declared he
did not believe it could be "a sound and rational trial in the sense
of the standards we've set for ourselves." As to knowing "how
much of a mockery it would have been," Freund said much de-
pended on "the remote possibility of finding twelve good men and
women who for some reason, perhaps because they had been under
hospital surgery that very weekend, had not been part of the
American public at that time."

Americans do have a rather extreme concept of the required
impartiality of jurors; foreign correspondents who sat through the
selection of the jury in the Ruby trial marveled at the procedure.
It seemed to them that the perfect juror would be the village idiot
who never read a newspaper, never listened to the radio or
watched TV (except for soap operas), was uninterested in what
went on around him, including the assassination of his President,
and never exchanged an idea with a neighbor, or even a bit of
gossip with his barber.

To remedy the fortunate shortage of such "citizens" even in the
United States, and to avoid having to recruit jurors exclusively
from a roster of patients emerging from anaesthesia, the most
simple solution would seem to be to seek jurors who are not badly
informed, rather than jurors who are not informed at all. This
idea apparently has not occurred to anyone. The *Columbia Journalism Review* thus offers without comment the case of a TV
network executive who, it says, "confessed to an impulse, when he
heard the statements of Dallas officials condemning Oswald, to
cut them off the air. He resisted the impulse, he says, because he
knew the competition would continue to carry the statements."
He might have partially corrected the situation that so under-
standably shocked him by assigning a commentator to stress the
premature character of such declarations and to analyze the weaknesses and contradictions in them.

In support of "a set of ethics or ground rules or principles
agreed upon between the press, the broadcasting medium and the
courts," Newton Minow remarked on the December 29 TV program that, "as it is now, the worst competitor in the news business
sets the standard." The former FCC chairman went on: "The

fellow who has the least amount of respect for integrity or self-discipline or self-restraint is the one who sets the norm because all the others are degraded down to his level." There is, moreover, the competition between individuals added to the competition between organizations, dehumanizing the journalist who ends up seeing in the greatest tragedies nothing more than the occasion for a professional triumph.

To me it seems especially unfortunate, in this regard, that the study prepared under the auspices of the Columbia University School of Journalism dealt so lightly with certain questions of personal and professional ethics as displayed in the light of the Dallas events.

The *Columbia Journalism Review* effort was billed as "a case study in the reflexes and conscious actions of professional journalists under the heaviest kind of pressure and emotional stress." But it did not comment on some of the actions and reflexes described in the study. One example: A veteran wire-service reporter, lucky enough to be sitting next to a radio telephone in a White House press car a short distance behind the President's limousine, dictated his flash while ducking under the dashboard "to avoid the blows" of the rival wire-service man, who tried in vain to get the phone from him, "clawing and pummeling."

The same reporter—who later received a Pulitzer Prize as his reward—relates himself how he commandeered a telephone at Parkland Hospital by barking at an employee: "The President has been hurt and this is an emergency call." I would not think that in a hospital the desire to beat the competition qualified as an "emergency." But perhaps I am a poor reporter, and I shall receive no Pulitzer Prize.

Far from discussing these questions, the Columbia study finds in the press behavior of November 22 "evidence that American journalism is developing a firmness of style, a sureness in taste that will enhance its reputation and value." At most it mentions "a few sour notes" and wonders in passing if journalism might "do anything more on its own to avoid possible infringements on individual rights." Except for that, "there has been well-earned praise in plenty for all branches of journalism," and "the *Review* joins this praise."

Charles T. Duncan, dean of the University of Colorado School of Journalism and former president of the Association for Education in Journalism, went even further. He issued a statement congratulating the American news media for a "superb performance throughout these black hours of shock and grief" and for their "unprecedented standard of professional competence and maturity." He expressed the opinion that the media "carried out their bitter but inescapably necessary task with such thoroughness, speed, accuracy and, withal, dignity and reverence as to renew and reaffirm public confidence in them."

One might ignore Duncan's enthusiasm with an indulgent shrug if his former and present duties were not of a nature to arouse some concern about the future. The attitude of the Columbia journalism school, as expressed in the *Columbia Journalism Review,* is not very reassuring, either, despite the respect inspired by the character of its dean, Edward W. Barrett. But these causes of worry were soon eclipsed by the appalling exhibition of conformity that the American press revealed to the world in its treatment of the Warren Report.

For some liberal newspapers and newsmen, a prime reason for their devout approval was the desire to support Earl Warren, the favorite target of the right-wing rabble. Nothing could be more significant, in this connection, than the September 28, 1964, article in the *New York Post* by its former editor, James Wechsler.

Wechsler frankly titled his piece "To Earl Warren." Although he claimed to have read the Report, he left to the editorial page the duty of celebrating its "penetrating research," its "massive documentation," its "thorough investigation," and "clear presentation." Wechsler's column goes beyond any rational pretexts, even though to satisfy his professional conscience he offers one or two of these in passing. It is an expression of personal devotion, an act of faith. Here, in fact, is why James Wechsler was convinced by the Warren Report:

What conceivable consideration could have induced Earl
Warren to sign this report if he had any real reservations
about its validity? What personal or political stake could
have inspired him to act as "front man" for any form of
whitewash or any rewriting of history? He is beyond political ambition. He is widely revered. His place in history is
already large. Only the Birchers and their frenzied associates brand him an enemy of the nation; if there were the
faintest substance to the theory of "right-wing conspiracy,"
Warren could only have been a beneficiary of such disclosure; his most violent critics would have been exposed
as assassins. What possible advantage could he derive from
absolving all branches of the lunatic right as well as all
varieties of the Marxist set from involvement in the assassination? One need hardly contend that he is infallible; but
it seems almost an indignity to affirm that he is incorrupt-
ible. Yet that must be said because the world air has been
so dismally poisoned during the long months in which he
has conducted the inquiry.

Everything Wechsler wrote about Earl Warren's character is
true, certainly, but he forgot the historical precedents in which
equally respected men took part in unjust actions because they
believed this would serve their country. In any case, does Wechsler
establish a principle that a journalist has to accept an argument
that appears to be false simply because it bears the signature of
an eminent man?

On the side of the less "liberal" press, the accent was placed on
the virtues of the investigation and the qualities of the Report
rather than on Earl Warren's personality. The *New York Journal-
American* had published some pertinent and even insidious questions during the investigation, mainly under Dorothy Kilgallen's
byline. But when the Report came out, there was room in the
Journal-American only for pure adulation: "The Warren Commission Report is a magnificent masterpiece of soundly reasoned
judgment. It is clear, judicial, calm and meticulous in its determi-
nations. All persons capable of restrained consideration of facts,
and of discarding conjecture based on spectacular rumor, will

accept the conclusion inevitably reached by the seven eminent Americans who with superb achievement realize their purpose: TRUTH."

Between the *Post* and the *Journal-American,* the *Times,* widely regarded as the best newspaper in the world, took a position that seemed to be more unacceptable than the other two put together.

The issue of September 28, with a special 48-page section containing much of the text of the Report, led off with James Reston's less than enthusiastic analysis on page one. "The central mystery of who killed the President has been answered by the Commission only in the process of raising a new catalogue of mysteries," Reston wrote amid some rather skeptical philosophical considerations on the theme that the Commission allowed "many vital questions" to remain. The *Times* editorial also showed a distinct tendency to veer from the general line. The first sentence duly qualified the Report as "convincing," but this was followed by a series of criticisms in which parts of the Report were labeled "curious," "of little value," and even "worthless." While declaring that the Commission had established an "admirable standard in the quest for truth," the *Times* expressed the view that, contrary to the official opinion that the case was closed, "their report in no way precludes others from investigating this tragedy."

A few days later, however, the tone had changed. A single example will show the extent of this change.

On October 3, in a Washington story based on reports from the U.S. Information Agency, Max Frankel noted that the conclusions of the Commission had inspired "widespread skepticism and outright disbelief in many newspapers throughout the world." Citing the USIA, the *Times* story said the opinions differed "not only between the political left and right in various countries but also from country to country," and that except for the Communist and pro-Communist press "papers tended to follow country rather than party lines." It reported that the negative view was predominant in France and, to a lesser degree, in Belgium and Austria; that doubts remained in Latin America; that there was skepticism in Japan and "doubt about the effectiveness of the Commission's argument" in the Philippines; that there were question marks in the headlines of "many Greek papers," etc.

The following day, however, the *Times* introduced a review of the world press reaction to the Report with the following observation: "Abroad, the findings were agreed with or questioned largely on the basis of right or left wing attitudes. . . ."

Thus contradicting the USIA as well as its own story of the day before, the *Times* now had only to choose the press quotations according to this new angle. This it did. Twelve foreign papers were quoted, among which only four were decidedly unfavorable to the Commission. All four, without exception, were Communist newspapers, carefully identified as such. The Japanese skepticism mentioned by Frankel was represented exclusively by the official Communist organ, *Akahata;* the negative attitudes dominant in France were illustrated by *L'Humanité;* and all Italian or Swedish criticism had its outlets in *L'Unità* and *"Ny Dag,* Stockholm (Communist)."

And yet the *Times* has always condemned McCarthyism.

18

OSWALD
AND THE MATHEMATICIAN

THE "BUCHANAN REPORT," much discussed in Europe, began appearing in the Paris weekly *L'Express* on February 20, 1964. I stress the date to show that I owe no apologies to Max Lerner, whose tirade against "amateur investigators" appeared more than two months before that. Lerner criticized the foreign critics of the investigation for "feeding the rapidly changing speculations from their fantasy world to millions of eager readers whose worst hostilities and fears about America are being confirmed." If Lerner had read the *L'Express* articles before writing this, I would have said he had perfectly understood Thomas Buchanan, if not Buchanan's eager readers.

Like Chester Himes, whose contribution to the confusion I pointed out earlier, Thomas Buchanan was an American in Paris. Françoise Giroud, coeditor of *L'Express,* introduced him, in presenting "The True Story of the Assassination," as "a very quiet American, 44 years old, a sensitive novelist, an artillery captain during the war, and a mathematician in charge of computer programming in a large firm in Paris." Then, before quoting an anonymous American publisher to the effect that no one could possibly refute his "brilliant argument," Mme. Giroud summed up and evaluated this argument as follows:

"Thomas Buchanan, scientific by training and by inclination, has gathered the facts, and it is strictly on the basis of the facts that he has undertaken a concise argument whose logical development is impressive."

The "Buchanan Report" assumes there were two assassins, iden-

243

tified as Assassin Number 1 and Assassin Number 2. The mathematician of *L'Express* does not say whether his choice of numbers reflects a hierarchy of values or a random selection, but he does inform us that numbers do not signify a chronological order: "The first shot," he tells us, "was fired by Assassin Number 2." While Assassin Number 1 surveyed the motorcade from the Depository Building, Assassin Number 2 was stationed on the railroad overpass ahead of the President. This theory had been suggested as early as December 1963 by Richard Dudman. Thomas Buchanan, who reasons "strictly on the basis of the facts," brought to it a previously unknown "fact," in the form of a regret: "It is regrettable," he wrote, "that Assassin Number 2 was only seen from behind, just before he disappeared, by the policeman who climbed up the embankment to the overpass immediately after the last shot."

Richard Dudman had based his theory of a second gunman not on alleged "witnesses" but on his reasoning about the number of bullets and the nature of the wounds. Even if Buchanan's policeman only glimpsed Assassin Number 2 from behind, he transformed the theory into a reality. What is therefore regrettable above all is that Buchanan believed he could settle the question in a single sentence without bothering to tell us why this Dallas policeman, after scaling the bridge, went on to Paris to inform Buchanan—and Buchanan alone—of what he had seen.

The following week *L'Express* published a story cabled by Buchanan from Dallas, where he had finally gone to look things over *after* describing them. There was no further mention of the policeman who unfortunately had seen only the assassin's back, nor of the assassin's back in general: "If the assassin [back included —L.S.] had been seen and if police had started to chase him, his pursuers would have had to scale a high wire fence which only a skilled athlete could have climbed before the first assassin [Buchanan means Assassin Number 2, by the numbering in *L'Express*—L.S.] disappeared in the warehouse on the other side."

Was Buchanan's policeman, then, a skilled athlete? The answer was later given by Buchanan himself in the original French edition of his book, *Who Killed Kennedy?* "A policeman *tried* to climb up the embankment at the overpass in the direction of the rail-road tracks but he was *stopped* by a high metal fence. . . ." (Italics mine.) Since the policeman did not succeed in his attempt, Buchanan's previous statement that he had "climbed up the embank-ment" was false, and the statement that Assassin Number 2 had been seen from the back before disappearing was also false. Buchanan therefore had nothing to regret, but he had not proved any-thing either, except for the gratuitousness of his statements.

Buchanan had consoled himself in his February 27 article, add-ing after his regrets: "There is one witness, however, who could have seen the gunman on the overpass. Perhaps he could even identify him. This witness is Jack Ruby."

What are the facts gathered on this point by the man who undertakes his "concise argument" strictly on the basis of the facts? Here they are: "Ruby was in the *Dallas Morning News* building. . . . In fact he was alone in a room looking out on both the Depository Building and the railroad overpass. . . . If Ruby, at this time, looked out the window, he must have seen the shot. . . ." If Ruby was able to have "seen the shot," that still would not explain how he could "perhaps even identify" the gun-man, since the author has taken care to tell us a page earlier that the overpass "is protected by a long wall behind which it is easy to hide from sight." But then Buchanan's field is mathematics, not optics.

In his story from Dallas the same Buchanan, however, seemed on the point of preparing another "proof" that would give Ruby a much more important role than that of a mere and faraway "eyewitness." For he had discovered that Assassin Number 2, if he fled in the right direction, needed "only two or three minutes" to "simply cross the street and disappear into the offices of the *Dallas Morning News,* the only building nearby." Would Assassin Number 2 then be Jack Ruby himself?

This in fact was the hypothesis suggested by Richard Dudman in *The New Republic* when he pointed out that, while Ruby was with the advertising staff at the *Dallas Morning News* before the shooting, and the employees found him in their office when they returned later, there was nobody in the room at the time of the assassination—and nobody could testify to Ruby's presence at that time. Novelist Chester Himes, we may recall, took the "reasoning" of Captain Fritz literally and "evacuated" the Depository Building. Confusing one department of the *Morning News* with the entire newspaper, mathematician Buchanan now evacuates the *Morning News* building for his purposes: It was, he writes in his book, "almost completely deserted because all the employees had gone outside to watch the motorcade go by."

As a matter of fact many employees had remained in the building, including those behind the counters in the lobby, the elevator operators, etc. Why then does Buchanan find it necessary to move out all the employees? Because the assassin then would have been able to "catch his breath, compose himself and find a valid reason to justify his presence in the building."

One could readily conclude from this that the assassin on the overpass was indeed Jack Ruby, whose "valid reason"—revision of an ad for his club—is already known. But the next sentence in Buchanan's book opens this to question. "What makes this hypothesis very interesting is the fact that Jack Ruby was in the *Morning News* building at that time." If Buchanan wants to emphasize "at that time," it could mean that Ruby had just arrived, and thus that he was the assassin. But if he means that Ruby was *already* there, and thus that he could not be the assassin, how would his presence in the building make the theory "very interesting"? Did Jack Ruby, if he was not the assassin, have anything to do with the breathing or composure of whoever was the assassin, and what valid excuse did he help find for *him?*

We arrive now at the second gunman, whom *L'Express* labels Assassin Number 1, after a brief interlude in which he is described as Accomplice Number 1. (The book rearranged the numbering system; it began by reversing the identification numbers of the assassins.)

Buchanan first details the nature of the relations between Assassin Number 1 and Lee Oswald, identified now as Accomplice Number 1: "He [the assassin] entered the Depository between the time it closed the night before and the time it opened the morning of the murder. He brought a snack with him. He gave

Oswald the task of bringing the rifle into the building, since Oswald would be less likely to attract attention arriving with a large package." This, at least, is what Buchanan saw on February 27 in the crystal ball he took for an electronic brain. When he looks into it again in his *L'Express* article of March 5, the vision is a bit clouded and the image summoned forth again gives a slightly different picture of the respective actions of the two men: "Oswald had let Assassin Number 1 into the Depository the night before the murder; he led him to the sixth-floor room, brought him the rifle, provided some food and kept on the lookout to make sure nobody entered the room."

This is the proper time to list quickly the other accomplices, all of them Dallas policemen, who play a part in Buchanan's "solution."

"If we call Oswald Accomplice Number 1, we have no difficulty in finding Accomplice Number 2," Buchanan writes. "This was the officer who gave the order to let Oswald leave the building." Number 3 is the one "who sent out the alarm about Oswald before his 90 co-workers had been rounded up." Buchanan, deducing that "this policeman already knew Oswald's role in the conspiracy," even considers his role "more important than that of the other accomplices." Number 4 is an officer in civilian clothes, and in a car, whose mission was to "follow Oswald in order to arrange for his arrest at the right moment." Accomplice Number 5 was Tippit. At the "agreed signal" (from Accomplice Number 4) he was to stop Oswald, cause him to draw his revolver, and then kill him in "self-defense."

Oswald, Buchanan discloses at this point, was intentionally allowed to go to his room after the assassination: *"The police already knew his address. . . .* One can therefore state that even before Oswald arrived there, the police knew where he was headed. But when he entered the room, *nobody was waiting for him there.* After the police broadcasts, the neighborhood probably was already surrounded. But nobody kept Oswald from going to get his pistol from his room. . . ."

Three comments: The italics are Buchanan's; none of the police broadcasts mentioned a neighborhood or an address or the name of Oswald; and when Buchanan says Oswald went to get his pistol, the "fact" on which he bases his "reasoning" is in this case the word of Captain Fritz. Buchanan says the police wanted Oswald to go home for the pistol because that would justify his execution by Tippit; but the policeman, an "inveterate bungler," was out-maneuvered and slain by Oswald.

Buchanan now returns to Assassin Number 1: "On November 22, 1963, Assassin Number 1 wore a police uniform." And he adds with dramatic subtlety: "Unless he has been killed since, I believe he still wears it."

The only policeman killed "since" was J. D. Tippit. Is Buchanan implying that Assassin Number 1 was none other than Accomplice Number 5? The next sentence indeed implicates Tippit in some activities outside of his role as Accomplice Number 5, but without specifying their nature very clearly. First, informing us that Assassin Number 1 left the scene of the crime "probably in a patrol car," the author notes that "we will speak again of a police car occupied by only one man, contrary to the rules." This was J. D. Tippit then, suddenly whisked from Oak Cliff to Elm Street. But is he the man who supposedly spent the night in the building, and did he then leave his patrol car nearby to get away after the crime? Or was he only coming to pick up his fellow assassin, offering him the extra seat in his car?

In either case, one wonders why the author appears so unjust toward Tippit, speaking of him as the "inveterate bungler," when he had carried out his mission perfectly as the unnumbered accomplice who helped Assassin Number 1 flee the scene, or as Assassin Number 1 himself. One might also wonder why, in the latter case, the absence of Tippit and his patrol car was not noticed all night and all morning, and why in the other case the assassin needed Tippit and his car at all to get away. Couldn't Accomplice Number 2—who, we recall, "gave the order to let Oswald leave"—do the same for the assassin, who even "wore a police uniform" and would have been able to remain on the scene without trouble?

Those who hoped the book would offer answers to these fascinating questions, left open in the articles in *L'Express*, found that the questions had disappeared because the "concise reasoning" of March 5 had been abandoned. Buchanan's book still finds it "inconceivable that a patrol car searching a neighborhood where an armed assassin was likely to be found would have only one man in it," but this patrol car is now kept within the boundaries of the Oak Cliff neighborhood, where Buchanan *knew* that the police *knew* the assassin was likely to be. There is no longer any connection between the fact that Tippit was alone and the departure of the assassin from the Depository Building. The author has finally discovered that the uniform he loaned to the assassin allows him to reverse his reasoning in *L'Express;* he explains with great satisfaction the benefits of his discovery by repeating the questions he has thereby disposed of: "But if he was in uniform, he had no need to leave the building. He could have remained inside the Depository, mingling with the police looking for the killer. Since only a man wearing a police uniform could pass unnoticed, this appears to be the solution. . . ."

It cannot be ruled out, obviously, that the real assassin was indeed a man in uniform, and the speculation even has some merit. The paradox here is that among all those who speculated on the Dallas events, Buchanan is the only one who fails to benefit from this speculation—presented in *L'Express* as incontrovertible fact. Buchanan says that Lee Oswald, in civilian clothes, was able to leave without trouble because Accomplice Number 2 gave the order. There is no reason, therefore, why Assassin Number 2 would have to wear a uniform to escape detection. Buchanan has already made the uniform unnecessary through his invention of Accomplice Number 2, just as the uniform makes unnecessary the escape, "probably in a patrol car."

Picking up the thread of the "deductions" born in the "rigorous mind" of our mathematician is not easy.

At the beginning we have a genuine fact, and only one: Oswald was able to leave the Depository Building without being stopped, even though the police chief affirmed that the building was immediately surrounded. Buchanan draws without hesitation on the entire Dallas Police Department in selecting the cast to match his script, but does not consider the possibility that Jesse Curry's men simply did a bad job on Elm Street, or that Jesse Curry had made up the story. A whole series of postulates in *L'Express* are based on Curry's word: "Almost immediately after the last shot, the police blocked all the exits of the building. . . . There was no panic among the police. . . . They were immediately led to the Depository. . . ."

I admit that I don't get the meaning of the following statement: "It is undeniable that the police were able to block all the exits of the building before he was able to leave since even Oswald was unable to get further than the second floor."

It might be impolite to remind Buchanan that some people still deny what he considers undeniable, and that among them is his colleague Nerin E. Gun, who wrote in a book published at the same time as his, by the same French publisher (*The Red Roses of Dallas*): "The police never thought of surrounding the building. . . ." This, incidentally, is equally false, since they did think of it but failed to do so. I am much more intrigued by the "proof" Buchanan offers here. If Oswald was not *able* to go further than the second floor, does that mean he first tried to leave and went back up for his Coke only *after* he was prevented from walking out? That would mean Accomplice Number 2, who gave the order to let Oswald leave, was inexplicably late in doing so. Could such a thing happen in a well-organized plot?

A curious character, indeed, this Accomplice Number 2, as seen by Thomas Buchanan, and depending on when he sees him.

In *L'Express,* this accomplice was the one who "gave the order." In the book, now under the name Accomplice Number 4, he is "the one who allowed Oswald to leave the building." Buchanan had begun by explaining in *L'Express* that "this order not only constituted a flagrant violation of procedures the police are required to follow in such circumstances; it constituted an act of disobedience to the personal order of the police chief." In the next paragraph, however, the same order is described by Buchanan as "a mistake which was not only a grave error of judgment, but an act of insubordination arousing suspicion of complicity in the assassination." The accomplice whom Buchanan had "no difficulty" finding a few lines before is now merely *suspected* of complicity. Shouldn't a mathematician such as Buchanan have chosen between the "error of judgment" and the "act of insubordination," since a less rigorous mind than his might find in this a certain contradiction? The question is settled only in the book, when Buchanan wonders why Curry did not "identify the policeman, order his arrest and prosecution, not for an error of judgment but for deliberate disobedience and complicity in the assassination."

To find Accomplice Number 3, again without difficulty, the author bases his argument on the fact that the police did not have adequate time to assemble the 91 Depository Building employees at the time they began the hunt for Oswald. "One thing is therefore certain," Buchanan concludes. "The policeman who sent out the alarm on Oswald before his 90 co-workers had been assembled and counted, already knew Oswald's role in the conspiracy, and he could only know it if he himself were in on the plot."

The distance between the true facts and this conclusion is spanned by an example of Buchananian logic that I quote in full (the parentheses also are Buchanan's):

> We are asked to believe that these 90 persons could have been assembled in one minute; that their boss, who was on the sixth floor of the building, could have been called down to have them pass in review; that he called the roll of these 90 people (undoubtedly from memory?) whose names he did not always know; that none of them had made use of the lunch hour to take care of personal matters; that none had gone to telephone friends about the assassination; that none had gone someplace where they could listen to the radio; that none had gone outside to see if anyone was wounded. No, all 90 employees were there except Oswald; and they were brought together in one minute! Such is the official version. If the reader believes this will not stand up, the conclusion is evident: Someone gave the order to arrest Oswald when there was nothing as yet to implicate him in the attack. . . .

One could perhaps appreciate the somewhat feverish eloquence of this diatribe if the author were merely trying to treat ironically the incoherent sputtering of the Dallas authorities. The amazing thing is that Buchanan is not being ironic; he takes the sputtering literally and builds his theory on it.

It was indeed absurd to give the impression, as Curry did on November 22, that the order for Oswald's arrest was sent out following a head count that revealed his absence. Contrary, however, to Buchanan's statement, it is absolutely false that this was the "official version" at the time he wrote his articles. Curry had eaten those words, among many others, on the day after the assassination; the only official version after that time—and up to September 27, 1964—was this: The alarm went out for Oswald's arrest, without any roll call, after Truly noticed the absence of the employee he had seen in the lunchroom a minute or so after the assassination. Buchanan mentions this version in an incidental way in *L'Express*, in the course of tilting at his windmill, but does not comment on it.

In his book, the author follows again the same "concise reasoning" that allows him to repeat that Accomplice Number 3 (rechristened Accomplice Number 5) is "the most important of all those we know about." He challenges the theory that "the absence of Oswald indicated his guilt." And for ironic emphasis: "While normally it is the *presence* of a suspect near the scene of the crime that indicates his guilt, this time it was his *absence*." (Buchanan's italics.)

But this was a case of absence *preceded* by presence—in other words, of an unexplained departure that could reasonably be interpreted as an escape and that made Oswald not guilty but suspect. If the police had not taken immediate measures to locate and question an employee who had been around at the time of the assassination and had then slipped away, this would have amounted to gross negligence.

Only an author without any knowledge of what went on in Dallas would need Buchanan's Accomplice Number 4.

This, says Buchanan, was a plain-clothes officer assigned to "follow Oswald," and his existence is shown by "the speed with which the police were informed of Oswald's route." In fact, he explains with that superb assurance shared by the mathematicians of *L'Express* and the caption-writers of *Life,* there was no question about it: "The police knew his route even before Oswald was arrested." How does Buchanan know that? Answer: "Even a cub reporter knows that in a manhunt of this kind, it is impossible for switchboard operators at headquarters to keep up with all the information called in, most of which is purely imaginary." A quick glance at Buchanan's book gives us the startling revelation of what has taken place: The author believes that the evidence on Oswald's movements obtained by the police *after* his arrest had been called into headquarters *before* the arrest, while Oswald was still on the move!

As we know, it was possible to retrace Oswald's route thanks to the ticket-punch mark on the bus transfer found in his pocket; reporters were able to question witnesses (bus driver McWatters, cab driver Whaley) and correct or refute Wade's mistakes and inventions. According to Buchanan, however, "the witnesses disappeared mysteriously when reporters sought to question them."

The masterpiece of the "Buchanan Report" appeared on March 12 in *L'Express*. This installment set out to prove nothing less than that Oswald had acted under the protection of the FBI, if not actually at its direction. The facts? "From a building belonging to the city government and administered by it, a municipal employee shoots at the President of the United States. . . ." Seven, eight times in the same article, the words are repeated: ". . . municipal employee . . . municipal book depository . . . city administration . . . official of the Dallas city government. . . ." In short, Oswald, known for his subversive opinions, obtained a city job in Dallas, "something which would not strike a European but must amaze every American citizen, since this is *impossible in the United States.*" (Italics are Buchanan's.)

There is unfortunately a serious flaw in this construction: It rests on a nonexistent foundation. Lee Oswald was not hired by the city government, as Buchanan declares; his job was not under the jurisdiction of any city department or agency. Despite its name, which might confuse a Frenchman but should not so easily mislead an American, the *"Depot de livres scolaires du Texas"* is a strictly private commercial enterprise, not connected in any way with the city or state government.

From this blunder, Buchanan leaps to the wildest conclusions.

Picturing Oswald as a city employee, he reasons that he could not have obtained the job without the "intervention of a governmental agency which had taken him under its protection." For those who might not have recognized immediately that this agency was the FBI, he offers some further comments: "From all the evidence, a man as conspicuous as Oswald could not have worked a month for the city unless a fairly high-placed authority came to the employer, *showed his badge and official identification,* and said to him: 'This Oswald you have hired is all right. Don't believe the stories they tell about him. We can't give you any explanation, but *we would like him to work here'. . . ."* (This time the italics are mine.)

In view of Buchanan's revelations, one can only be impressed by Roy Truly's stoic silence about this visit by the man with a badge. But Buchanan also maintains that Oswald was able to bypass "the investigation required by Texas anti-subversive laws." As manager and co-owner of the Depository, Truly must have had some difficulty hiding his bewilderment when he learned that the stock clerk he had hired at $50 a week to fill book orders until Christmas was a city employee whose employment violated Texas law!

Just before the appearance of his fourth installment, which contained these disclosures, Buchanan made his trip to Dallas. In two minutes he could have learned that the Depository was a private business and that no government official in Dallas or elsewhere had any reason to check on its employees. But on March 26, when he returned to Paris from Dallas (and from Washington, where, he bragged, he was received with great respect by the Justice Department and the Warren Commission), Buchanan hammered away at the same theme, but with an unexplained variation: "No one would have been able to obtain a municipal job for Oswald and keep him there without the approval of the city government or, moreover, without the desire of Dallas officials to make use of Oswald later on."

Thus, on March 26, it was the "Dallas officials" who wanted "to make use of Oswald." On March 12, those officials had kept him on the job only because a "fairly high-placed authority" with a badge had asked them to do so. True, Buchanan had not explained why the proud Texans, jealous of their rights, should have agreed to violate their own anti-Communist laws to please a federal representative, no matter how highly placed; nor why, having done so, they said nothing—and thereby offered themselves as scapegoats for the Washington plotters—when they discovered, at the moment of the assassination, the motive of the man with a badge who had said "we would like him to work here."

In dealing with Buchanan's "deductions" I have concentrated on the articles in *L'Express,* whose sensational presentation passed off these lucubrations as the product of a scientific mind.

As a whole, the only notable difference in the book (as first published in Paris) was the numbering of accomplices: Each is demoted two notches, beginning with Lee Oswald, who drops from Accomplice Number 1 to Number 3. But this amounts only to a kind of internal reorganization. Instead of having two different lists, one for assassins and the other for accomplices, Buchanan proves his talent as a computer programmer by unifying his system and reclassifying Assassins Number 1 and 2 as Accomplices Number 1 and 2.

The author, in any case, does hold to the total number of seven. He assigns no numbers to the many other accomplices he needs to carry out his plans, whose existence he does not explicitly recognize.

Thus we read in *L'Express* on March 5, concerning Tippit's mission: "Police had been cleared out of the neighborhood so that Accomplice Number 5 could operate freely." This notion remains intact in the book (in which Tippit becomes Accomplice Number 7): "So that he could accomplish his task without being disturbed, the police had been removed from the entire neighborhood."

I am not acquainted with the administrative procedures of the Dallas police, but I assume that to pull all patrolmen out of an area where they were customarily assigned, a considerable number of accomplices would have been required: inspectors, captains, sergeants, clerks, switchboard operators. Why not list them too? Buchanan at least should have conferred the title of Accomplice Number 8 on the officer in charge of the Oak Cliff section, since that officer must have been aware of the reasons for such an unusual move before being informed by Buchanan.

"Police had been cleared out of the neighborhood so that Accomplice Number 5 could operate freely." I reread this sentence with increasing uneasiness. In devoting an entire chapter to dismantling Buchanan's surrealist constructions, have I fallen into a trap? Could it be that the "Buchanan Report" was, after all, one of those gigantic hoaxes that sometimes hoodwink even serious journals?

This is certainly not the view of the Warren Commission. On the contrary: Its report, more than once, gives the impression of having been drafted as a personal reply to Thomas Buchanan. The Commission, for example, is so anxious to prove no conspiracy was required for Oswald to get out of the Depository Building that it paints an even more damning picture than I would have dared to imagine of the way the police "surrounded and searched" the building. It seems right, therefore, to credit Buchanan with the fact that, in waving his tattered red rag, he led the Washington bull out into the open.

The Commission also issued for Buchanan's benefit a previously unpublished speculation that, on one point, upsets everything that had passed for official truth before. This concerns the first police broadcast about the suspect and the origin of the information on which the broadcast was based. Buchanan had made this the special province of his Accomplice Number 3 (or 5, in the book). Placing this accomplice, without regard to his number, at the head of the list of culprits, he had gone so far as to charge: "The Dallas police know the name of this man, and have known it from the moment he gave the order to arrest Oswald." This was quite unpleasant for Captain Fritz, and perhaps the Commission wanted to rush to his aid by clubbing Buchanan in the following sample from the "Speculations and Rumors":

> *Speculation.*—A detailed and remarkably clear description of Oswald was sent over the police radio in Dallas at 12:36 p.m., November 22, 1963.
>
> *Commission finding.*—The radio logs of the Dallas Police Department and the Dallas County Sheriff's Office show

that no description of a suspect in the assassination of the President was broadcast before 12:45 p.m. on that day. No reference to Oswald by name was broadcast before he was arrested. The description of the suspect that was broadcast was similar to that of Oswald, but it lacked some important specific details such as color of hair and eyes. The information for the initial broadcasts most probably came from Howard Brennan, who saw Oswald in the window when he was firing the rifle.

I will have occasion to deal further with these speculations of the Commission, which are no more believable and no less irresponsible than those of Thomas Buchanan.

19

LEE HARVEY OSWALD

IF, AS MOST AMERICANS SEEM TO BELIEVE, it was Lee Oswald and Lee Oswald alone who killed John F. Kennedy, why did he do it?

District Attorney Wade, during Jack Ruby's trial, dodged the question of the defendant's motive, and this omission did not prevent him from getting the death penalty he needed to keep up his winning streak. True justice, however, does not permit evasion of the question of motive when a man is accused of murder. Still less can it be ignored when the accused has been convicted without a trial, by decision of a "factfinding agency," and when the authors of this decision ask for its endorsement by the public.

Many were said to have been impressed by the fact that the Warren Commission, after having decreed that "the shots which killed President Kennedy and wounded Governor Connally were fired by Lee Harvey Oswald," was honest enough to recognize later on in its conclusions that it "could not make any definitive determination of Oswald's motives."

Since that did not keep the Commission from deciding that Oswald was the assassin, I must admit that I was not so favorably impressed.

Although it was incapable of determining Oswald's motives, the Commission nevertheless enumerates some factors which "might have influenced his decision to assassinate President Kennedy." And it does not hesitate to include among these, along with the "urge to try to find a place in history," his "capacity for violence as evidenced by his attempt to kill General Walker."

There are also the explanations given at the beginning of the

258

nearly 50 pages that the Report devotes to the "possible motives" of Oswald:

> The Commission has considered many possible motives for the assassination, including those which might flow from Oswald's commitment to Marxism or communism, the existence of some personal grievance, a desire to effect changes in the structure of society or simply to go down in history as a well publicized assassin. None of these possibilities satisfactorily explains Oswald's act if it is judged by the standards of reasonable men. The motives of any man, however, must be analyzed in terms of the character and state of mind of the particular individual involved. For a motive that appears incomprehensible to other men may be the moving force of a man whose view of the world has been twisted, possibly by factors of which those around him were only dimly aware. . . .

In short, it is not necessary to explain before condemning; since the death of the accused made any psychiatric examination impossible, ordinary citizens need not worry about motive. The excuse suggested, and utilized by the Commission itself, is that Oswald's acts which cannot be explained might well have been explained by experts. Thus one can attribute to Oswald's insanity everything that defies common sense in the Commission's version of the events.

Here then is what I cannot help calling a monumental hypocrisy. While proclaiming Oswald the assassin, the Commission says it "did not draw any conclusions concerning Oswald's legal guilt." It simply "ascertained the facts surrounding the assassination." Questions having to do with the assassin's mental state were not included in that task, and could not have been: "Under our system of justice no forum could properly make that determination unless Oswald were before it."

Does this mean the Commission abstains from venturing into this domain to seek out theories likely to back up its charges? No. It means only that the Commission does not consider itself obligated to look for arguments to back up its theories, or even to take into account any arguments that might wreck those theories.

The Report goes to great lengths to persuade us that Oswald had "some quality about him that led him to act with an apparent disregard for possible consequences." The proof? "He defected to the Soviet Union, shot at General Walker, tried to go to Cuba and even contemplated hijacking an airplane to get there. He assassinated the President, shot Officer Tippit, resisted arrest and tried to kill another policeman in the process."

It's the old method, perfected behind the Iron Curtain, of coolly advancing the most gratuitous affirmations as if they were undeniable and universally accepted facts. Of the statements listed above, only one cannot be challenged: Oswald indeed defected to the Soviet Union in October 1959. I showed in previous chapters how weak or nonexistent was the evidence presented to support the other affirmations. Concerning Oswald's intention to hijack a plane, the Commission does not even claim it has the shadow of a proof. All it has is the word of Marina Oswald.

But the Commission not only tries to establish Oswald's "apparent disregard for possible consequences" by invoking his alleged but unproved acts; it also pretends to explain the improbability of those acts by invoking his "apparent disregard for possible consequences."

Thus in the same chapter devoted to Oswald's possible motives, the Report returns to the notebook in which, Marina declared, her husband kept a record of his preparations for the Walker assassination, including photographs of the area. According to the complacent widow, Oswald "forgot" the note in Russian that was to give the Commission so much comfort. but destroyed the notebook, "apparently after he thought that what he had written in his book might be proof against him," as Marina explained it. The Commission, however, was not frustrated by this; for "even after his wife told him to destroy the notebook, he removed at least some of the pictures which had been pasted in it and saved them among his effects, where they were found after the assassination."

Before commenting on the deeper meaning of these revelations by Marina, the Report gives us a brief extract from the transcript of her testimony (informing us proudly that she answered the first three questions without using the interpreter).

> *Question.*   After he brought the rifle home, then, he showed you the book?
> *Answer.*   Yes.
> *Question.*   And you said it was not a good idea to keep this book?
> *Answer.*   Yes.
> *Question.*   And then he burned the book?
> *Answer.*   Yes.
> *Question.*   Did you ask him why he had not destroyed the book before he actually went to shoot General Walker?
> *Answer.*   It never came to me, myself, to ask him that question.

Now the Commission's comment:

> Marina Oswald's testimony indicates that her husband was not particularly concerned about his continued possession of the most incriminating sort of evidence. If he had been successful and had been apprehended even for routine questioning, his apartment would undoubtedly have been searched, and his role would have been made clear by the evidence which he had left behind. Leaving the note and picture as he did would seem to indicate that he had considered the possibility of capture. Possibly he might have wanted to be caught, and wanted his involvement made clear if he was in fact apprehended. . . .

Various psychiatrists had already said as much, but they were not handing down a verdict. The Warren Commission at least ought to have explained why Oswald, pushing his "apparent disregard for possible consequences" to the point of wanting to be caught, lost that desire the minute he was captured.

Instead, the Commission compounds the inanity of its position by trying to give the impression that what had motivated Oswald was his desire to gain attention. Such an attitude on Oswald's part, the Report states with satisfaction, "was entirely consistent

with his wife's testimony." For here again, all the Commission has
is Marina's word, or "supposition" as she admits this time: "I
asked him," Marina said, "what for he was making all these en-
tries in the book and he answered that he wanted to leave a complete record so that all the details would be in it. . . . I am guess-
ing that perhaps he did it to appear to be a brave man in case
he were arrested, but that is my supposition.* * *"

The asterisks are those of the Report, which gives no other details about Marina's supposition. It is quite significant, however,
that the Commission's reasoning starts from one of her most un-
proven affirmations:

> The attempt on General Walker's life deserves close at-
> tention in any consideration of Oswald's possible motive
> for the assassination and the trail of evidence he left behind
> him on that occasion. While there are differences between
> the two events as far as Oswald's actions and planning are
> concerned, there are also similarities that should be con-
> sidered. The items which Oswald left at home when he
> made his attack on Walker suggest a strong concern for
> his place in history. If the attack had succeeded and Oswald
> had been caught, the pictures showing him with his rifle
> and his Communist and Socialist Worker's Party newspa-
> pers would probably have appeared on the front pages of
> newspapers or magazines all over the country, as, in fact,
> one of them did appear after the assassination. The circum-
> stances of the attack on Walker coupled with other indica-
> tions that Oswald was concerned about his place in history
> and with the circumstances surrounding the assassination,
> have led the Commission to believe that such concern is
> an important factor to consider in assessing possible moti-
> vation for the assassination.

What then happened to Oswald's concern about "his place in
history" once he had every newspaper, radio, and television screen
in the world at his disposal to satisfy it?

There is no room for consideration of this problem in the 888
pages of the Warren Report, which does not even tell us whether

Oswald, in his cell, expressed any desire to see the newspapers that were devoting entire pages to him. As for the commentators who had been aware from the beginning that this promised to be a stumbling block, they tried in vain to get around it.

In the Paris weekly *Le Nouveau Candide* (which had published, on November 28, the article by Chester Himes titled "I Do Not Believe in This Bargain Killer"), another American undertook to explain, a week later, why he did believe. Under the title "The Simplest Explanation," Bernard Frizell, chief of the NBC Paris bureau, wrote that he believed in Oswald's guilt because he considered him a "nut," and a "nut" had no need of rational motives to commit "irrational acts."

This explanation is simple enough, but far from explaining what needs to be explained. Frizell opposes American reasoning, "pragmatic rather than Cartesian," to the "traditional French prejudices," including the "imperiously French conviction" that "acts which have political consequences have political causes." I believe a Frenchman could tear himself away from the Cartesian prejudices that Frizell attributes to him, with a rather flattering American prejudice, and assume that President Kennedy was slain by a lone psychotic without reason other than his psychosis. Still, such a psychotic would have to act according to his psychosis.

Frizell's argument takes the form of an ingenious little treatise on the "nut," which he terms a "specifically American phenomenon," although, writing for a French magazine, he had no trouble naming the French slang equivalent, *le dingue*. What difference is there between the "nut" and the *dingue?*

"In general," says Frizell,

> a nut is an individual who without being insane, is unbalanced; he is a person afflicted with emotional instability and half-baked ideas which can lead him to commit irrational acts. No nation has a monopoly on *les dingues*, though it might seem after the assassination and the murder of the alleged assassin, that the United States has cornered the market. American nuts are a special breed. They are not at all like the Russian variety, the tormented

Raskolnikovs with their anguished sensitivity and keen sense of guilt. Nor are they like the French variety, with their political obsessions and their taste for intellectual rationalization, whether they are anarchist as in the past or O.A.S. [French Algerian terrorist organization] as in recent times. . . .

The picture is nicely drawn, but Bernard Frizell repeats in vain that American nuts are a special breed, nonpolitical and nonintellectual, living in their private jungle; to kill a President while acting as Lee Oswald is said to have acted is no more plausible in the United States than it would be in Europe.

It is not the portrait of the nut that I dispute; it could apply perfectly well to Lee Oswald, on condition that the word "nonpolitical" not be taken too literally.

Oswald was a loner, unequipped to meet the demands of society—any society—and certainly not up to political discussion. Those who gave him a chance to set forth his ideas, as did Michael Paine when he visited his children in Irving, generally found his opinions simple-minded if not childish. He called himself a Marxist. Nearly uneducated, no more aware of the laws of economy than of the rules of the English language, he certainly grasped little of *Das Kapital*—which he claimed to have discovered at the age of 15—apart from the title. Head stuffed with "leftist" clichés, in the pejorative sense that orderly members of the Communist Party apply to that word, Oswald undoubtedly would have been better off in Havana than in Moscow or in Minsk. But he wouldn't have lasted long in Havana, either, for there too they would have sent him off to work in socialist production, as they did in the Soviet Union, instead of placing him at the head of an army. I can easily imagine Oswald being executed by a Cuban firing squad for having set fire to a sugar-cane field after failing to get permission to go back to the United States.

The brilliant essayist Dwight Macdonald, who described himself as "a former Trotskyist who is now an anarchist-conservative with pacifist sympathies," probably was right when in a letter to

The New Republic he called Oswald "our baby"; even more so when he described him as a "bastard" of the left. But historian Gerald W. Johnson was no less perceptive in his reply to Macdonald: "It seems to me that he belonged neither to the Fascists nor to the Communists, but to something far more sinister, to wit, the Sour."

On the basis of their own political and psychological interpretations, Macdonald and Johnson had no difficulty believing in Oswald's guilt. It might seem plausible enough that this social misfit and misunderstood revolutionary could concentrate all the faculties of his unbalanced mind toward a "grand coup" such as the assassination of the President. What does appear totally unbelievable is that a man having made such a decision and carrying it out without regard for the consequences should then give up the demented pleasure he had purchased at the cost of his life—to play out his triumphant part. Is it really because, as Frizell suggests, Oswald was an American nut and "the American nut is not like any *dingue* in the world"?

The United States has produced only one variety of the unbalanced that one could say exists nowhere else, at least in this form and to this degree: the anti-Red maniac obsessed by a blind, superstitious, and hysterical conviction of the imminent triumph of an irresistible, pestiferous, all-powerful Communist menace.

Except for this species, America's nuts are not unique. While the history of political crime may include Russian, French, Italian, Irish, and other varieties, all of these have adapted to American soil according to the mood and immigration of the moment. Writing in *The Rebel* about what was then called in France *la propagande par le fait*, Albert Camus noted that in one year, 1892, there were more than 1,000 dynamite attacks in Europe, but also nearly 500 in America. There are no frontiers for this kind of epidemic, nor for those who carry the germs. Philosophical anarchists existed in Czarist Russia, and there were some tormented Raskolnikovs among the killers of the O.A.S., as well as quite a number of those "pure" nuts in their private jungles whom Frizell wrongly considers a "specifically American phenomenon."

Political assassination may be classified by all kinds of standards, and historians—not to mention psychiatrists—have made use of all of them. There is a distinction, for example, certainly not ir- relevant in the Dallas crime, between the abstract assassination (the victim is only a symbol, chosen for his position or other im- personal attributes) and the practical assassination (the victim is an object of personal hatred for the killer or his party). Particu- larly impossible to overlook in our case is the distinction between assassins who want to die and those who prefer to live.

Camus dealt at length with the case of the terrorists for whom "the taste for sacrifice matched the attraction of death" *(The Rebel)*. Psychiatrists have made somewhat similar statements con- cerning Oswald, in their own language and without waiting for the Warren Report. Thus Dr. Lewis Robbins, quoted by Walter Sullivan in the *New York Times:* "It is typical of the psychopathic criminal to leave a trail that makes his capture easy. In a sub- conscious way he wants to be caught."

But to Dr. Renatus Hartogs, who had examined the 13-year-old Oswald in 1953 and later boasted he had already found him "po- tentially dangerous," the case inspired an opposite view: "Those who commit political homicides," he told Fern Marja Eckman of the *New York Post,* "are cunning, conniving, capable even as chil- dren of formulating long-range plans. They harbor jealousy and mistrust much longer than other murderers. And when they strike, they strike with much greater viciousness."

Bitter rather than inspired, spiteful rather than fanatical, Lee Harvey Oswald would seem to belong in the category of the as- sassin who wants to live rather than the one who sacrifices himself. In any case, he must have been one or the other. What we are asked to believe by the Commission is that he was both.

If Lee Oswald was one of those political assassins who at least unconsciously want to die as well as kill, it would be perfectly understandable that he failed to cover his traces or prepare his escape after the crime. But such assassins do not deny their acts: They explain, proclaim, expound, harangue. Even Marinus van der Lubbe, with whom Oswald had something in common, tried to convince his judges that he had burned the Reichstag in the name of the German working class. Lee Oswald, on two occasions, had a chance no political assassin before him had ever enjoyed: the power to speak directly to the whole world through the TV microphones thrust at him. What did he do? The first time he complains of not having a chance to take a shower and change his clothes. The second time he shouts the name of a New York lawyer he wants to aid him.

Oswald, of course, could belong to the other group of terrorists, for whom escaping punishment adds to, rather than detracts from, the satisfaction they derive from their acts.

False revolutionaries, more criminal than political, whose sole faith is in their own superiority—such assassins have no need of the public: For them, the most intoxicating homage is the one *they* render to themselves. They therefore deny it all to the end, playing a game with everybody and trying to outwit their accusers if arrested. But since their madness is in the pride of their performance as well as in the repercussions of their act, they try not to be caught.

How can it be explained then that this man, who did not break down under 12 hours of interrogation, who was concerned with getting a lawyer and wanted one from New York because he did not trust the Dallas lawyers, in short, a man who showed he was ready to battle tooth and nail against the electric chair—how can it be explained that he first did everything possible to help the police send him there?

Will it be said that this chronic failure possessed as little talent for crime as for his other enterprises? When we think of the infantile way he used his aliases and false addresses, we might readily concede this. But it demonstrated that he intended, at least, to play it smart and that he was aware of what the revolutionary pamphlets call "the rules of conspiracy." Certain precautions are truly elementary: Even the clumsiest assassin, before going off to shoot the President, would have burned the pictures showing him with the murder weapon; checked the contents of his wallet to see that no card bearing the name A. Hidell was kept; and thought for five minutes about what he would do after firing the last shot.

Here then is the dilemma that no psychological or psychiatric explanation has even attempted to resolve, since most of the explanations have missed the point.

In a study that appeared December 12, 1963, in the Paris weekly *Les Nouvelles Littéraires,* Dr. Max Beucher, chief of the neuropsychiatric clinic at the University of Paris, refuted the argument that Oswald's innocence appeared likely "because fanatics confess, and he did not confess." This argument, he answered convincingly, would be valid only if Oswald could be aligned with the "passionate idealists." But Beucher finds Oswald "more *unstable* and more *secretive*" than the fanatics he places in that category, and he puts him in a different niche:

> There are, in fact, other psychopaths who live in a constant atmosphere of hatred and suspicion, distrust and concealment. They are always *against* the society they live in. They feel persecuted. They could kill someone who represents that society to avenge themselves. They also have a tendency to overestimate their importance and their intelligence. Without overestimating our own abilities, we believe that Oswald was one of these *persecuted psychopaths. . . .*

Professor Beucher concludes: "His secretiveness and his hatred, his arrogance and his conceit, marked by a twisted smile, could explain his denials concerning even the most self-evident facts. Oswald, at least as we know him from the press, could have killed and yet denied his crime."

I have no quarrel with this conclusion. I have already said, without employing the same terms and basing my statements on purely empirical considerations, that Lee Harvey Oswald appeared to be more of a "persecuted psychopath" than a "passionate idealist." And I do not rule out the possibility that a man of this type could take it into his head to kill the President. The point I raise here relates only to the following question: Granting that Oswald was a paranoid psychopath capable of denying "even self-evident facts," can we assume that it would also be consistent with his character to assist the authorities by personally handing over to them all the incriminating evidence?

This contradiction—and it is a contradiction, for madmen do have method in their madness—is crowned by the ultimate psychological improbability, which seems to have drawn scant attention though it is plain to see: While providing Wade, Curry, and Fritz with all the material evidence they were looking for, Oswald demonstrated an extraordinary talent for hiding the feelings that, to believe those who accused him, had led to the crime. For at no time before or after the assassination did Oswald show in any way that the name of Kennedy aroused the slightest emotion in him.

Some employees of the Depository reported that on the very morning of the assassination they had talked about the President in Oswald's presence. There was no reaction. When invited to join them to watch the motorcade go by, he answered something like "not yet," and they took his reply to mean he would join them later (this probably gave birth to the story about sending the elevator back up). Wouldn't this have been the time for him to laugh "very loud"—as Wade solemnly affirmed he did in the bus after the assassination? But not a muscle in Oswald's face betrayed any sign of what must have gone on in his head as he watched his colleagues go off to applaud the man he was supposedly preparing to kill, the man who (according to Max Lerner and others) was the "symbol *par excellence*" of all his obsessions.

The Warren Report reveals some startling testimony on this point. In itself that testimony suffices to destroy the 50 pages of psychological and political speculation that the Report devotes to Oswald's "background and possible motives." But the Commission passes over it without pausing, in the evident hope that it will go unnoticed.

This curious passage takes up six lines in a small subsection of the chapter on "The Assassin," which deals with Oswald's "Actions During and After Shooting." The Commission's purpose here is to prove that Oswald lied to Captain Fritz. He is said to have declared, in one of his unrecorded replies, that "at the time the President was shot he was having lunch with 'Junior'. . . ." The only colleague of Oswald known by this name, the Report goes on, was an employee named James Jarman, Jr. Now James Jarman, Jr., informed the Commission that he had not had lunch with Oswald, and had not even seen him while he was eating his lunch. But "Jarman did talk to Oswald that morning," the Report notes, and it thoughtlessly gives a quotation from Jarman's testimony:

> . . . He asked me what were the people gathering around on the corner for and I told him that the President was supposed to pass that morning, and he asked me did I know which way he was coming, and I told him, yes, he probably come down Main and turn on Houston and then back again on Elm. Then he said, "Oh, I see," and that was all.

A commission headed by the Chief Justice of the United States must be treated with respect, and I will therefore refrain from expressing in print my personal reaction to the fact that the Warren Commission, after receiving such testimony, whose truth it does not question, simply closes the quotation and moves on to something else. I have the right, however, not to follow the Commission's example, and to say Jarman's testimony signifies either that:

(1) Oswald, at the time people began to gather for the motorcade, actually did not know that Kennedy would pass in front of the Depository and thus could not have planned to take advantage of the building's location to kill him. Theoretically he might have made his decision after talking to Jarman (as a "nut" susceptible to sudden murderous impulses). But what could he have done in that case, other than throw a typewriter down at the President's car or toss a carton of books out the window? There would be no rifle available, and there would be nothing left of the Commission's theory, which presumes premeditation dating at least from the morning before, when Oswald asked Wesley Frazier to drive him to Irving that evening (so that he could get the rifle, the Commission says). In short, the testimony of James Jarman, Jr., in this interpretation, would clear Oswald. Or:

(2) Oswald, knowing perfectly well why people were gathering in the street and calculating the time remaining to prepare for the assassination, asked his colleague the question to prepare his alibi. If he were ever suspected, then, Jarman could testify—

as he later did—that Lee Oswald, shortly before the crime, did not even know the victim would pass the building. Should we see in this attitude the supreme subtlety of a methodical criminal who wants to escape the consequences of his act and takes all necessary precautions? Perhaps. But how can the Commission reconcile such subtlety—and such precautions—with the opposite picture of Oswald it has drawn?

And afterward, when the crime is accomplished? I don't need to comment on his ranting and his laughing "very loud" in the bus, since this exists only in the imagination of Henry Wade. That night, on the third floor of police headquarters, when a reporter asked him if he had killed the President, Oswald looked at him with astonishment and replied that he was accused only of having killed a policeman. I was not there, but I spoke to newsmen who were present. They were unanimous: no arrogance, no conceit, no twisted smile, only astonishment.

Was Oswald a great actor, or did the mention of the slain President—supposedly his victim—really create no particular emotion in him? Some journalists wanted to know more about this, and one asked Wade about it in his Sunday-night press conference. Although there would seem to have been no possible confusion, the District Attorney chose to misunderstand the question. And since the reporters were talking all at once, it went unanswered. Here is the passage I refer to, as recorded on tape:

> *Reporter.*   Did he display any animosity towards the President, in any conversation with any officers?
> *Wade.*   He was bitter toward all of the officers that examined him is what I've been told.
> *Reporter.*   Do you think he deserved . . .
> *Reporter.*   Let's finish the . . .
> *Wade.*   We have—that's about all.

There was more, fortunately. The Warren Report, in publishing the statements of the various officers who had taken part in Oswald's questioning, gives some precious information on the attitude of the presumed assassin when he was asked to comment on the personality or politics of his supposed victim. It will be well to recall at this point that none of the officers in question could be suspected of having the slightest personal desire to bring out information that might be favorable to Oswald.

Statement of Captain Fritz: "I asked him what he thought of President Kennedy and his family, and he said he didn't have any views on the President. He said 'I like the President's family very well. I have my own views about national policies. . . .' "

Again Captain Fritz: "Someone of the Federal officers asked Oswald if he thought Cuba would be better off since the President was assassinated. To this he replied that since the President was killed that someone else would take his place, perhaps Vice President Johnson, and that his views would probably be largely the same as those of President Kennedy."

Statement of FBI Agent James W. Bookhout: "Oswald stated that he has nothing against President John F. Kennedy personally; however in view of the present charges against him, he did not desire to discuss this phase further."

Statement of Secret Service Inspector Thomas J. Kelley: "Upon questioning by Captain Fritz, he said, 'I have no views on the President. My wife and I like the President's family. They are interesting people. I have my own views on the President's national policy. I have a right to express my views but because of the charges I do not think I should comment further.' Oswald said 'I am not a malcontent; nothing irritated me about the President.' "

Again Inspector Kelley: "I asked him if he thought that the President's assassination would have any effect on the Fair Play for Cuba Committee. He said there would be no change in the attitude of the American people toward Cuba with President Johnson becoming President because they both belonged to the same political party and the one would follow pretty generally the policies of the other."

A master criminal who never cracks, or a perfectly innocent man? He must have been one of the two; yet neither alternative fits the description of Oswald given by the Warren Commission.

20

THREE THEORIES

Among those who refused to accept the official doctrine of the solitary "nut," there were many who found a place for Oswald as conspirator or executioner in all kinds of plots whose secrets they alone possessed. Three general theories have emerged, and the first even had the originality of keeping out of politics. It was the "gangland-murder" theory, launched by a brilliant French-Italian-Hollywood journalistic school that took Jack Ruby as guide and discovered in the crime of Dallas the hand of Chicago.

For the well-known French novelist Serge Groussard, whose nine-page essay in the Paris daily *L'Aurore* was prefaced by the honest warning that it was "an entirely personal interpretation," there was no doubt about it: The assassination had been plotted by the Mafia (Groussard tosses out at random such names as Tony Accardo, Johnny Dio, Longie Zwillman), "which President Kennedy had relentlessly pursued and which is still the target, now more than ever, of his younger brother, Attorney General Robert F. Kennedy."

If Robert Kennedy was pursuing it "more than ever," it's hard to see what the Mafia gained by executing his brother. But Groussard doesn't stop there. Describing "the gangland of Chicago in 1963," with its new ranks of criminals "more savage than any before," he lends them two motives for killing the President: "For these tigers it would mean vengeance. And they believed it would also mean a weakening of their terrorized, leaderless foes." Recognizing that nothing changed after all, he is content to add, without specifying what then his "subject" is: "On this second point they were mistaken, but that is not our subject. . . ."

But he still has to explain how the underworld succeeded in organizing the assassination while failing to achieve its second goal.

According to Groussard, the Mafia felt more and more harassed and cornered, and became "carried away by its anger." Its decision was not sudden; "it must have decided months in advance to aim for the head—to slay the top Kennedy." Assigned to recruit a killer, Jack Ruby finds Oswald, who needs money. The Mannlicher-Carcano is ordered ("It is probable that neither Ruby nor the ex-Marine knew the intended use of the rifle, but the Mafia wanted them to have something to kill with"), although for some reason—difficult to explain where professional killers are concerned—no bullets are ordered along with it. "Then, in September, someone must have brutally informed Oswald that the time was coming when he would have to pay back the organization which had aided him. And he was made to understand that he would have to commit an important murder . . ." (*L'Aurore*, December 30, 1963).

How did the organization help Oswald, and what was its hold on him?

Groussard assumes that Ruby first "hooked him by providing the money to pay back the $436 he had borrowed from the State Department." This is not a very kind thing to say about the State Department, since it suggests the government was so insistent and uncompromising in demanding repayment that poor, frightened Oswald, forgetting that debtors' prisons no longer existed in the United States, was ready to throw himself into the arms of anyone to escape the sheriff. Groussard also mentions the "small remittances" that were wired to Oswald. This was based on a rumor officially denied well before the article appeared in *L'Aurore;* the remittances were therefore not merely small but nonexistent. And finally, "it would be impossible to explain without some mysterious assistance the way he was able to travel to Mexico."

Oswald's financial situation involves no mysterious or unexplained elements.

He was, of course, often reduced to living on his unemployment check, and even when he worked his wages were low. But he had no urgent need of more money. After their return to Texas, his wife and daughter were given free room and board at the Paine home, where he himself was fed on weekends. The birth of his second daughter cost him nothing; the welfare department paid the expenses. He lived frugally in Dallas, on sandwiches and milk; he did not smoke or drink; and he seldom bought new clothes. His room on North Beckley Avenue took only $8 a week out of his $50 paycheck. With his habit of thrift, if not stinginess, Lee Oswald even was able to save a little money.

Concerning the Mexican trip, a triple investigation (by American and Mexican officials and world news media) disclosed not only what Oswald did in Mexico but how he went there and how much he spent. He hitchhiked to Nuevo Laredo; took a Mexican bus (72 pesos or $5.75); stayed in Mexico City at the Hotel Comercio, in a $1.28-a-day room; ate in a nearby *loncheria* called La Esperanza, where dishes cost 25 or 30 cents. On September 27, the day after he arrived, Oswald went to the Cuban consulate to ask for a transit visa. This could not be provided, he was told, until he could show his Soviet visa, which also was refused. Mexico was then one of four Latin American countries still maintaining diplomatic relations with Cuba, but its police kept a close watch on anyone having the slightest connection with Castro's friends. Oswald thus was under Mexican surveillance from the time he showed up at the Cuban consulate. The Mexican police said Oswald had no suspicious contacts during his stay in Mexico apart from his two visits to the Cuban and Soviet consulates.

Now for the "personal interpretation" of the imaginative novelist Groussard:

> They probably kept Oswald going with small doses. The plan was to provide mere subsistence but make him hunger for the moment when, he was told, he would be showered with gold somewhere safe abroad. To con him some more the Mafia sent him to Mexico. He probably met some anonymous nabobs who received him briefly, as in a dream. He visited a clinic where he was told he would

undergo "afterward" an operation which would give him
a new face, and in a way, a new soul. . . .

After such preliminaries, Groussard has nothing more to do
than close his eyes and jump, like Lee Oswald:

> On Thursday, November 21, the thin young man with
> brown hair and complexion ravaged by acne received the
> revelation of his terrible mission. He surely was warned
> that if he tried to pull out of it, he would be quickly exe-
> cuted; and he had seen enough of the Mafia's power to
> know it wasn't an idle threat. . . .

I have already discussed in a special chapter the *two* theories of
Thomas Buchanan. Both make Oswald the accomplice and future
scapegoat of a gang he fell in with after his return from Russia
because this gang seemed "ready to give him a start, protect him,
and find him a job." The gang of Buchanan, however, is not the
gang of Groussard, and Buchanan offers something better than the
successors of Al Capone. Unfortunately, though we can easily
guess the general meaning and intention, the political conclusions of Buchanan's theories are as incoherent as their technical
assumptions.

As to the organizers of the plot, Buchanan initially offered his
readers the choice between the FBI (the March 12 article in
L'Express) and the "Dallas officials" (the March 26 article). To
judge from the summary in the issue of April 9, modestly entitled
"J'accuse," Buchanan finally seemed to have decided in favor of
the second version. This is because he had read in the meantime
an article in *U.S. News and World Report*, as well as a study on
"The Power Structure of Dallas" by a local sociologist, Carol
Estes Thometz. Reading between the lines something that was
in neither the book nor the article, Buchanan discovered the existence of a "Council of Citizens," which held the reins of power
in Dallas and which he also imagines to be secret, mysterious, ex-
pansionist, and imperialist, dedicated to the ultrareactionary
principles of the celebrated H. L. Hunt and subservient to the
worldwide interests of Texas oil magnates.

In fact, the Dallas Citizens' Council (not to be confused, of course, with the segregationist White Citizens' Councils of the South) took pride in the fact that H. L. Hunt was not a member. It was dominated by the local aristocracy of banks and insurance companies, not oil firms. (Dallas claims to serve as headquarters for more insurance companies than any other city in the world, including London, and has 22 large banks with a total capital of $2.5 billion.)

Several visiting French journalists, including myself, were able to determine personally, at a charming Thanksgiving dinner in an elegant home in University Park, how anxious local society was to prevent the world from accepting the idea that Dallas was the American capital of the extreme right-wing lunatic fringe. The civic leaders we met were eager to develop, on the contrary, the image of a great modern metropolis, a center of business and culture. The leaders of the Council, incidentally, were discreet but by no means anonymous, as Buchanan claimed. Its founder, and for a long time the most influential man in Dallas, was a banker named Robert L. Thornton, whose death in 1964 at the age of 83 brought about the postponement of the first session of Ruby's trial as a mark of mourning. The situation became even more open when the president of the Citizens' Council, Erik Jonsson, the wealthy head of a large precision-instruments firm, succeeded Earle Cabell as mayor. Among the active members of this group, which Buchanan practically accused of having organized the assassination of John F. Kennedy, was also the liberal Stanley Marcus, president of the Neiman-Marcus department store.

While the late Senator McCarthy is generally considered to have been a demagogue rather than a model for mathematicians, Buchanan never hesitates to borrow the method of insinuation by association. He expounds at length, for example, on the reactionary lucubrations of H. L. Hunt's 1960 novel, *Alpaca*. Except for the fact that Hunt lives in Dallas, one would look in vain in Buchanan's writings for the slightest indication of how the assassination of President Kennedy in 1963 was connected to the publication of *Alpaca* in 1960. But if the reader of Thomas Buchanan is sufficiently McCarthyized, he will have had, in one flash, two intuitions and three associations of ideas, the complete revelation of the ideological bases of the plot.

Buchanan's insistence on evoking the death of Italian oilman Enrico Mattei in connection with the Dallas crime—still under the title *"J'accuse"*—seems to indicate at last that the guiding principle is here.

Enrico Mattei, he notes at the start, died in Italy in a plane accident whose cause "has never been determined." Now Enrico Mattei "would without a doubt have been lynched if he had set foot in Texas." Is this to say that the two crimes are connected? Of course, replies Buchanan with all the eloquence of Joe McCarthy: "Before Kennedy, there had been Enrico Mattei." Let's be specific: "There is some reason to believe, in fact, that they [the assassins of Kennedy] were not engaged in their first crime." There is no need, apparently, to tell us what "some reason" may be. It is easier to continue and state: "I believe that *l'homme H* [he became "Mr. X" in the English edition of Buchanan's book— L.S.], who directed the plot against Kennedy could provide some clarification of the causes of this mysterious explosion" (the Mattei plane accident). Replying in his book to those who persisted in believing that Mattei's death was indeed an accident, Buchanan tops it off by this proof by analogy: "Is it so certain? It was, at all events, an accident which benefited the oil magnates of Texas who were the rivals of Mattei. And the assassination of Kennedy aids them in the same way . . ." (The suspension points are Buchanan's.)

What is jarring amid such blinding clarity is that the first paragraph of the article *"J'accuse"* begins: "Shortly before his assassination, President Kennedy and Mr. Khrushchev had signed a treaty putting an end to nuclear tests." Must the search for the "instigators of the assassination" nevertheless be limited to "Texas oil circles"? Apparently yes, since the sixth article in *L'Express* was titled "Battle to the Death Between Wall Street and Texas," which suggests that the "oil tycoons" could not rely on the "kings of finance" to have Kennedy assassinated in order to sabotage the détente.

In Buchanan's book, which follows the same geometrical progression as did his articles in *L'Express,* we finally come to this profession of faith: "I believe the assassination of the President was essentially provoked by the fear of the internal and international consequences which the Moscow treaty might touch off; disarmament which would dismember the industries on which the conspirators depend; an international détente which, according to them, would threaten nationalization of their oil investments abroad." Two pages later: "How could the assassination of the President *automatically* have benefited the plotters? [Buchanan's italics—L.S.] It is obvious that they made use of Lee Harvey Oswald for the specific purpose of increasing tension between the United States and Cuba, and above all between the United States and the Soviet Union, which was the main objective. . . ."

None of this explains why the dangers of the détente—which brought the risk, Buchanan tells us again, of causing a $50-billion reduction in the U.S. defense budget—should have set off the homicidal reaction of H. L. Hunt and his oil colleagues in Texas, while they apparently did not trouble the huge aeronautical firms of California, the steel interests of Pittsburgh, the missile makers, and other "cannon merchants."

I am not obliged, luckily, to make Buchanan's theories coherent. He himself summed up as follows the objectives of *l'homme H,* chief of the plot:

> Of the three principal enemies of *l'homme H*—Mattei, Kennedy and Khrushchev—the first was already eliminated. *L'homme H* undoubtedly thought he could get rid of the other two at the same time: The assassination of Kennedy by the "Communist" Oswald would be a double blow; it would discredit Khrushchev and reduce to nothing the efforts toward obtaining a détente.

Too bad Buchanan decided to stop at this point. He was so neatly arriving at the "obvious" collusion—"obvious" because it benefited both—between H. L. Hunt and Mao Tse-tung.

Parallel to the "reasoning" of Buchanan, but with a totally

opposed purpose, is the theory expressed (if one can use that word) in the magazine *American Opinion,* published by Robert Welch, the Massachusetts candymaker who founded the John Birch Society.

The author of this theory is a professor named Revilo P. Oliver (if Revilo—Oliver spelled backward—is the real "Christian" name supplied by his parents, then his problems began before he was born), whose state of health apparently does not prevent him from teaching Greek and Latin properly at the University of Illinois. For the professor, there isn't the slightest doubt that President Kennedy was killed by Oswald, and that Oswald was a professional agent of "the Conspiracy." The Conspiracy, of course, is the John Birch notion of the worldwide Communist plot whose members included former President Eisenhower and whose principal tool remains Chief Justice Warren. For those who might not realize the purpose of the Conspiracy, Oliver is happy to provide that information: It is "to disarm the United States and prepare it for occupation by Soviet troops and associated savages of the 'United Nations'. . . ."

There is no question about the assassin: Oswald was "trained in sabotage, terrorism and guerrilla warfare (including accurate shooting from ambush) in the well-known school for international criminals near Minsk," then brought to the United States "by our Communist-controlled State Department."

When it comes to the victim, however, the explanation requires more effort on Oliver's part. Kennedy had been denounced as "anti-American" by the extreme right-wingers who lamented that they could not call him "Rosenfeld" as they did Roosevelt (although they refrained from referring to Goldwater as Goldwasser). Aside from the famous "welcome" ad in the *Dallas Morning News* the morning of Kennedy's arrival, the city had been flooded with pamphlets showing full-face and profile photos of the President in the style of FBI posters; the black headline over the pictures was "Wanted for Treason." Among the "seditious activities" for which "this man" was condemned were his plan for "turning the sovereignty of the U.S. over to the Communist controlled United Nations," his giving "support and encouragement to the Communist inspired racial riots," and his having "illegally invaded a sovereign state with federal troops" (a reference to the Oxford, Mississippi, episode of 1962). Was Kennedy redeemed by death in the eyes of the Birchers?

Not at all. Revilo P. Oliver even takes pains to warn us that he does not believe in the maxim *de mortuis nil nisi bonum*, because "taboos"—such as speaking well of the dead—"are for barbarians" while "we are a civilized race." After which he devotes a long tirade to the memory of the President, which can only be read in small doses unless one has a strong stomach.

The Birchite analyst states that he does not approve of the assassination. The first reason is that Kennedy was President of the United States, a symbol of the nation; "to put the matter as clearly as possible, the crime would have been every bit as horrible and shocking, had it *(per impossibile)* been absolutely certain that on the very next day the President would be impeached, tried, convicted, removed from office, and executed for his own crimes." The second reason is that the assassination was "an act of violence both deplorable and ominous—as ominous as the violence excited by the infamous Martin Luther King and other criminals engaged in inciting race war with the approval and even, it is said, the active co-operation of the White House."

To put the matter as clearly as possible concerning the second reason as he had done for the first, Oliver cites another example of "deplorable and ominous" violence comparable to the assassination: ". . . the violence of the uniformed goons (protected by reluctant and ashamed soldiers) whom Kennedy, in open violation of the American Constitution, set into Oxford, Mississippi, to kick into submission American citizens, whom the late Mr. Kennedy had come to regard as his subjects."

Thus explaining the "two basic reasons why the American people were shocked and grieved by the assassination," the classicist of the Birch Society enumerates "a few of the hundred reasons why we shall never forget John F. Kennedy."

I will mention only the final two of the hundred:

He is the John F. Kennedy who installed and maintained

in power the unspeakable Yarmolinsky-McNamara gang in the Pentagon to demoralize and subvert our armed forces and to sabotage our military installations and equipment. He is the John F. Kennedy who, by shameless intimidation, bribery, and blackmail, induced weaklings in Congress to approve treasonable acts designed to disarm us and to make us the helpless prey of the affiliated criminals and savages of the "United Nations". . . .

His oration concludes:

So long as there are Americans, his memory will be cherished with distaste. If the United States is saved by the desperate exertions of patriots, we may have a future of true greatness and glory—but we shall never forget how near we were to total destruction in the year 1963. And if the international vermin succeed in completing their occupation of our country, Americans will remember Kennedy while they live, and will curse him as they face the firing squads or toil in a brutish degradation that leaves no hope for anything but a speedy death.

But then, why did the Conspiracy want to kill a man who gave it such support? And since the assassination seems to have saved the United States from "total destruction," why not give credit to the "desperate exertions of patriots" rather than blame the "international vermin"? Professor Oliver prefers not to consider the second question, but he takes up the first and suggests three possible explanations:

(1) "Kennedy was executed by the Communist Conspiracy because he was planning to turn American. For this comforting hypothesis there is no evidence now known."

(2) "The assassination was the result of one of the rifts that not infrequently occur within the management of the Communist conspiracy, whose satraps sometimes liquidate one another without defecting from the Conspiracy, just as Persian satraps, such as Tissaphernes and Pharnabazus, made war on one another without revolting or intending to revolt against the King of Kings."

(3) "The Conspiracy ordered the assassination as part of systematic preparation for a domestic take-over. If so, the plan, of course, was to place the blame on the 'right-wing extremists' (if I may use the Bolsheviks' code-word for informed and loyal Americans), and we may be sure that a whole train of 'clues' had been carefully planted to lead or point in that direction as soon as Oswald was safe in Mexico."

Summing it up: Revilo Oliver eliminates in one stroke the first "explanation." After having read three times the three columns of *American Opinion* that he devotes to the second, I think Oliver seems to admit that while it was possible that "Fidel arranged the assassination of Jack," he does not believe this explanation either, despite Tissaphernes, Pharnabazus, "Zinoviev (Apfelbaum)" and "Kamenev (Rosenfeld)." He does not conceal his preference for the third alternative, all the more possible in his eyes since, "aside from the Conspiracy's obvious need for some drastic means of checking the growth of American patriotism, there is the consideration that Kennedy was rapidly becoming a political liability." In fact, he tells us, the lid was about to blow off all sorts of scandals, concerning not only "secret shipments of secret munitions of war to the Soviet by the Administration" but "sadistic sexual perversions" and "the use of governmental powers for the importation and distribution of hallucinatory narcotics."

In short, the Conspiracy, angry because Kennedy was not "on schedule" (he had not yet been able to force through Congress those "Civil Rights" that were "a very vital part of the vermin's preparations for the final take-over"), sent the man from Minsk into action.

Oliver does not go into the events in Dallas, although he does find an opportunity to say Oswald was "walking directly toward the apartment of the Jakob Rubenstein (alias Jack Ruby) who later silenced him." His final revelation consists in explaining why "Comrade Oswald was careful to provide evidence that the rifle used in the assassination had been purchased by mail"; this was to create propaganda for banning the sale of firearms to the public, and to "reduce the occupational hazards to the Balubas,

Outer Mongolians, or other beasts who may form the 'international police force' that is to occupy the United States and butcher its white inhabitants. . . ."

It is time to bring out the mop, but to those readers who might think I should have done so before—perhaps believing I went to look for these quotations among the garbage of an insane asylum —I owe an explanation.

Revilo P. Oliver is not in a mental hospital. He is a professor of classical languages—of the humanities—at the University of Illinois, an influential member of the John Birch Society, a featured writer for the magazine put out by Welch (who hailed Oliver's article as a "superb commentary"). And it must be recalled that board members of the Birch Society include industrialists, bankers, scientists, professors, and even military personalities such as General Douglas MacArthur's former aide, Colonel Laurence E. Bunker.

It must also be recalled that on August 12, 1964, at Hershey, Pennsylvania—standing between former President Dwight D. Eisenhower and former Vice President Richard M. Nixon—Barry Goldwater, Republican candidate for President of the United States, publicly refused to repudiate that same John Birch Society.

21

SOME QUESTIONS OF
EVIDENCE

THIS BOOK IS NOT A BRIEF. Circumstances, it is true, have led me
to offer Lee Harvey Oswald a chance to defend himself, a chance
brutally denied him by Ruby, Wade, and Warren, each in his
own way. But I am not a defense lawyer, ignoring evidence that
might be unfavorable to the client or trying to minimize it. I
have no client, and moreover I feel no personal sympathy for
Oswald or his family. I ask nothing better than to be convinced—
but no matter how I turn the case around to see it from every
angle, I find nothing to show that Oswald was the assassin of
President Kennedy.

I admit the authorities proved he owned a rifle. So what? Thousands of Texans keep rifles in their homes, and most of them,
unlike Oswald, even buy bullets when they purchase their guns.
For Oswald, it apparently was enough to hold the rifle or pose
for photographs with it so that he could feel like a revolutionary
hero. The fact that he had not thought about buying the bullets
proves, in any case, that at the time he ordered the Mannlicher-
Carcano the idea had not come to him that he might really use
it one day.

This unexpected conclusion can be drawn from a mere glance
at the Klein's Sporting Goods ad as reproduced by the *New York
Times*.

Answering questions about the actual price Oswald had paid
for the rifle sent from Chicago on March 20, 1963, Captain Fritz
declared that the figure given earlier, $12.78, was erroneous. The
price paid was $19.95. But what then about the "6.5 mm Italian

285

military ammo, 108 rounds" (article No. E20-751) which, with a six-shot clip furnished free of charge, came to $7.50? Milton P. Klein, confirming that "A. Hidell" had ordered the rifle with telescopic sight for $19.95, had said nothing about ammunition. Strange though it might seem, could it have been that Oswald bought his Italian carbine without anything to load it with?

The answer is: Yes. Klein himself told me this when I called him in Chicago.

"You sent A. Hidell the $19.95 rifle?" I asked.

"Yes," he replied wearily.

"Was the order paid in advance?"

"Yes."

"Then it was accompanied by a money order for $19.95?"

"$19.95 plus shipping charges."

"Was there a separate money order for $7.50?"

There was a brief pause. Then he asked: "Why would there have been another money order for $7.50?"

"For the ammunition and the clip. Or were a clip and cartridges included in the $19.95 price?"

Another silence, but not for long:

"The price of $19.95 was only for the rifle and the telescopic sight. The order we shipped to the post-office box in the name of A. Hidell did not include any cartridges."

Thus, contrary to what had been thought, the investigators had not even proved that Oswald owned the "lethal weapon," since an unloaded rifle is not a lethal weapon. The authorities had never given the slightest hint as to when and where Oswald could have bought the Italian military bullets, without which the Mannlicher-Carcano was a harmless toy in his hands, and as to how many of them he had bought. The only ones ever mentioned were the three empty cartridges near the sixth-floor window and the one bullet that remained in the rifle. No bullets were found in the garage in Irving or in the room on North Beckley Avenue. Either Oswald was down to his last four bullets at the time of the assassination, or else he took special care to get rid of any other ammunition he had—while handing the authorities his giveaway assassin's picture, his correspondence with the Communist Party, his false credentials in the name of A. Hidell, etc. The third possibility, of course, is that the four bullets described by the investigators belonged to someone else.

I have found only one allusion to the origin of the cartridges in the Warren Report. This appears on page 555 and starts with a reference to the clip: "The rifle probably was sold without a clip; however, the clip is commonly available."

Those who do not consider the Warren Report a holy book which it would blasphemous—or worse, communistic—to question will be intrigued once more by the odd ambiguity of certain information that should have been pinned down precisely. Why does the Commission say the rifle *probably* was sold without a clip? Did none of Earl Warren's associates have time to make a phone call to Chicago and ask Milton P. Klein for the information I obtained in a matter of minutes? But the Commission also had the FBI's report, and it is impossible to believe that the agents who spent many hours at the headquarters of Klein's Sporting Goods could have forgotten to ask about the clip. I can see only one plausible explanation for this lack of precision: The Commission declares that the rifle *probably* was sold *without* a clip because it hopes the reader will take it that *perhaps* it was sold *with* a clip.

The serene indifference of the Warren Commission regarding the cartridges is even more startling.

Describing the one that was found in the clip, the Report says it was "readily available for purchase from mail-order houses, as well as a few gunshops." That would considerably narrow the field of investigation, even though the Commission seems to give the impression that the task would be beyond it by adding that "some 2 million rounds have been placed on sale in the United States." The FBI discovered in one day the mail-order house that had sent the rifle to A. Hidell; it should have been able in 10 months to find the firm that provided the cartridges, if there was such a firm. As to the "few gunshops" where Oswald might have bought the ammunition personally, these presented even less difficulty for a serious inquiry, since Oswald's whereabouts between March and November were known.

Incidentally, although the Report volunteers the irrelevant data about the number of rounds "placed on sale," it does not tell us how many were actually sold.

Drawing up an accurate list of those who bought such cartridges between March 20 and November 22 might have been costly and time-consuming, but is it presumptuous to say that it would have been worth the trouble, since it involved the assassination of the President of the United States? The FBI and the Commission wasted countless days of effort and hundreds of thousands of dollars in assembling tons of useless details that did not lead to important facts but buried them. Certainly the Commission and the FBI, before concentrating their attention on Oswald's biography, should have exhausted every possible avenue of inquiry— including those that seemed to lead to someone other than Lee Harvey Oswald.

The Report, for instance, prefers to ignore what its star witness, Marina Oswald, told the FBI on December 17, 1963. The FBI summed it up (Commission Exhibit 1403, Volume XXII of the Hearings): "Oswald did not have any ammunition for the rifle to her knowledge in either Dallas or New Orleans, and he did not speak of buying ammunition."

Nor does the Report mention the affidavit given to the FBI on December 9, 1963, by Mitchell Scibor, general production manager for Klein's Sporting Goods. Klein's was the logical place for Oswald to order cartridges when and if he wanted some, since he knew Klein's had them and offered 108 rounds with a clip for the relatively low price of $7.50. Scibor said the records were searched "in the variations of the name Hidell as well as in the name Lee Harvey Oswald" for the period "from February 22, 1963, the date that Klein's received the rifle in stock, to November 22, 1963," but that "no sales of ammunition were found under these names" (Exhibit 2957, Volume XXVI).

Now Oswald needed at least *one* 6.5 mm. (ex-7.65 mm.) bullet before April 10, when according to the Warren Commission he set out to shoot General Walker. If he did not order "it" by mail (FBI expert Frazier testified that "the ammunition that we have purchased for this rifle comes in 20-shot boxes"), where did he buy his ammunition?

In March 1964—only then, not before—the FBI started "an effort to locate a source of supply" where Oswald could have bought cartridges, by canvassing all possible outlets in the Dallas and Irving areas. They found only two places where this type of ammunition had been on sale—two Dallas gunshops, one run by John Thomas Masen and the other by John H. Brinegar. On March 11, 1964, "the photograph of Lee Harvey Oswald was exhibited to Mr. Masen and he advised he was unable to identify this individual as being a person to whom he had previously sold 6.5 ammunition." The FBI returned to Masen's Gun Shop on March 26, but with no more success: "Mr. Masen claimed he had never seen Lee Harvey Oswald, had no recollection of his ever having come to his place of business, and he had never sold any of this ammunition to Oswald." Brinegar gave exactly the same answers. March 12: "The photograph of Lee Harvey Oswald was exhibited to Mr. Brinegar and he stated he was not able to identify this individual as being a person to whom he had previously sold 6.5 ammunition." March 26: "Mr. Brinegar stated he did not know Lee Harvey Oswald, had no recollection of ever seeing him, and did not believe he had sold him any of this type ammunition" (Exhibit 2694, Volume XXVI).

None of the information given here is to be found in the Report, which devotes *one three-line sentence* in its nearly 900 pages to the absolutely essential question of Oswald's ammunition. The Warren Commission, of course, needs the space for Oswald's biography.

Compared to such a tremendous gap in the prosecution brief, several other points about the case that I have not yet discussed appear to be of secondary interest. I shall review them briefly, if only to show why I do not deal with them at greater length.

THE PARAFFIN TEST

It was a Cuban, Iturrioz Font, who apparently used paraffin for the first time to reveal traces of powder left by the firing of a weapon. That occurred in 1913. But it was another Latin American criminologist, the Mexican González Miranda, who developed the "paraffin test" as a method of discovering murders camouflaged as suicides, and then as a general means of determining whether a suspect recently fired a weapon. A shot leaves minute traces of nitrate on the skin exposed to the gases produced by the detonation, and a coating of paraffin brings the traces out of the pores.

The probative value of this test, internationally known today as the González test, is far from being universally accepted; its critics, in fact, are especially numerous in the United States.

The FBI *Bulletin,* for example, has on many occasions warned against drawing hasty conclusions solely on the basis of a paraffin test. The American experts believe the absence of powder traces does not suffice to clear a suspect, and their presence does not suffice to convict him. As early as 1935 the *Bulletin* had published a list of professions in which the paraffin test gave positive results although the subject had never touched a weapon: miners handling explosives, gardeners using certain fertilizers, etc. The police manual of Callan and Stephenson, first published in 1939, held that the test could at most serve as corroborative evidence and found its main advantage to be psychological: It "may frequently be used to obtain confessions from suspects." In the TV debate I mentioned earlier, Percy Foreman, president of the National Association of Defense Lawyers, said categorically: "There's no competent person in America who will give any credence to the paraffin test."

However probative or insignificant it may be, it is obvious that the González test cannot be simultaneously invoked and ignored. Yet this is what was done in Dallas: The investigation invoked the test when it served its purpose as evidence against Oswald but ignored it when it tended to clear Oswald.

In fact the paraffin tests on Oswald disclosed powder traces on his hands but not on his face. If the tests are to be trusted, this meant Oswald had fired a revolver that day but not a rifle, unless we assume that he performed his feat in the style of a circus star who fires from the hip instead of the shoulder. It followed that Oswald was not the assassin of the President, who was slain by bullets from a rifle, not from a revolver. But the Dallas investigators talked just the same of the "proof" of the paraffin test, and

made use of ambiguous references to Oswald's having fired a
"gun," without specifying whether they meant a rifle or a pistol.
The best example of this was provided by District Attorney
Wade's Sunday press conference:

> *Reporter.* What about the paraffin tests?
> *Wade.* Yes, I've got paraffin tests that showed he had
> recently fired a gun—it was on both hands.
> *Reporter.* On both hands?
> *Wade.* Both hands.
> *Reporter.* He recently fired a rifle?
> *Reporter.* A gun.
> *Wade.* A gun.

Wade cannot be charged with lying, since in avoiding the word
"rifle," he seemed to mean a revolver. But for the TV viewers and
even for most of the newsmen, the distinction was too subtle.
The *New York Times* being the only newspaper, as far as I know,
that published the entire transcript of the press conference, a good
many Americans still believe the paraffin tests "proved" that
Oswald shot the President.

The way he stressed that powder traces were found on both
hands shows well enough that this was exactly what Wade wanted.
Since a rifle shot releases gases behind the firing chamber, even
the presence of traces on both hands, which would tend to indicate use of a rifle, still could not compensate for the absence of
traces on the cheek and neck. Thus, if the D.A. was able to convict
Oswald in the eyes of the public with these tests, there was nothing
in them that could have supported his case in a courtroom.

The prosecution could not even have used the paraffin tests as
proof of Oswald's guilt in the Tippit murder: This would amount
to conceding at the same time the innocence of Oswald in the
assassination of President Kennedy.

The members of the Warren Commission were more aware
than Wade of how these attempts to prove too much could go
astray. They made a complete about-face on the question:

During the evening of November 22, the Dallas Police Department performed paraffin tests on Oswald's hands and right cheek in an apparent effort to determine, by means of a scientific test, whether Oswald had recently fired a weapon. The results were positive for the hands and negative for the right cheek. Expert testimony before the Commission was to the effect that the paraffin test was unreliable in determining whether or not a person has fired a rifle or revolver. The Commission has, therefore, placed no reliance on the paraffin tests administered by the Dallas police.

Appendix X of the Report, on "Expert Testimony," has a two-page section that describes the tests in greater detail. It summarizes the technical objections raised by the FBI against the González test, objections about which ex-FBI Agent Wade must have known when he presented the public with his "scientific" paraffin test. We could end the matter there if the editorial methods employed by those who prepared the Report did not reveal in an obvious way just what the Commission's main preoccupation was. In its explanations of chemistry designed to show the care exercised by the Commission in studying all aspects of the evidence, the Report offers only one direct passage in nontechnical language, from the testimony of FBI expert Cortlandt Cunningham:

> *Mr. Cunningham.*   I personally wouldn't expect to find any residues on a person's right cheek after firing a rifle due to the fact that by the very principles and the manufacture and the action, the cartridge itself is sealed into the chamber by the bolt being closed behind it, and upon firing the case, the cartridge case expands into the chamber filling it up and sealing it off from the gases, so none will come back in your face, and so by its very nature, I would not expect to find residue on the right cheek of a shooter.

In its subtle criticism of Henry Wade (subtle in that it questions his statements but not his methods of investigation), the

Commission admonishes the D.A. for his "mistaken statement that the paraffin test showed that Oswald had fired a gun," explaining that this "might have influenced prospective jurors." As if anyone still had any thought about jurors! The immediate and evident concern of the Commission, as expressed in its choice of the above passage, is to see that the careless publicizing of the paraffin tests would not lead the public to interpret the results in Oswald's favor.

THE SELF-BETRAYING DETOUR

In a book published in the United States as *Oswald: Assassin or Fall Guy,* whose main purpose seems to have been to sink a knife into J. Edgar Hoover, the German-American journalist Joachim Joesten attached much importance to a point he had already raised in the French weekly *Le Nouveau Candide* in January 1964. This concerns what he called "the self-betraying detour." Joesten declared:

> Instead of proceeding from Main Street to the underpass in a straight line, which would have been the normal and "logical" thing to do, the motorcade at the intersection of Main and Houston Streets embarked on a wholly uncalled-for double detour. It swung first to the right into Houston Street and then, after a one-block stretch, turned left into Elm Street, which like Main Street feeds into the triple underpass. The reader is invited to look carefully at the map, reproduced in the documentary section of this book, for it was this double detour which assured the success of the shooting.

I accepted the invitation and carefully examined the map in the "documentary section" of Joesten's book.

The map clearly shows, however, the opposite of what the author wants to prove. It confirms, in fact, that for traffic coming from the city and heading toward the Stemmons Freeway, the "normal" and "logical" access route, and moreover the one prescribed by the police, is along Elm Street and not Main Street.

For just beyond the underpass there is a concrete curb separating the two streets and a "No Turns" sign forbidding Main Street traffic from turning right into the Stemmons Freeway approach. I refer here, for my part, to the aerial photo in the Illustrations.

To explain away the fact that his argument is contradicted by his own map and his own photos, Joesten contends that "the feasibility of the turn is proven by the sign prohibiting it." True enough, though he admits that "traffic would have had to be halted on Elm to allow [the] motorcade to make the S turn across it." True also that "with all the police available, this slightly inconvenient but much safer route could easily have been arranged." Yet the planners of the motorcade route would have had to know in advance that it would be "much safer" not to pass in front of the Texas School Book Depository.

Since President Kennedy's concern, however, was not to escape assassination (see Chapter 13) but to make a good impression in Dallas, he had no reason whatsoever to break the city rules and have the police stop traffic while he made an illegal turn. Such a request, in fact, could only have caused local resentment.

Joesten tells us that he made this turn twice in a taxi, each time asking the driver to swing around from the Main Street extension toward the Freeway approach, at the point where the "curb" ends. This proves nothing except that two Dallas cab drivers were willing to risk fines in order to satisfy Joachim Joesten, and I hope he tipped them well. I performed a different test. I got into a taxi on Main Street and asked the driver to take me to the Trade Mart, giving him no other instructions. He turned right on Houston Street, made a left turn in front of the Depository Building, and went under the right arch of the underpass onto Stemmons Freeway—the same route followed by the motorcade.

Since Joesten, after all, did not undertake a general critique of the traffic regulations in Dallas, I do not believe anyone can call this a "preposterous itinerary" that "cries out for investigation and explanation."

Ascribing, however, the most "sinister meaning" to this "self-betraying detour," Joesten finds in it "a key element in raising suspicions of a conspiracy." And when he discovers, moreover, that the route published the morning of November 22 in the *Dallas Morning News* did not specifically mention the "detour," he seeks no further: "This is, indeed, the crux of the matter, the key to the mystery, the one detail that gives the whole show away. . . ."

Things are not *that* simple.

OSWALD, SECRET AGENT

There were rumors that Lee Oswald had been at one time in the pay of the CIA, which supposedly had hired the young political wanderer to infiltrate either pro-Castro groups or anti-Castro groups, or both. Attempts were made to prove also, on the basis of a name and telephone number found in his room, that he had connections with the FBI. Joachim Joesten, finding in this a chance to denounce J. Edgar Hoover as "an accessory after the fact," and as "one of the most maleficent forces in American public life," managed to weave all this into a single pattern: "Oswald, I am convinced, was an FBI agent provocateur, with a CIA background and connections."

Mrs. Marguerite Oswald even claimed her son had undergone special training in the Marines to become a secret agent and that it was in this capacity that he had gone off to Russia in 1959.

More convincingly, it was held that Lee Oswald, before obtaining permission to leave the Soviet Union with his Russian-born wife and child, had to make certain promises to the Soviet secret police. This would explain the surprising ease with which he was able to acquire the hard-to-get exit visas, just as his contacts with the FBI or the CIA explained the no less unusual facility with which he got his American passport in June 1963 in New Orleans.

Lee Oswald, of course, could well have worked for both Moscow and Washington, successively or at the same time, and he might have decided one day to pull away from these two in favor of Havana. Nerin E. Gun, in his *The Red Roses of Dallas*, unhesitatingly suggests that Oswald made a secret trip to Cuba during his visit to Mexico from September 26 to October 3, 1963. If we were to believe Gun, we would indeed have to conclude that Oswald had remarkable personal connections with Havana: at least plane connections.

While some of these theories are far-fetched, I do not exclude the possibility that Oswald had been contacted—and used at times —by American or Soviet secret services.

No matter what the Warren Report says, it is certainly amazing that a man with Oswald's past was able to get his passport in only 24 hours. His request, filed in New Orleans on June 24, 1963, gave his true identity and indicated as well, among the countries he planned to visit, the Soviet Union and Poland. The passport was issued to him the next day, June 25. Such promptness is certainly not the rule in the State Department's issuance of passports to citizens such as Lee Harvey Oswald.

The files of the State Department, the Report contends, contained no information "which might reasonably have led it to expect that Oswald would violate the laws of the United States when he went abroad." It adds piously: "State Department officials believed that in view of the Supreme Court decisions, the Department was not empowered to deny anyone a passport on grounds related to freedom of speech or to political association and beliefs."

This may be the way things are supposed to be, but it isn't the way things are. True, by 1963 it was no longer possible for some highly placed imbecile in the State Department to delight Communist propagandists throughout the world by preventing a Paul Robeson from singing "Ole Man River" in London or Stockholm. But before the Supreme Court declared such practices unconstitutional—in a *1964* decision—many Americans, such as those who had a bone to pick with the House Un-American Activities Committee, had to submit to petty harassment that Lee Harvey Oswald apparently escaped. Where Oswald is concerned, the extraordinary dedication to principle claimed by the State Department and accepted as such by the Warren Commission does not appear very convincing.

Although Oswald had expressed his "intention to expatriate himself" when he went to the U.S. Embassy in Moscow in 1959 (in fact he had explicitly pledged his allegiance to the Soviet

Union), the Report contends that no final decision had been made in his case, so that the question of expatriation did not arise when his passport request was under consideration.

The Report admits, however, that in 1963 the State Department still held that it had the right to refuse a passport to an American citizen if it believed his future activities abroad could be "prejudicial to the interests of the United States." It is certainly difficult to see how the State Department, guided by this principle, could have believed there was nothing questionable about issuing a passport to a man with Oswald's record, especially when he had stated his intention to return to the Soviet Union.

The Commission's explanations become truly suspicious when we see how the Report handles the possibility that Oswald could have passed military secrets to the Soviets, as he had openly declared he would. For the Commission, Oswald's statement about this was nothing more than "rash talk," which the authorities had no reason to be concerned about: "Although Oswald's statement in 1959 that he would furnish the Russians with information he had obtained in the Marine Corps may have indicated that he would disclose classified information if he possessed any such information, there was no indication in 1963 that he had any valuable information." That he had any valuable information in 1963, or in 1959?

The officer in charge of Oswald's radar unit, Lieutenant James E. Donovan, appeared before the Commission and his name is mentioned four times in the Report: as a witness to the inordinate pride of Oswald, his lack of political militancy, his technical ability, and his interest in world affairs. It is only when we turn to Volume VIII of the Hearings and look up Donovan's testimony that we find the lieutenant said something more. Oswald's defection, he declared, "necessitated a lot of change of aircraft call signs, codes, radio frequencies, radar frequencies."

Strange that the Report does not mention these troubles caused by Oswald's move to Moscow, in view of the fact that he knew the characteristics of certain new equipment and "that kind of stuff you cannot change." On September 13, 1960, the Marine Corps had not hesitated to change Oswald's discharge retroactively to "dishonorable." But we are expected to believe—and the Warren Report tries to make our belief easier by omitting Donovan's relevant testimony—that the State Department was too concerned with Oswald's rights to subject him to questioning or to initiate any investigation before handing over his passport.

Perhaps the most interesting contribution regarding this aspect of the Oswald affair came from Congressman Gerald R. Ford, in the first of 37 chapters in his *Portrait of the Assassin*.

This chapter, titled "The Commission Gets Its First Shock," describes what happened on January 22, 1964, when Texas Attorney General Waggoner Carr called J. Lee Rankin in Washington and told him he had received information that Oswald had been an "undercover agent" for the FBI. "The members of the Commission were hurriedly called into emergency session by the Chairman," Ford wrote. Gathered "around the eight-foot oblong table," they "looked at one another in amazement"; "the late hour and the complete disruption of everyone's personal plans added to the atmosphere of tension."

Ford cannot recall attending a meeting "more tense and hushed." The members of the Commission decided to ask Carr, Wade, and any other Dallas officials who might have knowledge of the allegations to come "at once" to Washington. They "slipped into the nation's capital with complete anonymity," but over the weekend the *New York Times* "got wind of part of the speculation." Furthemore, on the very day the Dallas officials met with the Commission, January 24, "Harold Feldman's article in *The Nation* magazine hit the newsstands" with "four pages of hard-to-answer questions."

Now, as Ford states, "members simply knew that the whole business was a most delicate and sensitive matter involving the nation's faith in its own institutions and one of the most respected federal agencies," but what was the Commission to do about it?

It seems the origin of the "rumor" was a *Houston Post* reporter named Lonnie Hudkins. "The dilemma of the Commission," Ford says, "was how to go about checking the allegation that the FBI was involved in this matter" while avoiding "plunging into the matter in some irresponsible manner that might jeopardize the

effectiveness of an important agency's future operations." Senator
John Sherman Cooper thought "we are under a duty to see what
Hudkins says about it." Senator Richard B. Russell agreed: "Of
course, we can get an affidavit from Mr. Hoover and put it in
this record and go on and act on that, but if we didn't go any
further than that, and we don't pursue it down to Hudkins or
whoever it is, there still would be thousands of doubting Thomases
who would believe this man was an FBI agent and you just didn't
try to clear it up and you just took Hoover's word." Chairman
Warren then decided: "We must go into this thing from both
ends, from the end of the rumormongers and from the end of
the FBI, and if we come into a *cul de sac*—well, there we are, but
we can report on it. . . ."

Well, there we are not. All the soul-searching reported by Congressman Ford remained purely theoretical. Lonnie Hudkins was
never heard by the Commission, which "just took Hoover's word."
General Counsel J. Lee Rankin had made it clear: "We do have
a dirty rumor that is very bad for the Commission, the problem,
and it is very damaging to the agencies that are involved in it and
it must be wiped out insofar as it is possible to do so by this
Commission." Rankin did not say it must be *investigated;* he said
it must be *wiped out*.

If, in spite of all this, I do not give more space to the question
of whether Lee Harvey Oswald was a secret agent, it is because
I have no ways and means of finding out what the Warren Commission refused to look for. But, above all, I wish to emphasize
again that this is not a basic question. For, whatever the Russians'
motives were in allowing Oswald and his family to leave, and whatever the State Department's were in granting a passport in 24
hours to an ex-defector who had vowed allegiance to the Soviet
Union, it would still remain to be proved that it was Oswald who
assassinated President Kennedy.

THE TWO RIFLES

Because Wade at first spoke of the rifle found in the Depository
as a Mauser, and did not identify it as a Mannlicher-Carcano until
the next day, some concluded that the police had found two rifles,

a German one and an Italian one, but had hastily disposed of the first when it found that only the second could be linked to Oswald.

Thomas Buchanan, naturally, had something even better for us: The "German Mauser" referred to by Wade was the rifle used by the assassin on the railroad overpass; this assassin, before running to the *Dallas Morning News* building, "threw away his still smoking weapon," and the police found it and turned it over to the D.A. As if this were not enough, Buchanan added that "in fact, it has even been proved that not one but two Carcanos were involved in the assassination." He apparently drew this conclusion from the Irving gunsmith incident, or perhaps he found it some where else in his imagination; I confess I could not follow the thread of his thinking. In any case, he informed us, the two weapons were "so similar that for a moment the police seem to have confused them."

The argument at the base of the two-rifles theory can be traced to the conviction that Wade, a former FBI agent, could not have mistaken a Mannlicher-Carcano for a Mauser. It can also be explained by the remarkable incompetence of the Dallas investigators, aggravated by their feverish desire to be seen on TV and get their names in the papers. Even though Wade continued to speak of a Mauser, the rifle shown Friday night on the third floor of police headquarters was actually a Mannlicher-Carcano.

What helped keep the theory alive later on was the embarrassment it seemed to have caused the Warren Commission.

In its "Speculations and Rumors" appendix, the Report lists as a "speculation": "The rifle found on the sixth floor of the Texas School Book Depository was identified as a 7.65 Mauser by the man who found it, Deputy Constable Seymour Weitzman." Then the Commission's "finding":

> Weitzman, the original source of the speculation that the rifle was a Mauser, and Deputy Sheriff Eugene Boone found the weapon. Weitzman did not handle the rifle and did not examine it at close range. He had little more than a glimpse of it and thought it was a Mauser, a German bolt-type rifle similar in appearance to the Mannlicher-Carcano. Police

laboratory technicians subsequently arrived and correctly identified the weapon as a 6.5 Italian rifle.

Since these "technicians," we gather from another "finding" on the same page, were Captain Fritz himself and Lieutenant Day, the above affirmation may yet present some difficulty. All the more so since, before we congratulate them on correctly identifying the weapon "subsequently" as a 6.5 Italian rifle, it should be remembered that this achievement was one that any school child could have equaled.

The Report's "Description of Rifle" tells us that the weapon found on the sixth floor was inscribed with various markings such as "MADE ITALY" and "CAL. 6.5." "These markings have been explained as follows," states the Report with scholarly precision: " 'MADE ITALY' refers to its origin; 'CAL. 6.5' refers to the rifle's caliber." Such a convincing explanation cannot be contested. The question remains whether Deputy Constable Weitzman did not know how to read, or whether he wasn't sharp enough mentally to understand that "MADE ITALY" referred to the origin of the rifle and "CAL. 6.5" to its caliber. If we are to accept the Commission's opinion in another part of the Report, the markings were easy to detect: In giving its reasons for rejecting the idea that the mysterious stranger at the Grand Prairie Sportsdrome could have been Oswald, the Commission notes that one witness had "examined the rifle briefly for some indication as to where it had been manufactured, but saw nothing, whereas the words 'MADE ITALY' are marked on the top of Oswald's Mannlicher-Carcano."

I am inclined to admit, nevertheless, that it took some time for the Dallas investigators to discover that a rifle marked "MADE ITALY" and "CAL. 6.5" was a 6.5-caliber Italian rifle . . . more time, in any case, than it took to rush to the nearest TV microphone. So I do not believe this is the most troubling mystery or even an essential point in the Oswald affair.

Perhaps I now have cleared the terrain enough to venture three general ideas that could pass for a theory, if one insists, and a fourth that should explain, even if one does not insist, what the Oswald affair has in common with *L'Affaire* of long ago, the Dreyfus case.

22

FOUR IDEAS

THE POPULAR FRENCH DICTIONARY *Petit Larousse,* referring to the Latin adage *Is fecit cui prodest* (the perpetrator of a crime is he who profits by it), wisely advises: "Caution should be used in applying this ancient axiom of law."

Caution is indeed necessary, because the principle has misled many an investigation and has sometimes resulted in gross miscarriages of justice. But this does not mean that in examining the Dallas affair we should go around looking for suspects among men, organizations, or circles with nothing to gain by the death of President Kennedy. Serge Groussard, for example, and the others who went to Chicago for their explanation of Dallas not only were unable to show any link between Oswald and the underworld, aside from their "personal interpretations" devoid of factual basis; they were obliged to admit that the change of command in the White House did not put an end to whatever problems the Mafia may have had.

Nor do I see how either the Communists (including those of Peking and Havana) or the anti-Communists (including those of Dallas) stood to gain by installing Johnson in place of Kennedy.

The weird prose of Revilo P. Oliver may show, of course, the degree to which hatred of Kennedy, mixed with a morbid fear of Communism, obsessed and unbalanced some fragile minds. And it would not have been entirely unexpected if some right-wing fanatic, steamed up by the furious propaganda strewn around the city, had taken up arms and waited at a window to get rid of the "traitor." Wasn't John F. Kennedy turning America the beau-

tiful over to the red (and black and yellow) hordes of world
Communism?

But this is not what happened on November 22. If Oswald was
the assassin, he was not this type at all; and if, as I believe, Oswald
was not the assassin, then there was a cold-blooded plot prepared
by efficient and methodical ringleaders who knew what they were
doing. We might suppose that these organizers, carried away by
their own propaganda, really saw treason in the nuclear test ban,
aid to Yugoslavia, noninvasion of Cuba, or participation in the
United Nations. But it would also have to be admitted that they
expected Lyndon Johnson to denounce the treaty of Moscow,
break relations with Yugoslavia, invade Cuba, and order UN headquarters in New York evacuated as soon as he moved into the
White House. Nothing could have encouraged a belief that Kennedy's Vice President would follow such a course.

The anti-Communists are not the only ones who would have
been disappointed by Johnson and would thus have had no reason
to eliminate Kennedy in his favor. It would have been the same
for the Communists, even those in Peking and Havana. For if they
had reason to fear any rapprochement between Washington and
Moscow as detrimental to themselves, they had no grounds for
believing that Lyndon Johnson, a conservative Texan but a
disciple of Franklin D. Roosevelt, would reject coexistence. As to
the possibility that the assassination might have been inspired by
the Kremlin, this could be imagined only as the result of a sudden
fit of insanity on the part of Khrushchev.

Then we have the oil millionaires. Joachim Joesten as well as
Thomas Buchanan rightly point out that H. L. Hunt and his
colleagues were afraid of losing their 27.5-per-cent tax credit,
which had been granted to the Texas oil industry on the pretext
of compensating for the depletion of oil resources. There is no
doubt that even though Kennedy and Johnson were elected on
the same platform, which explicitly condemned "financial privi-
lege," Johnson would be more likely than Kennedy to guarantee
the continuation of the Texans' special favors. Could this then
be the reason?

I will not go into any analysis of whether H. L. Hunt was ca-

pable of killing to avoid paying higher taxes. I prefer to note that
Hunt and his friends were not threatened with any immediate
action by Kennedy, nor were they necessarily saved from it by
Johnson. This is a decision that only the Congress can make. The
President may use his influence one way or the other, but he cannot act in Congress' place; and it is unlikely that Lyndon Johnson
would veto oil-tax legislation unfavorable to the Texas magnates.
Buchanan recalls that Kennedy was one of 29 Senators who in
1957 had supported the bill proposed by Senator Paul Douglas,
Democrat of Illinois, which would have taken away some of the
oil industry's privileges. If this was a vote for which H. L. Hunt
could never forgive Kennedy, how is it that he allowed Douglas
to stay alive?

Of all the possible objectives in the assassination, I find only
one that the organizers of a plot could reasonably have expected
to achieve: the defense of white supremacy in the South.

This, incidentally, is the only motive that Buchanan flatly rejects. "The racial question," he says in *L'Express,* "can be eliminated at the outset: although Johnson is a man of the South, he is
no Dixiecrat. It was the general view that he would pursue a policy
of gradual desegregation." And in his book: "Although Johnson
is a Southerner, there was little difference of opinion between him
and his predecessor concerning civil rights. . . . It is for this reason that I have not even bothered to consider the possibility that
Kennedy was assassinated by segregationists."

I do not intend to analyze the various ways one can approach the racial issue in the United States.

It is necessary to point out, however, that for Negroes as well
as for white racists what counts is not the passage of laws but their
enforcement. There were some excellent laws before those of
1964, and there was the decision of the Supreme Court ten years
earlier, but at the rate "gradual desegregation" had progressed in
Alabama or Mississippi, it would take a hundred years for Negroes
to become truly equal citizens. The Negroes—those of Harlem or
Chicago leading those of the South—do not want to wait even
one year. So-called gradual desegregation, in fact, offered an advantage to the racists: Legal but not enforced, and rejected in any

case by the masses of Negroes, it stamped as lawbreakers those who refused to be "reasonable" after a century of patience and whose violence—frightening some elements favoring "civil rights" in principle—was to create a "white backlash."

But with or without new laws, the President of the United States can throw his considerable powers into the balance on the side of the black minority and completely change the situation.

These are essentially economic powers: his decisions, for example, on where the federal government should build arsenals, bases, space projects, and dozens of other kinds of establishments that in many parts of the South, as poor as they are Southern, represent the difference between stagnation and prosperity. It is the chambers of commerce, not the churches, that consistently prove effective in bringing about adaptation to modern times; white ministers preach in a vacuum when they don't choose to preach *against* integration, but white businessmen realize that racial conflict is bad for business. And all are terrorized by the idea that the federal government might take action against them, not by sending in troops but by cutting off the money. Federal activities are more important to the economy of the South than to any other part of the country, and the South has been rather spoiled in that regard, thanks to the skillful political deals made by its Senators in Washington. Thus it is all the more vulnerable to Administration pressure. All that was needed to bring the South to its knees was a President willing to do so.

Was John F. Kennedy such a President? He did not appear to be so at Oxford, Mississippi, where he was content to follow—reluctantly—the precedent set by Eisenhower at Little Rock. He was even less so at Birmingham, where he tried, on the contrary, to appear only as a mediator. But there was something in the personality of John F. Kennedy that gave the impression that he might become, after November 1964, what he had not been in 1962 and 1963.

Perhaps the important fact here is that Kennedy could not seek another term in 1968. No one could really imagine him leaving office at the age of 51 with the main preoccupation of maintaining at all costs the unity of the monstrous hodgepodge known as the Democratic Party, as Eisenhower had done in 1964 for the Republican Party. Kennedy, a shrewd politician, was also a man who wanted to go down in history as a great president. Until 1964, in order not to jeopardize this ambition, which amounted to an ideal, the politician and party leader was obliged to maneuver. Once re-elected, he would have a free hand. The fact that he would have to leave the White House four years later would liberate him from the need to nurse his party, which is also the party of Senator James Eastland of Mississippi. He would know, at the same time, that it was a now-or-never situation.

In this century, the truly great American president will be the one who will use all the legal means at his command to prevent history from being written without him or against him amid bloody upheavals—the one who will impose racial equality once and for all.

I think what Negroes liked about Kennedy was his youth, his vitality, his apparent desire to confront problems squarely, even though the most often cited example of this determination had to do with the Cuban missile crisis of October 1962 and not the University of Mississippi crisis a short time before that. Negroes, in fact, expected more positive action from a John F. Kennedy than they had expected from an Adlai Stevenson or from other liberal leaders apparently closer to them in outlook. Certain characteristic reflexes on the part of the white racists showed that they, too, thought there was reason to fear what their colored victims were hoping for. They seemed convinced, in any case, that John F. Kennedy was the most dangerous enemy they had in the United States.

We will never know whether the racists' fears—the Negroes' hopes—would have been justified. The assassination of President Kennedy, a consecration of those fears and those hopes, was a tragic homage to the force of his personality.

In attributing the murder of President Kennedy to a racist conspiracy, I am only repeating what the entire world—the United States included—believed immediately after it heard the news.

The fact that this could not fail to be the universal and spontaneous reaction must have been a consideration of prime importance to the organizers of the plot. Their problem was not merely to succeed in the technical mission of executing the President; indeed they had to avoid what is usually considered a "perfect" assassination, that is, one that leaves no traces. Their problem was to make sure the assassination would be followed as quickly as possible by the arrest of an "assassin" who had no connection with the plotters.

Let us suppose for a moment that there had been no Oswald at the Texas School Book Depository, and that no one had been arrested.

With the country absolutely convinced that the crime could only have been the work of the racist extreme right, the first steps taken by President Johnson could well have ended the freedom these extremists had enjoyed. The FBI, so well informed about what goes on in the ludicrous Communist cells populated largely by its agents and informers, could no longer ignore the powerful racist groups, responsible for countless unpunished crimes such as the murders of the Negro girls in Birmingham. In short, the President's assassination, creating a wave of indignation against the racist killers and silencing their protectors in Congress, would inevitably boomerang against the plotters. It made sense only if public opinion could quickly be led to believe that someone else was to blame.

Lee Harvey Oswald, then, was a gift from heaven. Those who do not believe in gifts from heaven, or who believe that heaven distributes its gifts more judiciously, will therefore conclude that the whole blueprint of the assassination was based on the existence of Lee Harvey Oswald.

It is not even certain that the assassination was initially conceived in Dallas. One can easily imagine the plotters going through the list of cities President Kennedy planned to visit, Rule Number One being to strike during one of those propaganda trips in which vote-getting outweighed security precautions. But Rule Number Two—and, in my opinion, the *sine qua non*—was to consider only those cities where a scapegoat was available. I suppose that if Miami was on the list, they may have looked among the Cuban refugees: a former Bay of Pigs prisoner, for instance. The blame for the assassination could then be placed on his suffering and bitterness; better yet, "evidence" could be arranged to make of him a brainwashed Castro agent recruited in prison. The discovery in Dallas of Lee Oswald, the former pro-Soviet defector back in the country with a Russian wife and obscure political leanings, made it unnecessary to look any further.

In fact, whatever his behavior, the presence at the scene of the crime of an individual like Oswald sufficed virtually to guarantee that the conspirators could act with impunity.

We have imagined a Depository without Oswald, and have seen that an assassination under such conditions would have been unthinkable; even if the gunman took advantage of the incompetence of the police and escaped, the instigators would suffer mass reprisals imposed by public opinion. Let us suppose now that Oswald, instead of going off to be picked up at the Texas Theater, had disappeared. He would seem more guilty than ever, and all the more precious to the plotters. Let us suppose even that Oswald had remained with his Coke in the lunchroom, without leaving the building. That would change nothing, either, since the police would have learned soon enough who he was, and, if necessary, an anonymous telephone tip to Captain Fritz would have speeded things up.

The only real risk for the conspirators was that Oswald might go out to lunch in some nearby drugstore, or leave to watch the motorcade, or turn up among other employees at the moment of the crime. This risk, however, was reduced by what was known of Oswald's habits and character. He preferred to eat a sandwich at work, and he certainly wasn't the type to hang around street corners with pals. If on the other hand, to make sure he remained in the building, he was told to meet someone on some pretext in the lunchroom, it was hardly probable that someone else would enter that windowless room at the time the motorcade was going by. After all, the building *was* nearly deserted by this time.

I shall recapitulate (in Chapter 23) some of the facts impossible to explain other than by the existence of a plan to frame Oswald.

The Warren Report does not attempt to explain these facts. It prefers to dismiss them in advance by declaring that Oswald was not being hunted by the police at the time of his arrest.

This effort begins in a subdued tone, in a paragraph of the opening narrative where the dramatic note is sounded only in the final sentence:

> As Fritz and Day were completing their examination of this rifle on the sixth floor, Roy Truly, the building super-intendent, approached with information which he felt should be brought to the attention of the police. Earlier, while the police were questioning the employees, Truly had observed that Lee Harvey Oswald, 1 of the 15 men who worked in the warehouse [not including the em-ployees of the various publishing firms with offices in the building—L.S.], was missing. After Truly provided Os-wald's name, address, and general description, Fritz left for police headquarters. He arrived at headquarters shortly after 2 p.m. and asked two detectives to pick up the em-ployee who was missing from the Texas School Book De-pository. Standing nearby were the police officers who had just arrived with the man arrested in the Texas Theatre. When Fritz mentioned the name of the missing employee, he learned that the man was already in the interrogation room. The missing School Book Depository employee and the suspect who had been apprehended in the Texas The-atre were one and the same—Lee Harvey Oswald.

In its chapter on "The Assassin," the Warren Report pads the story with added detail and coats it with snatches of dialogue:

> Captain Fritz returned to police headquarters from the Texas School Book Depository at 2:15 after a brief stop at the sheriff's office. When he entered the homicide and rob-bery bureau office, he saw two detectives standing there with Sgt. Gerald L. Hill, who had driven from the theatre with Oswald. Hill testified that Fritz told the detective to get a search warrant, go to an address on Fifth Street in

Irving, and pick up a man named Lee Oswald. When Hill asked why Oswald was wanted, Fritz replied, "Well, he was employed down at the Book Depository and he had not been present for a roll call of the employees." Hill said, "Captain, we will save you a trip * * * there he sits."

It would have been interesting to know how Sergeant Hill had learned the name of the arrested suspect, but the Report does not go into that. Nor does it take up the mistake of Captain Fritz concerning the "roll call" of Depository employees, an assumption that fired the imagination of Thomas Buchanan but does not correspond with the segment of Roy Truly's testimony accepted by the Commission. At least the Report, in this instance, does not dodge another important contradiction:

> Although Oswald probably left the building at about 12:33 p.m., his absence was not noticed until at least one-half hour later. Truly, who had returned with Patrolman Baker from the roof, saw the police questioning the warehouse employees. Approximately 15 men worked in the warehouse and Truly noticed that Oswald was not among those being questioned. Satisfying himself that Oswald was missing, Truly obtained Oswald's address, phone number, and description from his employment application card. The address listed was for the Paine home in Irving. Truly gave this information to Captain Fritz who was on the sixth floor at the time. Truly estimated that he gave this information to Fritz about 15 or 20 minutes after the shots, but it was probably no earlier than 1:22 p.m., the time when the rifle was found. Fritz believed that he learned of Oswald's absence after the rifle was found. The fact that Truly found Fritz in the northwest corner of the floor, near the point where the rifle was found, supports Fritz' recollection.

The transcript of Roy Truly's testimony, in Volume VII of the Hearings, allows us to examine more closely what the Commission is talking about. The most striking element here is the fierce insistence of Joseph A. Ball, the assistant counsel who conducted the questioning, in trying to crush Truly's certainty about the time he recalled having reported Oswald missing.

The Depository manager had declared, as he had earlier told newsmen (including me), that he had become aware of Oswald's absence soon after returning from the roof:

> *Mr. Ball.* Did you make a check of your employees afterwards?
>
> *Mr. Truly.* No, no; not complete. No, I just saw the group of the employees over there on the floor and I noticed this boy wasn't with them. With no thought in my mind except that I had seen him a short time before in the building, I noticed he wasn't there.
>
> *Mr. Ball.* What do you mean "a short time before"?
>
> *Mr. Truly.* I would say 10 or 12 minutes.
>
> *Mr. Ball.* You mean that's when you saw him in the lunchroom?
>
> *Mr. Truly.* In the lunchroom.

Questioned by another assistant counsel, David W. Belin, in an earlier deposition (Volume III of the Hearings), Truly had already estimated the time he thought he had spent on the roof with Patrolman Baker. This statement matched his later testimony perfectly.

> *Mr. Belin.* About how long after these shots do you think it took you to go all the way up and look around the roof and come all the way down again?
>
> *Mr. Truly.* Oh, we might have been gone between 5 and 10 minutes. It is hard to say.

Truly's estimate was confirmed by Baker. "It was a little over 5 minutes," the motorcycle officer replied when Belin put the same question to him. Later the assistant counsel went back on the offensive:

> *Mr. Belin.* In this time sequence you mentioned you were on the roof more than 5 minutes, that could be 25 or 30 or 10 or 15 or what?

> Mr. Baker.   This, to my recollection, it seemed like I
> shouldn't have stayed up there over 10 minutes anyway,
> if that long.
> Mr. Belin.   So you would say somewhere between 5 and
> 10 minutes?
> Mr. Baker.   I just ran around up there looking for some-
> thing; I didn't find it and then we came on down.

When Ball went specially to Dallas, on May 14, to submit Roy
Truly to a new searching examination on this point, the Depository manager was finally thrown off balance. But the incredible—
and unprecedented—obstinacy with which the assistant counsel
had concentrated on that end left his "victory" somewhat unconvincing:

> Mr. Ball.   Now, about what time of day would you say
> is your best estimate that you told Captain Fritz of the
> name "Lee Oswald" and his address?
> Mr. Truly.   My best estimate would be a little before
> 1 o'clock—10 minutes.
> Mr. Ball.   The gun wasn't found until after 1 o'clock?
> Mr. Truly.   It wasn't found until after 1 o'clock?
> Mr. Ball.   No, it wasn't found until after 1 o'clock. I
> won't tell you exactly the time the gun was found, but
> I will say that the gun was not found until after 1 o'clock.
> Mr. Truly.   Well, I may be mistaken about where I
> learned they had found the gun. I thought it was on the
> sixth floor—it could have been some other place.
> Mr. Ball.   Captain Fritz said you didn't tell him that
> until after the gun was found [thus, according to the
> Report, after 1:22 P.M.—L.S.] and that seems to corre-
> spond with your memory too, is that correct?
> Mr. Truly.   It sure does, because I remember clearly that
> Captain Fritz was over at where the gun was found and
> I'm sure they must have found it or he wouldn't have
> been standing in that area when we came up there.
> Mr. Ball [apparently satisfied by this deduction, and with-
> out asking Truly how he knew the place where the gun

had been found—L.S.].   Now, if the gun was found after 1 o'clock, when was it that you discovered that Lee Oswald wasn't there?

Mr. Truly.   I thought it was about 20 minutes after the shooting—the assassination, but it could have been longer.

Mr. Ball.   In other words, you thought originally it might have been 10 minutes of 2 or so that you learned that?

Mr. Truly.   Ten minutes to 1.

Mr. Ball.   Ten minutes to 1?

Mr. Truly.   It was around 1 o'clock—that period of time after I came down from the sixth floor [*he means from the roof*—L.S.] to the first floor was rather hazy in my memory.

Mr. Ball.   You think it might have been after 1 when you first noticed he wasn't there?

Mr. Truly.   I don't think so—I don't feel like it was. It could have possibly been so.

Mr. Ball.   Well, if the gun was not found before 1:10, if it wasn't found before that, can you give me any estimate?

Mr. Truly.   That seems to be a longer time after the assassination.

Then the interrogator moved on to something else for a minute or two, but the attack was soon resumed, in an aggressive style never applied to such witnesses as Howard Brennan or Helen Markham, not to mention Marina Oswald.

Mr. Ball.   Then, if the gun wasn't found until after 1:10, you think it might have been as late as 1:05 or so before you discovered that Oswald wasn't there?

Mr. Truly.   It could be—it could have been.

Mr. Ball.   You have no exact memory as to the time you discovered he was not there?

Mr. Truly.   No, sir; I didn't believe after thinking things over—it was over in 15 or 20 minutes after the shots

were fired, but after retracing my trip to the roof and
the time delay and back, I would have to say that it was
farther along in the day than I had believed, so it could
have been 1 or 1:05 or something like that.

Mr. Ball.   Before you discovered Oswald wasn't there?

Mr. Truly.   That's right. . . .

It goes without saying that in any American court this method
of making a witness say something he obviously does not believe
would have touched off some angry scenes with opposing lawyers,
and the judge would have sustained their objections. We can
console ourselves that the Warren Commission was not a court and
that here it had delegated its powers to Joseph A. Ball, which
saved the Chief Justice from having to preside at the destruction
of a witness. But Ball's almost desperate insistence makes it difficult to believe that the Commission's replacement of Roy Truly's
story by Howard Brennan's was dictated by a sudden and exclusive
concern with the truth.

The Hearings also reveal an important fact and a curious incident.

The important fact is that Truly, before bringing his information to Fritz on the sixth floor, had disclosed Oswald's absence to
Deputy Chief George L. Lumpkin, who was on the main floor.
"And I remember Chief Lumpkin talking to two or three officers,"
Truly said, "and I stepped back and he went ahead and told them
a few things—it could have been 2 or 3 or 4 minutes." It was only
after this that Lumpkin took him to see Fritz.

The curious incident has to do with an unidentified reporter
who spoke to Truly on the sixth floor. The Commission confirms,
without comment, that reporters—or persons claiming to be reporters—were tramping around freely on this same floor, where
the police supposedly were still seeking prints and clues. After
he talked to Fritz, Truly declared, a reporter approached him and
asked, "What about this fellow Oswald?" This surprised Truly
because, he said, he had "talked rather low" to Fritz. Could the
reporter have obtained his information from one of the detectives
Lumpkin had spoken to after receiving the report from Truly?

It certainly would be of interest to know exactly what this conversation of "two or three or four minutes" was all about, and whether Lumpkin had initiated any action (after all, he was Deputy Chief) before escorting Truly to see Fritz. When we check the list of witnesses heard by the Commission, we find that Lumpkin is among the missing.

But there is the testimony of Captain Fritz, taken on April 22 by the same assistant counsel of the Commission, Joseph A. Ball— a Joseph A. Ball quite unlike the interrogator who was going to take care of Truly. Fritz had begun by giving the information used by Ball against Truly, although he was unable to give the exact time:

> *Mr. Ball.*   While you were there [*on the sixth floor—* L.S.] Mr. Truly came up to you?
>
> *Mr. Fritz.*   Yes, sir; where the rifle was found. That was about the time we finished Mr. Truly came and told me that one of his employees had left the building, and I asked his name and he gave me his name, Lee Harvey Oswald, and I asked his address and he gave me the Irving address.
>
> *Mr. Ball.*   This was after the rifle was found?
>
> *Mr. Fritz.*   Yes, sir; after the rifle was found.
>
> *Mr. Ball.*   Another witness has testified that the rifle was found at 1:22 p.m., does that about accord with your figures or your memory?
>
> *Mr. Fritz.*   Let's see, I might have that here. I don't think I have that time.

Ball did not follow this up. Nor did he follow up Fritz's version of what he did after receiving the information from Truly. And yet this version was rather different from the story told by the Warren Report, based on the testimony of Sergeant Gerald Lynn Hill two weeks earlier.

> *Mr. Ball.*   How long did you stay at the Texas School Book Depository after you found the rifle?
>
> *Mr. Fritz.*   After he told me about this man almost, I left immediately after he told me that.

> Mr. Ball.   You left almost immediately after he told
> you that?
>
> Mr. Fritz.   Almost after he told me that man, I felt it
> important to hold that man.
>
> Mr. Ball.   Did you give descriptions to Sims and Boyd
> [these were the two detectives with Fritz—L.S.]?
>
> Mr. Fritz.   Yes, sir; I told them to drive me to city hall
> [location of police headquarters—L.S.] and see if the
> man had a criminal record and we picked up two other
> officers and my intentions were to go to the house at
> Irving. When I got to the city hall, I asked, because,
> I will tell you why I asked because while we were in the
> building we heard that our officer had been killed,
> someone came in and told me, I asked when I got to my
> office who shot the officer, and they told me his name
> was Oswald, and I said, "His full name?" And they told
> me and I said, "That is the suspect we are looking for
> in the President's killing."

It is possible, of course, that the homicide chief rearranged the
tale slightly in his own favor. But why didn't Ball question him
further on this? Why didn't he try to establish, for example, how
much time had elapsed between Fritz's talk with Truly and his
"almost immediate" departure? By the Commission's own calculations, Fritz and the two detectives must have left the Depository
Building shortly before 2 P.M. If Fritz reacted to Truly's report as
promptly as he claims to have done, that would time Truly's visit
to the sixth floor not at 1 o'clock and not at 1:22, but closer to 2,
a good deal more than Ball had obtained from Truly even when
he had him on the ropes.

Here, again, is what Truly had to say when Ball tried to set a
trap for him:

> Mr. Ball.   In other words, you thought originally it
> might have been 10 minutes of 2 or so that you learned
> that [the fact that Oswald was absent—L.S.]?
>
> Mr. Truly.   Ten minutes to 1.
>
> Mr. Ball.   Ten minutes to 1?

> *Mr. Truly.*   It was around 1 o'clock....

Perhaps the Warren Commission had good reasons for preferring Sergeant Hill's picturesque account to the involved explanation of Captain Fritz, but one would like to know them . . . as
well as the reasons why in its Report the Commission makes no
mention of the testimony of Detective C. W. Brown, who offers
a third version, in complete contradiction to the two others.

Questioned by Belin, this detective of Fritz's homicide bureau
had been assigned on November 22 to bring a group of Depository employees to headquarters to take statements. He was accompanied by Detective B. L. Senkel. One of the employees was
Oswald's immediate superior, William H. Shelley.

> *Mr. Brown.*   . . . Detective Senkel and I took these em-
> ployees to the city hall, and in this group of employees I
> was talking to a Mr. Shelley, and got an affidavit from
> him, when the officers brought in Lee Harvey Oswald.
> And there were several cameramen following these
> boys also in front of them, and they opened the door to
> where I was interviewing; Mr. Shelley looked up and he
> said, "Well, that is Oswald. He works for us. He is one
> of my boys."
>
> *Mr. Belin.*   What did you do or say?
>
> *Mr. Brown.*   We got up and got out of the room so they
> could put Oswald in there in the room we were using.
>   We just had two small interview rooms there, and I
> let them put him in there.
>   Then as we got outside, of course, the phones were
> ringing. I answered the phone. It was Captain Fritz. He
> was still at the scene on the sixth floor of the School
> Book Depository, and I told him that the officers had just
> brought in a suspect that had shot the police officer, and
> told him about Mr. Shelley telling me that this boy that
> was identified was Lee Harvey Oswald, was also an em-
> ployee there.
>   He said, "I will be right up in a few minutes."
>
> *Mr. Belin.*   Where was Captain Fritz at this time?

> *Mr. Brown.*   He was still at the scene of the shooting, at
> the Texas School Book Depository. He called from there.

This version, to be found in Volume VII of the 26-volume set,
will be news to those who read only the Warren Report, which
ignores it entirely. The Report sticks to the fictionalized account
of Sergeant Hill, a story unknown up to then but proclaimed the
official truth as of September 27, 1964.

Brown's version had one advantage over the story chosen by
the Commission: It was easy to verify. And was this done? Shelley
was questioned four days after Brown had testified. The transcript
contains no question about Brown's statement that Shelley had
identified Oswald as soon as he arrived at headquarters. But when
Ball questioned Shelley a second time a month later, checking on
other points, the confirmation popped up without being invited.

Shelley had just told Ball that he had last seen Oswald at the
Depository 10 or 15 minutes before noon. "Did you ever see him
again?" Ball persisted, seeking only Shelley's word that he had
not authorized Oswald to quit work for the day. But Shelley did
not take the question in this limited sense, and replied: "At the
police station when they brought him in." Ball quickly explained
that he was talking about the Elm Street building; there was no
further reference to the encounter at police headquarters.

Nor was the incident mentioned in the interrogations of Captain Fritz and Sergeant Hill, although Fritz had not told of the
phone conversation with Brown, and Hill had not reported Shelley's identification of Oswald. In order to learn what actually
happened, the Commission might at least have questioned the
other Depository employees who were with Shelley at headquarters when Oswald was brought in. I found no such interrogations
in the transcripts. Nor did the Commission find it worthwhile to
hear Brown's partner, Detective B. L. Senkel, although he also was
the detective who had taken Bonnie Ray Williams' first statement
that day.

I shall cite here, and not only for the record, the comic touch
added to all this by Jesse Curry in his appearance before the Commission. On April 22, 1964, the chief of the Dallas police had not

yet heard about the way Sergeant Hill was supposed to have surprised Fritz on November 22.

>   *Mr. McCloy.*   I would want to go back for a little while
>   on one thing.
>   How did it happen the description was broadcast so
>   quickly after the event? Can you explain the circum-
>   stances under which——
>   *Mr. Curry.*   I am merely giving an opinion here.
>   *Mr. McCloy.*   Yes.
>   *Mr. Curry.*   I think the reason it was when they found
>   out at the Texas School Book Depository that this em-
>   ployee when they were checking employees and they
>   found out this employee was missing, that they presumed
>   he must or could have had some connection between
>   the shooting of the President and the fact that he was
>   not present at this time.
>   *Mr. McCloy.*   Can you describe the mechanics or the
>   machinery by which this did get on to, this material on
>   to the broadcast, that is——
>   *Mr. Ball* [*Rankin conducted the questioning, but Ball at-
>   tended the session*—L.S.].   Could I go off the record
>   on it?
> (Discussion off the record.)

There is nothing funny, after all, in this comic touch. It was
hard enough before to accept what the Warren Commission was
asking us to believe: that the events related by Sergeant Hill could
have happened without the story getting out to the eager newsmen. And a good story it was: the boss giving orders to go and
pick up someone somewhere in Irving, when his man was already
sitting handcuffed in the next room. True, Fritz might not have
found the circumstances flattering, and Hill might have been
afraid to displease Fritz. But there were also the two detectives
who had come with Fritz, the two others who were waiting in his
office, and those who had brought in Oswald. And now we learn
not only that nobody in Dallas leaked the story to the press, but
that nobody breathed a word of it to Chief Curry. Even without

Detective C. W. Brown giving the lie to the version accepted by the Warren Commission, that version becomes utterly unbelievable in the light of Curry's testimony, which still supported the Truly version five months after the event.

When we see how Ball barged in to prevent Curry (through a "discussion off the record") from spilling more beans in answering McCloy's imprudent question, there is not much left to say except to congratulate Thomas Buchanan.

For I cannot find any explanation but this: that the Commission panicked when reading in the "Buchanan Report" about the accomplice who had given the order to arrest Oswald and therefore, according to Buchanan, was one of the chief agents of the plot. As I said before, Buchanan's list of accomplices is pure fiction, and his whole construction needed very little pushing to collapse (as indeed it did the first time someone pushed it). Yet for a Commission that was seeking not the facts but arguments to convince world opinion, what mattered was not the plausibility of Buchanan's affirmations but their impact on the readers. By trying to prove that Oswald was already under arrest when the police started looking specifically for him, the Commission hoped to get rid of Buchanan's imaginary accomplice and squelch at the same time any idea that Oswald had been deliberately chosen as a "patsy."

Unfortunately for the Commission, Buchanan's phantoms would have vanished even without the hocus-pocus of Ball and his colleagues. Their clumsy efforts convince us instead that Oswald was the scapegoat not only of the plotters but also of the Warren Commission.

Oswald's behavior after the assassination no longer seems incomprehensible, in fact, if we proceed from the assumption that he was innocent. I believe that Oswald, captive of his past and his own mentality as well as of the net woven around him by the conspirators, suddenly felt his fate closing in after he looked down the barrel of Baker's pistol and learned the President had been shot. And this time he had very good reason for his feelings of persecution.

From this moment on, Oswald acted like a hunted animal, and

nothing he did makes sense. He began by escaping not *to* but *from* something, going nowhere but to a movie theater, probably because of the darkness there—forgetting that the lights could be turned on. If he had stopped to think for a minute, he would have realized that his flight was stupid and could only be used against him. But for Oswald, this was not a time for thinking: He was fleeing not the police but the Furies.

And if he really had a revolver in his pocket as he wandered through the streets of Oak Cliff, he might well have been capable of slaying an officer who stopped him for jaywalking.

The third idea I would like to suggest as a hypothesis has to do with distinguishing between the plot to kill the President and the plot to kill Oswald.

Despite some disturbing elements in the story he told Chief Justice Warren on June 7, 1964, at the Dallas jail, I do not believe Jack Ruby acted simply on an uncontrollable impulse. But I have already said in Chapter 13 that I also do not believe that Ruby and Oswald knew each other, let alone conspired together against Kennedy. I then emphasized in Chapter 14 that Ruby, far from having the trust of the organizers of the plot, seemed to be only a tool of the plotters, possibly without being fully aware of it. I would add here that, contrary to the assumption of many who believe there was more to Oswald's murder than Ruby told, I do not believe the plotters killed Oswald to silence him; and I would suggest that those who organized the assassination of the President were not necessarily the same ones who arranged the murder of the alleged assassin.

Suppose that Oswald had been involved in a conspiracy. I doubt that he could have known the inner workings of the plot and its leaders, any more than Ruby; his mental deficiencies could not have been overlooked by any qualified conspirator. Thus it seems unlikely that Oswald would have had much to say if he had decided to talk. The plotters, naturally, still had good reason to keep Oswald from going to court. But this was only because a trial revealing the inanity of the prosecution case would backfire and result in a new investigation.

Such a prospect was one to upset a number of influential groups that played no part in the President's assassination. I refer to the authorities responsible for the investigation; indeed, all the authorities responsible for all the investigations, but primarily the Dallas police department and District Attorney's office. For them, a trial ending in acquittal of Oswald would have amounted to a personal disaster. If nothing worse, they would be compromised morally and scorned professionally. In certain cases where clearly illegal acts had been committed in the probe, administrative penalties or even court proceedings appeared inevitable. For those who were guilty of such acts and who risked at least the end of their careers, the instinct for survival would dictate that the trial be prevented—in other words, that the defendant be done away with.

Thus it does not seem illogical to assume the existence of two independent plots, though one was the consequence of the other: a plot to assassinate the President, conceived by a racist clique and carried out by as yet unknown executioners, with Oswald as scapegoat; and a plot to get rid of the accused assassin, with Jack Ruby as executioner, the motive being not to silence Oswald but to prevent his trial.

Unlike the first plot, the second required little preparation and, except insofar as the killer was concerned, no directly illegal acts —at least by Dallas standards.

In the Ruby trial, for example, we were carefully frisked from head to toe before being allowed into the courtroom. But in the corridor leading from the prison elevator to the courtroom, where Ruby passed several times a day, nobody bothered with the chaos created by the TV crowds. Many times I saw strangers, without either of the two required press cards attached to their lapels, come up the stairway and stand near the cameras to watch Ruby go by. They were not searched or even asked to identify themselves. If Ruby was not slain in the corridor outside the courtroom as Oswald had been slain in the basement of police headquarters, it was not because security precautions were any better but because his trial gave no one cause for alarm.

There was no need for special arrangements to enable Jack Ruby to walk up to Lee Oswald that Sunday morning. It was enough to let things go on as before, as on Friday, for example, when Ruby was able to enter police headquarters at will and meet Oswald face to face that very night. The only problem was to lead the lachrymose strip-tease impresario and devoted police headquarters hanger-on to do on Sunday what he had not thought of doing Friday night—that is, to become a hero or an avenger or, to use the term he chose in talking to Earl Warren, a "martyr."

When the Chief Justice went to visit him in jail along with Representative Ford and J. Lee Rankin, Ruby poured out a flood of tortured explanations, pathetic justifications, transparent tricks, and unintended admissions. Dorothy Kilgallen, who said she had obtained a copy of the 102-page transcript "from sources close to the Warren Commission," published this extraordinary document in three consecutive issues of the *New York Journal-American*, August 18–20, 1964. It is contained in Volume V of the Hearings.

One could point out all sorts of interesting items in it, but two aspects impressed me most: (1) Ruby did not mind at all being asked about his possible connections with Oswald before the murder; he even insisted that the question be put to him again with the aid of a lie detector, because "just to say no isn't enough." (2) Ruby became argumentative, confused, and angry at his lawyer when the latter suggested that a conversation he had had with a policeman might have been connected with his homicidal impulse.

Ruby had first talked at length about his activities on the day of the assassination, concentrating on his business with the two local newspapers in preparing the ads that were to announce that his club would close as a sign of mourning. He wanted his questioners to know that he had made his decision to close the place out of devotion to "our beloved President" (he rarely pronounced the word "President" without the accompanying "beloved"), despite his difficult financial situation and without regard to what his competitors might do.

Now we come to his visit to the *Dallas Times Herald* at 2 A.M. Saturday morning. He was going there, he explained, to check on the position his ad had been given and also to show the employees how to use the "twist-board," an exercise gadget he was planning to promote by mail. On the way he heard a car horn honk at him. He stopped and saw a Dallas policeman named Harry Carlson sitting in his car with Kathy Kay, a Carousel Club stripper. Ruby joined them. ("I thought a lot of Harry Carlson as a police officer," he commented.) They discussed the assassination, and the two told Ruby he was "a great guy" to close his club and how bad it was that others remained open. It was an emotional scene.

> *Mr. Ruby.*   And they talked and they carried on, and they thought I was the greatest guy in the world, and he stated they should cut this guy inch by inch into ribbons, and so on.
>
> And she said, "Well, if he was in England, they would drag him through the streets and would have hung him." I forget what she said.
>
> I left them after a long delay. They kept me from leaving. They were constantly talking and were in a pretty dramatic mood. They were crying and carrying on . . .

Here Ruby interrupted himself suddenly. He had noticed that his lawyer, Joe Tonahill, had scribbled something on a slip of paper and passed it to someone. Ruby asked to see the paper, and it was handed to him. He began to read it, exclaimed "That is untrue," and then repeated three times that the questioning would get nowhere "unless you get me to Washington."

> *Mr. Ruby.*   Unless you can get me to Washington immediately, I am afraid after what Mr. Tonahill has written there, which is unfair to me regarding my testimony here—you all want to hear what he wrote?
> *Chief Justice Warren.*   Yes; you might read it. If you need glasses again, try mine this time (handing glasses to Mr. Ruby) .

Mr. Ruby (putting on glasses).   "This is the girl"——

Mr. Tonahill.   "Thing," isn't it?

Mr. Ruby.   "This is the thing that started Jack in the shooting."

Mr. Tonahill.   Kathy Kay was talking about Oswald.

Mr. Ruby.   You are lying, Joe Tonahill. You are lying.

Mr. Tonahill.   No; I am not.

Mr. Ruby.   You are lying, because you know what motivated me. You want to make it that it was a premeditation.

Mr. Tonahill.   No.

Mr. Ruby.   Yes; you do.

Chief Justice Warren tried in vain to get Ruby to drop his quarrel with Tonahill and proceed with his story. Ruby was not yet finished with Tonahill, and demanded that he explain his "lie":

Mr. Ruby.   Because the reason why, Joe knows from the time that I told Attorney Belli, and the story I wanted to tell on the stand, and Mr. Tonahill knows this isn't the time. The thought never entered my mind. He knows it.

Mr. Tonahill.   I didn't say the thought entered your mind. I didn't say that.

Mr. Ruby.   You are inferring that.

Mr. Tonahill.   Unconsciously, maybe, is what l meant to say.

Mr. Ruby.   Why go back to Friday, Joe?

Mr. Tonahill.   You are going to come right down——

Mr. Ruby.   Why go back to Friday? That set me off. Then it is a greater premeditation than you know is true.

Mr. Tonahill.   I don't say it is premeditation. I never have. I don't think it is.

Mr. Ruby.   Because it never entered my mind when they talked about, the officer, cutting him into bits. You would like to have built it up for my defense, but that is not it. I am here to tell the truth.

Mr. Tonahill.   The psychiatrist said that to me.

> *Mr. Ruby.*   You want to put that into my thoughts, but
> it never happened. I took it with a grain of salt what he
> said at that particular time.
>
> Well, it is too bad, Chief Warren, that you didn't get
> me to your headquarters 6 months ago.

Just how would the situation have been changed if Ruby had
been taken to the Chief Justice's "headquarters" six months
earlier? Ruby didn't say, and nobody asked him. Yet this seems to
be a passage of major importance. On the one hand Ruby clearly
showed he was aware of his vulnerability on this point, not only
because it would constitute—as Ruby understood—a proof of
premeditation, but also because it could never be brought up
in Dallas. On the other hand, what Tonahill had written on the
slip of paper had never been introduced at the trial, and the
psychiatrist who had told Tonahill the idea could have pene-
trated Ruby's mind unconsciously had not been called as a
witness. A few weeks before the transcript was published in the
Journal-American, Melvin Belli had already alluded in an interview with *Fact* magazine to a policeman and his friend who "got
him to approve the idea of having Oswald lynched." The lawyer
even observed: "They picked Ruby because they knew what a
weak-minded guy he was." Why was there no talk of this at the
trial? Was this the deal that left Melvin Belli out in the cold when
the verdict came in and made him so angry?

In the few lines concerned with this aspect of the Ruby episode, the Warren Report seems at first to limit its remarks to informing us that the policeman was named Olsen, not Carlson, and
that the real name of Kathy Kay was Kay Helen Coleman.

We also learn, true enough, that "6 weeks after the assassination, Olsen left the Dallas Police Department and married Miss
Coleman," but we search in vain for any comment on the reasons for the departure, if not for the marriage. The scene described
by Ruby is only briefly mentioned in the Report, principally to
tell us that "Mrs. Olsen denied and Olsen did not recall the remarks ascribed to them." We glean one other fact a few pages
later: On the following night, shortly after 11 P.M., Harry Olsen

(Carlson) and Kay Coleman (Kathy Kay) were on the sidewalk in front of the Carousel Club when Ruby walked in, and "exchanged greetings" with him.

Since the Warren Commission apparently was unable to keep its secrets even when it wanted to, the *New York Post* had published on August 20 the transcript of Jack Ruby's testimony of July 18, when the FBI had submitted him to the lie-detector test he had requested.

The significance of a test of this kind, to the extent that it has any value at all, obviously depends on the choice of questions. Despite the importance that the Carlson-Kay incident had in Ruby's June 7 testimony, the FBI examiners did not ask a single question about it. They had no trouble obtaining categorical "no's" to questions that seemed more important to them: "Did you assist Oswald in the assassination of President Kennedy?" "Did you shoot Oswald in order to silence him?" And they did not forget some grotesque questions borrowed from the bureaucratic catechism of Washington, solemnly asking whether Ruby or members of his family were—or ever had been—members of the Communist Party or of "any group that advocates the violent overthrow of the United States Government."

There was, however, one revealing moment in the lie-detector session. Ruby had admitted at the trial that, on returning home Saturday morning, he might have said to George Senator, with whom he shared an apartment, that someone should "do away with Oswald." The FBI questioner asked: "Did you tell anyone on Saturday you were going to shoot Oswald?" Ruby's reply: "No." The examiner repeated the question, and this time there was silence. Then Ruby explained that if he spoke of "doing away with Oswald," he never said it was he who would do it, and he had not suggested that Senator should kill him either. It can be seen, nevertheless, that Ruby's conversation with the policeman and the stripper had made enough of an impression on him so that when he went home, after having checked on the Carousel Club's advertising and demonstrated his "twist-board" for newspaper employees, he spontaneously started talking about the need to "do away with Oswald."

A careful study of the transcript of the lie-detector test brings out an implicit confirmation of Ruby's premeditation in the murder of Oswald.

Ruby answered negatively when the examiner asked whether he had a revolver with him when he went to police headquarters Friday night. He replied no less plainly in the affirmative when asked whether he had $2,200 in his pocket Sunday morning because he had not been able to deposit the money in his bank. He had already given this explanation earlier, saying that he carried a revolver that day because he had no safe at home and was holding the club receipts in his pocket. But these receipts could only have been from the Thursday-night business, because the club had been closed since then. Ruby thus carried $2,200 on him all day Friday, including Friday night, without carrying a revolver. But the revolver suddenly seemed necessary to him when he left his apartment Sunday morning.

Was the money in greater danger on Sunday than on Friday, or did Jack Ruby have another reason for taking his revolver along that morning?

In my numerous discussions with American friends about the Oswald affair, the most trying moment always came not when I attacked the errors and falsehoods in the investigation but when I questioned that Washington ever intended to get at the truth.

"What?" they cried, somewhat indignant. "You mean that nobody in Washington would have the courage or moral integrity to face disagreeable facts? Not even Chief Justice Warren, who has proved his independent spirit in not knuckling under to the pressure of hatemongers constantly threatening him with death? Not even Attorney General Robert Kennedy, who had not only justice to uphold but also a brother to avenge?"

This is not a question of courage. Nor is it a question of moral integrity, since what may be immoral to some is not necessarily so to others. But there is a certain blind concept of patriotism that Americans have not yet learned to guard against, and which in Europe is pejoratively identified with the *Raison d'Etat.*

The *Raison d'Etat,* according to the neutral *Petit Larousse,* is "the reason of high priority invoked in a State when one does things contrary to law and justice." Such a "reason of high priority" was not hard to recognize in the Oswald affair. The assassination of President Kennedy could have been the signal, the occasion, or the excuse for disorders whose effect would have been to weaken the United States and upset the world balance of powe1. But nothing of the kind took place; the American constitutional system survived the test victoriously. To reopen the debate would have meant reopening the wound, and the ship of state might have been tossed back to the reefs it had just passed safely by.

Perhaps a less admissible, but equally understandable, factor is closely allied to this general conception of the *Raison d'Etat.* It is even possible to see in it the foundation of a third plot, not unlike the second, but which fortunately required no victim: a conspiracy of silence.

Distinguished persons and important institutions, apparently believing this was their patriotic duty, lent their names and reputations to support the affirmations and attitudes based on Oswald's guilt. The FBI, for example, with its easily traced leaks, compromised itself to the point that any recognition today of Oswald's innocence would profoundly shake the confidence of the American people in that agency. Added to the interest of the country, therefore, were the interests of the individuals and institutions who believed their prestige and power were indispensable to the nation's survival.

This would not be the first time such a situation has arisen in the world. "If Dreyfus is innocent, then our generals are guilty," cried Paul Déroulède, a French "Birchite" of the day, on the eve of the trial in Rennes in 1899. The military judges who then condemned Captain Dreyfus for "high treason," but granted there were "extenuating circumstances," had tried to save the generals without bearing down too hard on Dreyfus. "A compromise between discipline and their consciences," commented Georges Clemenceau.

The compromise was much easier 65 years later in Washington. Lee Harvey Oswald is dead and buried; there is no innocent man in prison whose suffering could weigh on consciences. And there is no Esterhazy in the Oswald affair: Nobody among those who believe in Oswald's innocence is able to accuse anyone else by name. Why then make a fuss about it? There is no judicial error to rectify, since there never was a court decision. Of course there is the Warren Commission and its Report, calling Lee Harvey Oswald the assassin of the President. But the Commission was not a court, we are told, its Report is not a verdict, and there is no more need to rehabilitate Oswald than there was to defend him.

On September 21, 1899, two days after Captain Alfred Dreyfus —pardoned but not rehabilitated—had been given his freedom, General Galliffet, the Minister of War, issued an order of the day:

> The incident is closed. The military judges, respected by all, have pronounced their verdict with complete independence. We bowed to their decision without hesitation, just as we bow now to the act of mercy performed by the President of the Republic. There should be no further question of reprisals against anyone. I repeat: The affair is ended.

L'Affaire did not end until July 12, 1906, when the judicial error was officially recognized and the innocence of Dreyfus solemnly proclaimed. If it *had* ended seven years earlier, as General Galliffet wished, the stain on the honor of France would never have been erased.

23

THE CLIPBOARD MYSTERY

IN ITS POSTHUMOUS INDICTMENT of Lee Harvey Oswald, the Warren Commission makes some unintentional disclosures and raises questions it never deals with. I have titled this chapter "The Clipboard Mystery"; I might as well have called it "The Mystery of the Jumping Shells" or "The Mystery of the Manic-Depressive Marksman." What all of these mysteries have in common is that they prove there never was a serious investigation of the assassination.

The clipboard incident takes up 11 lines in a section of the chapter on "The Assassin" that offers, the Report proudly declares, "additional testimony linking Oswald with the point from which the shots were fired."

This concerns Charles Givens, a Depository employee who the Commission says was last to see Oswald in the building before the assassination, at about 11:55 A.M. At this time, Givens said, Oswald was on the sixth floor and was heading toward the elevator carrying a clipboard, which held book orders to be filled. It was Givens who claimed Oswald had uttered the historic words about sending the elevator back up, a request made less picturesque but more believable in the Warren Report's version: Oswald had only asked his colleague not to forget to close the elevator gate.

And now we come to the 11 lines:

> The significance of Givens' observation that Oswald was carrying his clipboard became apparent on December 2, 1963, when an employee, Frankie Kaiser, found a clipboard hidden by book cartons in the northwest corner of the

sixth floor at the west wall a few feet from where the rifle had been found. This clipboard had been made by Kaiser and had his name on it. Kaiser identified it as the clipboard which Oswald had appropriated from him when Oswald came to work at the Depository. Three invoices on this clipboard, each dated November 22, were for Scott-Foresman books, located on the first and sixth floors. Oswald had not filled any of the three orders.

This rather dramatic closing sentence seems designed to show that Oswald had not stayed on the sixth floor to finish his work; it implies that instead of filling the book orders he was preparing for the assassination. But he might as well have been sitting on a carton of books, daydreaming while waiting for lunchtime. People sometimes do that sort of thing in offices, when they can get away with it.

None of the seven Commission members and none of their thousands of panegyrists seem to have noticed the incredible information contained in that paragraph. On December 2, 1963, we are told—that is, ten days after the assassination and eight days after Oswald's murder, a board 12 by 9 inches, with a clip that would prevent it from sliding under a crate or against a wall, was discovered for the first time in the room where the police search had been concentrated. Either the sixth floor was never thoroughly searched or evidence tending to incriminate Oswald was placed there after the search.

I suppose that if the Warren Commission can be made to accept the idea that it is not above criticism, and that it has a duty to explain what obviously needs explaining, it will choose as the lesser evil the negligence of the investigators. Since these investigators included the FBI, Earl Warren will have a difficult time with J. Edgar Hoover, but the alternative is worse. Meanwhile, the Commission appears cheerfully unaware that there could be any dilemma. And this is not the only example.

The Commission makes much of the number of witnesses who saw the rifle or even the assassin in person, and who identified not only the building and the floor but also the exact window from which the shots were fired. These witnesses, the Commission says, quickly informed the police. The Report notes on page 71 that some employees on the fifth floor heard the sound of the ejected shells falling on the floor above them: "After pausing for a few minutes, the three men ran downstairs. Norman and Jarman ran out of the front entrance of the building, where they saw Brennan, the construction worker who had seen the man in the window firing the gun, talking to a police officer, and they then reported their own experience." But they have vanished by page 79, where the Report states, as if they had never existed:

> Shortly after the assassination, police officers arrived at the Depository Building and began a search for the assassin and evidence. Around 1 p.m. Deputy Sheriff Luke Mooney noticed a pile of cartons in front of the window in the southeast corner of the sixth floor. . . . Searching that area he found at approximately 1:12 p.m. three empty cartridge cases on the floor near the window. When he was notified of Mooney's discovery, Capt. J. W. Fritz, chief of the homicide bureau of the Dallas Police Department, issued instructions that nothing be moved or touched. . . .

The Commission must have found this quite normal, since it offers no comment. Perhaps it even felt entitled to some praise for the minute detail of its description of Luke Mooney's activities. But what this passage actually tells us is that the police, who were informed shortly after 12:30 exactly where the assassin had been seen (or heard), tried very hard to keep away from that spot. Deputy Sheriff Mooney *discovered* the southeast corner *around* 1 P.M. Then no one had acted on the information provided by Brennan, Norman, Jarman, and others by hurrying to the sixth floor and the corner they had pointed out. On the contrary, the police who invaded the building spread out everywhere *except* on the sixth floor. To judge from the Commission's story, Mooney just happened to glance over at the southeast corner by chance some 25 minutes after the police had been given the information by witnesses. What remarkable intuition!

And it is useless to search through the Warren Report for an explanation of the following anomaly: At about 12:45 P.M. the police radio broadcast the description "most probably" based on the information furnished by Brennan, who had seen "the man in the window," but the police, "around 1 p.m.," still hadn't thought of taking a look at that window.

The farce is only beginning. Mooney "noticed" the pile of cartons "around 1 p.m." What did he do then? The Report tells us that he searched "that area," but it was only at "approximately 1:12 p.m." that he found the shells. Now these shells had not rolled out of sight under some boxes. The Report specifies that they "richocheted between the boxes and the wall until they came to rest to the west of the window," which means they were in plain view. Did Mooney suffer from severe myopia? Had he lost his glasses? If not, how did he spend those 12 minutes after he *noticed* the pile of cartons and before he *discovered* the shells?

The situation is utterly absurd. It is inconceivable that no one had gone to the sixth floor before 1 o'clock, inconceivable that the pile of cartons was discovered only by chance, inconceivable that it could have taken 12 minutes to find the shells. And remember those other unseemly details from the preceding chapters: the traveling chicken bones, for example, and the invisible paper bag. What actually went on there? I don't know, but any man of common sense could look any Warren Commission member in the eye and say: It is impossible to believe that these events happened in the way you describe them.

The Commission, however, does not worry about that. The Report imperturbably mixes the impossible with the improbable without ever seeming to realize what it is saying, and without noticing that its own statements can only inspire renewed speculation. I prefer not to speculate, but no speculation could be more unacceptable than the Commission's version of the activities on the sixth floor after the assassination; one can indeed conceive of the possibility that the evidence found on the sixth floor—including the rifle and the shells—was part of an over-all staging.

In any case, to conclude from the scandalous gaps in the investigation that there was no evidence pointing to any suspect but Oswald is to mock the public as well as justice.

If one accepts the suggestive picture provided by the Report, and if one recalls the discovery of the clipboard 10 days afterward in the room "searched" by Dallas police, deputy sheriffs, and Secret Service and FBI agents, it would not be an exaggeration to suppose that among the evidence gone undetected were the footprints, the fingerprints, the gloves, the handkerchief, the calling card of another suspect—or even this other suspect himself, in person.

Furthermore, the grotesque manner in which the "investigation" was carried out on the sixth floor, while the President was dying at Parkland Hospital, is complemented by the farce performed on the sidewalks of Elm Street.

In the first chapter I mentioned the mystery of the unsealed building. Even before the Warren Report certified that the Depository Building had not been searched, it was evident that contrary to Jesse Curry's statements it had not been "surrounded" either. The fact is that the police on the scene did not attempt in any way to make use of their opportunity to catch the assassin inside the building.

It would seem that the Commission should have studied the reasons and established the blame for such unheard-of negligence. It is conceivable—though not easy to believe—that it was due to the professional incompetence of *all* the local and federal officers involved; but it could also be explained by the desire (not necessarily preconcerted) to let the assassin escape. I insinuate nothing; I am saying only that the possibility existed and that it should have been examined.

But the Commission, of course, had other worries. Thomas Buchanan had said (see Chapter 18) that the building was sealed off immediately after the shots. He had also stated, following Richard Dudman and Mark Lane, that other shots were fired from the railroad overpass. The task the Commission seems to have considered paramount was to convince Buchanan's readers that the assassin was indeed in the Depository Building, but that he could have walked out of the building at will long after he had fired the shots.

Thus the Report notes that Forrest V. Sorrels, a Secret Service agent who had been in the motorcade and had followed the President to the hospital, "returned to the Depository Building about 20 minutes after the shooting, found no police officers at the rear door and was able to enter through this door without identifying himself." The Commission, rather than showing distress at this, appears pleased with Sorrels' testimony: It would force Thomas Buchanan to shut his mouth.

Since I never attached any weight to Buchanan's affirmations, I had no need of the Commission's assistance in order to believe that the doors *were* open, but I would have appreciated some explanation as to *why* they were open.

"Some spectators at Houston and Elm Streets," the Report declares, "did see a rifle being fired in the direction of the President's car from the easternmost window of the sixth floor on the south side of the building. Other witnesses saw a rifle in this window immediately after the assassination. Three employees of the Depository, observing the parade from the fifth floor, heard the shots fired from the floor immediately above them."

The Report does not mention here the testimony of Motorcycle Patrolman Marrion L. Baker, whose attention was drawn to the building when he "saw pigeons flutter upward" from it as the shots echoed, and who might have shouted a warning or a call for help to the many other officers nearby before rushing inside with revolver in hand. But we do learn that the famous Brennan who, according to the Report, "saw 70 to 85 percent of the gun when it was fired and the body of the man from the waist up" lost no time and "quickly reported his observations to police officers." There was also a 15-year-old boy, Amos Lee Euins, who saw the assassin at the sixth-floor window and "immediately after the assassination" reported this to Police Sergeant D. V. Harkness.

How did the police react? As far as Harkness is concerned, he radioed a message to headquarters at 12:36: "I have a witness that says that it came from the fifth floor of the Texas Book Depository Store." The Report notes that the boy had correctly located the floor as the one "under the ledge," the sixth, but that Sergeant Harkness had made a mistake in his "hasty count of the floors," as he later admitted. Sergeant Harkness, in any case, took no action on the basis of what he had learned, and headquarters issued no instructions.

The employees Harold Norman and James Jarman, Jr., according to the Report, ran out of the building a few moments after the shots were fired, saw and heard Brennan telling his story to a policeman, and gave the same officer the information they had. From the context it seems the officer concerned was W. E. Barnett, who had been stationed at the Houston-Elm intersection for the motorcade. We owe him and an unidentified sergeant the following burlesque skit:

> . . . W. E. Barnett . . . testified that immediately after the shots he went to the rear of the building to check the fire escape. He then returned to the corner of Elm and Houston where he met a sergeant who instructed him to find out the name of the building. Barnett ran to the building, noted its name, and then returned to the corner. . . .

So that the reader will miss none of the spice of the story, I refer him to the photograph (see Illustrations) showing the name of the building written in large letters across the top of the door, and easily read from a distance. And I don't have to point out the futility of Barnett's "check" of the fire escape when all the other, more comfortable exits were open to the assassin.

We find, on the same page where Barnett's exploits are recorded, the beginning of the adventures of Inspector Sawyer.

At the time he sent his message to headquarters relaying the report of Amos Euins, Sergeant Harkness noticed that the car of Inspector J. Herbert Sawyer was parked in front of the building. But he did not know, the Report says, "whether or not two officers with Sawyer were guarding the doors." Sawyer himself told the Commission that at 12:34 he had heard a call on his police radio that the shots had come from the Depository Building. Here is his story as told in the Report:

> He then entered the building and took the front passenger elevator as far as it would go—the fourth floor. After inspecting this floor, Sawyer returned to the street about

3 minutes after he entered the building. After he returned to the street he directed Sergeant Harkness to station two patrolmen at the front door and not let anyone in or out; he also directed that the back door be sealed off.

The Report, observing that this was "no earlier than 12:37 p.m. and may have been later," does not comment on Inspector Sawyer's strategy, wasting three minutes by going to the fourth floor *before* putting guards at the doors. Nor does it have anything to say about the way Sergeant Harkness carried out the belated orders, although the Commission knew from Sorrels' testimony there was still no one at the back door at about 12:50.

The transcripts of the 26-volume set add new enigmas to the mysteries, while also providing some noteworthy detail on the care with which the police refrained from blocking the exits and getting to the sixth floor.

The testimony of Captain Fritz in Volume IV offers a perfect illustration. Questioned by Joseph A. Ball, the Dallas homicide bureau chief declared that he went from the hospital to the Depository, arriving with his two detectives at 12:58. Several officers, he said, were there in front of the building. Keep in mind that Sergeant Harkness had relayed Euins' report at 12:36 and that, even though Harkness was wrong in speaking of the fifth floor, he had at least given a specific floor. At almost the same time (in any case, according to the Commission, before 12:45), Brennan had informed the police outside that the shots had come from the sixth floor.

> *Mr. Ball.*   What did you do when you got to this building?
> *Mr. Fritz.*   Some officer told us they thought he was in that building, so we had our guns——
> *Mr. McCloy.*   Thought who was in the building?
> *Mr. Fritz.*   The man who did the shooting was in the building. So, we, of course, took our shotguns and immediately entered the building and searched the building to see if we could find him.

Mr. Ball.   Were there guards on the doors of the building at that time?

Mr. Fritz.   I am not sure, but I don't—there has been
some question about that, but the reason I don't think
that—this may differ with someone else, but I am going
to tell you what I know.

Mr. Ball.   All right.

Mr. McCloy.   By all means.

Mr. Fritz.   After I arrived one of the officers asked me if
I would like to have the building sealed and I told him
I would.

Mr. Ball.   What officer was that?

Mr. Fritz.   That is a uniformed officer, but I don't know
what his name was, he was outside, of course, I went
upstairs and I don't know whether he did because I
couldn't watch him.

Mr. Ball.   Then what did you do?

Mr. Fritz.   We began searching the floors, looking for
anyone with a gun or looked suspicious, and we searched
through hurriedly through most all the floors.

Mr. McCloy.   Which floor did you start with?

Mr. Fritz.   We started at the bottom; yes, sir. And, of
course, and I think we went up probably to the top.

In Volume VII we have the testimony of Patrolman Welcome
Eugene Barnett. The last two shots, he said, convinced him the
gunman was on the roof of the building (from where he stood
he could not see the windows), and he believed he would probably try to get away by the fire escape. Seeing nobody there, he
looked no further and returned to the front of the building on
Elm Street. The scene involving the building's name was enacted
at that point.

"I broke and ran to the front and got the name of it. There
were people going in and out at that time. I ran back and told
him [the sergeant—L.S.] the name of it. . . ."

Since the "people going in and out" made use of the main entrance and not the fire escape, Barnett asked them nothing. But

then a construction worker ran up to him and said: "I was standing over there and saw the man in the window with the rifle."
Barnett says he kept the worker with him in front of the entrance
"until they took him across the street to the courthouse."

This story should now be compared with the one told by the
construction worker—that is, by Howard L. Brennan himself. It
appears in Volume III of the Hearings.

Brennan, replying to questions put by David W. Belin, described how the police first directed their search to the west side
of the building, although he had seen the gunman in the southeast corner window.

> *Mr. Belin.*   After you saw that, what did you do?
>
> *Mr. Brennan.*   I knew I had to get to someone quick to
> tell them where the man was. So I ran or walked—there
> is a possibility I ran, because I have a habit of, when
> something has to be done in a hurry, I run. And there
> was one officer standing at the corner of the Texas Book
> Store on the street. It didn't seem to me he was going in
> any direction. He was standing still.
>
> *Mr. Belin.*   What did you do or what did you say to him?
>
> *Mr. Brennan.*   I asked him to get me someone in charge,
> a Secret Service man or an FBI. That it appeared to me
> that they were searching in the wrong direction for the
> man that did the shooting.
>   And he was definitely in the building on the sixth floor.
> I did not say on the sixth floor. Correction there.
> I believe I identified the window as one window from
> the top.
>
> *Mr. Belin.*   All right.
>
> *Mr. Brennan.*   Because, at that time, I did not know how
> many story building it was.
>
> *Representative Ford.*   But you did say to the policeman
> it was a window on the second floor from the top?
>
> *Mr. Brennan.*   Right.
>
> *Mr. Belin.*   And then what happened?
>
> *Mr. Brennan.*   He——
>
> *The Chairman.*   May I ask there. By the second floor from

the top, do you mean the one directly underneath the top
floor?

Mr. Brennan.   Underneath the top floor, excluding the
roof, yes, sir.

Mr. Belin.   And then what happened, sir?

Mr. Brennan.   He said, "Just a minute." And he had to
give some orders or something on the east side of the
building on Houston Street. And then he had taken me
to, I believe, Mr. Sorrels, an automobile sitting in front
of the Texas Book Store.

Mr. Belin.   And then what happened there?

Mr. Brennan.   I related my information and there was
a few minutes of discussion, and Mr. Sorrels had taken
me then across the street to the sheriff's building.

Mr. Belin.   Did you describe the man that you saw in
the window?

Mr. Brennan.   Yes; I believe I did.

The story gets more and more curious. The Report, which contains nothing about this portion of Brennan's account, does say
that Sorrels returned to the Depository 20 minutes after the shooting. Brennan, perhaps, made a mistake about the name of the
officer he had spoken to. He may have confused Inspector Sawyer
with Secret Service Agent Sorrels, for example; Sawyer did have
his car parked in front of the building. But Sorrels, whose testimony may be found in Volume VII, confirmed not only that he
had arrived at the building and walked in the back door without
being questioned, "20 or 25 minutes" after the assassination; he
also confirmed that he was indeed the man to whom Brennan had
told his story and who had taken him to the sheriff's office.

Sorrels declared that after having asked Truly to prepare a list
of employees he had left by the front door and inquired on the
sidewalk: "Did anyone here see anything?" Someone pointed out
Brennan, saying: "That man over there." Sorrels continued: "He
was out in front of the building and I went right to him."

Agent Sorrels—the permanent Secret Service representative in
Dallas—repeated for the Commission the story he had been told

by Brennan, including the description of the man at the window:
". . . he appeared to be a slender man, he had on what appeared
to be a light jacket or shirt or something to that effect [Oswald
did not wear a jacket at this time, and his shirt was dark brown—
L.S.], and that he thought he could identify him—said he was
slender build." Asking if there were other witnesses, Sorrels was
led to "a young colored boy there, by the name of Euins," and
he took both witnesses "over to the sheriff's office where we could
get statements from them."

The testimony of Inspector Sawyer is in Volume VI. Compared
—by me, not by the Commission—with the account given by
Agent Sorrels, it brings us back to the mystery surrounding the
initial description of the suspect broadcast by the police radio, a
mystery I touched on in Chapter 22.

As the Report says, Inspector Sawyer first went to the fourth
floor, which he believed was the top floor since the elevator went
no further.

> *Mr. Belin.*   Now Inspector, what did you do then?
>
> *Mr. Sawyer.*   Well, I didn't see anything that was out of
> the ordinary, so I immediately came back downstairs to
> check the security on the building.
>
> *Mr. Belin.*   When you say check the security on the build-
> ing, what do you mean by that?
>
> *Mr. Sawyer.*   Well, to be sure it was covered off properly,
> and then posted two men on the front entrance with
> instructions not to let anyone in or out.
>
> *Mr. Belin.*   What about the rear entrance?
>
> *Mr. Sawyer.*   Well, I also had the sergeant go around and
> check to be sure that all of those were covered, although
> he told me that they were already covered.
>
> *Mr. Belin.*   When was the order given to cover the front
> entrance of the building?
>
> *Mr. Sawyer.*   Well, they had it covered when I got there.
> There were officers all around the front. The only thing
> I don't think had been done by the time I got there,
> was the instructions not to let anybody in or out.

We also learn from Sawyer's testimony, for the first time, just who it was who broadcast the famous description on the police radio "immediately after 12:43 and before 12:45": Inspector J. Herbert Sawyer.

> *Mr. Sawyer.*   That description came to me mainly from one witness who claimed to have seen the rifle barrel in the fifth or sixth floor of the building, and claimed to have been able to see the man up there.
>
> *Mr. Belin.*   Do you know this person's name?
>
> *Mr. Sawyer.*   I do not.
>
> *Mr. Belin.*   Do you know anything about him, what he was wearing?
>
> *Mr. Sawyer.*   Except that he was—I don't remember what he was wearing. I remember that he was a white man and that he wasn't young and he wasn't old. He was there. That is the only two things that I can remember about him.
>
> *Mr. Belin.*   What age would you categorize as young?
>
> *Mr. Sawyer.*   Around 35 would be my best recollection of it, but it could be a few years either way.
>
> *Mr. Belin.*   Do you remember if he was tall or short, or can't you remember anything about him?
>
> *Mr. Sawyer.*   I can't remember that much about him. I was real hazy about that.
>
> *Mr. Belin.*   Do you remember where he said he was standing when he saw the person with the rifle?
>
> *Mr. Sawyer.*   I didn't go into detail with him except that from the best of my recollection, he was standing where he could have seen him. But there were too many people coming up with questions to go into detail. I got the description and sent him on over to the Sheriff's Office.
>
> *Mr. Belin.*   Inspector, do you remember anything else about this person who you say gave you the primary description?
>
> *Mr. Sawyer.*   No, I do not, except that I did send him

with an escort to the Sheriff's Office to give fuller or
more complete detail.

In short, the only thing that Inspector Sawyer remembered was
precisely what Agent Sorrels contradicted. Sorrels, reporting that
he had personally conducted Brennan and Euins to the sheriff's
office, made no reference to Sawyer; and Sawyer certainly could
not have been thinking of Sorrels, the Secret Service's permanent
representative in Dallas, when he explained the cooperative arrangement he had set up with the sheriff's office: ". . . we set up
a group of officers and deputy sheriffs who were to take charge
of the witnesses and take them over to see that affidavits were taken
from them. They were more or less an escort service so the witness
wouldn't get away." Thus, if it was Brennan who gave the description to Sawyer, we would have to assume that after judging
his evidence important enough to radio to headquarters (although
not important enough to warrant sending anyone to the sixth
floor), the Inspector, contrary to his statement, did not turn him
over to his "escort service," but let him stand around on the sidewalk until Sorrels found him.

The testimony in the Hearings allows us to see why the Report
dares not go beyond "most probably" in tracing the original description to Brennan, and why it also chooses not to name the
officer who was supposed to have taken it down.

Absolutely nothing, in fact, of what Inspector Sawyer said about
his mysterious informer would indicate Brennan; there is at least
one very good reason to believe, on the contrary, that this informer
could *not* have been Brennan. A steamfitter working on a construction job, Brennan was wearing a protective helmet. This
detail was unusual enough to be noticed by Sorrels, Patrolman
Barnett, and others who easily recalled "the construction worker."
The only exception was Inspector Sawyer, despite Belin's efforts
to guide him along the right path. It is conceivable that Sawyer
took down the description, broadcast it, and discussed it with the
headquarters dispatcher without paying attention to the age of
his witness (Brennan was 45, by the way, and looked older), or the

color of his hair or eyes. But is it possible that he would not have noticed the helmet?

A further indication that Sawyer's informant was not Brennan may be found in the discrepancy between Sawyer's radio messages and statements made by Brennan before the Commission.

To the few who paid $76 for the 26 volumes in the set and the fewer still who read them, Volume XXI of the Hearings offers a rather interesting document entitled "Sawyer Exhibit No. A." This is the transcript of the Dallas police radio messages between 10:25 A.M. and 12:53 P.M., November 22. Notes written in the margin identify the code: 531 is the designation of headquarters and 9 is Inspector Sawyer. The time is 12:43 P.M.

> 9-531   The wanted person in this is a slender white male about thirty, five feet ten, one sixty five, carrying what looked to be a 30-30 or some type of Winchester.
>
> 531-9   It was a rifle?
>
> 9-531   Yes, a rifle.
>
> 531-9   Any clothing description?
>
> 9-531   Current witness can't remember that.
>
> 531   Attention all squads, description was broadcast and no further information at this time.

Howard L. Brennan did not offer a description of the rifle in any of his statements. He never referred to a 30-30 or "some type of Winchester." When Belin asked him what type of rifle it was, he replied: "I am not an expert on guns. It was, as I could observe, some type of high-powered rifle."

Perhaps Sawyer took it upon himself to imagine a description of the rifle, apparently assuming the suspect had left the building with the weapon under his arm. But it is incredible that he would have omitted a description of clothing for which he was asked and which he would have been able to provide had the "current witness" been Brennan. Although Brennan was silent about the rifle, he was not reticent in talking about the suspect's clothing. He had already given some details to Sorrels—and as we have seen, these did not fit Oswald. Before the Commission, he boasted of having drawn the attention of police at the lineup Friday night to the fact that the man he pointed out "was not dressed in the same clothes that I saw the man in the window." He confirmed again that "the man in the window" wore "light colored clothes, more of a khaki color," and "if it was a white shirt, it was on the dingy side." How could he have been the witness who, according to Sawyer, remembered no details about clothing?

Leafing through the systematically but not always cleverly expurgated *New York Times* selection of the Hearings issued as a pocketbook under the title *The Witnesses,* I found the facsimile of an FBI report of June 3, 1964, which, though published in the 26-volume set as Commission Exhibit 2585, had escaped me earlier.

This report had been prepared by the FBI, following a special request by the Commission, "on claims made by Thomas G. Buchanan in book *Who Killed Kennedy."* It confirms, incidentally, what I have said before (see Chapters 18 and 22) regarding the Commission's worries about Buchanan's claims in general, and his insinuations about the police broadcast in particular. Here we see that the FBI *on June 3, 1964,* still did not attribute the first police description—not even "probably"—to Brennan. The only explanation given by the FBI is that "this suspect [as described in the police broadcast—L.S.] was reportedly seen running from the Texas School Book Depository after the assassination," which means that the FBI, contrary to the Commission, did take seriously a deposition made by Deputy Sheriff Roger D. Craig, mentioned below. The June 3 FBI report, at the same time, foils Joseph A. Ball's desperate efforts (see Chapter 22) to destroy Truly's testimony, since it adds: "It is also noted that inquiry has shown that Oswald did not become a suspect until he was reported missing from the book building at approximately 12:50 p.m."

Only one argument remains in favor of the theory that Brennan was Sawyer's informant.

Brennan said the uniformed officer to whom he had spoken at first (identified by the context—and by the Commission—as our Welcome E. Barnett) had taken him to a parked car where he had met Sorrels. Sorrels, however, said he was leaving the building when Brennan was pointed out to him, and Barnett, in turn, did not say he had led the "construction worker" to a car but that he kept him in front of the building entrance. It would have been necessary, nevertheless, to give some consideration to the argument involving the car—if the questioning of Brennan on this point had not created a tangle that neither the reader nor the Commission could hope to unravel. It seems there were *two* cars parked (or, as Brennan says, "sitting") in front of the entrance, and the witness constantly confuses them to the consternation of the Commission's assistant counsel. Since, moreover, he seems sometimes to place one or the other car not at the curb but at the very doorstep of the building, it is impossible in the final analysis to conclude that Brennan really went to Sawyer's car and talked to *him*.

A Brennan-Sawyer-Sorrels-Barnett confrontation certainly would have helped solve the problem, but this idea never occurred to the Commission.

There are some other aspects of the investigation that should be mentioned before we go on to the eight findings or "proofs" on which the Commission claims to base its case against Oswald.

The Commission judged it expedient to dispose of certain public statements made by officials by burying them as anonymous "rumors" in the "Speculations and Rumors" appendix. Among them: "There were other people present in the lunchroom at the time that Baker and Truly saw Oswald there" (Chief Curry); Oswald was with other employees "until they went downstairs to watch the President go by" (Captain Fritz); "Oswald was stopped by police as he left the building and was permitted to pass after he told them he worked in the building" (Curry, Fritz, and District Attorney Wade).

Conversely, although the introduction to the appendix says its purpose is to "clarify the most widespread factual misunderstandings," the Report often chooses to upgrade a figment of some eccentric or plainly lunatic mind. I cannot imagine, for example, why the Report considers it necessary to honor with a correction a "rumor" that I never heard: "The headquarters detachment of the U.S. Army, under orders from [Secretary of Defense Robert S.] McNamara's office, began to rehearse for the funeral more than a week before the assassination."

At the same time the Commission turns the other way when it comes to examining any situation that could set it on a trail not leading to Lee Harvey Oswald.

I described in Chapter 4 the alternative suggested by the episode of the Irving gunsmith and the way it is dodged in the Report. There are several other curious or disturbing incidents that the Commission mentions and examines in the same spirit: that is, by refusing to consider the possibilities they suggest and by considering the job done when it has established that the person mentioned in the given incident could not have been Oswald. The possibility suggested by these oddly parallel incidents is this: the existence of a false Oswald.

There was the case of the expert rifleman whose obnoxious manners caused a scandal at the Sportsdrome in Grand Prairie—and helped the customers at the rifle range remember him.

The stranger (see Chapter 3) made himself conspicuous by his marksmanship, his foreign rifle with telescopic sight, and his ostentatiously casual way of firing at others' targets. He was also remembered, it seems, for looking like Oswald. Two of those involved—Malcolm Price, a Sportsdrome employee, and Garland Slack, a customer—have remained convinced that the man was definitely Oswald. They appeared on the two-hour CBS television program on September 27, 1964:

"We were shooting the targets," Slack recalled, "and someone else kept shooting my target before I ever got to put a bullet in. . . . And that happened not only one time but about three times. So I went to the fellow [Price—L.S.] and told him, I'm paying two bits for targets and putting them up and somebody's shooting a hole in them before. So we got to looking at who it was, and it was this fellow that turned out to be Oswald."

But the stranger, as I have said and as the Commission easily proved, could not have been Oswald. Wasn't this a reason for trying to find out who the man was? This bizarre customer, who did not act like a timid soul averse to public attention, never showed up again. Why not, when all the papers were talking about him and all the TV cameras were at his command? Was he a manic-depressive, sometimes overexcited and at other times morose? If so, the period of overexcitement still had not returned long after this incident, so that he was not led to seek attention again.

There is also the tale of the "automobile demonstration" as the Warren Report calls it. One Albert Guy Bogard, a Lincoln-Mercury salesman in Dallas, told the Commission that early on the afternoon of November 9, 1963, a prospective customer had tried out a car on the Stemmons Freeway, driving at 60 to 70 miles an hour; the man explained to Bogard that "in several weeks he would have the money to make a purchase." The Report adds that "Bogard asserted that the customer gave his name as 'Lee Oswald,' which Bogard wrote on a business card. After Oswald's name was mentioned on the radio on November 22, Bogard assertedly threw the card in a trash can, making the comment to coemployees that he supposed Oswald would no longer wish to buy a car."

But while clearly implying that Bogard lied—as it did in the case of the Irving gunsmith, Dial Ryder—the Commission recognizes that his testimony "received corroboration." The Warren Report names two salesmen, Frank Pizzo and Eugene M. Wilson, who remembered "an instance when the customer described by Bogard was in the showroom." Another salesman, Oran Brown, whom Bogard asked to take care of a customer for him if he arrived when Bogard was not in, even remembered the name of the customer: "Brown stated that he too wrote down the customer's name and both he and his wife remember the name 'Oswald' as being on a paper in his possession before the assassination."

The Commission, however, is not upset: ". . . Pizzo, who saw Bogard's prospect on November 9 and shortly after the assassination felt that Oswald may have been this man, later examined pictures of Oswald and expressed serious doubts that the person with Bogard was in fact Oswald. While noting a resemblance, he did not believe that Oswald's hairline matched that of the person who had been in the showroom on November 9."

I agree entirely with the Commission in rejecting the idea that Bogard's prospect was Lee Harvey Oswald, but since I am not convinced that Bogard—whose testimony is supported by that of the Browns—lied in saying that the stranger had given his name as Lee Oswald, this—together with Pizzo's description—is precisely what troubles me. For, unlike the Commission, I cannot help considering suspicious the series of coincidences, in the weeks before the assassination, which tended to attract attention to the man who would later be presented as the assassin:

(1) A stranger has a telescopic sight mounted on a rifle by an Irving gunshop, gives his name as "Oswald," then disappears;

(2) A stranger resembling Oswald attracts attention to himself and his foreign scope-equipped rifle at a Grand Prairie rifle range, then disappears;

(3) A stranger resembling Oswald proves his ability as a driver, announces that "in several weeks he would have the money" to buy a car, gives his name as "Lee Oswald," then disappears.

Add to this the story told by Deputy Sheriff Craig, summarized as follows by the Report:

> Roger D. Craig, a deputy sheriff of Dallas County, claimed that about 15 minutes after the assassination he saw a man, whom he later identified as Oswald, coming from the direction of the Depository Building and running down the hill north of Elm Street toward a light-colored Rambler station wagon, which was moving slowly along Elm toward the underpass. The station wagon stopped to pick up the man and then drove off.

The Commission's comment: "Craig may have seen a person enter a white Rambler station wagon 15 or 20 minutes after the shooting and travel west on Elm Street, but the Commission concluded that this man was not Lee Harvey Oswald, because of the overwhelming evidence that Oswald was far away from the building by that time."

All right, he didn't see Oswald—but wouldn't it have been advisable to locate the station wagon and its passengers? And the strange customers of the gunshop, the rifle range, and the car dealer?

I repeat that, not being a mathematician like Thomas Buchanan,

I will not allow my imagination to run wild and I insinuate nothing. I am stating only that the Commission had the duty to consider the possibility that a false Oswald had been employed before the assassination to stack the evidence against the real one. It even had the duty to consider the possibility that a man resembling Oswald was the assassin.

In any case, no official agency in the United States has the right to contend there was no evidence suggesting that someone other than Oswald was the assassin, because no official agency in the United States ever tried to find such evidence or even condescended to look at it when it was spread out before its eyes.

24

THE EIGHT PROOFS OF THE WARREN REPORT

INSTRUCTED BY PRESIDENT JOHNSON on November 29, 1963, to "satisfy itself that the truth is known as far as it can be discovered," the Warren Commission announced on September 27, 1964, that "the shots which killed President Kennedy and wounded Governor Connally were fired by Lee Harvey Oswald."

No ifs or buts, no qualifying terms to indicate a recognition of the possibility of human error and to salvage an appearance of humility. The President's Commission on the Assassination of President Kennedy was no more afraid of the sin of pride than it was of injustice. Its excuse was that it did not judge, it only "determined" and "concluded." But there was no appeal from the verdict it handed down. The government of the United States, the bar, the press, the churches, the universities, the liberals, the conservatives—all of them, following the lead of the Chief Justice of the United States, demanded that this verdict be accepted as final. On what basis?

In the Report's preliminary summary affirming that Oswald killed Kennedy, the Commission explains that its "conclusion" (it prefers this word to "verdict") is based on the following considerations:

> (a) The Mannlicher-Carcano 6.5-millimeter Italian rifle from which the shots were fired was owned by and in the possession of Oswald.
>
> (b) Oswald carried this rifle into the Depository Building on the morning of November 22, 1963.

(c) Oswald, at the time of the assassination, was present at the window from which the shots were fired.

(d) Shortly after the assassination, the Mannlicher-Carcano rifle belonging to Oswald was found partially hidden between some cartons on the sixth floor and the improvised paper bag in which Oswald brought the rifle to the Depository was found close by the window from which the shots were fired.

(e) Based on testimony of the experts and their analysis of films of the assassination, the Commission has concluded that a rifleman of Lee Harvey Oswald's capabilities could have fired the shots from the rifle used in the assassination within the elapsed time of the shooting. The Commission has concluded further that Oswald possessed the capability with a rifle which enabled him to commit the assassination.

(f) Oswald lied to the police after his arrest concerning important substantive matters.

(g) Oswald had attempted to kill Maj. Gen. Edwin A. Walker (Resigned, U.S. Army) on April 10, 1963, thereby demonstrating his disposition to take human life.

Two more considerations, contained in other paragraphs, complete the summary of the Commission's case against Oswald. They are not listed in the alphabetical sequence above, but I will add them in that form:

(h) Oswald killed Dallas Police Patrolman J. D. Tippit approximately 45 minutes after the assassination. This conclusion upholds the finding that Oswald fired the shots which killed President Kennedy and wounded Governor Connally. . . .

(i) Within 80 minutes of the assassination and 35 minutes of the Tippit killing Oswald resisted arrest at the theatre by attempting to shoot another Dallas police officer.

All of these points are condensed and recapitulated in the final paragraph of the Report's chapter on "The Assassin." The climax of a trial in which there were no rights for the defense—only for the prosecution—this final paragraph sums up the accusation, and convicts the accused, in eight *findings:*

> On the basis of the evidence reviewed in this chapter, the Commission has found that Lee Harvey Oswald (1) owned and possessed the rifle used to kill President Kennedy and wound Governor Connally, (2) brought this rifle into the Depository Building on the morning of the assassination, (3) was present, at the time of the assassination, at the window from which the shots were fired, (4) killed Dallas Police Officer J. D. Tippit in an apparent attempt to escape, (5) resisted arrest by drawing a fully loaded pistol and attempting to shoot another police officer, (6) lied to the police after his arrest concerning important substantive matters, (7) attempted, in April 1963, to kill Maj. Gen. Edwin A. Walker, and (8) possessed the capability with a rifle which would have enabled him to commit the assassination. On the basis of these findings the Commission has concluded that Lee Harvey Oswald was the assassin of President Kennedy.

Here we have it all clearly stated and properly enumerated; the eight *findings* can now be reviewed one by one to decide whether they carry the necessary weight to justify the conclusions of the Commission.

1. LEE HARVEY OSWALD OWNED AND POSSESSED THE RIFLE USED TO KILL PRESIDENT KENNEDY AND WOUND GOVERNOR CONNALLY.

Few people will dispute that Lee Harvey Oswald was the owner of a Mannlicher-Carcano purchased by mail from Klein's Sporting Goods of Chicago under the name A. J. Hidell. What is far from proved, however, is the statement that the Mannlicher-Carcano was the murder weapon.

In Chapter 4 I discussed at length the ballistic reports and the experts' conclusions. The experts declared that the "nearly whole bullet" and the two fragments they examined had been fired from the rifle that the police said they had found partly hidden behind some cartons on the sixth floor of the Depository. Jurors must evaluate even the statements of experts. If there had been a trial, the prosecution experts would have been matched, no doubt, by other experts brought in by the defense, who would have held that proper ballistic identification cannot be obtained with mere fragments. I repeat, nevertheless, that I do not intend to dispute the opinions of Frazier and Nicol that the "nearly whole bullet" and the fragments were fired from the Mannlicher-Carcano.

But to contend, as the Commission does, that Oswald's rifle was "used to kill President Kennedy," it is not enough to show that a bullet and some fragments were fired from the rifle. It must first be established that this bullet and these fragments actually were the ones that struck the victim.

The need for this preliminary determination generally does not impress the public, for the simple reason that in most cases there is no question about the bullets to be identified; either they are recovered from the victim's body or they are found at the scene of the crime in a position that can be explained logically and gives rise to no argument. In the case of President Kennedy, none of the bullets identified by the experts were furnished by the autopsy. The two fragments were found on the front seat "after the Presidential car was returned to Washington." As to the "nearly whole bullet," the solid part of the ballistic evidence, it raises a major problem that no honest investigation can choose— and should be allowed—to ignore.

The initial statements of the investigators said it had been found on a stretcher, and everybody assumed they meant the stretcher on which Kennedy had been placed. Even so, counsel for the defense would have been able to raise grave doubts. It was not impossible, of course, that the bullet had lost its force in passing through the President's body or even at the moment of impact, and that it had fallen into his clothing and rolled out later when he was put on the stretcher. But the prosecution would have had to prove this through experts subjected to cross-examination. It would have to explain convincingly—more convincingly than the defense with its opposing experts—that the wounds were of such a nature as to justify the assumption that the bullet could have lost its force, and that the condition of the bullet corresponded to the nature of the wounds. Otherwise, there was indeed a serious possibility that a bullet fired from Oswald's Mannlicher-Carcano had been smuggled onto the President's stretcher after the crime.

By informing us now that the "nearly whole bullet" was found not on Kennedy's stretcher but on Governor Connally's, the Warren Report changes the situation completely—for the worse.

The Report states:

> A nearly whole bullet was found on Governor Connally's stretcher at Parkland Hospital after the assassination. After his arrival at the hospital the Governor was brought into trauma room No. 2 on a stretcher, removed from the room on that stretcher a short time later, and taken on an elevator to the second-floor operating room. On the second floor he was transferred from the stretcher to an operating table which was then moved into the operating room, and a hospital attendant wheeled the empty stretcher into an elevator. Shortly afterward, Darrell C. Tomlinson, the hospital's senior engineer, removed this stretcher from the elevator and placed it in the corridor on the ground floor, alongside another stretcher wholly unconnected with the care of Governor Connally. A few minutes later, he bumped one of the stretchers against the wall and a bullet rolled out.

The Report adds that Tomlinson "was not certain whether the bullet came from the Connally stretcher or the adjacent one," but tells us finally that "the Commission has concluded that the bullet came from the Governor's stretcher." It eliminates the possibility that the bullet could have come from Kennedy's stretcher because this stretcher had been placed in "a completely different location from the site where the nearly whole bullet was found."

The picture originally drawn, while raising numerous questions and requiring much more evidence than had been given, allowed the Commission (theoretically at least) to start from the presumption that this bullet was one that had hit the President.

In the Report's new version, such a presumption is out of the question. If the Warren Commission wanted to be taken seriously, it should have assumed that the bullet was the one that had hit the Governor. Even this would not have been easy to prove: The bullet, "slightly flattened but otherwise unmutilated," supposedly passed through Connally's chest, "shattering his fifth rib," and traveled on through his right wrist, shedding small fragments of metal "upon striking the firm surface of the bone," and leaving "a tiny metallic fragment embedded in the Governor's leg"—all of this while remaining "nearly whole." In any case, where then was the first, nonfatal bullet that had struck the President? The Warren Commission calmly answers: on Connally's stretcher; it was the same "nearly whole bullet."

One could write pages about this miraculous bullet and its extraordinary voyage, whose vicissitudes (when brought to light, as they were most effectively by Vincent J. Salandria, a Philadelphia lawyer) seem to have been borrowed from the fables of Baron Munchausen.

It must be noted, at least, that the Commission's theory was rejected by several medical experts whose depositions are reproduced in the Hearings even though they are ignored in the Report. In addition, while the Report rather arbitrarily affirms the existence of "very persuasive evidence from the experts to indicate that the same bullet which pierced the President's throat also caused Governor Connally's wounds," it does not conceal the formal disagreement of Connally himself and grants that "Governor Connally's testimony and certain other factors have given rise to some difference of opinion as to this probability."

The Commission thus officially admits that this is not a demonstrated fact but a simple "probability," and a doubtful "probability" at that. Yet it apparently did not consider the issue of great importance, since "it is not necessary to any essential findings of the Commission to determine just which shot hit Governor Connally."

Such an opinion is thoroughly stupefying. It certainly is not only "necessary" but absolutely *essential*, if we are to give the slightest credit to the "findings" of the Warren Commission, to determine whether or not the bullet that struck Governor Connally was one of those that hit the President. I do not wish to go into the various possibilities—all contrary to the Commission's conclusions and implying unpleasant considerations about its methods—that arise if, as is probable, the bullet was *not* the same. What must be emphasized here is that the Commission admits it did not establish beyond doubt that the bullet found on the Governor's stretcher had first hit the President. The Commission thus has no right to say that *all* the bullets that struck the President were identified as having been fired from Oswald's Mannlicher-Carcano. Nor can it say that Oswald's Mannlicher-Carcano was the only murder weapon, if indeed it was a murder weapon at all.

Even if it had been established beyond a reasonable doubt that Oswald's rifle *was* the murder weapon, this would not prove that Oswald was the assassin. Hundreds of crimes have been committed with weapons belonging to others, often for that very reason: in order to incriminate them. The law, taking this into consideration, demands that the prosecution prove that the owner of the weapon had it in his possession at the time of the crime and that it was actually he who used it. The pronouncement in Finding Number 1 that Oswald both "owned and possessed" the rifle seems intended to suggest that ownership constitutes possession, but that is not the case. Thus, aside from the questions raised by the unexplained bullet, the probative value of Finding Number 1 depends entirely on the validity of Findings 2 and 3.

2. LEE HARVEY OSWALD BROUGHT THIS RIFLE INTO THE DEPOSITORY BUILDING ON THE MORNING OF THE ASSASSINATION.

I have devoted an entire chapter to the problem of the paper bag. It shows that the only two witnesses who had seen the bag on the morning of the assassination described it as too small to have contained a rifle, even dismantled. Nor did they recognize the wrapping left in plain view near the window, according to the Report, which fails to answer the question of when it was discovered. No witnesses saw Oswald bring the package into the building, and none saw him with it inside the building at any time.

The Commission's Finding Number 2 takes into account neither the missing witnesses nor the denials of the two existing witnesses. But the Report does, at least, admit that the package could not have contained a fully assembled rifle. The Commission therefore would still have to convince us that Lee Oswald had the time and the opportunity to reassemble his rifle with the care necessary to assure the success of his undertaking.

It is quite unlikely that Oswald could have accomplished this task during working hours: The sixth floor, we are told, was occupied by workers putting in a new floor, and it is hard to picture Oswald locked in a toilet putting his rifle together and then walking through the corridors and stairways with one end of the weapon protruding from the bag.

The Report, by the way, does not try to suggest this. Instead, it assumes that Oswald assembled the rifle after his co-workers went downstairs to have lunch or watch the motorcade. On the basis of Charles Givens' testimony, that would have allowed him to start the operation no earlier than 11:55 A.M. The shooting took place at 12:30. But Oswald did not have 35 minutes available, for two reasons: (a) before concentrating his attention on the rifle, he had to construct his barricade of book cartons; (b) during part of the time, Bonnie Ray Williams, according to the Report, was eating his chicken lunch on the same floor.

Bonnie Ray Williams, the Report says, had gone down with the others, but he "returned to the sixth floor at about noon to eat his lunch and watch the motorcade." Elsewhere the Report says this took place "shortly after noon." Since Bonnie Ray Williams, moreover, said his lunch might have lasted "maybe 12 minutes," and the Report at another point specifies that Williams' meal took place "at least 15 minutes before the assassination," we can conclude that Williams was on the sixth floor from about 12:03 to 12:15.

There is no problem about how Oswald must have used the eight minutes between Givens' departure and Williams' return: He had to build his barricade.

This was no easy task. The Report says that "the arrangement of boxes at the window from which the shots were fired was studied to determine whether Oswald required any assistance in moving the cartons to the window." The Report answers its question by saying that "most of those cartons had been moved there by other employees" to clear the floor being repaired. Roy Truly, as the Report states, confirmed there were "quite a lot of cartons" in the southeast corner; but he also added that they were placed there at random without any particular pattern. A glance at the photo published in the Report (see Illustrations) suffices to show that this "shield of cartons"—as the caption describes it—indicates a very definite pattern. Each of the boxes shown weighed 50 pounds, the Report tells us. Oswald had to move them, line them up in a different way, take cartons from other stacks to build new stacks, and close up the gaps. It would not be an exaggeration to say this effort required all of those eight minutes between Givens' departure and Williams' arrival.

Did he have time enough to assemble the rifle in the remaining 15 minutes after Williams departed?

"A firearms expert with the FBI assembled the rifle in 6 minutes using a 10-cent coin as a tool," the Report declares. The mention of the dime is probably aimed at giving the impression that it was child's play for the expert, but in fact it accidentally brings up another question: Since no tools were found at the scene, Oswald himself must have used a dime to put the weapon together. The Report fails to tell us whether Oswald had a dime on him—though it says he had $13.87 when he was arrested (apparently Oswald thought that would be enough to cover the costs of his escape). Perhaps the "assassin" used his fingernails to tighten the screws of the rifle he was preparing to fire at the President of the United States.

Oswald had no opportunity to play with his Mannlicher-Carcano after he had left New Orleans two months earlier, and it must have taken him more time to do the job than was needed by the FBI expert. Still, we might have assumed that in the remaining 15 minutes before the motorcade's arrival, that is, with nine minutes more than the six required by the expert, Oswald could have done the job—if those nine extra minutes had not been reduced to two by the testimony of star witness Howard Brennan.

Waiting for "about 7 minutes" for the President to arrive, Brennan "noticed a man at the southeast corner window of the sixth floor, and observed him leave the window 'a couple of times,' " the Report declares.

Since Brennan observed the man leaving the window a couple of times, this means the man must have been in sight the rest of the time. Brennan, whose powers of observation are not questioned by the Commission, did not say the man was handling a rifle when he saw him. Since it is not likely the assembly job was carried out in brief stages each time the man stepped away from the window, the man had already finished the job when Brennan noticed him, seven minutes before the motorcade arrived. This gunman, who would prove the equal of the champions of the National Rifle Association, was thus only slightly less skilled than the FBI expert in assembling the weapon: It took him eight minutes instead of six. This is saying a lot for Lee Harvey Oswald; in fact, a little too much.

The Commission was not unaware of the problem, since it reserved the means of replying to objections of that kind by invoking another possibility: Oswald, it suggests, was not necessarily restricted to such a tight schedule; behind his "shield of cartons," he could have been working on the rifle while Williams ate his chicken.

This suggestion, in fact, is precise enough to be termed a hypothesis. It appears in two different places in the Report. Describing Bonnie Ray Williams' meal (and this is probably why it had to move the location of that meal away from the southeast corner window), the Commission ascertains that "Williams saw no one on the sixth floor during this period, although the stacks of books prevented his seeing the east side of the building." The other allusion is even more to the point. In the section where the arrangement of boxes as a gun rest is described, the Report states: "A person seated on the fourth carton could assemble the rifle without being seen from the rest of the sixth floor because the cartons stacked around the southeast corner would shield him."

I shall limit myself to quoting an excerpt from the testimony of Bonnie Ray Williams. Joseph A. Ball was asking the questions when Commission member Allen W. Dulles interrupted:

> *Mr. Dulles.*   I would like to ask one question here. When you were on the sixth floor eating your lunch, did you hear anything that made you feel that there was anybody else on the sixth floor with you?
>
> *Mr. Williams.*   No, sir; I didn't hear anything.
>
> *Mr. Dulles.*   You did not see anything?
>
> *Mr. Williams.*   I did not see anything.
>
> *Mr. Dulles.*   You were all alone as far as you knew at that time on the sixth floor?
>
> *Mr. Williams.*   Yes, sir.
>
> *Mr. Dulles.*   During that period of from 12 o'clock about to—10 or 15 minutes after?
>
> *Mr. Williams.*   Yes, sir. I felt like I was all alone. That is one of the reasons I left—because it was so quiet.

The reader can decide for himself whether Oswald could have assembled his rifle under those conditions—not only without being troubled in his own mind by the presence of an intruder but without making the slightest sound. But it should be recalled that the question arises only if one accepts: (a) the Commission's assumption concerning the contents of the package, rather than the description of the package given by the two who had seen it; (b) the testimony of Detective Studebaker as to the location where Williams had his lunch, rather than that of the six policemen who arrived on the scene before him.

It is time also to point out that a major element of the mystery of the paper bag has been definitively solved by the Warren Commission—in Oswald's favor.

I admitted in Chapter 8 that one of the most troubling aspects of the case was the fact that Oswald, contrary to his habit, went to Irving on Thursday night, without calling in advance. I also wrote—and I repeat it here, even though the Report suggests the contrary—that Ruth Paine herself wondered, and asked me, what could have been the reason for his unexpected visit. The explanation of the "curtain rods" was difficult to believe, and the only answer that seemed possible in the absence of other information was that Oswald had gone there to get his Mannlicher-Carcano. The Commission did not miss the chance to make use of this, and its Report informs us: "In deciding whether Oswald carried a rifle to work in a long paper bag on November 22, the Commission gave weight to the fact that Oswald gave a false reason for returning home on November 21, and one which provided an excuse for the carrying of a bulky package the following morning."

Now the Commission knew perfectly well—and was the only one to know it, since this part of Marina Oswald's testimony, unlike the rest, was never leaked out—that Lee Oswald had an important reason for going to Irving. The Commission refers to it elsewhere in the Report: "Although his visit was a surprise, since he arrived on Thursday instead of Friday for his usual weekend visit, both women [Marina Oswald and Ruth Paine—L.S.] testified that they thought he had come to patch up a quarrel which he had with his wife a few days earlier when she learned that he was living in Dallas under an assumed name."

Finally, in its chapter devoted to the personality and "possible motives" of Oswald, the Report gives us a complete, detailed, and in my opinion entirely convincing explanation of the profound reasons for Oswald's visit. Marina had told the Commission about her argument with her husband on the telephone when he had reproached her—quite unjustly, in fact—for having asked for Mr. Oswald when she called him on Sunday, November 17, instead of using the alias, Mr. Lee, which he had never told her about. "On Monday he called several times," Marina testified, "but after I hung up on him and didn't want to talk to him he did not call again. He then arrived on Thursday." The Commission does not indicate any dissatisfaction with Marina's explanation. On the contrary, the Report remarks with good reason that "the events of that evening [Thursday night—L.S.] can best be appreciated through Marina Oswald's testimony." It then quotes the following extract:

> Q. Did your husband give any reason for coming home on Thursday?

A. He said that he was lonely because he hadn't come the preceding weekend, and he wanted to make his peace with me.

Q. Did you say anything to him?

A. He tried to talk to me but I would not answer him, and he was very upset.

Q. Were you upset with him?

A. I was angry, of course. He was not angry—he was upset. I was angry. He tried very hard to please me. He spent quite a bit of time putting away diapers and played with the children on the street.

Q. How did you indicate to him that you were angry with him?

A. By not talking to him.

Q. And how did he show that he was upset?

A. He was upset over the fact that I would not answer him. He tried to start a conversation with me several times, but I would not answer. And he said that he didn't want me to be angry at him because this upsets him.

On that day, he suggested that we rent an apartment in Dallas. He said that he was tired of living alone and perhaps the reason for my being so angry was the fact that we were not living together. That if I want to he would rent an apartment in Dallas tomorrow—that he didn't want me to remain with Ruth any longer, but wanted me to live with him in Dallas.

He repeated this not once but several times, but I refused. And he said that once again I was preferring my friends to him, and that I didn't need him.

Q. What did you say to that?

A. I said it would be better if I remained with Ruth until the holidays, he would come, and we would all meet together. That this was better because while he was living alone and I stayed with Ruth, we were spending less money. And I told him to buy me a washing

machine, because two children it became too difficult
to wash by hand.

Q. What did he say to that?

A. He said he would buy me a washing machine.

Q. What did you say to that?

A. Thank you. That it would be better if he bought
something for himself—that I would manage.

I do not intend to discuss here the character of Marina Oswald. Still it is worth recording what the Report thus reveals
about the state of mind of a man supposedly preparing to kill
the President. Nothing in Marina's story would indicate that
Oswald, who must have been watching all the time for the moment when he could go off to the garage to dismantle and wrap
up his rifle, had anything on his mind other than their marital
crisis. Marina, like Ruth Paine, confirmed also that there was no
mention that night of President Kennedy, and it is obvious from
reading the above account that if Oswald was obsessed by problems, these concerned his own home and not the White House.

Marina went to bed two and a half hours after her husband,
and the Report tells us that "she did not speak to him when she
joined him there, although she thought that he was still awake."

What was worrying Lee Oswald, alone in bed and unable to
sleep for two and a half hours while he waited for his wife to
join him? The fate of the world? The emancipation of the working class? The menace of Yankee imperialism to Fidel Castro?
The Report does not make any such claim. While declaring that
"the Commission does not believe that the relations between
Oswald and his wife caused him to assassinate the President,"
it does not entirely preclude the possibility that John F. Kennedy
might not have been assassinated at 12:30 P.M. Friday if Marina
Oswald, at 11:30 P.M. Thursday, had been willing to settle their
problems in bed.

The Commission, in any case, admits it was impressed by the
intimate details revealed by Marina about that night. It even
seems to accept the idea that Oswald went to Irving on Thursday
because he was obsessed by his marital troubles and could not

wait any longer to talk to his wife. Why then does it hold against him the fact that he gave a "false reason" to Wesley Frazier?

Oswald, withdrawn and sullen, had little in common with anyone, least of all with the 19-year-old Texan who interested him only to the extent that he saved him bus fare. In giving such weight to the argument of the "false reason," does the Commission mean to suggest that Oswald ordinarily would have confided to Frazier that things were not going well between him and his wife, that he was unhappy about it, and that he hoped to make up with her that night and perhaps make a new start in life?

3. LEE HARVEY OSWALD WAS PRESENT, AT THE TIME OF THE ASSASSINATION, AT THE WINDOW FROM WHICH THE SHOTS WERE FIRED.

During his famous press conference on November 24, District Attorney Wade made a series of insinuations that struck me at the time as particularly irresponsible.

After announcing that "the purpose of this news conference is to detail some of the evidence against Oswald for the assassination of the President," after emphasizing that he intended to "go through the evidence piece by piece for you," Wade produced an immediate sensation with "Number One," as he listed his first item. I quote:

> First, there was a number of witnesses that saw the person with the gun on the sixth floor of the bookstore building, the window—detailing the window—where he was looking out.
>
> Inside this window the police found a row of books, cases, boxes, hiding someone sitting in the window, from people on the same floor looking in. On the window were some boxes where, in the little circle around the window, by the bookcases, some boxes where, apparently the person was sitting, because he was seen from that particular window.
>
> On this box that the defendant was sitting on, his palm print was found and was identified as his. . . .

To the extent that we can make sense of this gibberish, it can signify only one thing: The D.A. was seeking to create the impression that it had been established, through witnesses, that "the person with the gun," the man "seen from that particular window," was Lee Harvey Oswald.

Reporters and commentators were aware that "a number of witnesses" had seen the barrel of a rifle appear and disappear at a window of the building, and one of their colleagues in fact was among those witnesses. But they knew that no one could have identified "the person with the gun" from the street. The *Dallas Morning News* on Saturday morning published a photo of the assassin's position in the southeast corner. Since the assassin was leaning his rifle not directly on the window ledge but on the boxes he had arranged for this purpose, his head, while he was firing, necessarily remained some distance from the window and therefore in the shadows.

This is why the paper relegated to an inside page the following item: "A few people outside the building, like H. L. Brennan, a 44-year-old steamfitter, actually got a glimpse of the gunman. 'After the first shot, I looked up and saw him. The gun was sticking out the window. I saw him fire a second time. He was a slender guy, a nice-looking guy. He didn't seem to be in no hurry,' said Brennan."

Newsweek magazine thus was wrong when it said on October 5, 1964, in its panegyric on the Warren Report: "The Commission also had the testimony of a witness never publicly heard from before—an eyewitness to the shooting itself. He is steamfitter Howard L. Brennan. . . ." In fact, Brennan's statement had appeared the day after the crime, with and without his name, in all the papers—but nobody had given it much attention because it was impossible to imagine then that it could be presented one day as the cornerstone of a verdict.

Among the publications that mentioned Brennan's testimony at the time, I will quote only from one—*Newsweek* itself:

In an article titled "Oswald and the Weight of Evidence," in the issue of December 9, 1963, we find a paragraph clearly referring to Brennan, although *Newsweek*'s editors, showing how little importance they attached to it, didn't even bother to mention his name: "At that moment, witnesses saw a rifle disappear into a sixth-floor corner window. One saw a man as well. 'I can't identify him,' he said, 'but if I see a man who looks like him, I'll point him out.' Later, he looked over a police lineup of four men—and chose Oswald."

Now the Warren Report picks up these faded and forgotten scraps of "news" and makes them its most sensational revelation: Lee Harvey Oswald was caught in the act by Howard L. Brennan.

Brennan makes his appearance in the Warren Report as early as page 5:

> One eyewitness, Howard L. Brennan, had been watching the parade from a point on Elm Street directly opposite and facing the building. He promptly told a policeman that he had seen a slender man, about 5 feet 10 inches, in his early thirties, take deliberate aim from the sixth-floor corner window and fire a rifle in the direction of the President's car. Brennan thought he might be able to identify the man since he had noticed him in the window a few minutes before the motorcade made the turn onto Elm Street.

Three pages later, however, we find the first mention of the achievement of Deputy Sheriff Luke Mooney, who "noticed" the barricade of boxes [at one o'clock—L.S.] and "squeezed through the boxes and realized immediately [at 1:12—L.S.] that he had discovered the point from which the shots had been fired" because "on the floor were three empty cartridge cases." It goes on: "A carton had apparently been placed on the floor at the side of the window so that a person sitting on the carton could look down Elm Street toward the overpass and scarcely be noticed from the outside."

Despite this somewhat troublesome note, the Commission returns with all of its enthusiasm to Brennan, who has the place of honor in the section titled "Eyewitness Identification of Assassin." Brennan declared, we read, that "Lee Harvey Oswald, whom he had viewed in a police lineup on the night of the assassination, was the man he had seen fire the shots from the sixth-floor window of the Depository Building."

Unfortunately for the Commission, here too we will soon detect a false note, and this one is especially strident.

Brennan testified that it seemed to him the man he had seen "was standing up and resting against the left window sill." In his first statement he had "promptly told a policeman" the height of the man but not his weight. It is true that in a second statement to police later the same day, he had given the weight but omitted the height. In any case Brennan believed the gunman had been standing, while the Report is compelled to admit that "the half-open window, the arrangement of the boxes, and the angle of the shots virtually preclude a standing position."

Such a contradiction should have signaled the quick end of a wonderful witness. For the Commission, however, it is just a small mistake on one single detail, and Brennan remains nevertheless the most observant of observers, the most informative of informants.

The Report, incidentally, has an explanation for Brennan's mistake. "Since the window ledges in the Depository Building are lower than in most buildings, a person squatting or kneeling exposes more of his body than would normally be the case. From the street, this creates the impression that the person is standing. Brennan could have seen enough of the body of a kneeling or squatting person to estimate his height." Here we are referred to the photographs taken by Thomas C. Dillard "a few seconds after the assassination," one of which shows the corner window and, at a window below, two of three employees who were on the fifth floor (see Illustrations). I go back to the same piece of evidence, for opposite reasons.

According to the Report, the two employees give the impression of standing, but in fact one was squatting and the other kneeling. It seems to me that the young man on the left is leaning his elbows on the window ledge, which would be impossible for a person standing unless the window sills in the building were unusually *high;* as to the other employee, he seems to be sitting on a chair.

Dillard's pictures prove something else to me. Only the face of the man on the left, whose head is partly outside, is clearly visible. The face of the other man, whose head is a few inches farther inside, is more difficult to make out. Behind them is only darkness, and this is even more true of the window above, where we can recognize the form of one of the boxes that we know was placed directly on the sill. Sitting or squatting, anyone using these boxes as a gun rest, and kept therefore to a corresponding distance from the window, could indeed "scarcely be noticed from the outside."

And why, given the major role it assigns its "eyewitness," didn't the Commission carry out the tests that would seem to be dictated by the situation?

Chief Justice Warren took the trouble to check in person whether it was possible to hear, on the fifth floor, shells dropping overhead. But when it comes to the eyewitness testimony of Brennan, we are given hypotheses, or suggestions on how to interpret a photo. The Commission could have easily verified the validity of Brennan's testimony, and it seems incredible that this was not done. It had only to place him on the same concrete wall on the southwest corner of Elm and Houston Streets one day at 12:30, when the Texas sun strikes almost perpendicularly down the façade of the Depository Building; place a stranger in the position of the assassin behind the half-closed window; and then ask our "eyewitness" to (1) describe the man, and (2) pick him out of a real lineup.

For we come now, precisely, to the circumstances in which Howard L. Brennan "identified" Oswald as the man in the window. The Report offers on this subject a page so involved that it is hard to follow Brennan and even harder to follow the Commission following Brennan. The jumble can be reduced to the following statements, in the words of the Report:

(a) "During the evening of November 22, Brennan identified Oswald as the person in the lineup who bore the closest resem-

blance to the man in the window but he said he was unable to
make a positive identification."

(b) "In an interview with FBI agents on December 17, 1963,
Brennan stated that he was sure that the person firing the rifle was
Oswald."

(c) "In another interview with FBI agents on January 7, 1964,
Brennan appeared to revert to his earlier inability to make a positive identification."

(d) "In his testimony before the Commission, Brennan stated
that his remarks of January 7 were intended by him merely as
an accurate report of what he said on November 22."

(e) "Brennan told the Commission that he could have made a
positive identification in the lineup on November 22 but did not
do so because he felt that the assassination was 'a Communist
activity, and I felt like there hadn't been more than one eyewitness, and if it got to be a known fact that I was an eyewitness, my
family or I, either one, might not be safe.' "

(f) "When specifically asked before the Commission whether or
not he could positively identify the man he saw in the sixth-floor
window as the same man he saw in the police station, Brennan
stated, 'I could at that time—I could, with all sincerity, identify
him as being the same man.' "

(g) "Prior to the lineup, Brennan had seen Oswald's picture
on television and he told the Commission that whether this affected his identification 'is something I do not know.' "

In spite of all this, and while avoiding comment on the fact
that Brennan had seen Oswald on television before he was asked
to point him out in the lineup, the Report comes to the following
conclusion, a model of either scrupulous fairness or palpable dis-
honesty:

> Although the record indicates that Brennan was an ac-
> curate observer, he declined to make a positive identifica-
> tion of Oswald when he first saw him in the police lineup.
> The Commission, therefore, does not base its conclusion
> concerning the identity of the assassin on Brennan's subse-
> quent certain identification of Lee Harvey Oswald as the

> man he saw fire the rifle. Immediately after the assassina-
> tion, however, Brennan described to the police the man
> he saw in the window and then identified Oswald as the
> person who most nearly resembled the man he saw. The
> Commission is satisfied that, at the least, Brennan saw a
> man in the window who closely resembled Lee Harvey
> Oswald, and that Brennan believes the man he saw was in
> fact Lee Harvey Oswald.

In my opinion, this masterpiece of casuistry is intended to allow
the Commission to make use of the ultraquestionable "testimony"
of Howard L. Brennan while at the same time reserving a virtuous
disclaimer to silence critics: "The Commission, therefore, does not
base its conclusion . . ."

For the press and the public, the hidden reservations of the Report's editors could not weaken the conviction that the Commission had "turned up an eyewitness who saw Oswald shooting the
President from the Texas School Book Depository." This quotation happens to be from *Newsweek,* but nearly all American newspapers and magazines carried the sensational "information" in
similar terms. This was obviously what the Commission wanted.
The Report, in fact, after building an escape route behind the
moral fortifications of page 145, does not restrain itself further
in speaking of Brennan. On page 250, for instance, the Report
unhesitatingly repeats that Brennan "made a positive identification of Oswald as being the person at the window."

The Commission, however, found two witnesses whose testimony had really not been published before, as far as I know.

Ronald Fischer and Robert Edwards, we learn, were on the
sidewalk not far from the wall where Brennan was sitting. They
did not see the shots being fired, but they saw a man near the
window shortly before the motorcade arrived. "Fisher and Edwards did not see the man clearly enough or long enough to identify him," the Report admits, but it quickly adds that "approximately 1 week after the assassination, according to Fischer, policemen showed him a picture of Oswald." And the Report proudly
quotes Fischer's response a week after the assassination, as he
looked at Oswald's picture: "I told them that that could have been

the man * * * That that could have been the man that I saw in
the window in the School Book Depository Building, but that I
was not sure."

The Commission's conclusion is that the testimony of Fischer
and Edwards "is of probative value, however, because their limited description is consistent with that of the man who has been
found by the Commission, based on other evidence, to have fired
the shots from the window."

Other evidence? Summing up its reasons for declaring that
Oswald "was present, at the time of the assassination, at the win-
dow from which the shots were fired," the Report again stresses
Brennan's testimony:

"An eyewitness to the shooting immediately provided a description of the man in the window which was similar to Oswald's actual appearance. This witness identified Oswald in a lineup as the
man most nearly resembling the man he saw and later identified
Oswald as the man he observed."

As to the other "findings" given in the summary, here they
are:

(a) "Fingerprint and palmprint evidence establishes that Oswald handled two of the four cartons next to the window and also
handled a paper bag which was found near the cartons." We need
only recall here the testimony of the Commission's own experts.
"While the age of a print cannot be generally determined," the
experts had stated, "this palmprint must have been relatively
fresh, because the carton was constructed of cardboard, an ab-
sorbent material." But when called upon to determine the maximum age of the print in question, the two experts gave estimates of
a day and a half (Arthur Mandella, of the New York police) and
three days (Sebastian Latona, of the FBI). Such prints could not
possibly prove that Oswald was at the window *at the time of the
shooting.*

(b) "Oswald was seen in the vicinity of the southeast corner of
the sixth floor approximately 35 minutes before the assassination
and no one could be found who saw Oswald anywhere else in the
building until after the shooting." This argument is so obviously
ridiculous that it requires no comment.

(c) "Oswald's known actions in the building immediately after the assassination are consistent with his having been at the southeast corner window of the sixth floor at 12:30 p.m." The Commission refers here to the tests it conducted to refute the suggestion that Roy Truly and Patrolman Baker might have furnished an alibi for Oswald. As I have shown in Chapter 1, the alibi was actually proved rather than refuted by one of the tests, and even in the other one all the Commission gained by a very few seconds' margin was the right to say that it was at least not impossible for Oswald to have been on the sixth floor at the time of the shooting. The reasoning of the Warren Commission now is that since there is, after all, a small chance that Oswald *could* have been at the window, then he *must* have been there. This type of argument also requires no comment.

4. LEE HARVEY OSWALD KILLED DALLAS POLICE OFFICER J. D. TIPPIT IN AN APPARENT ATTEMPT TO ESCAPE.

Like Finding Number 3, this one depends essentially on "eyewitnesses"—a plethora of "eyewitnesses": "Two eyewitnesses who heard the shots and saw the shooting of Dallas Police Patrolman J. D. Tippit and seven eyewitnesses who saw the flight of the gunman with revolver in hand positively identified Lee Harvey Oswald as the man they saw fire the shots or flee from the scene. . . ."

The first "eyewitness" to the murder itself was, of course, Helen Markham. Chapter 5 contains all that I have to say about her. I would only like to add that in the case of Mrs. Markham, as with Brennan, the Commission built some inconspicuous emergency exits along its tortuous route. Thus, after writing that "the Commission considers her testimony reliable," the Report's authors continue:

"However, even in the absence of Mrs. Markham's testimony, there is ample evidence to identify Oswald as the killer of Tippit."

As "ample evidence" the Commission produces its second "eyewitness," William Scoggins, a taxi driver who was having lunch in his cab parked on Patton Avenue near the corner of Tenth Street. He watched as a police car pulled up alongside a man on the sidewalk, saw the man approach the car and the policeman get out; then he heard three or four shots and saw the officer fall. When the gunman started toward Patton Avenue, revolver in hand, Scoggins hid behind the cab and the man passed on the other side, within 12 feet of him.

"The next day," the Report states, "Scoggins viewed a lineup of four persons and identified Oswald as the man whom he had seen the day before at 10th and Patton. In his testimony before the Commission, Scoggins stated that he thought he had seen a picture of Oswald in the newspapers prior to the lineup identification on Saturday. He had not seen Oswald on television and had not been shown any photographs of Oswald by the police."

The Report does not say why the lineup was not held for Scoggins until Saturday. While congratulating the Commission, on the other hand, on its well-grounded suspicion of the Dallas police, which led it to inquire whether the police had shown the witness any photos before the lineup, I cannot help wondering what difference that would have made, since he had already seen the picture in the newspapers. But the Commission, as we saw in connection with Brennan and Mrs. Markham, has its own ideas on what constitutes a valid identification.

It even seeks to recover—partially at least—a third "eyewitness" to the Tippit murder, one whom the Dallas police had crossed off the list before.

Domingo Benavides, a truck driver, saw the man fire and the officer fall. It was he who then notified headquarters by using the radio in Tippit's car. But he said he did not believe he could identify the man, so the Dallas police did not take him before a lineup. That fails to prevent the Report from registering with satisfaction that Domingo Benavides testified before the Commission that "the picture of Oswald which he saw later on television bore a resemblance to the man who shot Officer Tippit."

The Commission nevertheless does not place Benavides among the nine "eyewitnesses" who it contends "positively identified" Oswald, the first two being Helen Markham and William Scoggins.

Leading the seven others were Barbara and Virginia Davis.

The first "was not sure whether she had seen his picture in a newspaper on the afternoon or evening of November 22 prior to the lineup," although her stepsister insisted she had not seen television or newspapers before identifying him. Next came Ted Callaway and Sam Guinyard: Both identified Oswald in a lineup Friday afternoon as the man they had seen walking on Patton Avenue "with a revolver held high in his right hand." Finally we have Warren Reynolds, Harold Russell, and Pat Patterson, who also saw a man holding a revolver, although the Report does not say what the man was doing with it.

After informing us without comment that these witnesses were questioned by the FBI "2 months after the shooting," the Report tells us how they "identified" Oswald at that time:

> Russell and Patterson were shown a picture of Oswald and they stated that Oswald was the man they saw on November 22, 1963. Russell confirmed this statement in a sworn affidavit for the Commission. Patterson, when asked later to confirm his identification by affidavit said he did not recall having been shown the photograph. He was then shown two photographs of Oswald and he advised that Oswald was "unquestionably" the man he saw. Reynolds did not make a positive identification when interviewed by the FBI, but he subsequently testified before a Commission staff member [after recovering from his bullet wound in the head—L.S.] and, when shown two photographs of Oswald, stated that they were photographs of the man he saw.

The Report does not try to justify the Commission's notions about the meaning and validity of identifications made two months after the fact, on the basis of one or even two pictures showing a man whose every feature had been engraved for all time in the minds of the whole world by press and television.

It does, at least, devote five lines to an attempt to justify the validity of the lineup method of identification:

> The Dallas Police Department furnished the Commission with pictures of the men who appeared in the lineups

with Oswald, and the Commission has inquired into general lineup procedures used by the Dallas police as well as the specific procedures in the lineups involving Oswald. The Commission is satisfied that the lineups were conducted fairly.

This, however, was not the opinion of Oswald, as we can also read in the Report. FBI Agent James W. Bookhout, for example, wrote that during his interrogation on the night of November 23, "Oswald complained of a lineup wherein he had not been granted a request to put on a jacket similar to those worn by some of the other individuals in the lineup."

The Saturday lineup, probably the one referred to by Oswald, is described elsewhere in the Report by the cab driver William Whaley, who had driven Oswald to Oak Cliff on Friday afternoon. According to Whaley, "five young teenagers" were displayed with Oswald, whom he identified without difficulty. But he commented in testifying before the Commission, "you could have picked him out without identifying him by just listening to him because he was bawling out the policeman, telling them it wasn't right to put him in line with these teenagers and all of that and they asked me which one and I told them. . . ." The Report comments neither on the complaint recorded by Bookhout nor on the fact that Oswald attracted attention to himself by his behavior. But we are told that Whaley's memory is "inaccurate," since there were only three men, not five, with Oswald in the lineup, and only two of them were 18, while the third was 26.

If Whaley did not remember the exact number of men in the lineup, and was wrong about the age of one of them, does this mean that his entire account is unacceptable and that, contrary to his statement, the lineup was carried out without incident?

From the way the Report presents—and criticizes—his testimony, this appears to be the conclusion the Commission would like us to draw. This impression becomes a certainty when we examine the transcript of the Hearings. We perceive then that, not content with treating Whaley's testimony as if there were nothing significant in it, the Warren Report dodges the fact that his story was supported by several other persons, including two Dallas policemen.

Detective Walter E. Potts of the Dallas homicide bureau attended the lineup (or showup as it is sometimes called) on Saturday afternoon. Here is part of his testimony, contained in Volume VII of the Hearings:

> *Mr. Potts.*   Well, he was complaining all during the showup. He had on a T-shirt and the rest of them didn't have on T-shirts, and he was complaining, "Well, everybody's got on a shirt and everything, and I've got a T-shirt on"—he was very belligerent about the showup. He wouldn't cooperate in any way. He was just making all kinds of commotion out there and he was doing more of the talking than anybody.
>
> *Mr. Ball.*   What kind of commotion was he making?
>
> *Mr. Potts.*   Well, he was doing a lot of talking about him being in a T-shirt, and "nobody else has got on a T-shirt and I've got on a T-shirt, this is unfair," and all that. . . .

Detective James R. Leavelle, also of the homicide bureau—it was he who was walking at Oswald's right, handcuffed to him, when Jack Ruby fired his shot—attended two of the three Friday lineups as well as the one on Saturday.

> *Mr. Leavelle.*   In one instance—now, I am not positive which one it was, Oswald was in a T-shirt, having the other shirt removed upstairs where they were going to send it to the FBI laboratory for tests, and the rest of them, I believe, had on shirts. He was the only one that had on a T-shirt and I recall—I am not sure but I think it was the last one where he was raising cain about being up there with a T-shirt and wouldn't be quiet.
>
> *Mr. Ball.*   What did he say?
>
> *Mr. Leavelle.*   He said it wasn't fair, him being showed up in a T-shirt and being photographed in a T-shirt and all that. I don't know what he didn't say; he went on all the time.

What remains then of the nine "eyewitnesses" of the Tippit case who the Commission says "positively identified" Oswald?

We can eliminate at the outset, as having no significance whatsoever, all the "identifications" made two months later, on the basis of photographs, by witnesses whose memories had to be prodded by the Commission, when its job should have been on the contrary to subject them to scrutiny. Nothing remains, either, of the "identifications" made at the Saturday lineup, and this applies especially to William Scoggins, the second "eyewitness" to the actual murder. Concerning the three lineups on Friday, the last cannot possibly be accepted: it took place at 7:40 P.M., when extra editions of the newspapers were already out with pictures of Oswald and when he had already been shown on television; a tape of his appearance in the third-floor corridor had been replayed several times during the afternoon. But it is obvious that even an identification made in the first lineup, at 4:05, could not have any probative value, if only because of the bruises on Oswald's face. It is regrettable that the Warren Commission, which published two pages of Oswald's photo album showing the family in Minsk, did not consider it equally important to publish the pictures of the individuals who were in the lineups with Oswald. The Commission thus lost a chance to show that these lineups really were "conducted fairly."

Volume VII of the Hearings also contains the testimony of several policemen, an employee of the city jail, and a prisoner who were in the lineups with the suspect. Their testimony shows that the procedure was so obviously unfair that it would have been impossible for anyone to overlook Oswald.

We learn, for example, that at each of the lineups, a detective asked each man his name, age, occupation, and address. In principle, this is a routine procedure, although elsewhere more impersonal questions are asked, with the sole purpose of allowing the suspect's voice to be heard. In this case, the routine method ignored the purpose and violated the basic principle of any lineup. None of the "eyewitnesses" had ever heard the voice of the man they were asked to identify, and there was thus no reason to ask him to speak. If the police were really after the truth, there was good reason, on the contrary, not to ask questions during the lineup: The answers might influence the witnesses who were supposed to base their decisions only on the evidence of their *eyes*.

The Commission never established exactly what questions Oswald was asked and what his answers were. But we can get an idea from some of the testimony, such as that of Detective Richard L. Clark of the Dallas vice squad.

With his colleague W. E. Perry, Clark appeared in the first lineup at the request of Captain Fritz. They had removed their neckties, but this laudable precaution was negated by the clothes they were given to wear: a red vest for Clark and "a sports coat hanging there" for Perry. Clark—blond, blue-eyed, about 5 feet 11 inches tall—had never been in a lineup before.

> *Mr. Ball.* Now, back to the first showup, did the detective ask you any questions? Ask your name and address and occupation?
> *Mr. Clark.* Oh, in the showup?
> *Mr. Ball.* In the showup.
> *Mr. Clark.* Yes, sir.
> *Mr. Ball.* What did he ask you?
> *Mr. Clark.* He asked me my name.
> *Mr. Ball.* What did you tell him?
> *Mr. Clark.* I don't remember what I told him.
> *Mr. Ball.* Did you give him your real name?
> *Mr. Clark.* No, sir.
> *Mr. Ball.* Fictitious name?
> *Mr. Clark.* Yes, sir.
> *Mr. Ball.* Ask you your occupation?
> *Mr. Clark.* Asked my occupation.
> *Mr. Ball.* What did you tell him?
> *Mr. Clark.* I don't recall. All of them are fictitious.
> *Mr. Ball.* Fictitious?
> *Mr. Clark.* Yes, sir.

The fourth man in the first lineup, Don R. Ables, a civilian employee in the city jail, disclosed that he had never been in a lineup before, that he had not been told he would be asked questions, and that he improvised his replies. He too had forgotten what he had said. The Commission, however, finds it "fair" that these participants in a lineup, without warning, were compelled to invent answers on the spot when asked their names and occupations, at the risk of revealing to an attentive observer that they were lying.

Oswald himself did not lie. This can be seen, notably, in the deposition of Detective Richard M. Sims, who attended all the lineups on Friday but not on Saturday. He was asked about the first Friday lineup, the only one that could be taken seriously, since it was the only one in which the persons asked to make the identification—I am thinking especially of Ted Callaway—had not seen Oswald before on television or in the papers.

> *Mr. Ball.*   How did Oswald act at this showup; tell me what he did and what he said?
> *Mr. Sims.*   Well, he just acted more or less like the other —acted natural.
> *Mr. Ball.*   Answered the questions?
> *Mr. Sims.*   Yes, sir.
> *Mr. Ball.*   Did he protest any?
> *Mr. Sims.*   No, sir.
> *Mr. Ball.*   Did he say that he had a T-shirt on and no one else had a T-shirt on?
> *Mr. Sims.*   No, sir; now, I think the showup that I didn't conduct the next day, I believe he refused to answer questions or said something about a T-shirt or something.
> *Mr. Ball.*   He didn't say anything of that sort [*on Friday* —L.S.]?
> *Mr. Sims.*   No, sir; he acted normal, with the other showups I was in.
> *Mr. Ball.*   He answered the questions?
> *Mr. Sims.*   Yes, sir; he did.

We can easily see what the Commission chose not to notice. According to its Report, this first lineup took place at 4:05, more than two hours after the arrest. By this time, except for infants and patients under anaesthesia, the entire population of Dallas knew that the assassin had fired from a window of the Depository Building and that the suspect was an employee there. Many must have already been familiar with his name, repeated incessantly on every wave length, in homes and offices, on car radios, and on transistors in the streets. In short, if Oswald told the truth—while the others improvised their answers, more or less skillfully—he identified himself as clearly as he did the day after, when he "raised cain."

Did the detective who conducted the showup ask Oswald his name and where he worked? Here is James Leavelle's testimony on this point:

> *Mr. Ball.*   Who conducted the showup questioning?
> *Mr. Leavelle.*   I probably asked the questions, yes.
> *Mr. Ball.*   What questions?
> *Mr. Leavelle.*   Normally, I would not have asked names in this case because for fear of her [*Helen Markham, the guest of honor at this first lineup*—L.S.] remembering the name, so, or might have heard the name, so, probably asked how old they were, what occupation, anything so they could speak and let me hear the sound of their voice.
> *Mr. Ball.*   Did any of them say they were police officers?
> *Mr. Leavelle.*   No, no; the officers gave some other occupation.

Leavelle apparently recalled nothing precisely, and merely reconstructed what he "normally" must have done. Assistant Counsel Ball carefully refrained from going into the question any further. Two days later, Clark and Perry, the two detectives who had been in the lineup, testified that Leavelle had indeed asked their names. But Ball did not call Leavelle back to confront him with Perry and Clark. He learned on the same day, in questioning Daniel Gutiérrez Luján, that the questions by Leavelle at the Saturday lineup did include the place of work.

Gutiérrez was the fourth man in the Saturday lineup, the man who allowed the Warren Report to "prove" triumphantly how in-

accurate Bill Whaley had been because he was 26 and not a teen-
ager like the others.

Gutiérrez had spent three years in jail for possession of narcotics. He had been arrested again on November 21 on a similar
charge. On Saturday, he told Ball, a policeman went up to the
jail (above police headquarters) and "told me to stand up and I
stand up and he looked at me and said, 'Come out.'" Gutiérrez,
thus deliberately chosen from among the others available, was so
unlike Oswald physically that it is worth going into detail here if
only to show how Ball tried to minimize the differences and uphold the theory of the "fairness" of the lineups.

> *Mr. Ball.*   What is your size? What is your weight?
> *Mr. Luján.*   Weigh about 170.
> *Mr. Ball.*   What is your height?
> *Mr. Luján.*   About 5'8".
> *Mr. Ball.*   And your hair is dark?
> *Mr. Luján.*   Black.
> *Mr. Ball.*   It is black hair. And your eyes?
> *Mr. Luján.*   Brown.
> *Mr. Ball.*   And brown, and your complexion?
> *Mr. Luján.*   Olive.
> *Mr. Ball.*   Are you of Mexican descent?
> *Mr. Luján.*   Yes, sir.
> *Mr. Ball.*   You are very fair in color for a Mexican.
> *Mr. Luján.*   Yes.
> *Mr. Ball.*   You have fair skin, haven't you?
> *Mr. Luján.*   Yes.

But I wanted to get to the nature of the questions asked in the
lineup, the rule being that the same questions are put to each of
the men.

> *Mr. Ball.*   Did the detective ask your name?
> *Mr. Luján.*   Yes, sir.
> *Mr. Ball.*   And did you tell him your name?
> *Mr. Luján.*   Yes, sir.
> *Mr. Ball.*   Did he ask your occupation?

> *Mr. Luján.*   Yes, sir.
> *Mr. Ball.*   What did you tell him?
> *Mr. Luján.*   Working for S. & F. Meat Co.

Thus the Warren Commission has been told that Lee Oswald, already marked by the bruises and the sneer on his face, was probably led moreover to give his name and to say that he worked at the Texas School Book Depository. But it still maintains the lineups were fair—quite logically, in fact, since it also accepts identifications made by witnesses who had seen Oswald before on television, even identifications based on examination of photos two months later. I beg to disagree. And I respectfully suggest to the learned lawyers of the Warren Commission that they read a book by Patrick M. Wall, written as a doctoral thesis for the New York University School of Law. Entitled *Eyewitness Identification in Criminal Cases*, and drawing upon the highest legal authorities, it lists some of the "improper procedures" that make lineups—and other methods of eyewitness identification— "grossly suggestive" or even, according to a description quoted from a British report of 1925, "little more than a farce." Every one of these "improper procedures" was used against Oswald.

One last remark about the Commission's "eyewitnesses." While on page 176 of the Report the quoted passage limits them modestly to nine, a reproduction of Commission Exhibit No. 1968 on page 164 (see Illustrations) seems to indicate there were more. Exhibit No. 1968 is a photograph purporting to show the "location of eyewitnesses to the movements of Lee Harvey Oswald in the vicinity of the Tippit killing." Printed on the photograph are their names—13 of them. Thus there are four "eyewitnesses" more in the photo than in the text. Where did they come from?

According to the statement of one of the additional four, Mrs. Mary Brock, she saw neither the shooting nor the revolver in the hand, but simply "a white male" going by "at a fast pace with his hands in his pockets." Assuming this "white male" had something to do with the case, was he Oswald? "When interviewed by FBI agents on January 21, 1964, she identified a picture of Oswald as being the same person she saw on November 22." Another of the four extra "eyewitnesses" presented in Exhibit No. 1968 is

Domingo Benavides, whom we have met. The third one, William Arthur Smith, "told a Commission staff member that he saw Oswald on television the night of the murder and thought that Oswald was the man he had seen running away from the shooting." He had not said so before because "on television Oswald's hair looked blond," but when the FBI later showed him a picture, he said "it looked more like him [Oswald] than it did on television." Finally there is L. J. Lewis. Here is what the Report itself tells us about him: "L. J. Lewis said in an interview that because of the distance from which he observed the gunman he would hesitate to state whether the man was identical with Oswald."

Aside from the "eyewitnesses," the Commission invokes three other arguments to bolster its Finding Number 4.

Two have to do with the revolver. As in the case of the Mannlicher-Carcano, the fact that the Commission is able to prove that Oswald had bought a Smith and Wesson .38 by mail from a Los Angeles firm does not mean that he used it to kill. And here the Report cannot call upon ballistic identification, as it did in the case of the rifle. For the bullets taken from Tippit's body had inconsistent characteristics, which "made identification impossible," according to the Report.

The last argument consists in the fact that: "Shortly after Tippit was slain, policemen found a light-colored zipper jacket along the route taken by the killer as he attempted to escape."

In its relatively objective editorial of September 28, 1964, the *New York Times* already had found this jacket of "little value as evidence since so many witnesses gave conflicting testimony as to its color." The Report itself seems to hesitate in mentioning it because, speaking of the jacket's discovery and its identification before the Commission by Captain W. R. Westbrook, it systematically keeps to the "light-colored" description. It is only in the "Speculations and Rumors" section that we find it described as "light-gray."

Marina Oswald, naturally, identified the jacket found by Captain Westbrook as her husband's, but since she also "identified" the rifle and the revolver, her identifications mean nothing. Earlene Roberts, the housekeeper at 1026 North Beckley Avenue, who had seen Oswald when he went there to get it, said that "it seemed to her that the jacket Oswald wore was darker" than the one found. Cab driver Scoggins thought the man he had seen wore a "lighter" jacket than the one he was shown, and Ted Callaway recalled that it "had a little more tan to it."

The description broadcast on the police radio at 1:22 on the man wanted for the murder of Tippit mentioned, the Report declares, that he wore "a white jacket, white shirt and dark slacks."

Patrolman J. M. Poe, identified (without any trouble in this instance) as the man who broadcast the 1:22 description, testified that the information had been supplied to him by Mrs. Markham and Barbara Davis. Now even though the Report carefully refrains from pointing it out, two elements in the description contradict both what we already know on the subject of Oswald and what the Commission confirms. Not only the "white" jacket is at issue, but also the "white" shirt: Oswald was wearing a brown sport shirt, impossible to mistake for a white one.

The story of Oswald's shirt, imprudently brought up by the Commission, has another strange twist.

Patrolman Poe testified that the description of Tippit's assassin given by Mrs. Markham specified that he wore a "white jacket." This is indicated on page 175 of the Report. On page 176, after noting that the "eyewitnesses vary in their identification of the jacket," the Report states: "Mrs. Markham and Barbara Davis thought that the jacket worn by the slayer of Tippit was darker than the jacket found by Westbrook." How does it happen that a "white jacket" could have been darker than "a light-colored jacket"?

To conclude our discussion of Finding Number 4: Even if the Commission had convinced us that Oswald shot Tippit, it would still have to prove that the murderer of the policeman was necessarily the assassin of the President. The Commission's argument is that Oswald killed Tippit "in an apparent attempt to escape." Yet no one—the Commission no more than I—knows why Tippit, alone in his patrol car, "pulled up alongside a man walking in the same direction." The Commission states that "it is conceivable, even probable, that Tippit stopped Oswald because of the description broadcast by the police radio." This statement is ridiculous. The description broadcast by the police, as we have seen, did not mention clothing, shoes, manner, or any other distinctive trait enabling identification of a man approached from behind in a car. And this occurred several miles from the scene of the crime, in a neighborhood where Tippit (unless he was informed about Oswald, a hypothesis the Commission avoids like the plague) had no reason to seek the suspect.

In short, the Commission cannot contend that Oswald was seeking to "escape," because it cannot show that Tippit was trying to arrest him.

5. LEE HARVEY OSWALD RESISTED ARREST BY DRAWING A FULLY LOADED PISTOL AND ATTEMPTING TO SHOOT ANOTHER POLICE OFFICER.

In Chapter 6, I described "The Mystery of the Texas Theater" and the assorted contradictions in the statements of Patrolman M. N. McDonald. In the editorial mentioned in that chapter, the *New York Times* didn't seem very satisfied either:

> The second sequence of events, involving the murder of Patrolman J. D. Tippit and Oswald's capture in a movie theater, is reasonably certain, but not every detail is as strongly supported by evidence as are the circumstances of President Kennedy's death. . . . It is also curious that, since there were six or seven people on the theater's main floor and an equal number in the balcony, only two came forward to testify to the commission. . . .

The *Times,* true enough, dutifully adds that these are only "weaknesses" and "small gaps in the evidence" that in its view "do not materially alter the outline of the facts as reconstructed in the report." But from the moment the *Times* admits that McDonald's testimony ought to have been confirmed by the theater patrons, it can only conclude that the testimony of McDonald alone does not suffice. If the newspaper does not consider the circumstances of the arrest of major importance, the Warren

Commission did: It made them the basis of one of the eight counts of its verdict.

In the form the Commission gives to its Finding Number 5, it runs up against some facts established by the Report itself.

For nothing in the Report backs up the statement that Oswald "resisted arrest by drawing a fully loaded pistol and attempting to shoot another police officer": He struck McDonald "between the eyes with his left fist"; only then, according to McDonald, did he draw a gun from his waist. If Oswald had wanted to resist arrest by slaying a policeman about to apprehend him, he would have had the pistol in his hand long before this and he would have shot the moment the policeman turned toward him from the aisle.

Finding Number 5 thus contradicts the Commission's own evidence. But, in any case, it would not constitute proof of guilt in the assassination of the President.

It may be customary to take resistance to arrest into account as circumstantial evidence against a suspect. But it is also admitted that such resistance, especially when it reveals neither premeditation nor method, but rather an irrational and clumsy reaction of anger, may constitute an indication of innocence. Compared to the methodical assassin of Elm Street, and the cold-blooded killer of Tenth Street, the man in the Texas Theater seemed remarkably slow on the trigger. Perhaps it proves nothing either way. There is certainly no foundation for transforming Oswald's childish behavior at the theater into a proof that he killed President Kennedy.

6. LEE HARVEY OSWALD LIED TO THE POLICE AFTER HIS ARREST CONCERNING IMPORTANT SUBSTANTIVE MATTERS.

Finding Number 6 proves even less, and may be dismissed with a minimum of respect for its sponsors not only because it is illogical and irrelevant but also because it has been formally retracted by the Commission itself.

When the Report refers to Oswald's "lies," it means the statements of the accused which, since they were not recorded on

tape or by a stenographer, are known to us only through the recollections of various policemen who questioned Oswald. While the
Commission apparently saw nothing reprehensible in that fact
(and was not shocked to learn that the man suspected of having
killed the President had been questioned for a total of 12 hours
in the absence of a lawyer), it is neither a fair nor a regular procedure to hold a defendant accountable for remarks attributed to
him by his interrogators when it is impossible to know their
context and still less their exact terms. It does not speak for the
sincerity or seriousness of a "factfinding agency" when the skimpy,
belated, and unsubstantiated reminiscences of the interrogators
are accepted as full and incontrovertible evidence.

Justifying its Finding Number 6, the Report states that Oswald's "untrue statements" during interrogation had "probative
value in deciding the weight to be given to his denial that he
assassinated President Kennedy and killed Patrolman Tippit."
It explains: "Since independent evidence revealed that Oswald
repeatedly and blatantly lied to the police, the Commission gave
little weight to his denials of guilt."

I don't know where the Commission found the "independent"
evidence of Oswald's lies; the only "evidence" available in the
Report is the testimony of the various *nonindependent* police
interrogators. But the Commission, at least, admits its argument
about Oswald's "lies" is meant only to justify its refusal to heed
his "denials of guilt." Assuming those denials could actually be
neutralized in this way, the Commission might ignore them; but
it cannot go beyond that to transform a stalemate into a victory
by slyly and surreptitiously turning the inconclusiveness of Oswald's denials into positive evidence of guilt.

In any case, Oswald's "lies" can be used as evidence against
him only in the context of that "consciousness of guilt" once invoked in a trial that Chief Justice Warren surely would not
choose as a model.

It was Judge Webster Thayer who saw this kind of reasoning
as sufficient ground to send Nicola Sacco and Bartolomeo Vanzetti
to the electric chair. Felix Frankfurter, then a Harvard Law
School professor, asked at the time what basis Thayer had for

affirming that the "consciousness of guilt" shown by the lies of Sacco and Vanzetti was "consciousness of murder rather than of radicalism." Would not Justice Frankfurter, if he were alive, direct the same question today to Chief Justice Warren on the subject of Oswald?

In addition, it cannot be presumed that Oswald believed he was obliged to tell the truth to hostile police whom he scorned and blamed for not providing him with a lawyer; as the Report says, he was "overbearing and arrogant throughout much of the time between his arrest and his own death."

Thus, Proof Number 6 in the end proves nothing. Indeed, it is rather astonishing that the Commission dared to include Oswald's "lies" as one of its eight officially proclaimed proofs on page 195 of the Report, for on page 180 it declares: "Oswald's untrue statements during interrogation were not considered items of positive proof by the Commission."

7. LEE HARVEY OSWALD ATTEMPTED, IN APRIL 1963, TO KILL MAJ. GEN. EDWIN A. WALKER.

The lack of evidence for this charge, and indeed the absence of any plausibility in it, were discussed in Chapter 10. And assuming that Oswald had fired (so inaccurately) at General Walker, how would that constitute evidence that he shot President Kennedy?

The idea, apparently, is that the attempt on Walker demonstrated Oswald's "disposition to take human life" and "his capacity for violence." This is summed up in Chapter VII of the Report, where "possible motives" of Oswald are discussed in a striking sentence that is in itself sufficient to destroy Proof Number 7: "The Commission has concluded that on April 10, 1963, Oswald shot at Maj. Gen. Edwin A. Walker (Resigned, U.S. Army), demonstrating once again his propensity to act dramatically and, in this instance, violently, in furtherance of his beliefs."

In furtherance of which beliefs is Oswald supposed to have slain Kennedy? The Report gives us the following details:

> . . . Oswald did not lack the determination and other traits required to carry out a carefully planned killing of

another human being and was willing to consummate such a purpose if he thought there was sufficient reason to do so. Some idea of what he thought was sufficient reason for such an act may be found in the nature of the motive that he stated for his attack on General Walker. Marina Oswald indicated that her husband had compared General Walker to Adolph Hitler. She testified that Oswald said that General Walker "was a very bad man, that he was a fascist, that he was the leader of a fascist organization, and when I said that even though all of that might be true, just the same he had no right to take his life, he said if someone had killed Hitler in time it would have saved many lives."

Unlike Earl Warren, I am not inclined to accept Marina Oswald's word as sacred, but I am ready to admit that Oswald was against fascists and that he might have been led to undertake some action against a Walker. Would the same reasoning have led him to kill a Kennedy?

It is surely rare to see a conclusion so totally demolished by those who propose it. This, however, is what the Commission achieves when it tries to convince us that Lee Oswald killed President Kennedy *because* he tried to kill General Walker. Did Oswald see John F. Kennedy as another Adolph Hitler, or as another Edwin Walker? We read in the same section of the Report that "shortly before the assassination Oswald had expressed approval of President Kennedy's active role in the area of civil rights." (A witness named Frank Krystinik, who talked politics with Oswald one night, said he had "admitted that the United States was superior to the Soviet Union in the area of civil liberties and praised President Kennedy for his work in that connection.") But the conclusion of the chapter, nonetheless, is that Oswald "demonstrated a capacity to act decisively and without regard to the consequences when such action would further his aims of the moment," and that he was therefore "a man capable of assassinating President Kennedy."

Since one searches in vain, from start to finish of the Warren Report, for a single word on the "aims of the moment" Oswald

believed he would serve by killing Kennedy, the Commission—
to the extent that it brings up the attempt on Walker—seems
to prove, if anything, that Oswald could not have been the assassin
of President Kennedy.

8. LEE HARVEY OSWALD POSSESSED THE CAPABILITY WITH A RIFLE
WHICH WOULD HAVE ENABLED HIM TO COMMIT THE ASSASSINATION.

The falsity of this statement has been established once and for
all by the Warren Commission itself in seven pages (189 to 195)
of its Report. I have analyzed them, as well as other data, in
Chapter 3. I still cannot help marveling at the amazing sleight
of hand the authors of the Report dared to perform to give the
impression that Oswald could easily have done better than three
masters of the National Rifle Association.

The Hearings, furnishing details that do not appear in the Report, help unmask what was already clearly visible to anyone who
did not feel it his patriotic duty not to see it.

There are, for instance, the flagrant contradictions concerning
the condition and quality of the weapon. Ronald Simmons testified that the Mannlicher-Carcano found on the sixth floor was
"quite accurate," and gave an affirmative reply when asked
whether the rifle was "as accurate as the current American military
rifles." Marine Master Sergeant James A. Zahm repeated twice
that the shots from the Depository were "easy," and he added each
time that he took into account not only Oswald's experience but
also the quality of his weapon. And Marine Major Eugene D.
Anderson suggested the same in assuring the Commission that the
shots were not "particularly difficult."

Anderson, however, explained the drop in Oswald's Marine
target scores (from 212 to 191) by commenting that, between 1956
and 1959, his rifle had probably been "banged around in normal
usage." Had nothing of the kind happened to the second-hand
Mannlicher-Carcano? Sebastian Latona of the FBI, who was
called on not to discuss Oswald's skills but to explain why there
were no prints on the rifle, gave an opinion somewhat different
from the others presented above.

> *Representative Boggs.*   A weapon of this type, in your
> examination do you find a lot of other prints on it as
> well? You do not?
> *Mr. Latona.*   No. First of all the weapon itself is a cheap
> one as you can see. It is one that——
> *Representative Boggs.*   Is what?
> *Mr. Latona.*   A cheap old weapon. The wood is to the
> point where it won't take a good print to begin with
> hardly. The metal isn't of the best, and not readily sus-
> ceptible to a latent print.

Granting that Latona is only an expert on fingerprints, perhaps
we should not attach too much importance to his description of
the Mannlicher-Carcano rifle as "a cheap old weapon" when the
superexpert Ronald Simmons found it as accurate as the current
American military rifles. But Robert A. Frazier, FBI firearms
expert who testified at the same session and who was the fourth
specialist called in by the Commission on the question of Oswald's
abilities as a rifleman, was even more explicit than Latona about
the rifle. He was questioned by Melvin Aron Eisenberg, assistant
counsel:

> *Mr. Eisenberg.*   Does this weapon show—how much use
> does this weapon show?
> *Mr. Frazier.*   The stock is worn, scratched. The bolt is
> relatively smooth, as if it had been operated several times.
> I cannot actually say how much use the weapon has had.
> The barrel is—was not, when we first got it, in excellent
> condition. It was, I would say, in fair condition. In
> other words, it showed the effects of wear and corrosion.
> *Mr. Eisenberg.*   Is this weapon——
> *The Chairman.*   I didn't get that last.
> *Mr. Frazier.*   It showed the effects of wear and corrosion.

After a brief digression concerning the dimensions of the rifle,
John J. McCloy—who had already shown his familiarity with firearms in other interrogations—asked for details.

> *Mr. McCloy.*   When you examined the rifle the first time,

you said that it showed signs of some corrosion and wear?

Mr. Frazier.   Yes, sir.

Mr. McCloy.   Was it what you would call pitted, were the lands in good shape?

Mr. Frazier.   No, sir; the lands and the grooves were worn, the corners were worn, and the interior of the surface was roughened from corrosion and wear.

None of the Commission members or staff thought of taking advantage of the fact that both Frazier and Simmons were in the room and might have conferred to let the Commission know whether the rifle was or was not in good condition. Having failed to ask them to do so, the Commission should have abstained from speaking of Oswald's rifle as a perfect weapon, omitting the fact that one of its chief experts had spoken of it as virtually a piece of junk.

At least as far as the weapon is concerned, the aces of the National Rifle Association were on an equal basis with the gunman of Elm Street, since they used the same rifle. But the testimony of Simmons unwittingly reveals that the champions' task was arbitrarily made easier through the conditions of the tests.

Noting that none of the three masters had missed the first target, Simmons said "this was to be expected, because they had as much time as they desired to aim at the first target." But the gunman in the Depository did not have all the time he might have desired for his first shot. The way he had arranged his position by the window, as described by the Commission, he had to wait for the Presidential car to turn the corner from Houston Street and begin moving along Elm Street, and then act quickly. Contrary to the Commission's riflemen, then, Oswald would have had hardly any more time for his first shot than for the others.

Simmons' testimony also provides some valuable information, not given in the Report, on the significance of the title "master" accorded by the National Rifle Association. This title, Simmons explained, is conferred only on "highly qualified riflemen" who have "participated in national match competitions." All three riflemen who took part in the Commission tests, Simmons said, were masters. Two were civilian gunners in the Army Small Arms Division and the third was a military specialist with "considerable background as a rifleman."

It is clear that even if these three authentic champions had succeeded in firing as well as or better than the Elm Street gunman, this would have proved nothing. What might be relatively easy for such specialists, practicing every day, would remain in all likelihood beyond the talents of an amateur with little training in the previous four years and no practice at all for the last two months, as the Commission states. Although the Warren Commission pretends not to be aware of it, the results of the tests showed that the specialists did not do as well as the amateur. Was it then a question of sheer luck? This seems to be the only theory one can decently uphold after the Commission tests—if one absolutely wants to consider Oswald guilty. But the Commission prefers to hide behind the "opinions" of its four personal experts and maintain that Oswald's feat was child's play, even though the tests proved the opposite.

Trying perhaps to compensate for his unfavorable opinion of the rifle, this is exactly what Robert Frazier implied.

Representative Hale Boggs of Louisiana asked Frazier if in his opinion only an "expert marksman" could have squeezed off the shots that came from the Depository Building. After energetically answering no, Frazier explained that all the work in fact was done by the telescopic sight: "I mean it requires no training at all to shoot a weapon with a telescopic sight once you know that you must put the crosshairs on the target and that is all that is necessary."

I am a poor marksman, but with this lesson from Mr. Frazier on what to do with the crosshairs, I can hardly wait to enter into competition against the masters of the National Rifle Association.

I would feel reassured, however, before signing up for a match, if Frazier were to explain why four of the six shots fired by the three masters missed the second target, even though these aces were using a telescopic sight. Didn't they know "you must put the crosshairs on the target"?

After careful study of the Warren Report and an attentive review of the eight findings it advances as evidence of Oswald's guilt, I arrived at the following conclusions:

(1) Oswald owned an Italian Mannlicher-Carcano 6.5-caliber carbine, but it is not certain that he had the cartridges needed to make it a murder weapon. It is also not certain that the assassination was in fact committed with this weapon, inasmuch as we cannot be sure that the bullets that killed President Kennedy and wounded Governor Connally were the ones recovered and identified.

(2) It is not likely that Oswald could have carried his dismantled rifle to the Depository Building on the morning of the assassination in the package described by witnesses, and it is completely implausible that he could have assembled it with the requisite care in time for the shooting.

(3) There is no basis whatsoever for the statement that Oswald was at the window from which the shots were fired. The alleged identification by an "eyewitness" is grotesque and the alleged indirect proofs are without probative value.

(4) The "eyewitness" identifications of Oswald as the murderer of Tippit are without probative value, and there is no basis for the affirmation that the killer of Tippit, whoever he may have been, was necessarily the killer of President Kennedy.

(5) The exact circumstances of Oswald's arrest in the Texas Theater are not known, but it is established that his resistance to arrest consisted of a blow with his fist. Furthermore, the fact that he struggled with police in the theater in no way proves that Oswald was the assassin of President Kennedy.

(6) The fact that Oswald lied to the police is without significance, except insofar as any reference to his interrogation can only call attention to the illegal conditions under which the questioning was conducted.

(7) There is no genuine proof to support the affirmation that Oswald tried to kill Walker. And if he were in fact the author of that attempt, this would be an additional reason for not considering him the assassin of President Kennedy, for such an act would

prove he needed a reason to kill, and he had none in the case of the President.

(8) Confirming the deductions suggested by his mediocre Marine record and his lack of opportunity to practice with the weapon, the Warren Commission definitively proved through the tests it carried out that Lee Harvey Oswald did not have the skill required to commit the assassination.

In view of these findings—and recalling the lack of any real effort to capture the assassin immediately after the shooting, or to find and preserve evidence, or to find and follow all possible paths of inquiry—I conclude that it is logically untenable, legally indefensible, and morally inadmissible to declare Lee Harvey Oswald the assassin of President Kennedy.

New York-Paris, January 1965

AMERICAN POSTSCRIPT

This book originally was to have been published first in the United States; on March 11, 1964, even before I got in touch with Les Editions de Minuit in Paris for the French edition, the contract for the American edition had been signed with a large New York publisher. But then came the publication of the Warren Report on September 27, 1964, and the enthusiasm of my New York publisher ebbed perceptibly.

By that time, I had not only finished writing the story of the Dallas investigation, but also had described the FBI leaks and the disturbing circumstances under which the Warren Commission had started its work: more leaks; more reckless statements, including some by the Chairman of the Commission, who thought it proper to make public his personal opinion about testimony still unpublished; the very choice of the first witnesses to be heard and the indecent stardom conferred on Marina Oswald; finally, and above all, the fact that the Commission deliberately turned away from an honest search for the truth when it decided to prohibit cross-examination. In short, I had already expressed a number of misgivings about the Warren Commission, and after reading its Report, I found that things were even worse than I had imagined.

What really appeared unacceptable to my New York publisher was my conclusion that since the Commission did not establish Oswald's guilt beyond a reasonable doubt, Oswald was to be considered innocent.

399

"The problem," I was told in a letter dated November 4, 1964, "is that the Warren Report has put the Oswald matter in a different light from what I had expected, and I'm now convinced that any book which attempts to question Oswald's guilt would be out of touch with reality and could not be taken seriously by responsible critics. This is by no means to say that the Warren Report is not without flaws—its treatment of the evidence, its indifference to many of the ambiguities which are evident in its pages, and its tendentiousness are clear. But for all this and for all the confusion earlier in Dallas, it is inconceivable that Oswald might yet be proven innocent. . . ."

As is already obvious, the author of this letter does not belong among the smug, sanctimonious and—most of all—ignorant troubadors of the Warren Report. He expressed the hope that I would give him "the credit to believe that I am not speaking here out of patriotic motives or in order to abet a conspiracy of silence." I do give him that credit. But . . .

"I am certain," his suggestion was, "that on the basis of your present research, you could, as I've often told you, prepare a most interesting and useful book which would take the question of Oswald's guilt as pretty well established, but which would then seriously question the great flaws in American criminal procedure which the Oswald affair has illuminated, all the way from the Dallas police station to the Supreme Court. No one could have been dealt with less fairly than Oswald was, and had he remained alive one would have hoped for his acquittal in the higher Courts on constitutional grounds. That the Warren Report doesn't make this plain is I think a very bad mark against it, and if you would agree to revise your material so as to focus on this aspect of the case, I'm certain that we could in time produce a book which would be of great interest in itself and great use to the country."

I did not agree, but I could see the point; I bear no grudge against the author of the letter who, at the publisher's direction, "reluctantly" released me from the contract. My own point is simply that no matter how useful a different approach might be to the cause of reform of American criminal procedure, I cannot consider the guilt of any man—even such a wretched and unpleasant character as Oswald seems to have been—as "pretty well established" when I feel it is not established at all.

Like the writer quoted above, a few American journalists— very few—have dared to criticize the Warren Commission's methods, sometimes in terms that seem to exclude the possibility of attaching any faith to its conclusions. But after recognizing its obvious partiality, after citing crushing examples of its omissions and distortions, they nevertheless support the affirmation to which those manipulations were meant to lead: that "Lee Harvey Oswald was the assassin of President Kennedy."

In "A Critique of the Warren Report," published in *Esquire*, Dwight Macdonald set out to demonstrate that it is possible to believe in Oswald's guilt *in spite of* the Commission. "Perhaps I can rescue the Warren Report from its authors," he wrote after stating flatly: "Partisanship does infect the Report, however, and it won't do to pretend otherwise. In two ways. *The Prosecutor's Brief:* accepting or rejecting testimony according to how it fits into what the Commissioners want to prove. And *The Establishment Syndrome:* the reflexive instinct of people in office to trust other officials more than outsiders, and to gloss over their mistakes." The author of *Against the American Grain* did not deny that the "tone" of the Report was that of "the advocate, smoothing away or sidestepping objections to his 'case,' rather than the impartial judge or the researcher welcoming all data with detached curiosity." But he believed that if the Report "obscures the strong points of its case," it remains that "many are very strong."

Macdonald thus joined Murray Kempton, who, in *The New Republic* of October 10, 1964, denounced the Warren Report as a "case for the prosecution," yet concluded that the Prosecution's "immense" statement was also "almost indisputable." According to Kempton, the Report "drastically narrowed the area of doubt," and "what doubts remain turn out to be less about Oswald's guilt than about the method of his judges." Kempton was aware that the Report sought to "elevate the implausible to the probable," and he added, "that is the kind of thing we expect, not from judges but from prosecutors of the better sort." But if he regretted the absence of defense counsel ("it is to test such cases that we have an adversary system of criminal justice"), he did not believe that the validity of the evidence was thereby weakened. This was undoubtedly because, while reproaching the Commission for having played the role of prosecutor, he was convinced that it was a prosecutor "of the better sort," or again, as he writes a few lines further on, "a highly responsible prosecutor." The sad truth is that the Warren Commission employed methods rarely used by even a moderately responsible prosecutor.

In the May 1965 issue of the New York University *Law Review,* which contains a 120-page "Symposium on the Warren Commission Report," Paul L. Freese, of the California bar, studies the treatment of some witnesses whose depositions did not fit "a conclusion previously made."

Freese takes, for example, the case of Arnold Louis Rowland, who watched the motorcade with his wife from Houston Street, between Elm and Main, and thought he had seen a man with a rifle at the *southwest* corner window of the sixth floor, while the *southeast* window, "the one they say the shots were fired from," was occupied by a Negro "hanging out that window at that time." Was the Negro Bonnie Ray Williams, watching the street while eating his chicken? I don't know; Rowland said "it seemed to me an elderly Negro," and I have not used his testimony in examining the mystery of the chicken bones. The point here, anyhow, is the way the Commission got rid of such an unwelcome witness—whose testimony, as Freese viewed it, suggested "the existence of an accomplice" and the possibility that "if true, a valuable link in tracing a broader conspiracy had been overlooked."

The Commission, Freese notes, "rejected the suggestion by impeaching the witness." It claimed, for instance, that the presence of the second man was not mentioned in Rowland's interviews with the FBI in Dallas, and thus implied that he invented it for his appearance in Washington. Rowland's answer was that he had indeed told the FBI: "They just didn't seem interested at all. They didn't pursue the point. They didn't take it down in the notation as such."

Freese's comment is that such an attitude on the part of the

FBI would conform "to an observable 'bias' which attorneys and investigators develop in pursuing a question, well defined in their own minds." And he remarks that "before rejecting the credibility of Rowland, one might expect that the Commission would summon the agents with their notes to determine their recollection or basic records concerning the many interviews." Well, the Commission did not. And when it heard Mrs. Rowland, Freese adds, it "betrayed a desire to discredit her husband rather than confront the implications of his testimony."

Freese's concern seems to be that the Commission's "investigative approach" was "incomplete" and that "the resort to impeachment of character smacks of a prosecutor's approach rather than that of one committed to the ascertainment of the truth." But like Dwight Macdonald and Murray Kempton, and though he does not eliminate the possibility that Oswald might not have acted alone, Freese believes that the Commission ascertained the truth in spite of its wrong approach:

> As the arbiter of its own procedures, and without any responsible agency or party critically examining its investigative hypotheses or its method of handling witnesses, the Commission was by design made susceptible to error through following any bias existing or developed by its own investigation. And, in the investigation of possible accomplices at the scene, there is evidence that it was victim of its own bias. It was a victim not in the sense that it failed to find the truth, but in the sense that it blinded itself from making the complete effort and assessment it otherwise attempted on all significant questions.

The fact is, however, that lawyer Freese, who recognizes that the Warren Commission was "vulnerable to the 'Dreyfus case' suspicion," admits a few pages later that the Commission's bias was its very *raison d'être:*

> Any number of tribunals might have amassed a record to satisfy the objective student of Oswald's guilt, and probably a congressional or Texas legislative committee could

have satisfied itself and some of the public that there was no complicity. The real task of the Warren Commission, however, was not to *find* the truth but to *appear to have found the truth* to the satisfaction of the largest possible number of people here and abroad. Despite the eminence of its members, the talents of its staff, and the prodigious factual development of its efforts, it could not escape the necessity of having been created for this assignment. . . . (Italics Freese's.)

A similarly open admission, coupled with some even more suggestive statements, appears in one of the other contributions to the same Symposium.

The author, Robert F. Cushman, associate professor of government at New York University, has no complaints as far as the working methods of the Commission are concerned. As a matter of fact, he thinks the methods were so efficient that "it seems hard to avoid the conclusion that such an agency was more apt to arrive at the truth than any other possible investigative agency," including "the twelve men of a trial jury" or "the grand jury which the Commission, in a sense, was designed to supplant." And he therefore expresses the opinion that "the very excellence of this kind of agency poses a threat to our traditional adversary system of justice."

But Professor Cushman, at least, does not indulge in the hypocritical excuses made by the Commission apologists and by the Commission itself. He declares bluntly that "while nominally an executive agency, in the mind of the public the Commission was a kind of court, designed to determine, once and for all, who killed President Kennedy." And he asks some refreshingly candid questions: "Suppose Mrs. [Marguerite] Oswald, for instance, suspecting that the Commission was going to issue a report naming her son as the President's assassin, sued to enjoin the publication of the report. Or, suppose that after the Commission had made its report she sued for damages, arguing that since he had not been found guilty in a court of law, and since they were not performing a legitimate governmental function, it was libel to pronounce him

a murderer. . . ." Even more easily, and I wonder why she didn't,
Mrs. Marguerite Oswald could have filed libel suits against any
of the major newspapers, magazines, wire services, or television
networks that called her son "the President's assassin" without
adding the precautionary adjective "alleged," compulsory in the
U.S. in the absence of a court decision. And if Mrs. Oswald's law-
suit had wound up before the Supreme Court, what would Chief
Justice Earl Warren have said or done?

The most important point in Professor Cushman's analysis is
the conclusion that the Warren Commission simply could not
afford to reach any other verdict than Oswald's solitary guilt, because any other verdict would have put the Commission in a
dreadful situation:

> Suppose, for example, the Commission had turned up
> evidence that someone else—some unanticipated subject—
> might have killed President Kennedy. Or, what is prac-
> tically the same, suppose it turned up one or more accom-
> plices to the killing. What does it do? Does it back grace-
> fully out of its role as chief investigator, letting the normal
> law enforcement agencies take over? Does it turn its in-
> formation over to the Dallas police? If so, it ceases to serve
> the function of satisfying public curiosity. If not, what of
> the rights of this new suspect? He could be granted im-
> munity and forced to testify, but it is unlikely that that
> would serve the public interest. Could they investigate
> him as they did Oswald? His past? His relationships? His
> private papers? Could they announce that he was guilty of
> killing the President? That he was not guilty? That he
> was insane? . . .

In short, Professor Cushman states, "the Commission, apparently without realizing it, was in the anomalous position of having
its very existence depend upon a particular answer to those questions which it was set up to investigate—namely, that Lee Harvey
Oswald, acting alone, assassinated President Kennedy." He then
pushes aside the various compliments paid to the Commission, by
himself as well as by others, to sound this clear warning: "Surely

the injection into our system of justice of an agency based on such a preconception poses a threat to impartial justice worthy of the most careful consideration."

Though I am impressed by Professor Cushman's conclusion, I do have some trouble following him through his premises. If I understand him correctly, he thinks that the Commission's "anomalous position" is dangerous in principle, but that no harm was done in fact this time because, happily, Oswald was guilty anyhow. How does Cushman know this? Because the Commission says so? But Cushman himself admits that the Commission, whether it realized it or not, was in no position to say otherwise. Then what good is its word? One purpose of this Postscript is to ask those Americans not blinded by adoration, jurists like Freese or Cushman, journalists like Macdonald or Kempton, to explain how they manage to reconcile their devastating criticism with their final approbation.

It is useless to debate with Louis Nizer, who simply turns everything upside down and then hides behind a display of virtuous indignation against those who do not repeat after him that black is white and white is black. Nizer pontificates:

> The word prejudice derives from the Latin *prejudicare* —to judge before one has the facts. Those who have so judged before they read the report may not wish their judgments interfered with by fact. They will persist in theories which exploit rumors and inconsistent statements made in the early turmoil. No one is as blind as he who will not see, and sight can be blocked by neurotic adherence to a conviction in which one has an investment of pride or a more sordid interest. We may expect, therefore, that those who cannot be dented by information will continue to carp and propagandize. They will insist that the failure to explain everything perfectly taints all that is explained. They will put the minor factors of the unknown or unknowable against major revelations. They will not joust fairly, by offering facts to be tested against facts, but will utilize a question or a doubt as if it were equivalent to

disproof. In this sense the report will not end all speculation. But in the historic sense, now that all the facts
available have been quarried and justly evaluated, the report will dispose convincingly of the major questions. This
is the incalculable service rendered by the Commission.
This is its achievement in effectuating domestic tranquility
and overcoming foreign skepticism. This is its contribution
to history. . . .

Also among the uninhibited mythmakers we find Harrison E.
Salisbury, who wrote a similar "special introduction" to another
popular paperback edition of the Report.

The word "mythmakers," incidentally, is Salisbury's, and he
applies it to all who do not consider the Warren Report "a hard-
rock basis of fact," including me. But the way Salisbury includes
me is a perfect example of how *his* myths are made, for after
naming Mark Lane and Thomas G. Buchanan, he lists "Leo
Sauvage, a writer for *Le Figaro* of Paris, who views the killing
as the product of a conspiracy linking police, gangsters and right-
wingers." As a *Times* correspondent in Moscow, Harrison E.
Salisbury used to lean backward—or leftward—in order to be
fair to *Pravda*. Too bad he didn't show the same concern for
Le Figaro. In my cables I had criticized the incoherence of the
Dallas investigation, the impudence of the Washington "leaks,"
the weaknesses of the Warren Report. I did not develop any
theories, and I remember having specifically ridiculed, as I do
again in this book, the "gangland-murder" theory imagined by
other French (also Italian and even American) journalists. As
for Buchanan, with whom Salisbury conveniently packages me,
I first demolished his lucubrations in the French magazine *Preuves*
in an article published in English in September 1964 by *The
New Leader*. Harrison E. Salisbury wrote his "special introduction" in October.

It is indeed a sad fact that the Warren Report has been circulated among American readers mostly in the form of the two
paperbacks endowed with the Soviet-style prefatory brainwashing
by Nizer the jurist or Salisbury the journalist.

Salisbury, by the way, seems to have mastered the strategy of the "Big Lie" as well as the tricks of Madison Avenue. He is not above using alliterative formulas in the tradition of my friends, the press agents of the Ringling Bros. and Barnum & Bailey Circus. Thus, the Warren Report is not only "toweringly clear"; it is "comprehensive, careful, compendious and competent." At the Circus they have the "Prodigious Procession of Pageantry" or the "Ringling Department of Screwballs in a Scintillating Siege of Silliness."

But Salisbury also fearlessly faces and "answers" some genuine questions. For example: "How could Oswald, who had no special qualifications as a marksman, have fired three shots at a moving target at such a distance and angle with such accuracy? Demonstrations by a moderately skilled person showed that no genuine difficulty was imposed in duplicating the feat. But the legend-builders overlook this." What Salisbury overlooks is the simple fact that, outside his voluntary or involuntary dream world, the "moderately skilled person" consisted of three masters of the National Rifle Association, and the demonstrations showed they had genuine difficulty in duplicating the feat of the alleged assassin, who had no qualifications at all as a marksman. But then Harrison E. Salisbury is no legend-builder.

As he puts it (italics and parenthesis are his): "If you know for a fact (as the Warren Commission has now established) that *all* the shots came from the Depository sixth-floor window from a gun wielded by Oswald, a whole train of conflicting clues, theories and bits of evidence (. . .) falls by the wayside." He repeats that in his eyes, the Warren Commission has had "little trouble" in "establishing, for example, beyond question that all the shots came from Oswald's gun; that it *was* Oswald's gun; that Oswald himself purchased it; and, of course, that Oswald himself fired the shots."

Of course, of course . . . If Harrison E. Salisbury is so sure about it, would he be willing, by chance, to confront one of the "myth-makers" or "legend-builders" about this last "fact," which the Commission had so little trouble in establishing "beyond question"?

To establish, "of course, that Oswald himself fired the shots," the Warren Commission relied on Howard L. Brennan. The reader who has gone through the twenty-four chapters of this book knows the facts about Howard L. Brennan, and thus can make up his own mind about Harrison E. Salisbury as well. There is one thing I should mention here. I have asked why the Warren Commission—instead of coaxing the public, through its speculations, into accepting Brennan's testimony—did not submit its "eyewitness" to a direct test in order to *prove* that he really was able to describe and identify, from the sidewalk, someone behind the sixth-floor window. In a recent book to which I shall return presently, Edward Jay Epstein informs us that the test actually took place, but the Commission preferred not to inform the public about its results. And for good reasons: Epstein quotes Assistant Counsel Joseph A. Ball as telling him that when he tried a reconstruction on March 20, 1964, he "found that Brennan had difficulty *seeing* a figure in the window." (Italics mine.)

Americans are not alone in the world: Siding with Nizer and Salisbury is Arthur L. Goodhart, K.B.E., Q.C., who contributes the lead piece to the "Symposium on the Warren Commission Report" published by the NYU *Law Review*.

Goodhart thinks the extraordinary efficiency of the Commission's investigation and the marvelous fairness of its methods have not been appreciated *enough*. "The public has never become aware of the full extent and the thoroughness of the work done by the Commission," for "the Report issued by the Commission, admirable though it was as a narrative, tended to screen from the reader the extreme care with which each witness was examined." Goodhart believes, for example, that "the importance of Mrs. [Marina] Oswald's evidence has not been sufficiently realized." As to the methods, he thinks that the Commission, in setting up its "own machinery," was "outstandingly successful." The reader, who has seen in the various chapters of this book how the Commission's interrogators went out of their way in order *not* to ask the obvious questions, will appreciate the terms in which Goodhart praises the Commission's General Counsel, J. Lee Rankin: "Much, if not most, of the credit for the success of the Commission must be ascribed to him because the skill and courtesy with which he examined the witnesses left little uncertainty concerning the facts for which they were testifying."

Yet even the blind sycophant, precisely because he is blind, will unwittingly give the show away, and that is what happens to Arthur L. Goodhart, K.B.E., Q.C. Trying to justify the Commission's holding its sessions in private, he ingenuously explains that the Commission knew in advance what it was going to find: "If it had seemed probable that the evidence would lead to a positive conclusion in regard to a conspiracy, or that someone besides Oswald had independently taken part in killing the President, there would have been stronger reasons for calling attention to the evidence at a public hearing as this would have enabled the public to judge how much weight should be given to it. But no such immediate publicity need be given to negative evidence that leads nowhere. . . ."

Besides the contribution of Marina Oswald and the "skill and courtesy" of J. Lee Rankin in examining the witnesses, two things impressed Arthur L. Goodhart most.

The first was the appointment of Walter E. Craig. Though it is "not entirely clear" to the British jurist why the Commission reversed its stand, he repeats all of the Report's promotional material concerning the opportunities offered Craig, as if what was theoretically developed on paper really happened. The fact is, of course, that while we do find an occasional reference in the Hearings to the presence of an "observer" representing Craig, none of these "observers" ever posed a question that might have scored a point in Oswald's favor. An incident that occurred on March 12, 1964, seems especially relevant here. Completing his questioning of taxi driver William Whaley, Assistant Counsel Joseph A. Ball (somewhat overstepping his role, it seems) declared "The witness is excused." Congressman Gerald R. Ford, substituting for Warren as Chairman, interrupted to ask a certain Lewis F. Powell, Jr., if he had any statement to make. This was Powell's reply: "Mister Chairman, I think I might say just this: I am here representing Mr. Walter Craig, as I think the Commission understands. I have been here the last two days. In a conversation with Mr. Rankin yesterday morning we agreed that rather than my asking questions directly to witnesses, I would make suggestions to Mr. Ball or to one of his associates. . . ." Since Arthur L. Goodhart, K.B.E., Q.C., obviously preferred not to check what he had decided to believe, this conception of "cross-examination" could not disturb him. It therefore did not prevent him from seeing the appointment of Walter E. Craig through the eyes of Louis Nizer: "This is more than a British Tribunal would have done in the circumstances, but the Commission probably felt that the appointment of Mr. Craig was an additional guaranty that every possible step had been taken to ascertain the truth." May I say that I have a higher opinion of British tribunals than does Arthur L. Goodhart, K.B.E., Q.C.?

I am even less open to the second point that impressed Mr. Goodhart. "It is inconceivable," he writes, "that if Mr. Kennedy, who was the most devoted of brothers, had felt that there had been the least evidence, or even any rational suspicion, of a conspiracy to assassinate the President, or that anyone other than Oswald had murdered him, he would not have insisted that further steps should be taken to see that justice was done. If he has not questioned the conclusions reached in the Report, it seems extraordinary that others should do so."

What seems extraordinary to me is that this type of medieval reasoning could still be not only heard but recommended in the 20th century. Robert Kennedy's approbation cannot substitute for evidence in support of the speculations and accusations of the Warren Report; this would be true even if the former Attorney General had not admitted, or rather boasted, that he had not read the Report. But Goodhart is not the only one to contend that a point of view should be accepted because of the authority or the prestige of the source that expresses it. I have mentioned, for example, James Wechsler's lecturing foreign correspondents for failing to base their interpretation of the facts, as he did, on the personality of Earl Warren. "European journalists," he wrote, "have a special responsibility to tell their readers the nature of the man who conducted this inquiry, and whose name gives so much weight and meaning to its findings." My own conception of journalistic responsibility—and ethics—is to examine everything honestly and carefully, and if anything appears erroneous, incoherent, or otherwise unconvincing, to say so, whatever the source.

In this orgy of aggressive and ecstatic conformism, the Anglo-Saxon solidarity was perhaps best expressed in the *Atlantic Monthly* in March 1965 by Lord Devlin.

Former Justice of the High Court, Queen's Bench Division, and former Lord of Appeal, Lord Devlin is now chairman of the Press Council. For him, the Warren Report was "a monumental work" and "an outstanding achievement": "Each fact is to be found in its proper place to sustain each conclusion. The minor conclusions support the major, and on the major the verdict rests." The *verdict?* And it *rests?* Well, at least Lord Devlin thinks there is no *alternative:* "Perhaps one day the critics will produce one. If they can suggest one that is even faintly credible, they will deserve more public attention than they are likely to get by making charges of suppression that are more than faintly ridiculous." Lord Devlin and the other distinguished members of the Warren Commission club—at the Opera they used to call it *claque*—will deserve more public respect if they can bring themselves to confront precise charges with arguments instead of righteous indignation.

The feeling, however, that there is no "alternative" has played an important part also in the attitude taken by nonmembers of the *claque,* like Dwight Macdonald and Murray Kempton. "Who else could have done it?" was Macdonald's ultimate argument each time we discussed the case. In his *Esquire* piece he maintained that all "conspiracy theories" face a *dilemma:* "Either (A): Some or all of the many investigators knew about a conspiracy in advance, perhaps were part of it, or discovered it later and then covered it right up again. Or (B): They knew of no conspiracy, were part of none, and although one existed, their best efforts were unable to find any trace."

I would like to invite Dwight Macdonald to consider that there is a third alternative. (C): Some or all of the many investigators knew of no conspiracy and were part of none, but did not make the slightest effort to find any trace of such a conspiracy because they assumed that their job—not as members or as protectors of a conspiracy but as representatives of the American Establishment —was only to prove the guilt of Oswald (without a doubt the best solution politically). Macdonald himself points out "a conclusion [that] may be drawn from the Warren Report," namely, that "the Commission drew back from a line of inquiry that would have discredited the Dallas cops, and more important, the FBI and the Secret Service." How does this conclusion fit in with either Horn A or Horn B of Macdonald's "dilemma"?

While writing the present Postscript, I read a fascinating book called *Inquest,* by Edward Jay Epstein. Begun as a master's thesis in government at Cornell University, it took as its primary subject, in the words of the author, "the Warren Commission, not the assassination itself." The exceptional value of *Inquest* lies in the fact that Epstein succeeded in interviewing five of the seven members of the Commission (the two he missed were Senator Russell and Chief Justice Warren), General Counsel J. Lee Rankin, eight of fourteen Assistant Counsel, and the senior U.S. Air Force historian who had special responsibility for writing the Report.

All of these coauthors of the Warren Report, until then, had remained wrapped in majestic silence, with the sole exception, as far as I know, of Congressman Gerald R. Ford. Described on the jacket as "a Member of the Warren Commission," Congressman Ford, while scornfully dismissing "the Mark Lanes, Sauvages, Feldmans, Buchanans, *et al,*" did not think it unethical to publish a $6.95 report of his own, *Portrait of the Assassin.* But the others preferred to say "No Comment!" At last, though, they agreed to talk to Epstein, and Assistant Counsel Wesley J. Liebeler even seems to have let the author have a copy of a 26-page memorandum criticizing the Report's chapter on "The Assassin," which, according to Epstein, he had submitted to the Commission on September 6, 1964.

I suppose there will be some denials and rectifications, though at the time of this writing the "yelling 'misquote,'" as *Newsweek* called it, has been remarkably anonymous. Epstein, in any case, gathered enough inside information on the workings of the Commission to trace the "Limits of the Investigation" as well as the

"Limits of the Investigators." The results allow him to define the "Dominant Purpose" of the Warren Commission in terms that add a subjective explanation to the objective conclusions that I have arrived at in this book.

"If the explicit purpose of the Commission," Epstein writes, "was to ascertain and expose the facts, the implicit purpose was to protect the national interest by dispelling rumors. These two purposes were compatible so long as the damaging rumors were untrue. But what if a rumor damaging to the national interest proved to be true? The Commission's explicit purpose would dictate that the information be exposed regardless of the consequences, while the Commission's implicit purpose would dictate that the rumor be dispelled regardless of the fact that it was true." Epstein's conclusion is that "in a conflict of this sort, one of the Commission's purposes would emerge as dominant." Is there any doubt about which one that would be?

What Epstein doesn't say is that this "dualism in purpose" applied to the Assistant Counsel individually as well as to the Commission as a whole.

Thus Wesley J. Liebeler's 26-page memorandum, which Epstein says was written on the weekend of September 5, 1964, after Liebeler had read the galley proofs of Chapter IV of the Report ("The Assassin"), mentions some of the major weaknesses pointed out in this book. An example: Liebeler, according to Epstein, was fully aware of the misleading character of the statement concerning the presence of the rifle in the Paines' garage "until the morning of the assassination." And he found the Report's assertions concerning "Oswald's Rifle Capability," as I do, to be "contrary to the evidence." The memorandum, Epstein says, was argued against by Norman Redlich, who had written that chapter, but in the end "some changes were made." Perhaps it was indeed worse in the original version, but as far as I am concerned I still see in the Report all the untrue and misleading assertions Liebeler is said to have denounced on September 6. Then what good did his memo do?

There is a frightening reply which, if Epstein is correct in quoting Liebeler, Norman Redlich is said to have given Liebeler concerning the rifle tests: "The Commission judged it is an easy shot, and *I* work for the Commission." Redlich, apparently, used a similar formula in regard to Mrs. Markham. According to Epstein, when Liebeler, who had checked her denials against the tape recording of her interview with Mark Lane (see Chapter 5), told Redlich that her testimony was "contradictory" and "worthless," Redlich is said to have replied: "The Commission wants to believe Mrs. Markham and that's all there is to it." Willingly or unwillingly, the fact is that Liebeler agreed, since Helen Markham remained one of the Commission's three star witnesses.

I have nothing, personally, for or against Wesley J. Liebeler, whom I don't know and whom I choose as an example only because of the part he plays in Epstein's book. The Warren Report says he was graduated, cum laude, from the University of Chicago Law School in 1957 and was managing editor of the University of Chicago *Law Review*. Epstein says he "considered himself 'definitely not establishment,'" and "sometimes played the role of devil's advocate on the [Commission] staff." I recall, however, the way he investigated the mystery of the Irving gunsmith (see Chapter 4), and I conclude that when he was not criticizing the Report (secretly, at least up to the publication of the Epstein book), Liebeler too had times when he seemed to say to himself: "*I* work for the Commission." After all, his reason for protesting the text of Chapter IV of the Report was that such methods "could seriously affect the integrity and credibility of the entire report." There was still no consideration of truth or justice; only of public relations.

While I have added or cut a few lines here and there, I did not have to revise any of the arguments in my book, as first published in Paris in March 1965. Indeed, from the day of publication of the 26-volume set of the Commission's Hearings and Exhibits, on November 23, 1964, one could say about the Oswald case what Felix Frankfurter had written in 1927 about the case of Sacco and Vanzetti: "There are no legal mysteries about the case which a layman cannot penetrate. The issues that are involved and the considerations relevant to their solution are within the comprehension of anyone who feels responsibility for understanding them."

One major document, however, was not made available until 1966: the FBI report of December 9, 1963, which can be consulted now at the National Archives in Washington, as Vincent J. Salandria—first, I believe—discovered on February 26, 1966. There is also a "Supplemental Report" by the FBI, dated January 13, 1964, excerpts of which were first quoted in Epstein's *Inquest.* The FBI report, whose conclusions—Oswald, lone killer—had been immediately leaked out to the press, served as the general basis for the Warren Report, but with one startling exception. The exception concerns the President's wounds, and thus the origin of the bullets that struck him. It is now official that the famous December 18, 1963, "leak" (which the Warren Commission "unmade" on September 27, 1964, as if we were already in 1984, not even acknowledging its past existence as a "speculation" or as a "rumor") was indeed the version of the FBI.

Most American newspapers, of course, knew it from the start, though none of them recalled it after 1964. We had to wait for May 29, 1966, to find the first direct reminder, in the *Washington Post,* that "this report was confirmed prior to publication by the FBI." We may also notice the fact that up to the very date of the publication of the Warren Report, the U.S. Information Agency was distributing throughout the world a document (see Illustration No. 1) contradicting the Warren Commission, clearly on the basis of the FBI report: "First Shot Hits Mr. Kennedy in Back.... Second Shot Wounds Governor Connally. . . ." For final confirmation, see the National Archives in Washington.

Though I cannot feel sorry for the members and supporters of the Warren Commission, they are certainly in a pathetic position. Most medical experts and some of the FBI witnesses had rejected the possibility that the same bullet caused the President's and Governor Connally's wounds. But the Commission had omitted or misused their testimony in order to maintain that possibility. Vincent J. Salandria, on the basis of this flagrant contradiction, concluded in the March 1966 issue of the magazine *Liberation,* harshly but not unfairly: "The Warren Commission appears to have involved itself wittingly or unwittingly in fabrication and withholding of vital evidence." In the light of the "diametrically

opposed findings" given by the reports of the FBI and of the Warren Commission regarding the results of the autopsy, Edward J.
Epstein sums up the "dilemma" in no less significant terms: "On
one hand, if the FBI reports distorted such a basic fact of the
assassination, doubt is cast on the accuracy of the FBI's *entire*
investigation; indeed the Commission's investigation and conclusions were, in the final analysis, predicated on the accuracy of
the FBI reports. The second horn of the dilemma is even more
painful, for, if the FBI's statements on the autopsy are accurate,
then the autopsy findings must have been changed after January
13. This would mean that the document in the Warren Report
which purports to be the original autopsy report is not. . . ."

Such a situation would be funny if it weren't so tragic. I foresaw, when I mentioned the mystery of the clipboard (see Chapter 23), that the day the Warren Commission could be made to
answer questions it would have to impugn the professional competence of the FBI in order to justify itself. The open conflict
about the autopsy findings has brought us to this point sooner than
I expected. As of this writing, the FBI has said "No Comment!,"
but "sources close to the Warren Commission" (as the Washington specialists in "leaks" would say) have already started dis-
paraging the FBI in terms seldom heard before. In the June 13,
1966, issue of *Newsweek,* for example, "Commission staffers" are
credited with the following explanation: "The FBI version was
not an autopsy report at all but hardly more than hearsay: it came
from two agents who watched part of the autopsy, heard the
doctors talk of their difficulty in tracing the bullet's path, and
dashed out to phone in their incomplete report of a 'back'
wound. . . ."

The Warren Commission indeed must have a very low opinion
of the FBI. It must have an even lower opinion of the American
people, who are supposed to believe that the much celebrated
FBI prepared an official report for the President, leaked it out to
the world, communicated it to the U.S. Information Agency, and
confirmed it again more than one month later, basing absolutely
crucial information on just one phone call, before all the facts
were in. In this book I have recorded many shortcomings in the

FBI investigation, but I refuse to believe that the FBI representative who attended the autopsy (and who certainly must have had some professional competence to be assigned such a responsible job in the first place) would not have gone back after the phone call to check what happened afterward and get *all* the facts together before submitting his report to his superiors. I even refuse to believe that these superiors did not double-check the agent's report before making it a key part of their own reports.

I hope, in any case, that if Harrison E. Salisbury has a chance to correct his "special introduction" to the Warren Report some day, he will not forget to include among his list of "mythmakers" the man who, according to the Warren Commission, must be the greatest mythmaker of us all: J. Edgar Hoover.

Quite a few editors in quite a few American publishing houses have tried to have this book accepted by their firms. I am as grateful to them, though they failed, as I am to Bram Cavin, of The World Publishing Company, who succeeded. I also wish to thank Myron Kolatch, executive editor of *The New Leader,* who had the courage to break the American silence in publishing, on November 22, 1965, and in two later issues, the main points of *The Oswald Affair.* Finally, I wish to express my gratitude to Mrs. Sylvia Meagher, author of an indispensable *Subject Index to the Warren Report* and the only person in the world who really knows every item hidden in the 26 volumes of Hearings and Exhibits. With total unselfishness, Mrs. Meagher has always been available, to me as to others, for any needed information, verification, or reference.

New York, June 1966